MERCURY READER

a custom publication

Writing Responsibly:
Communities in Conversation

Pearson Learning Solutions

New York   Boston   San Francisco
London   Toronto   Sydney   Tokyo   Singapore   Madrid
Mexico City   Munich   Paris   Cape Town   Hong Kong   Montreal

Senior Vice President, Editorial and Marketing: Patrick F. Boles
Senior Sponsoring Editor: Natalie Danner
Development Editor: Mary Kate Paris
Assistant Editor: Jill Johnson
Operations Manager: Eric M. Kenney
Production Manager: Jennifer Berry
Rights Manager: Jillian Santos
Art Director: Renée Sartell
Cover Designers: Kristen Kiley, Blythe Russo, Tess Mattern, and Renée Sartell

Cover Art: "Gigantia Mountains & Sea of Cortes," by R.G.K. Photography, Copyright
© Tony Stone Images; "Dime," courtesy of the Shaw Collection; "Open Book On Table
Edge w/Pencil," courtesy of PhotoAlto Photography/Veer Incorporated; "Open Book
On Table Near Table's Corner," courtesy of Fancy Photography/Veer Incorporated;
"Scrabble Pieces and a Die," by G. Herbst, courtesy of PlainPicture Photography/Veer
Incorporated; "Binary codes in bowls," by John Still, courtesy of Photographer's
Choice/Getty Images; "Close-up of an open book," courtesy of Glowimages/Getty
Images; "College Students Sitting At Tables," courtesy of Blend/PunchStock; "Red and
blue circles," courtesy of Corbis Images; "Laptop screen showing photograph of
landscape," courtesy of Martin Holtcamp/Getty Images; "Apples flying," courtesy of
Arne Morgenstern/Getty Images.

Printed in the United States of America.

Please visit our website at *www.pearsoncustom.com.*

Attention bookstores: For permission to return any unsold stock, contact us at
pe-uscustomreturns@pearson.com.

Pearson Learning Solutions, 501 Boylston Street, Suite 900, Boston, MA 02116
A Pearson Education Company
www.pearsoned.com

ISBN 10: 0-558-62740-4
ISBN 13: 978-0-558-62740-9

Contents

I. Preface

Dear Students,

Welcome to the Writing Program at Loyola University Chicago. In UCWR 110 (Writing Responsibly), we teach writing as a tool for discovery and communication. We want you to use writing to learn while you are learning to write. We teach writing as a recursive process and believe that good writers are constantly engaged in rethinking and rewriting. We also believe that writers benefit from reader feedback; therefore, our writing seminar stresses peer-editing and review during the writing process. We want this seminar to introduce you to the conventions of academic writing and to prepare you to write effectively in your university courses as well as in your professional lives. Towards those goals, this semester's focus will be on learning the building blocks of academic argument. Those include summarizing, synthesizing, analyzing multiple points of view, and creating and supporting statements of position.

In order to help you master these foundational writing skills, *Writing Responsibly: Communities in Conversation,* the custom text used in all UCWR 110 classes, includes a collection of essays chosen to exemplify and articulate the principles of good writing. These essays will not only raise the question of how arguments are discovered, supported and amplified; they will also offer instruction in writing for various audiences and rhetorical situations. *Writing Responsibly*, used in conjunction with the required handbook, Rebecca Moore Howard's *Writing Matters*, will help you to develop flexible strategies for generating, revising, and editing your writing. In addition to focus on structure, clarity, and grammar, this course will help you learn responsibility to your readers, responsibility to your sources, and responsibility to yourselves as writers. We hope this course and its textbooks will engage you and encourage you to share ideas in a forum that extends beyond the classroom.

Best wishes for an exciting and productive semester.

Victoria Anderson, Ph.D.
Writing Program Director

Argument: Non-Traditional Model

Argument and Persuasion

A hundred and fifty years ago, many prominent Americans were engaged in a heated debate over slavery. Abolitionists (opponents of slavery) cited the Declaration of Independence, claiming that "all men are created equal" and decrying an institution that allowed one person to be the property of another. Slaveholders pointed to the Bible, claiming that the Old Testament identified certain races as "sons of Cain," destined to be enslaved throughout history. Eventually the slavery issue was settled by the Civil War, but prior to and during that conflict, speakers and writers engaged in **argument** about the legitimacy of slavery. Put simply, argument refers to the presentation of a claim (e.g., that slavery should be abolished) and evidence (e.g., citations from the Declaration, stories of mistreated slaves) to support it. Those engaged in argument seek to persuade their audience to accept a certain position or take a certain action. While argument and persuasion are not precisely synonymous, their purposes are similar. **Persuasion** seeks to sway an audience, often employing appeals to emotion; **argument** seeks to justify a position, always employing appeals to reason and sometimes appeals to emotion as well. As in the case of the abolition debate, the most effective arguments involve appeals to both reason and emotion. In this chapter, we will discuss three models of argument: **Rogerian**, based on the work of psychologist Carl Rogers; **Toulmin**, based on the work of philosopher Stephen Toulmin; and **Aristotelian** or **classical**, based on the work of the great philosopher Aristotle.

Although slavery has not been an issue for over a century, race remains one of the most debated issues in contemporary society. Most of the examples in this chapter will be drawn from this issue.

In examining arguments about race, we will refer to a chapter from Maya Angelou's memoir *I Know Why the Caged Bird Sings*. Titled "Graduation," it recounts the day in 1940 on which Angelou graduated from the Lafayette County Training School, a segregated school in Arkansas. This piece (included at the end of this chapter) serves as an effective example of argument that is not presented in traditional argument form. Written as a narrative, "Graduation" nonetheless argues vehemently against the racism that supported legal segregation in schools during the first half of this century. It still resonates today, despite the demise of legal segregation, because issues of affirmative action and racial equality continue to be part of our national debates. ✱ He was born as a slave in mainland lived with aunt then trad. him later on 1852

Evidence

Both argument and persuasion share one crucial quality: Their claims must be supported by evidence. That evidence may take the form of reasoning, appeals to authority, reference to statistics or facts, or appeals to the audience's needs or values. Regardless of the nature of the supporting evidence, that support must be presented for an argument to be legitimate. This is what differentiates argument from mere **statement of opinion**. In contemporary society, statement of opinion is often mistaken for argument. If you listen to talk-radio programs or tabloid television, you hear endless unsubstantiated opinions presented as if they were full-blown arguments. Such programs do little except reinforce existing beliefs shared by the audience precisely because no argument is taking place. The key to convincing an audience of the legitimacy of a claim lies not in stating the claim but in supporting it with evidence. This chapter will explore the various kinds of support used to justify claims made in arguments.

Inductive and Deductive Reasoning

In constructing arguments based on rational rather than emotional appeals, it is necessary to understand the distinction between the two primary types of reasoning. **Inductive reasoning** involves moving from specific evidence to a general conclusion, while **deductive reasoning** moves from a general statement to specific conclusions. Using inductive reasoning to persuade her audience of the lack of

3

equity in segregated schools, for example, Angelou bases her argument on a collection of specific pieces of evidence:

Evidence: Segregated schools are poorly funded.

Segregated schools have outdated facilities.

Segregated schools train students for menial jobs.

Conclusion: Segregated schools are inherently unequal to white schools.

A deductive approach, on the other hand, involves presenting a **syllogism**. A syllogism comprises three parts: the **major premise** (a general statement about a category or class), the **minor premise** (a specific statement about one member of that category or class), and the **conclusion** (derived about the specific member). If presented in the form of a syllogism, Maya Angelou's argument against segregation might look like this:

Major premise: Segregation is always unjust.

Minor premise: The school system of Stamps, Arkansas was segregated in the 1940s.

Conclusion: The school system of Stamps, Arkansas in the 1940s was unjust.

Looking at Angelou's piece in this way illustrates the interrelationship between rational arguments and emotional appeals. While the syllogism is valid, the real persuasive power of "Graduation" lies in the emotional response it engenders in readers. Similarly, the emotional appeal would lose its effectiveness if the rational argument were not valid.

As you are probably aware from looking at this syllogism, it is necessary for the major premise to be valid in all cases if the conclusion is to be viable. For example, if it were demonstrated that segregation was not always unjust, then the conclusion would no longer follow. The conclusion would then have to be amended.

Audience

All models of argument emphasize **audience**. Because the most basic goal of argument is to convince the audience of the legitimacy of a claim, the arguer must be aware of the knowledge, values, and needs of the audience. In seeking to convince her readers to fight racism, for example, Angelou must consider a variety of audiences. Some will be entirely sympathetic to her position, some antithetic, and many will fall somewhere between those two extremes. Her task in making an argument is to appeal to common **beliefs** and **values** of her audience. By focusing on the aspirations of the children of Stamps, Angelou seeks to appeal to beliefs and values shared by everyone in her audience, namely that children represent the hope of a culture. This appeal makes her argument more convincing even to those who might believe in segregation.

Acknowledging/Rebutting Opposition

Acknowledgment of opposing arguments is an essential component of any audience-based model of argument. Acknowledging the opposition enhances the arguer's credibility and strengthens the argument as well. Regardless of the nature of the rebuttal, it is essential to the strength and validity of the argument that opposing views be aired and dealt with.

Of course, on some issues the credibility of one position has been so eroded that there is little if any validity left in it. Legal segregation, for example, has been judged an entirely untenable practice since the civil rights movement of the 1960s. Thus Maya Angelou does not need to acknowledge opposing views in order to establish her credibility; her piece (indeed, the entire book in which it appears) highlights past injustices in order to eradicate any remnants of unjust practices that remain, as well as to prevent such injustices from recurring in the future.

Current arguments in favor of retaining racial considerations in public college and university admissions, however, do need to acknowledge the opposition. Opponents of such admissions policies frequently refer to Martin Luther King's call for judging people by the content of their character rather than the color of their skin. If you are arguing to retain racial considerations, you must acknowledge that color does play a role in such admissions programs. In rebutting the "color-blind" argument, you might point to unequal educational opportunities for many minority students in elementary and high schools. This inequity, you might argue, requires redress when these students apply to college.

The Rogerian Model of Argument

In preparing an argument it is important to consider various approaches to argument and persuasion. Two of the more common approaches used today are the **Rogerian** and the **Toulmin** models. While this chapter focuses primarily on the Toulmin model, the Rogerian model is worth studying for its emphasis on common ground. This model was developed from psychologist Carl Rogers's work on conflict. Noting that adversarial arguments often result in opponents becoming entrenched in their own positions, Rogers suggested an approach that seeks common ground in order to negotiate a mutually acceptable position. Using the Rogerian model, you would first acknowledge your opposition and assert its validity, and then find a common ground from which all sides can view the issue. Finally, you would present evidence to establish your position as the most reasonable. Arguments for and against racial considerations in college admissions provide an example of the Rogerian model. An outline of the argument might look something like this:

A. **Acknowledge opposing position** that racial considerations in public college and university admissions do not result in each student's being judged solely on merit (i.e., some minority students may be admitted over equally qualified non-minority students).

B. **Find common ground**, namely that both sides are interested in eliminating racial inequities.

C. **Present evidence** that the benefits of racial considerations in public college and university admissions outweigh the costs (i.e., racial considerations at this level address inequities in elementary and secondary education).

Arguers who use the Rogerian approach truly seek to persuade their audience rather than to win an argument. However, not all persuasive pieces lend themselves to the Rogerian approach. When the opposition is generally discredited, it is difficult to acknowledge its validity. Thus in an argument such as Angelou's against segregation, the Rogerian model would not be appropriate. For Angelou's purposes, the Toulmin model is more appropriate.

The Toulmin Model of Argument

In 1958, philosopher Stephen Toulmin published *The Uses of Argument*, a book that challenged traditional logic-based argument models. Toulmin based his model on the adversarial process of a courtroom, in which each position is challenged openly and judged by a third party. Toulmin's model emphasizes the audience of an argument, and charges the arguer with not only providing support for his or her position, but with acknowledging and rebutting the opposition as well. The key to the Toulmin model is a strong link between the thesis and the evidence supporting that thesis. The primary components of the Toulmin model are **claim** (thesis), **grounds** (evidence or emotional appeal), and **warrant** (assumption linking claim to grounds).

Claims

If you are arguing for retaining racial consideration in public college and university admissions, you may seek to persuade your audience in several ways. In addressing those who argue for purely merit-based admissions, you may simply want to establish that this position is valid and must be considered in any debate. You also may want to convince those who call racial considerations a form of racism that you simply seek to level the playing field for students who have been denied opportunities in elementary and secondary school. Or you may seek to convince those who agree with you to take such actions as picketing institutions that have eliminated racial considerations, engaging in letter-writing campaigns to major newspapers, or petitioning legislators to retain racial considerations.

The purpose of an argument is embedded in the claim, the point that the arguer wants to make. The thesis of an argument, whether stated or implied, presents the claim. Claims can be divided into three primary categories: claims of fact, claims of value, and claims of policy. The type of claim depends on the purpose of the argument; in turn, the structure and development of the argument depends largely on the type of claim being presented.

Claims of fact are assertions about the existence of a certain condition. In an argument about racial considerations, proponents and opponents alike may wish to establish certain facts about such policies in order to frame their arguments. Competing claims of fact regarding this issue include the following:

Claim 1: Racial considerations offer preferential treatment to some students based on color rather than on merit exclusively.

Claim 2: Educational inequities at the elementary and secondary levels reduce opportunities for many African-American students.

In each case, the claim must be supported by data, hard evidence that establishes the existence of the condition stated in the claim.

Claims of value are statements of judgment regarding the worth of something. While Maya Angelou does present claims of fact in "Graduation" (e.g., that facilities in black schools were inferior to those in white schools), she also addresses issues of values. A claim of value made in Angelou's "Graduation" might read,

Claim: Segregating black children in schools is morally repugnant.

Often based on tastes or moral beliefs, claims of value must be supported by establishing criteria by which the judgments are made.

Claims of policy are calls to action. One of Maya Angelou's goals in writing "Graduation" was to eliminate school segregation. The following claim of policy reflects that goal:

Claim: Segregation in public schools must be eliminated.

Claims of policy must be supported by reasons for taking a specific action. Reasons for eliminating segregation, according to Angelou, include the equality of black and white children and the rights of all children to pursue their dreams.

In order for a claim to be effective, the terms of the claim must be clearly defined. For example, the above claim refers to public schools only, meaning that the argument is aimed at schools funded by state and local governments, not by private organizations.

Grounds

Grounds, also called *support* or *supporting evidence*, comprise everything the arguer offers to justify a claim. Grounds may include **facts, data, statistics, opinions of experts or affected individuals, examples**, and **appeals to emotion**. The nature of the grounds normally depends upon the type of claim being presented.

Facts offered in support of a claim should be irrefutable. That the black Lafayette County Training School has a dirt playground and no sports equipment while the white Central School has a paved playground and a variety of equipment is a fact that Maya Angelou can point to in her implicit argument against segregated schools.

Data and *statistics* offer numerical evidence to support a claim. Arguers must be careful, however, to recognize that statistics can be interpreted in different ways. Recently, for example, a good deal of attention has been paid to the depression and suicide statistics of homosexual teenagers. Those arguing for homosexual rights point to the statistics as evidence of the effects of ostracism on young gays and lesbians, while those arguing that homosexuality is abnormal use the same statistics to demonstrate the troubled state of mind and the guilt of homosexual teenagers. If you wish to make a convincing argument for retaining racial considerations in public college and university admissions, you must be careful to offer statistics that are less open to interpretation. Or you can offer the opinion of recognized experts.

The *opinion of experts* is valuable not only to support a particular interpretation of statistics but also to lend credibility to a claim. The opinion of someone whose expertise in a community is acknowledged is far more valuable than that of an uninformed person. In arguing for racial considerations, for example, the opinion of a respected educator or sociologist would offer strong support for the claim.

The *opinion of affected individuals* is also effective. In "Graduation," Angelou writes of her reaction to a speech by Edward Donleavy, a white politician who reminds his audience of their second-class status:

> The man's dead words fell like bricks around the auditorium and too many settled in my belly. . . . It was awful to be a Negro and have no control over my life. It was brutal to be young and already trained to sit quietly and listen to charges brought against my color with no chance of defense. We should all be dead.

These descriptions of the author's state of mind after being belittled by Donleavy offer convincing support for her position on the human impact of segregation.

Examples provide support for claims if they can be used in such a way that the audience draws generalizations from them. Angelou's example of a segregated school, if readers consider it representative, will support her claim.

Appeals to emotion differ from other grounds in that they do not rely on logic. Instead, appeals to emotion attempt to forge a link between the arguer and the audience by focusing on the needs of the audience or the values shared with the audience. Appealing to the values of her audience, Maya Angelou focuses on the industriousness and aspirations of the children in Stamps. She is proud of her own academic record:

> No absences, no tardiness, and my academic work was among the best of the year. . . . I could say the preamble to the Constitution even faster than Bailey. . . . I had memorized the presidents of the United States from Washington to Roosevelt in chronological as well as alphabetical order.

And she implies that both she and her classmates aspired to be more than "carpenters, farmers, handymen, masons, maids, cooks and baby nurses"; indeed, her brother Bailey wants to become a lawyer, even though it means that he must "first pay penance for his skin by picking cotton and hoeing corn and studying correspondence books at night for twenty years." Americans are known to value industriousness and aspirations; therefore, by emphasizing both qualities in her piece, Angelou uses her audience's own values to support her position.

Warrants

Perhaps the least familiar of the three components of the Toulmin model, the **warrant** is nonetheless crucial to the success of an argument. Put simply, the warrant is the assumption or belief, shared by the arguer and the audience, that underlies the entire argument. A warrant can be considered a guarantee for the argument, or, as Toulmin himself referred to it, a bridge between the claim and the grounds. Maya Angelou's argument, including the warrant, might look like this:

Claim:	Segregation is wrong.
Grounds:	Segregation results in poorer facilities for black students; segregation denies qualified black students higher education; segregation dehumanizes black people.
Warrant:	Any system advocating inequality or dehumanization is wrong.

If the audience shares Angelou's assumptions about equality and humanity, then her claim and grounds will be convincing.

Backing

Warrants such as those just illustrated are *implicit*; that is, they are obvious to any reasonable person. Occasionally, however, it is necessary to make the warrant *explicit*. Consider, for example, the 1954 Supreme Court decision in *Brown v. Board of Education of Topeka, Kansas*. The claim represented in that decision is similar to Angelou's: Segregation is unconstitutional. The grounds are also similar: Segregation results in poorer facilities for black students. In 1954, however, it was necessary that the warrant be spelled out: Separate facilities are inherently unequal. At the time, such an assumption was not common; thus the Court had to make the warrant clear. Whether the warrant is explicit or implicit, if it effectively links the grounds to the claim, then the argument will itself be effective.

If the warrant is not explicit, that is if it is not necessarily shared by the audience, then it must be supported by **backing**. Just as the grounds support the claim, the backing supports the warrant. As with other evidence, backing can take several different forms. Chief Justice Earl Warren, for example, in offering backing for the warrant on which the *Brown* decision was based, cited the fact that during the time of the 1896 *Plessy v. Ferguson* decision, in which the Court ruled that separate facilities were not inherently unequal, public education did not serve the purpose it did in 1954. Calling late nineteenth-century education "rudimentary," Warren noted that rural schools often combined several grades, that often the school year was a mere three months long, and that compulsory attendance was not enforced. In 1954, on the other hand, education was "the very foundation of good citizenship" as well as a necessary component to success in the workplace. Warren also cited the opinion of experts in his warrant, noting that psychologists in the 1950s agreed that segregation implied inferiority and therefore impeded black children's motivation. This backing for the Court's argument was necessary precisely because assumptions about the role of education and the effects of segregation had changed substantially between 1896 and 1954.

Qualifiers
Another significant term used in the Toulmin model is the **qualifier**. Consider the absolute nature of the following claim: *All* public college and university admissions policies based on racial considerations address previous educational inequities. To render this claim invalid, a single example of an upper-middle-class minority student who has benefited from such a policy would suffice. A strategy that you might use then is to attach a qualifier to the claim:

> **Qualified claim:** In most cases, public college and university admissions policies based on racial considerations address previous educational inequities.

Amending claims to include qualifiers can facilitate an argument by heading off opposing claims before they can be made.

The Aristotelian Model of Argument

The earliest analyses of argument in Western thought can be found in the writings of the ancient Greeks, particularly Aristotle. Aristotle's *Rhetoric* identifies three means by which an arguer attempts to persuade an audience: **logos**, or rational appeals; **ethos**, or emphasis on the integrity of the arguer; and **pathos**, or emotional appeals. As these terms indicate, traditional Aristotelian argument focuses not only on appeals to reason but to emotion and to integrity or credibility as well.

Logos

Considered the most important category of proof by rhetoricians from Aristotle to the present, *logos* appeals to the rational mind. *Logos* refers to the internal consistency of the argument, as well as to its reliance on reason and common sense. The *logos* of an argument favoring racial considerations in public college and university admissions policies is illustrated by the testimony of experts regarding the impact of such policies, as well as statistics suggesting inequities in elementary and secondary education.

Categories of Logical Proof

Logical proof in an argument can be presented in a number of ways. The nature of the claim, the type of grounds, and the nature of the warrant all determine the type of proof or line of reasoning employed to support the warrant. We will discuss six specific lines of reasoning: **argument from generalization**, **argument from definition**, **argument from cause**, **argument from sign**, **argument from analogy**, and **argument from parallel case**.

Argument from generalization is also known as *inductive reasoning*. Generalization involves offering a series of examples that when taken together support a position. For example, when Angelou points to a class full of bright, ambitious students whose aspirations are denied because of segregation, it is reasonable to conclude that segregation is unjust. The resulting argument would look like this:

Argument: Segregation denies the aspirations of bright, ambitious students.

Support: All of the bright, ambitious students at the Lafayette County Training School were denied opportunities because of segregation.

Argument from definition calls upon the arguer to establish a common understanding of key terms with the audience. If such an understanding does not exist, then the argument cannot proceed. Chief Justice Earl Warren, in his decision in *Brown v. Board of Education*, found it necessary to define public education in order to make his case. Claiming that public education in the 1950s was designed to prepare students for citizenship, he then made the case that separate facilities placed unconstitutional burdens on blacks relegated to those facilities. Taken as an argument itself, Warren's definition can be outlined as follows:

Argument: Segregated schools are by definition unequal.

Support: Segregated schools do not offer black children the opportunity to learn good citizenship, one of the functions of public education.

Argument from cause posits that a specific action results in a specific effect. In presenting a causation argument, it is necessary to link the cause to the effect; the audience must be convinced that the situation presented is not coincidence. Maya Angelou, in arguing that limited opportunities for black children was an effect of segregation in schools, establishes the relationship between inferior schools and limited opportunity. Her argument from cause would look like this:

Argument: Segregated schools limited the career opportunities of black children.

Support: Black schools had few facilities and fewer programs to prepare students for a variety of careers.

Argument from sign focuses on symptoms or indicators of a particular condition. Some of the most obvious signs with which we are familiar are symptoms of disease: stuffy nose, a cough, and a fever are signs of a cold. Although there is not always a causal relationship between the sign and the condition indicated, argument from sign can nevertheless be effective. You might argue, for example, that racially intolerant attitudes are a sign of a campus that is homogeneous, or lacking in diversity. The lack of diversity may not have caused the intolerant attitudes; nonetheless, the attitudes signify a homogeneous campus community. The argument from sign would look like this:

Argument: Racially intolerant attitudes are a sign of a homogeneous campus.

Support: On campuses lacking in diversity, racially intolerant attitudes are prevalent.

Argument from analogy uses an object or situation to represent an unrelated object or situation. The power of the analogy normally rests in the imagery it suggests, but at times rational connections between the two things strengthen the analogy. In taped conversations about the Watergate cover-up, White House Counsel John Dean referred to the growing scandal as a cancer eating at the presidency. Such an analogy is powerful in its imagery, but there is little real resemblance between a cancer-ridden body and the office of the presidency. An argument from analogy that calls on more rational connections would read as follows:

Argument: Like a field planted year after year with only one crop, a homogeneous campus community yields little growth.

Support: Lack of diversity makes the campus atmosphere less productive, just as overplanting a single crop year after year makes the soil less productive.

Argument from parallel case is used regularly in courts of law. Whenever an attorney cites a precedent, she is arguing from parallel case. Based on comparisons between objects or conditions with shared characteristics, argument from parallel case asks the audience to believe that what has happened in one situation can be expected to happen in another. A faulty argument from parallel case was made by the defendants in *Brown v. Board of Education*. The defense cited the 1896 *Plessy v. Ferguson* case in which separate facilities were not deemed inherently unequal. As noted previously, however, Chief Justice Warren and a majority of the Court rejected that argument, citing changing circumstances. In this case, the defense position, that conditions in 1954 replicated those in 1896, was declared faulty. A valid argument from parallel case might read as follows:

Argument: Segregated public schools in Little Rock, Arkansas in 1960 were inherently unequal.

Support: The Supreme Court ruled in 1954 that segregated public schools in Topeka, Kansas were inherently unequal.

Avoiding Logical Fallacies
As the example from *Brown v. Board of Education* indicates, not all arguments, even if the arguments follow a specific model, are valid. In addition to falling prey to such errors as failing to acknowledge changing times, arguers can also fall into what are known as **logical fallacies**. Such fallacies occur when the arguer is not careful in matching the grounds to the claim, or when the warrant is either irrelevant to the claim and support or is based on insubstantial backing. Logical fallacies include the following:

Post hoc reasoning assumes that simply because a phenomenon or an event precedes another, the first is the cause of the second. If a white student is denied admission to a public university which uses racial considerations in admissions decisions, the admissions policy is not necessarily the cause for denial. Any number of other causes, from the student's test scores to her intended major program of study, might have contributed to the decision.

Non sequitur (Latin for "it does not follow") is illustrated by Edward Donleavy in "Graduation" when he assumes that because he considers black students to be less than human, they will not be demoralized by his remarks. He does not take into account the limitations of his own experience, the pride of the graduates, or the heritage of the black population of Stamps.

Either/or assumes the possibility of only two diametrically opposed outcomes. To argue that colleges either maintain high admissions standards or foster racial diversity is to ignore other possibilities, for example that considering a number of criteria, including both academic standards and race, might result in a diverse institution with high standards.

Hasty generalization is also called jumping to conclusions. Just because integration of Central High School in Little Rock, Arkansas resulted in federal intervention, there was no reason to assume that all integration programs would require National Guard troops. Some communities were better prepared to abide by the *Brown v. Board of Education* decision than others.

Begging the question involves assuming that a conclusion is valid and using that conclusion as part of the argument. Donleavy in "Graduation" begs the question implicitly when he assumes that all black students aspire to be sports figures. Assuming that his conclusion is valid, he cannot see that there is no evidence to support it.

Ad hominem (Latin for "to the man") is an attack made on a person's character rather than on the position the person has taken. To discredit an opponent of affirmative action because she is in the midst of a messy divorce is to avoid the issue at hand.

Appeal to faulty authority involves attributing expertise on an issue to someone whose expertise lies in a different area. Supporting affirmative action because a leading show-business celebrity does is an example of this fallacy.

Red herring is a term for intentional diversion of attention away from an issue. Many segregationist leaders in Arkansas in the early 1960s committed this fallacy by calling up the specter of communism when confronted with civil rights activists demanding integrated schools.

False analogy ignores the fact that two analogous things or situations are not alike in all respects. Many historians now consider the analogy of the melting pot to be essentially false. While the many nationalities that make up this country, like the ingredients in a melting pot do, exist in harmony, they do not blend to become indistinguishable from one another.

It is obvious that maintaining the integrity of a logical argument is often a challenge. The legitimacy of the argument depends upon a sound relationship among the claim, the grounds, and the warrant.

Ethos

Ethos is often equal in importance to logos in an argument because it establishes the credibility and sincerity of the author. *Ethos* establishes a relationship between the arguer and the audience that supports the rational appeal of the argument. Any argument is enhanced if its author is deemed to have integrity, expertise, and a fair-minded approach. For example, Maya Angelou's *ethos* is established both within and without "Graduation." Within the essay she establishes her credibility by clearly presenting herself as one who has suffered the inequities of segregation; she has first-hand experience of her subject. A brief look at Angelou's biography also establishes her *ethos:* Growing up in the segregated South and San Francisco, she overcame numerous obstacles to become the first black female conductor on the San Francisco cable cars, to excel as an accomplished writer and actor, and to be chosen to compose and present the ceremonial poem at President Bill Clinton's first inauguration. Her experience creates sympathy in her audience, and her credentials lend credibility to her position. The establishment of credentials refers to a form of ethical proof called **argument from authority.**

Argument from authority is used to support the logical argument by calling upon the opinions of experts in the field. Because it is possible to find experts to support any number of positions in a given argument, establishing the credibility of the expert is essential. As discussed in the section on grounds, the expert should possess appropriate credentials and be respected in the field. Of course it is also essential that the authority's expertise be relevant to the topic at hand. Arguments against public school segregation after 1954 exemplify argument from authority:

Argument: Segregated schools are inherently unequal.

Support: The United States Supreme Court decided this point in 1954.

18

For an argument to have sound ethical appeal, it is necessary for the arguer to establish his or her own integrity, as well as the integrity of authorities cited in support of the claim.

Pathos

Pathos is perhaps the most familiar type of proof found in everyday arguments. Appealing strictly to the emotions of the audience, *pathos* can strengthen an otherwise sound rational argument by engaging the audience on a more personal level. A purely emotional argument is rarely convincing; however, expanding the appeal of an argument beyond *logos* and *ethos* can enhance it. Emotional appeals, if legitimately related to the claim, will strengthen a purely rational argument. The reason for this is simple: Human beings make decisions based on emotion as well as on reason. Indeed, sometimes emotional concerns outweigh reasonable concerns. Maya Angelou uses emotional appeals effectively in "Graduation" when she describes how she felt after Edward Donleavy's speech:

> Graduation, the hush-hush magic time of frills and gifts and congratulations and diplomas, was finished for me before my name was called. The accomplishment was nothing. The meticulous maps, drawn in three colors of ink, learning and spelling decasyllabic words, memorizing the whole of *The Rape of Lucrece*—it was for nothing. Donleavy had exposed us.

The demoralization of a young girl whose hopes only recently had included heading "for the freedom of open fields" supports the implicit argument against segregation that permeates Angelou's piece. By allowing her audience to focus not on statistics and principles but rather on a real girl's disillusionment with her life and her race, she brings the issue into clearer focus for her readers by providing a personal touch.

Language and Pathos

"Graduation" also illustrates the significance of language in *pathos*. When considering the meaning of words, it is important to distinguish between *denotation*, the dictionary definition of the word, and *connotation*, the implied meaning or emotional overtones of the word. The word *group*, for example, is rather neutral in both denotation and connotation; it refers to a number of people with some common purpose. Change the word to *gang*, however, and while the dictionary meaning may remain essentially the same, the sinister implications of the word, the sense of danger or violence, cannot be ignored. Thus a newspaper account referring to a *group* of civil rights activists creates a different image than one referring to a *gang* of activists. Angelou uses connotation when she asks why her brother has to "pay penance for his skin" in order to become a lawyer. Her reference to penance calls up religious images of sinning against God, thereby heightening the impact of this condemnation of segregation. Similarly, when she describes the demeanor of the principal and the teachers during Donleavy's speech, she writes, "the ancient tragedy was being replayed." Tragedy is often considered the highest form of drama; ancient tragedy, particularly Greek tragedy, is considered the model for everything that has followed. The implication Angelou makes, then, is that this is much more than simply an uncomfortable moment for these school officials; the scene has universal implications.

Emotional Proof

Arguments from emotion fall into two categories: **motivational appeals** and **appeals to values**. Each appeal can strengthen a rational argument.

Motivational appeals rely on an understanding of people's needs and desires. In addition to basic biological needs such as food and shelter, people also have needs for safety, for belonging, for self-expression, and so on. In "Graduation," Maya Angelou appeals to her readers' need to be perceived as good, to be approved of. When Angelou presents her arguments on the effects of segregated schools on black children, she taps into her readers' need to think themselves good, moral people. Her appeal might be presented as follows:

Argument: You should share my condemnation of segregation.

Appeal: Moral people condemn segregation, and you want to be considered a moral person.

Appeals to values rely on commonly held beliefs about what is good or desirable. (Appeals to values are similar to claims of value in the Toulmin model.) Political campaigns throughout the past two decades have focused on terms such as "family values," which, while vague and often ill-defined, nonetheless resonate with many voters. By calling upon a value shared by the audience, an arguer can strengthen a rational argument. Angelou, for example, is aware of the values of her primary audience, American readers, when she focuses on the career aspirations and the industriousness of her classmates. If her readers agree that these qualities are consistent with American values, then it is difficult for them to reject Angelou's position on segregated schools. Her argument can be outlined as follows:

Argument: Segregated schools were bad for black Americans.

Appeal: Segregated schools interfered with students' aspirations and industriousness, qualities that are valued in American society.

These lines of argument can be employed in any number of combinations. Most successful arguments will balance *logos, ethos,* and *pathos* in such a way that audiences are convinced not only by reason, but by authority and emotion as well.

READING AND WRITING ARGUMENTS

Now that you understand the nature of argument, you can employ that understanding in analyzing written arguments and in composing your own arguments. Using the previous discussion of the components of an effective argument to focus on specifics, you should be able to use the following advice to read argumentative texts with a critical eye.

Reading Arguments Critically

A critical reader creates a dialogue with a text by considering the author's ideas, making observations, asking questions, analyzing the author's perspective in relation to those of others, forging connections between different selections—in short, the critical reader *responds* to what the writer is saying. Responding effectively to an argument normally involves three activities: **understanding the topic**, **evaluating the evidence**, and **considering alternative perspectives**.

Understanding the Topic

A well-written argument will provide you with enough information to understand the topic at hand. But the writer is obviously presenting the material from his or her own perspective. Therefore, in order to effectively read and understand another's argument, you must first take stock of your own knowledge of the topic. This activity involves considering what you already know about the topic, clarifying your perspective on the topic, and recalling what else you may have read about the topic. If you discover that your knowledge is quite limited, you may want to investigate the topic further by talking to other students or professors and by reading about the topic in newspapers or magazines. When you begin reading the argument itself, try to identify background information presented within it. Maya Angelou, for example, describes the playground at the Lafayette County Training School and explains that the facilities at the white Central High School are far superior. Regardless of her judgment on the unfairness of these inequities, Angelou has provided readers with a sense of the conditions under which black and white children attended school prior to the *Brown v. Board of Education* decision.

More traditionally argumentative pieces include information on the topic early in the essay, often in the first paragraph.

Understanding the topic also includes identifying the claim, the grounds, and the warrant of the argument. Not all arguments are presented according to the Toulmin model, but it is possible to apply the model to most arguments. Thus the first thing to do after establishing your understanding of the piece is to highlight the author's statement of the claim. While many arguments feature clear statements of claim, some do not. Chief Justice Earl Warren, for example, states the claim clearly in his majority opinion in *Brown*: "Separate educational facilities are inherently unequal." Maya Angelou, on the other hand, never states her claim explicitly. In this case, you should state her implied claim in your own words. Those words might echo Warren's, or they might be more emotional: "Racism, as illustrated in segregated schools, demoralizes worthy black children" is one possibility.

Recognizing the grounds, or support for the claim, is the next step in reading an argument critically. The previous discussion of supporting evidence identifies several kinds of support found in Angelou's "Graduation": her identification of the industriousness and aspirations of black children, her description of the unequal facilities, and her account of the emotional toll of Donleavy's speech. Chief Justice Warren cites the changing nature of public education between 1896 and 1954, decisions in recent cases involving segregated educational facilities, and the opinions of psychologists on the effects of inferior education.

Identifying the warrant is usually a more difficult task that involves interpretation. Among Angelou's warrants are assumptions that all children should be provided with equal educational opportunities, that industriousness and aspirations are valuable American qualities, and that segregation is morally wrong. None of these warrants is stated explicitly, but a reader familiar with the Toulmin model of argument should be able to infer them from reading Angelou's narrative.

In order to facilitate your dialogue with the text, it is important to do more than simply read and identify elements passively. Underline or highlight claims and grounds; summarize them in the margins of the text; make note of questions you have regarding your understanding of certain items. If the selection includes terms that you do not understand, look them up. Often understanding one key term can turn an incomprehensible paragraph into a model of clear prose.

Evaluating the Evidence

As readers, we often take one of two contradictory approaches to a text. The first approach assumes that if the piece is published, then it must be right, so we will not question it. The second, usually occurring when we read something expressing a position contrary to our own, is simply to dismiss the argument without considering its merits. Neither approach is conducive to critical reading. In the first case, while publication lends a certain credibility to an argument, it is possible to find published arguments featuring opposing views on almost any topic. In the second case, it is necessary to understand that most published arguments are presented in the hope of continuing a dialogue on the issue. Thus to dismiss the argument out of hand is to cut off conversation. The critical reader should neither assume that the author has all the answers nor that the author has none. Instead, the critical reader evaluates the evidence presented by the author in support of the claim. This is precisely what Chief Justice Warren does in his decision on the *Brown* case. Part of the evidence presented to the Court was a precedent, the 1896 *Plessy v. Ferguson* case in which separate facilities were ruled not inherently unequal. In evaluating the legitimacy of that evidence, Warren (speaking for the majority) notes that the nature and purposes of public education differ profoundly in 1896 and 1954 and that psychologists have in the meantime identified the negative impact of unequal treatment. Thus the *Plessy* case is not deemed a legitimate precedent, and it is rejected as grounds. While it may not be easy to determine the legitimacy of grounds or warrants in the arguments you read, you can measure them against the grounds you offer for your own position as well as those offered by people making opposing claims.

It is worth noting that you can reject the grounds and warrant in an argument without rejecting the claim itself. Many of us have been in the position of agreeing with a certain claim but bemoaning the fact that the grounds are insufficient to support it. You may support capital punishment, for example, but find unconvincing the argument that asks how you would feel if you were directly affected by a capital crime. Your judgment will not reflect your position on the issue, only your evaluation of the evidence. It is always wise to distinguish between your agreement with a claim and your evaluation of the legitimacy of the grounds.

Considering Alternative Perspectives

Because a published argument is usually designed to further the dialogue about a certain issue, you should consider reading alternative arguments in order to assess the effectiveness of the original argument you have read. It is only after considering an issue from multiple perspectives that you can consider yourself truly capable of taking a position on that issue. For Chief Justice Warren, of course, it was necessary to consider alternative arguments; his job (and the job of his colleagues on the Supreme Court) was to examine the grounds for a number of different claims regarding segregated schools. After reading "Graduation," you might consider alternative perspectives on one of the responses to segregation, affirmative action. In the past three decades affirmative action has come under fire not only from white conservatives but from black activists as well. While writers such as Henry Louis Gates and Orlando Patterson have written extensively about the value of affirmative action, it has been criticized by writers such as Shelby Steele and Dinesh D'Souza. Perhaps the most valuable result of reading alternative perspectives on an issue is the realization that few issues lend themselves to only two opposing positions. More often than not, a number of positions between the two extremes exist as well, and they can enlighten readers to the complexity of most arguments.

Once you have established an understanding of the topic, evaluated the evidence, and considered alternative perspectives, you should be prepared to respond to the argument. If that response is to take the form of a formal essay, then the following guidelines should be helpful.

Writing Arguments

Writing argumentative essays is not entirely different from writing other types of essays. Indeed, argumentative essays often employ narrative, definition, cause-and-effect, and other rhetorical strategies. The writing process itself is similar as well: You will engage in prewriting, composing, revising, and editing—just as you do in all of your formal writing. Argumentative essays, however, involve a more refined process of writing. Just as in reading arguments, in writing them you must understand the topic, evaluate the evidence, and consider alternative perspectives. In writing arguments, you engage in the same specific activities associated with reading arguments critically:

> **Understanding the topic**: Read extensively about the issue and develop your own claim.

> **Evaluating the evidence**: Determine what evidence supports your claim and decide upon an organizational strategy.

> **Considering alternative perspectives**: Identify the most convincing arguments in opposition to your claim and address them.

Understanding the Topic

If you are to write a convincing argument on any topic, you must be familiar with the issues involved. While you may be able to engage in informal debate about a topic, it is unlikely that you can compose a well supported essay without doing some formal research. Reading newspaper articles, editorial columns, letters to the editor, and magazine pieces; talking with representatives of organizations involved in the issue; and attending relevant meetings will help you to familiarize yourself with the multiple perspectives from which the issue can be considered. Just as Chief Justice Warren had to review a number of precedents before writing his decision in *Brown v. Board of Education*, you must become familiar with the background of your topic before writing your argument. It is even conceivable that you may change your position on the issue after researching it. Regardless of whether your research alters or solidifies your position, however, your task once you have completed your preliminary review of the issue is to develop a claim, or thesis, that you think is defensible.

For the purposes of this discussion, consider the following scenario: A toxic waste dump has been proposed for your community. After investigating the impact such facilities have had on other communities, you either oppose or support its construction. This example not only taps into a heated current debate, but it also involves issues of health, the environment, and economics, thus offering the opportunity to support the claim (whether in opposition to or in support of the dump) from a number of different perspectives. One possible thesis on this topic is the following:

Thesis: Because of its impact on the economy, health, and the environment, a toxic waste dump should not be built in this community.

Whether or not you open your essay with the explicitly stated claim is a decision that should wait until later; it is normally best to concentrate on developing the argument itself before considering how to present it to your audience.

At this point, however, it is important to remember that failure to understand your audience can undermine an otherwise strong argument. As mentioned earlier, it is essential to recognize the needs and values of the audience as you compose your argument; remember, the most basic goal of argument is to convince the audience of the legitimacy of a claim. Thus the advice offered previously is worth repeating: Some audiences will be entirely sympathetic to your position, some will be antithetic, and many will fall somewhere between those two extremes. Your task in making an argument is to appeal to the **beliefs** and **values** of your audience. If you can find common beliefs and values, your task will be easier. For example, most members of a community will be sensitive to the economic impact of a toxic waste dump; a facility providing both jobs and tax dollars is an attractive prospect. You will be more persuasive, then, if you can address economic concerns. Perhaps you might balance the economic advantages of a dump with the increased costs of health care, loss of work due to illness, and decline of property values in order to appeal to those whose position stems from their sense of economic values.

Evaluating the Evidence

The evidence you choose to ground your argument depends not only on the nature of the claim itself but also on the needs and values of your audience. For example, if your community has demonstrated environmental awareness through recycling programs and conservation of land, then the environmental argument will be particularly appealing to them. If the community normally considers economic issues of primary importance, then the economic impact of the dump should be emphasized. Maya Angelou's audience is one that appreciates human-interest stories—her book is a memoir. Thus her appeal in "Graduation" is an emotional one, unlike Chief Justice Warren's rational appeal aimed at a legal audience. The nature and presentation of your evidence will also depend on your audience.

Suppose that you have determined from your reading on the subject and your knowledge of the people in the community that while economic issues are important to them, their primary concerns involve health and the environment. The following evidence, then, would be appropriate:

Evidence: Toxic waste dumps have been known to pollute the environment.

Increases in serious illnesses, including cancer, have been associated with toxic waste dumps.

Communities in which toxic waste dumps have been built have experienced a decline in property values and a loss of businesses.

In order to convince your audience of the legitimacy of this evidence, you will have to provide information such as examples of communities in which toxic waste dumps have been built, the opinion of experts on the relationship between the dumps and disease, and analyses of the economic impact of the dumps. The strength of your argument will depend in large part on how effectively you present this material. Pages of statistics with little narrative to break them up, for example, will likely confuse or bore all but the most technical audiences. Failure to make your warrant clear also will result in an unconvincing argument. While it is hardly necessary to state explicitly that the community values health, the environment, and a sound economic base, it will be necessary to establish the relative value of each of these features to a community. If you evaluate your evidence as conscientiously as you would that of an argument you were reading, your argument should be sound.

Considering Alternative Perspectives

When you are reading an argument, you consider alternative perspectives in order to evaluate the argument's effectiveness and to gauge your response to it. When writing an argument, you consider the opposition in order to strengthen your presentation. If you have conducted thorough research prior to making your claim, you should be aware of the alternative perspectives that might challenge you. Because of the significance of precedent in supporting a legal argument, for example, Chief Justice Warren addresses the *Plessy v. Ferguson* case explicitly in his argument, rebutting *Plessy's* claim by discussing the altered nature of public schools. You may have discovered evidence that toxic waste dumps bring needed tax revenues and jobs to the communities in which they are situated. If you are to argue successfully against the dump, you must address this evidence. If you can point to a decline in property values and a loss of other small businesses, then you have effectively countered the impact of the evidence.

Opposing view:	Dumps are an economic boon to communities because they generate tax revenues and increase employment.
Acknowledgment/ Rebuttal:	While dumps do provide taxes and jobs, their positive economic impact is mitigated by a decline in property values and a loss of other businesses.

What happens, however, if you do not have sufficient evidence to refute the economic claim? In this case, it will probably be necessary to revise your evidence to emphasize only health and environment, and to acknowledge that while dumps do have positive economic impact, their overall negative impact is more significant:

Opposing view:	Dumps are an economic boon to communities because they generate tax revenues and increase employment.

Acknowledgment/
Rebuttal: While dumps are economically valuable to
                        a community, their negative impact on
                        environment and health outweighs any
                        economic benefits.

Whether you acknowledge alternative perspectives or rebut them, including them in your argument reveals not only that you are well versed in the subject, but also that you are fair-minded.

Composing the Paper

Once you have a clear idea of your position and the evidence you will use to support it, you can determine how to present your argument to your audience. At this stage you can rely on what you have learned about writing essays in general, using a few tips related specifically to argumentative writing.

Drafting an Introduction/Statement of Thesis

A variety of options exist for introducing an argument. You may want to begin with an anecdote, a brief story that engages your audience. You may want to begin with a statement of your thesis, establishing from the first sentence that you take this issue seriously. You may choose to use your introduction to establish the background of the issue and save your thesis until the essay's conclusion, after presenting evidence in favor of your position. These decisions will depend in large part on your audience. If your audience includes families in the community, for example, a well-chosen anecdote may drive home to them the real impact the dump will have on their lives. If the audience is less personally involved in the issue, however, you may choose to simply state your position. And if you want to persuade your audience without their necessarily being aware of it, you can wait until the end to state your claim, bringing the audience to your conclusion through your presentation.

Your introduction also depends on the nature of the subject and the argument itself. It may be necessary, for example, to define terms in your introduction, or to provide background information that may not be familiar to your audience. If the subject is particularly controversial, it may be necessary to acknowledge the legitimacy of various alternative perspectives before beginning the argument.

Deciding how to introduce the argument is not simply a stylistic decision. The effectiveness of the argument itself will be influenced by the way in which it is introduced.

Organizing the Evidence
Since it is the evidence that ultimately convinces most audiences, the decision on how to organize that evidence is a crucial one. As in determining how to introduce the argument, audience considerations are important. An unfriendly audience may need to be led step-by-step to your conclusion. In that case, you may want to begin with the least significant item of evidence and move to the most significant. This strategy assumes that if you can convince your audience to agree with you in small increments, then the audience will have no choice but to accept your claim at the end. Of course, the decision on how significant any piece of evidence is rests with the audience. A community overwhelmingly concerned with a high unemployment rate, for example, may consider the economic implications of a toxic waste dump far more significant than any long-term environmental impact. Moving from the environmental to the health and then to the economic evidence might be the most effective organizational strategy for this audience.

If your evidence includes something especially compelling, you may want to reverse this organization and start with the strongest piece of evidence. Suppose your evidence includes a report from a prestigious university indicating that the groundwater within several miles of every toxic waste dump built in the past decade has become contaminated. This evidence may be so powerful that you want to present it to your audience first, placing the rest of your evidence in a supporting role to this, the star witness. The advantage of such an organizational strategy is that you all but convince your audience with your first piece of evidence, making it easier for them to accept your other, less compelling evidence.

What do you do if the opposite is true? If there is a particularly strong opposing argument, you may wish to deal with that argument first. If you delay your rebuttal until you have presented your own evidence, you may have already lost your audience. It is possible that your audience will read your entire argument distracted by their curiosity about how you will deal with the opposition. Thus it is sometimes wise to present the opposing argument first, acknowledging its legitimacy, and then refuting its claims before moving on to your own evidence. The advantage of this approach is that you clear your audience's minds of distraction at the same time that you present yourself as a fair-minded person.

If you keep in mind both the audience and the nature of your evidence as you determine your organizational strategy, you should be able to construct a solid foundation on which to base your claim.

Concluding

A conventional conclusion to an argumentative paper will sum up the evidence and reinforce the thesis. If you have chosen to save your thesis for the end of the paper, however, the thesis will be stated explicitly for the first time in the conclusion. Other alternatives include returning to an anecdote used in the introduction, perhaps by completing the story based on the evidence you have amassed. You also may wish to issue a call to action in your conclusion. If you believe that your audience has been convinced, for example, that the toxic waste dump should not be built in the community, you may conclude with a call to join the movement opposing the dump. Whether you sum up, state the thesis for the first time, complete an anecdote, or issue a call to action, you want to make sure that your conclusion leaves your audience thinking seriously about your position—if not convinced that it is the right position.

Revising and Editing

The guidelines for revising a written argument are essentially the same as those for any other kind of paper: make sure that the thesis is clear, whether explicitly stated or implied; make sure that the organization is coherent and the evidence sound; and make sure that the conclusion is consistent and forceful. In particular, in revising an argumentative paper you should ask yourself the following questions:

1. Is your thesis clear, your position evident?

2. Is the audience provided with sufficient background on the topic?

3. Are all relevant terms defined?

4. Is the relevance of each item of evidence to the thesis made clear?

5. Are all underlying assumptions identified?

6. Are opposing views acknowledged and satisfactorily rebutted?

7. Is the organization of evidence effective?

8. Is the conclusion forceful and consistent with the thesis and evidence?

When you are ready to edit your paper, remember the earlier discussion of *pathos*. The effectiveness of your argument depends in part on the audience's perception of you as author. One of the surest and easiest ways to undermine your effectiveness is to ignore mechanical, grammatical, spelling, and format issues. At best your audience will be distracted by errors; at worst they will question the credibility of a writer either unwilling or unable to conform to the most basic conventions of standard written English. While it is obviously the argument itself that convinces the audience, a carefully edited paper will tell your audience that you not only care about your topic, but that you are a competent writer as well.

BIBLIOGRAPHY

Brockreide, Wayne, and Douglas Ehninger. "Toulmin on Argument: An Interpretation and Application." *The Quarterly Journal of Speech* 46 (1960): 44–53.

Fahnestock, Jeanne, and Marie Secor. "Teaching Argument: A Theory of Types. *College Composition and Communication* 34 (1983): 20–30.

Kaufer, David S., and Christine M. Neuwirth. "Integrating Formal Logic and the New Rhetoric: A Four-Stage Heuristic." *College English* 45 (1983): 380–389.

Kneupper, Charles W. "Teaching Argument: An Introduction to the Toulmin Model." *College Composition and Communication* 29 (1978): 237–241.

Toulmin, Stephen. *The Uses of Argument.* New York: Cambridge UP, 1964.

—————, Richard Rieke, and Allan Janik. *An Introduction to Reasoning.* New York: Macmillan, 1979.

Winder, Barbara E. "The Delineation of Values in Persuasive Writing." *College Composition and Communication* 29 (1978): 55–58.

Graduation

Maya Angelou

Maya Angelou (1928–) was born in St. Louis, Missouri, with the name Marguerite Johnson, but grew up with her grandmother in Stamps, Arkansas, from the age of 3. Her traumatic childhood included being raped at age 8 by her mother's boyfriend, after which she became mute for five years. She was shuttled back and forth between mother and grandmother, living for a brief time also with her father and running away to join a group of homeless children. At age 16 she gave birth to her son, Guy. She went through many life changes in the decades that followed, including success as a dancer and actor as well as experiences as a cook, a prostitute, and a chauffeur. Increasingly she focused on her writing, which includes four books of poetry and four plays, as well as the five autobiographical novels for which she is best known: I Know Why the Caged Bird Sings *(1970),* Gather Together in My Name *(1974),* Singin' and Swingin' and Gettin' Merry Like Christmas *(1976),* The Heart of a Woman *(1981), and* All God's Children Need Traveling Shoes *(1986). Angelou is an influential African-American author who has received many honors and fellowships. The essay "Graduation" is excerpted from* I Know Why the Caged Bird Sings, *which describes her early childhood. This essay focuses on the period in her life when she was learning what it meant to be black in a world dominated by whites, where discrimination affected not only her school but her whole world.*

The children in Stamps trembled visibly with anticipation. Some adults were excited too, but to be certain the whole young population had come down with graduation epidemic. Large classes were graduating from both the grammar school and the high school. Even those who were years removed from their own day of glorious release were anxious to help with preparations as a kind of dry run. The junior students who were moving into the vacating classes' chairs were tradition-bound to show their talents for leadership and management. They strutted through the school and around the campus exerting pressure on the lower grades. Their authority was so new that occasionally if they pressed a little too hard it had to be overlooked. After all, next term was coming, and it never hurt a sixth-grader to have a play sister in the eighth grade, or a tenth-year student to be able to call a twelfth-grader Bubba. So all was endured in a spirit of shared understanding. But the graduating classes themselves were the nobility. Like travelers with exotic destinations on their minds, the graduates were remarkably forgetful. They came to school without their books, or tablets or even pencils. Volunteers fell over themselves to secure replacements for the missing equipment. When accepted, the willing workers might or might not be thanked, and it was of no importance to the pregraduation rites. Even teachers were respectful of the now quiet and aging seniors, and tended to speak to them, if not as equals, as beings only slightly lower than themselves. After tests were returned and grades given, the student body, which acted like an extended family, knew who did well, who excelled, and what piteous ones had failed.

Unlike the white high school, Lafayette County Training School distinguished itself by having neither lawn, nor hedges, nor tennis court, nor climbing ivy. Its two buildings (main classrooms, the grade school and home economics) were set on a dirt hill with no fence to limit either its boundaries or those of bordering farms. There was a large expanse to the left of the school which was used alternately as a baseball diamond or a basketball court. Rusty hoops on the swaying poles represented the permanent recreational equipment, although bats and balls could be borrowed from the P.E. teacher if the borrower was qualified and if the diamond wasn't occupied.

Over this rocky area relieved by a few shady tall persimmon trees the graduating class walked. The girls often held hands and no longer bothered to speak to the lower students. There was a sadness about them, as if this old world was not their home and they were bound for higher ground. The boys, on the other hand, had become more friendly, more outgoing. A decided change from the closed attitude they projected while studying for finals. Now they seemed not ready to give up the old school, the familiar paths and classrooms. Only a small percentage would be continuing on to college—one of the South's A & M (agricultural and mechanical) schools, which trained Negro youths to be carpenters, farmers, handymen, masons, maids, cooks and baby nurses. Their future rode heavily on their shoulders, and blinded them to the collective joy that had pervaded the lives of the boys and girls in the grammar school graduating class.

Parents who could afford it had ordered new shoes and ready-made clothes for themselves from Sears, Roebuck or Montgomery Ward. They also engaged the best seamstresses to make the floating graduating dresses and to cut down secondhand pants which would be pressed to a military slickness for the important event.

Oh, it was important, all right. Whitefolks would attend the ceremony, and two or three would speak of God and home, and the Southern way of life, and Mrs. Parsons, the principal's wife, would play the graduation march while the lower-grade graduates paraded down the aisles and took their seats below the platform. The high school seniors would wait in empty classrooms to make their dramatic entrance.

In the Store I was the person of the moment. The birthday girl. The center. Bailey had graduated the year before, although to do so he had had to forfeit all pleasures to make up for his time lost in Baton Rouge.

My class was wearing butter-yellow piqué dresses, and Momma launched out on mine. She smocked the yoke into tiny crisscrossing puckers, then shirred the rest of the bodice. Her dark fingers ducked in and out of the lemony cloth as she embroidered raised daisies around the hem. Before she considered herself finished she had added a crocheted cuff on the puff sleeves, and a pointy crocheted collar.

I was going to be lovely. A walking model of all the various styles of fine hand sewing and it didn't worry me that I was only twelve years old and merely graduating from the eighth grade. Besides, many teachers in Arkansas Negro schools had only that diploma and were licensed to impart wisdom.

The days had become longer and more noticeable. The faded beige of former times had been replaced with strong and sure colors. I began to see my classmates' clothes, their skin tones, and the dust that waved off pussy willows. Clouds that lazed across the sky were objects of great concern to me. Their shiftier shapes might have held a message that in my new happiness and with a little bit of time I'd soon decipher. During that period I looked at the arch of heaven so religiously my neck kept a steady ache. I had taken to smiling more often, and my jaws hurt from the unaccustomed activity. Between the two physical sore spots, I suppose I could have been uncomfortable, but that was not the case. As a member of the winning team (the graduating class of 1940) I had outdistanced unpleasant sensations by miles. I was headed for the freedom of open fields.

Youth and social approval allied themselves with me and we trammeled memories of slights and insults. The wind of our swift passage remodeled my features. Lost tears were pounded to mud and then to dust. Years of withdrawal were brushed aside and left behind, as hanging ropes of parasitic moss.

My work alone had awarded me a top place and I was going to be one of the first called in the graduating ceremonies. On the classroom blackboard, as well as on the bulletin board in the auditorium, there were blue stars and white stars and red stars. No absences, no tardinesses, and my academic work was among the best of the year. I could say the preamble to the Constitution even faster than Bailey. We timed ourselves often: "WethepeopleoftheUnited-Statesinordertoformamore perfectunion . . . " I had memorized the Presidents of the United States from Washington to Roosevelt in chronological as well as alphabetical order.

My hair pleased me too. Gradually the black mass had lengthened and thickened, so that it kept at last to its braided pattern, and I didn't have to yank my scalp off when I tried to comb it.

Louise and I had rehearsed the exercises until we tired out ourselves. Henry Reed was class valedictorian. He was a small, very black boy with hooded eyes, a long, broad nose and an oddly shaped head. I had admired him for years because each term he and I vied for the best grades in our class. Most often he bested me, but instead of being disappointed I was pleased that we shared top places between us. Like many Southern Black children, he lived with his grandmother, who was as strict as Momma and as kind as she knew how to be. He was courteous, respectful, and soft-spoken to elders, but on the playground he chose to play the roughest games. I admired him. Anyone, I reckoned, sufficiently afraid or sufficiently dull could be polite. But to be able to operate at a top level with both adults and children was admirable.

His valedictory speech was entitled "To Be or Not to Be." The rigid tenth-grade teacher had helped him write it. He'd been working on the dramatic stresses for months.

The weeks until graduation were filled with heady activities. A group of small children were to be presented in a play about buttercups and daisies and bunny rabbits. They could be heard throughout the building practicing their hops and their little songs that sounded like silver bells. The older girls (nongraduates, of course) were assigned the task of making refreshments for the night's festivities. A tangy scent of ginger, cinnamon, nutmeg and chocolate wafted around the home economics building as the budding cooks made samples for themselves and their teachers.

In every corner of the workshop, axes and saws split fresh timber as the woodshop boys made sets and stage scenery. Only the graduates were left out of the general bustle. We were free to sit in the library at the back of the building or look in quite detachedly, naturally, on the measures being taken for our event.

Even the minister preached on graduation the Sunday before. His subject was, "Let your light so shine that men will see your good works and praise your Father, Who is in Heaven." Although the sermon was purported to be addressed to us, he used the occasion to speak to backsliders, gamblers, and general ne'er-do-wells. But since he had called our names at the beginning of the service we were mollified.

Among Negroes the tradition was to give presents to children going only from one grade to another. How much more important this was when the person was graduating at the top of the class. Uncle Willie and Momma had sent away for a Mickey Mouse watch like Bailey's. Louise gave me four embroidered handkerchiefs. (I gave her three crocheted doilies.) Mrs. Sneed, the minister's wife, made me an underskirt to wear for graduation, and nearly every customer gave me a nickel or maybe even a dime with the instruction "Keep on moving to higher ground," or some such encouragement.

Amazingly the great day finally dawned and I was out of bed before I knew it. I threw open the back door to see it more clearly, but Momma said, "Sister, come away from that door and put your robe on."

I hoped the memory of that morning would never leave me. Sunlight was itself still young, and the day had none of the insistence maturity would bring it in a few hours. In my robe and barefoot in the backyard, under cover of going to see about my new beans, I gave myself up to the gentle warmth and thanked God that no matter what evil I had done in my life He had allowed me to live to see this day. Somewhere in my fatalism I had expected to die, accidentally, and never have the chance to walk up the stairs in the auditorium and gracefully receive my hard-earned diploma. Out of God's merciful bosom I had won reprieve.

Bailey came out in his robe and gave me a box wrapped in Christmas paper. He said he had saved his money for months to pay for it. It felt like a box of chocolates, but I knew Bailey wouldn't save money to buy candy when we had all we could want under our noses.

He was as proud of the gift as I. It was a soft-leatherbound copy of a collection of poems by Edgar Allan Poe, or, as Bailey and I called him, "Eap." I turned to "Annabel Lee" and we walked up and down the garden rows, the cool dirt between our toes, reciting the beautifully sad lines.

Momma made a Sunday breakfast although it was only Friday. After we finished the blessing, I opened my eyes to find the watch on my plate. It was a dream of a day. Everything went smoothly and to my credit. I didn't have to be reminded or scolded for anything. Near evening I was too jittery to attend to chores, so Bailey volunteered to do all before his bath.

Days before, we had made a sign for the Store, and as we turned out the lights Momma hung the cardboard over the doorknob. It read clearly: CLOSED. GRADUATION.

My dress fitted perfectly and everyone said that I looked like a sunbeam in it. On the hill, going toward the school, Bailey walked behind with Uncle Willie, who muttered, "Go on, Ju." He wanted him to walk ahead with us because it embarrassed him to have to walk so slowly. Bailey said he'd let the ladies walk together, and the men would bring up the rear. We all laughed, nicely.

Little children dashed by out of the dark like fireflies. Their crepe-paper dresses and butterfly wings were not made for running and we heard more than one rip, dryly, and the regretful "uh uh" that followed.

The school blazed without gaiety. The windows seemed cold and unfriendly from the lower hill. A sense of ill-fated timing crept over me, and if Momma hadn't reached for my hand I would have drifted back to Bailey and Uncle Willie, and possibly beyond. She made a few slow jokes about my feet getting cold, and tugged me along to the now-strange building.

Around the front steps, assurance came back. There were my fellow "greats," the graduating class. Hair brushed back, legs oiled, new dresses and pressed pleats, fresh pocket handkerchiefs and little handbags, all homesewn. Oh, we were up to snuff, all right. I joined my comrades and didn't even see my family go in to find seats in the crowded auditorium.

The school band struck up a march and all classes filed in as had been rehearsed. We stood in front of our seats, as assigned, and on a signal from the choir director, we sat. No sooner had this been accomplished than the band started to play the national anthem. We rose again and sang the song, after which we recited the pledge of allegiance. We remained standing for a brief minute before the choir director and the principal signaled to us, rather desperately I thought, to take our seats. The command was so unusual that our carefully rehearsed and smooth-running machine was thrown off. For a full minute we fumbled for our chairs and bumped into each other awkwardly. Habits change or solidify under pressure, so in our state of nervous tension we had been ready to follow our usual assembly pattern: the American national anthem, then the pledge of allegiance, then the song every Black person I knew called the Negro National Anthem. All done in the same key, with the same passion and most often standing on the same foot.

Finding my seat at last, I was overcome with a presentiment of worse things to come. Something unrehearsed, unplanned, was going to happen, and we were going to be made to look bad. I distinctly remember being explicit in the choice of pronoun. It was "we," the graduating class, the unit, that concerned me then.

The principal welcomed "parents and friends" and asked the Baptist minister to lead us in prayer. His invocation was brief and

41

punchy, and for a second I thought we were getting back on the high road to right action. When the principal came back to the dais, however, his voice had changed. Sounds always affected me profoundly and the principal's voice was one of my favorites. During assembly it melted and lowed weakly into the audience. It had not been in my plan to listen to him, but my curiosity was piqued and I straightened up to give him my attention.

He was talking about Booker T. Washington, our "late great leader," who said we can be as close as the fingers on the hand, etc. . . . Then he said a few vague things about friendship and the friendship of kindly people to those less fortunate than themselves. With that his voice nearly faded, thin, away. Like a river diminishing to a stream and then to a trickle. But he cleared his throat and said, "Our speaker tonight, who is also our friend, came from Texarkana to deliver the commencement address, but due to the irregularity of the train schedule, he's going to, as they say, 'speak and run.' " He said that we understood and wanted the man to know that we were most grateful for the time he was able to give us and then something about how we were willing always to adjust to another's program, and without more ado—"I give you Mr. Edward Donleavy."

Not one but two white men came through the door offstage. The shorter one walked to the speaker's platform, and the tall one moved over to the center seat and sat down. But that was our principal's seat, and already occupied. The dislodged gentleman bounced around for a long breath or two before the Baptist minister gave him his chair, then with more dignity than the situation deserved, the minister walked off the stage.

Donleavy looked at the audience once (on reflection, I'm sure that he wanted only to reassure himself that we were really there), adjusted his glasses and began to read from a sheaf of papers.

He was glad "to be here and to see the work going on just as it was in the other schools."

At the first "Amen" from the audience I willed the offender to immediate death by choking on the word. But Amens and Yes, sir's began to fall around the room like rain through a ragged umbrella.

He told us of the wonderful changes we children in Stamps had in store. The Central School (naturally, the white school was Central) had already been granted improvements that would be in use in the fall. A well-known artist was coming from Little Rock to teach art to them. They were going to have the newest microscopes and chemistry equipment for their laboratory. Mr. Donleavy didn't leave us long in the dark over who made these improvements available to Central High. Nor were we to be ignored in the general betterment scheme he had in mind.

He said that he had pointed out to people at a very high level that one of the first-line football tacklers at Arkansas Agricultural and Mechanical College had graduated from good old Lafayette County Training School. Here fewer Amen's were heard. Those few that did break through lay dully in the air with the heaviness of habit.

He went on to praise us. He went on to say how he had bragged that "one of the best basketball players at Fisk sank his first ball right here at Lafayette County Training School."

The white kids were going to have a chance to become Galileos and Madame Curies and Edisons and Gauguins, and our boys (the girls weren't even in on it) would try to be Jesse Owenses and Joe Louises.

Owens and the Brown Bomber were great heroes in our world, but what school official in the white-goddom of Little Rock had the right to decide that those two men must be our only heroes? Who decided that for Henry Reed to become a scientist he had to work like George Washington Carver, as a bootblack, to buy a lousy microscope? Bailey was obviously always going to be too small to be an athlete, so which concrete angel glued to what country seat had decided that if my brother wanted to become a lawyer he had to first pay penance for his skin by picking cotton and hoeing corn and studying correspondence books at night for twenty years?

The man's dead words fell like bricks around the auditorium and too many settled in my belly. Constrained by hard-learned manners I couldn't look behind me, but to my left and right the proud graduating class of 1940 had dropped their heads. Every girl in my row had found something new to do with her handkerchief. Some folded the tiny squares into love knots, some into triangles, but most were wadding them, then pressing them flat on their yellow laps.

On the dais, the ancient tragedy was being replayed. Professor Parsons sat, a sculptor's reject, rigid. His large, heavy body seemed devoid of will or willingness, and his eyes said he was no longer with us. The other teachers examined the flag (which was draped stage right) or their notes, or the windows which opened on our now-famous playing diamond.

Graduation, the hush-hush magic time of frills and gifts and congratulations and diplomas, was finished for me before my name was called. The accomplishment was nothing. The meticulous maps, drawn in three colors of ink, learning and spelling decasyllabic words, memorizing the whole of *The Rape of Lucrece*—it was for nothing. Donleavy had exposed us.

We were maids and farmers, handymen and washerwomen, and anything higher that we aspired to was farcical and presumptuous.

Then I wished that Gabriel Prosser and Nat Turner had killed all whitefolks in their beds and that Abraham Lincoln had been assassinated before the signing of the Emancipation Proclamation, and that Harriet Tubman had been killed by that blow on her head and Christopher Columbus had drowned in the *Santa María*.

It was awful to be Negro and have no control over my life. It was brutal to be young and already trained to sit quietly and listen to charges brought against my color with no chance of defense. We should all be dead. I thought I should like to see us all dead, one on top of the other. A pyramid of flesh with the whitefolks on the bottom, as the broad base, then the Indians with their silly tomahawks and teepees and wigwams and treaties, the Negroes with their mops and recipes and cotton sacks and spirituals sticking out of their mouths. The Dutch children should all stumble in their wooden shoes and break their necks. The French should choke to death on the Louisiana Purchase (1803) while silkworms ate all the Chinese with their stupid pigtails. As a species, we were an abomination. All of us.

Donleavy was running for election, and assured our parents that if he won we could count on having the only colored paved playing field in that part of Arkansas. Also—he never looked up to acknowledge the grunts of acceptance—also, we were bound to get some new equipment for the home economics building and the workshop.

He finished, and since there was no need to give any more than the most perfunctory thank-you's, he nodded to the men on the stage, and the tall white man who was never introduced joined him at the door. They left with the attitude that now they were off to something really important. (The graduation ceremonies at Lafayette Country Training School had been a mere preliminary.)

The ugliness they left was palpable. An uninvited guest who wouldn't leave. The choir was summoned and sang a modern arrangement of "Onward, Christian Soldiers," with new words pertaining to graduates seeking their place in the world. But it didn't work. Elouise, the daughter of the Baptist minister, recited "Invictus," and I could have cried at the impertinence of "I am the master of my fate, I am the captain of my soul."

My name had lost its ring of familiarity and I had to be nudged to go and receive my diploma. All my preparations had fled. I neither marched up to the stage like a conquering Amazon, nor did I look in the audience for Bailey's nod of approval. Marguerite Johnson, I heard the name again, my honors were read, there were noises in the audience of appreciation, and I took my place on the stage as rehearsed.

I thought about colors I hated: ecru, puce, lavender, beige and black.

There was shuffling and rustling around me, then Henry Reed was giving his valedictory address, "To Be or Not to Be." Hadn't he heard the whitefolks? We couldn't *be,* so the question was a waste of time. Henry's voice came out clear and strong. I feared to look at him. Hadn't he got the message? There was no "nobler in the mind" for Negroes because the world didn't think we had minds, and they let us know it. "Outrageous fortune"? Now, that was a joke. When the ceremony was over I had to tell Henry Reed some things. That is, if I still cared. Not "rub," Henry, "erase." "Ah, there's the erase." Us.

Henry had been a good student in elocution. His voice rose on tides of promise and fell on waves of warnings. The English teacher had helped him to create a sermon winging through Hamlet's soliloquy. To be a man, a doer, a builder, a leader, or to be a tool, an unfunny joke, a crusher of funky toadstools. I marveled that Henry could go through with the speech as if we had a choice.

I had been listening and silently rebutting each sentence with my eyes closed; then there was a hush, which in an audience warns that something unplanned is happening. I looked up and saw Henry Reed, the conservative, the proper, the A student, turn his back to the audience and turn to us (the proud graduating class of 1940) and sing, nearly speaking,

"Lift ev'ry voice and sing
Till earth and heaven ring
Ring with the harmonies of Liberty . . . "

It was the poem written by James Weldon Johnson. It was the music composed by J. Rosamond Johnson. It was the Negro national anthem. Out of habit we were singing it.

Our mothers and fathers stood in the dark hall and joined the hymn of encouragement. A kindergarten teacher led the small children onto the stage and the buttercups and daisies and bunny rabbits marked time and tried to follow:

"Stony the road we trod
Bitter the chastening rod
Felt in the days when hope, unborn, had died.
'Yet with a steady beat
Have not our weary feet
Come to the place for which our fathers sighed?"

Every child I knew had learned that song with his ABC's and along with "Jesus Loves Me This I Know." But I personally had never heard it before. Never heard the words, despite the thousands of times I had sung them. Never thought they had anything to do with me.

On the other hand, the words of Patrick Henry had made such an impression on me that I had been able to stretch myself tall and trembling and say, "I know not what course others may take, but as for me, give me liberty or give me death."

And now I heard, really for the first time:

"We have come over a way that with tears
has been watered,
We have come, treading our path through
the blood of the slaughtered."

While echoes of the song shivered in the air, Henry Reed bowed his head, said "Thank you," and returned to his place in the line. The tears that slipped down many faces were not wiped away in shame.

We were on top again. As always, again. We survived. The depths had been icy and dark, but now a bright sun spoke to our souls. I was no longer simply a member of the proud graduating class of 1940; I was a proud member of the wonderful, beautiful Negro race.

Oh, Black known and unknown poets, how often have your auctioned pains sustained us? Who will compute the lonely nights made less lonely by your songs, or the empty pots made less tragic by your tales?

If we were a people much given to revealing secrets, we might raise monuments and sacrifice to the memories of our poets, but slavery cured us of that weakness. It may be enough, however, to have it said that we survive in exact relationship to the dedication of our poets (include preachers, musicians and blues singers).

II. Foundations of Argument

From Rhetorica
(*Rhetoric*)

Aristotle

Book I

1

Rhetoric is the counterpart of Dialectic.[1] Both alike are concerned with such things as come, more or less, within the general ken of all men and belong to no definite science. Accordingly all men make use, more or less, of both; for to a certain extent all men attempt to discuss statements and to maintain them, to defend themselves and to attack others. Ordinary people do this either at random or through practice and from acquired habit. Both ways being possible, the subject can plainly be handled systematically, for it is possible to inquire the reason why some speakers succeed through practice and others spontaneously; and every one will at once agree that such an inquiry is the function of an art.

Now, the framers of the current treatises on rhetoric have constructed but a small portion of that art. The modes of persuasion are the only true constituents of the art: everything else is merely accessory. These writers, however, say nothing about Enthymemes, which are the substance of rhetorical persuasion, but deal mainly with nonessentials. The arousing of prejudice, pity, anger, and similar emotions has nothing to do with the essential facts, but is merely a personal appeal to the man who is judging the case. Consequently if the rules for trials which are now laid down in some states—especially in well-governed states—were applied everywhere, such people would have nothing to say. All men, no doubt, *think* that the laws should prescribe such rules, but some, as in the court of Areopagus, give practical effect to their thoughts and forbid talk about nonessentials. This is sound law and custom. It is not right to pervert the judge[2] by moving him to anger or envy or pity—one might as well warp a carpenter's rule before using it. Again, a litigant has clearly nothing to do but to show that the alleged fact is so or is not so, that it has or has not happened. As to whether a thing is important or unimportant, just or unjust, the judge must surely refuse to take his instructions from the litigants: he must decide for himself all such points as the law-giver has not already defined for him.

. . .

Rhetoric is useful (1) because things that are true and things that are just have a natural tendency to prevail over their opposites, so that if the decisions of judges are not what they ought to be, the defeat must be due to the speakers themselves, and they must be blamed accordingly. Moreover, (2) before some audiences not even the possession of the exactest knowledge will make it easy for what we say to produce conviction. For argument based on knowledge implies instruction, and there are people whom one cannot instruct. Here, then, we must use, as our modes of persuasion and argument, notions possessed by everybody, as we observed in the *Topics*[3] when dealing with the way to handle a popular audience. Further, (3) we must be able to employ persuasion, just as strict reasoning can be employed, on opposite sides of a question, not in order that we may in practice employ it in both ways (for we must not make people believe what is wrong), but in order that we may see clearly what the facts are, and that, if another man argues unfairly, we on our part may be able to confute him. No other of the arts draws opposite conclusions: dialectic and rhetoric alone do this. Both these arts draw opposite conclusions impartially. Nevertheless, the underlying facts do not lend themselves equally well to the contrary views. No; things that are true and things that are better are, by their nature, practically always easier to prove and easier to believe in. Again, (4) it is absurd to hold that a man ought to be ashamed of being unable to defend himself with his limbs, but not of being unable to defend himself with speech and reason, when the use of rational speech is more distinctive of a human being than the use of his limbs. And if it be objected that one who uses such power of speech unjustly might do great harm, *that* is a charge which may be made in common against all good things except virtue, and above all against the things that are most useful, as strength, health, wealth, generalship. A man can confer the greatest of benefits by a right use of these, and inflict the greatest of injuries by using them wrongly.

2

Rhetoric may be defined as the faculty of observing in any given case the available means of persuasion. This is not a function of any other art. Every other art can instruct or persuade about its own particular subject-matter; for instance, medicine about what is healthy and unhealthy, geometry about the properties of magnitudes, arithmetic about numbers, and the same is true of the other arts and sciences. But rhetoric we look upon as the power of observing the means of persuasion on almost any subject presented to us; and that is why we say that, in its technical character, it is not concerned with any special or definite class of subjects.

Of the modes of persuasion some belong strictly to the art of rhetoric and some do not. By the latter I mean such things as are not supplied by the speaker but are there at the outset—witnesses, evidence given under torture, written contracts, and so on. By the former I mean such as we can ourselves construct by means of the principles of rhetoric. The one kind has merely to be used, the other has to be invented.

Of the modes of persuasion furnished by the spoken word there are three kinds. The first kind depends on the personal character of the speaker; the second on putting the audience into a certain[4] frame of mind; the third on the proof, or apparent proof, provided by the words of the speech itself. Persuasion is achieved by the speaker's personal character when the speech is so spoken as to make us think him credible. We believe good men more fully and more readily than others: this is true generally whatever the question is, and absolutely true where exact certainty is impossible and opinions are divided. This kind of persuasion, like the others, should be achieved by what the speaker says, not by what people think of his character before he begins to speak. It is not true, as some writers assume in their treatises on rhetoric, that the personal goodness revealed by the speaker contributes nothing to his power of persuasion; on the contrary, his character may almost be called the most effective means of persuasion he possesses. Secondly, persuasion may come through the hearers, when the speech stirs their emotions. Our judgements when we are pleased and friendly are not the same as when we are pained and hostile. It is towards producing these effects, as we maintain, that present-day writers on rhetoric direct the whole of their efforts. This subject shall be treated in detail when we come to speak of the emotions.[5] Thirdly, persuasion is effected through the speech itself when we have proved a truth or an apparent truth by means of the persuasive arguments suitable to the case in question.

There are, then, these three means of effecting persuasion. The man who is to be in command of them must, it is clear, be able (1) to reason logically, (2) to understand human character and goodness, in their various forms, and (3) to understand the emotions—that is, to name them and describe them, to know their causes and the way in which they are excited. It thus appears that rhetoric is an offshoot of dialectic and also of ethical studies. Ethical studies may fairly be called political; and for this reason rhetoric masquerades as political science, and the professors of it as political experts—sometimes from want of education, sometimes from ostentation, sometimes owing to other human failings. As a matter of fact, it is a branch of dialectic and similar to it, as we said at the outset.[6] Neither rhetoric nor dialectic is the scientific study of any one separate subject: both are faculties for providing arguments. This is perhaps a sufficient account of their scope and of how they are related to each other.

. . .

A statement is persuasive and credible either because it is directly self-evident or because it appears to be proved from other statements that are so. In either case it is persuasive because there is somebody whom it persuades. But none of the arts theorize about individual cases. Medicine, for instance, does not theorize about what will help to cure Socrates or Callias, but only about what will help to cure any or all of a given class of patients: this alone is its business: individual cases are so infinitely various that no systematic knowledge of them is possible. In the same way the theory of rhetoric is concerned not with what seems probable to a given individual like Socrates or Hippias, but with what seems probable to men of a given type; and this is true of dialectic also. Dialectic does not construct its syllogisms out of any haphazard materials, such as the fancies of crazy people, but out of materials that call for discussion; and rhetoric, too, draws upon the regular subjects of debate. The duty of rhetoric is to deal with such matters as we deliberate upon without arts or systems to guide us, in the hearing of persons who cannot take in at a glance a complicated argument, or follow a long chain of reasoning. The subjects of our deliberation are such as seem to present us with alternative possibilities: about things that could not have been, and cannot now or in the future be, other than they are, nobody who takes them to be of this nature wastes his time in deliberation.

3

Rhetoric falls into three divisions, determined by the three classes of listeners to speeches. For of the three elements in speech-making—speaker, subject, and person addressed—it is the last one, the hearer, that determines the speech's end and object. The hearer must be either a judge, with a decision to make about things past or future, or an observer. A member of the assembly decides about future events, a juryman about past events: while those who merely decide on the orator's skill are observers. From this it follows that there are three divisions of oratory—(1) political, (2) forensic, and (3) the ceremonial oratory of display.[7]

10   Political speaking urges us either to do or not to do something: one   10 of these two courses is always taken by private counsellors, as well as by men who address public assemblies. Forensic speaking either attacks or defends somebody: one or other of these two things must always be done by the parties in a case. The ceremonial oratory of display either praises or censures somebody. These three kinds of rhetoric refer to three different kinds of time. The political orator is concerned with the future: it is about things to be done hereafter that he advises, for or against. The party in a case at law is concerned with the past; one man accuses the other, and the other defends himself, with reference to things already done. The ceremonial orator is, properly speaking, concerned with the present, since all men praise or blame in view of the state of things existing at the time, though they often find it useful also to recall the past and to make guesses at the future.

Rhetoric has three distinct ends in view, one for each of its three kinds. The political orator aims at establishing the expediency or the harmfulness of a proposed course of action; if he urges its acceptance, he does so on the ground that it will do good; if he urges its rejection, he does so on the ground that it will do harm; and all other points, such as whether the proposal is just or unjust, honourable or dishonourable, he brings in as subsidiary and relative to this main consideration. Parties in a law-case aim at establishing the justice or injustice of some action, and they too bring in all other points as subsidiary and relative to this one. Those who praise or attack a man aim at proving him worthy of honour or the reverse, and they too treat all other considerations with reference to this one.

Book II

1

We have now considered the materials to be used in supporting or opposing a political measure, in pronouncing eulogies or censures, and for prosecution and defence in the law courts. We have considered the received opinions on which we may best base our arguments so as to convince our hearers—those opinions with which our enthymemes deal, and out of which they are built, in each of the three kinds of oratory, according to what may be called the special needs of each.

But since rhetoric exists to affect the giving of decisions—the hearers decide between one political speaker and another, and a legal verdict *is* a decision—the orator must not only try to make the argument of his speech demonstrative and worthy of belief; he must also make his own character look right and put his hearers, who are to decide, into the right frame of mind. Particularly in political oratory, but also in lawsuits, it adds much to an orator's influence that his own character should look right and that he should be thought to entertain the right feelings toward his hearers; and also that his hearers themselves should be in just the right frame of mind. That the orator's own character should look right is particularly important in political speaking: that the audience should be in the right frame of mind, in lawsuits. When people are feeling friendly and placable, they think one sort of thing; when they are feeling angry or hostile, they think either something totally different or the same thing with a different intensity: when they feel friendly to the man who comes before them for judgement, they regard him as having done little wrong, if any; when they feel hostile, they take the opposite view. Again, if they are eager for, and have good hopes of, a thing that will be pleasant if it happens, they think that it certainly will happen and be good for them: whereas if they are indifferent or annoyed, they do not think so.

There are three things which inspire confidence in the orator's own character—the three, namely, that induce us to believe a thing apart from any proof of it: good sense, good moral character, and goodwill.

False statements and bad advice are due to one or more of the following three causes. Men either form a false opinion through want of good sense; or they form a true opinion, but because of their moral badness do not say what they really think; or finally, they are both sensible and upright, but not well disposed to their hearers, and may fail in consequence to recommend what they know to be the best course. These are the only possible cases. It follows that any one who is thought to have all three of these good qualities will inspire trust in his audience. The way to make ourselves thought to be sensible and morally good must be gathered from the analysis of goodness already given:[8] the way to establish your own goodness is the same as the way to establish that of others. Good will and friendliness of disposition will form part of our discussion of the emotions,[9] to which we must now turn.

15   The Emotions are all those feelings that so change men as to   15
affect their judgements, and that are also attended by pain or pleasure. Such are anger, pity, fear and the like, with their opposites. We must arrange what we have to say about each of them under three heads. Take, for instance, the emotion of anger: here we must discover (1) what the state of mind of angry people is, (2) who the people are with whom they usually get angry, and (3) on what grounds they get angry with them. It is not enough to know one or even two of these points; unless we know all three, we shall be unable to arouse anger in any one. The same is true of the other emotions. So just as earlier in this work we drew up a list of useful propositions for the orator, let us now proceed in the same way to analyse the subject before us.

Book III

1

In making a speech one must study three points: first, the means of producing persuasion; second, the style, or language, to be used; third, the proper arrangement of the various parts of the speech. We have already specified the sources of persuasion. We have shown that these are three in number;[10] what they are; and why there are only these three: for we have shown that persuasion must in every case be effected either (1) by working on the emotions of the judges themselves, (2) by giving them the right impression of the speakers' character, or (3) by proving the truth of the statements made.

Enthymemes also have been described, and the sources from which they should be derived; there being both special and general lines of argument for enthymemes.[11]

Our next subject will be the style of expression. For it is not enough to know *what* we ought to say; we must also say it *as* we ought; much help is thus afforded towards producing the right impression of a speech. The first question to receive attention was naturally the one that comes first naturally—how persuasion can be produced from the facts themselves. The second is how to set these facts out in language. A third would be the proper method of delivery; this is a thing that affects the success of a speech greatly; but hitherto the subject has been neglected. Indeed, it was long before it found a way into the arts of tragic drama and epic recitation: at first poets acted their tragedies themselves. It is plain that delivery has just as much to do with oratory as with poetry. (In connexion with poetry, it has been studied by Glaucon of Teos among others.) It is, essentially, a matter of the right management of the voice to express the various emotions—of speaking loudly, softly, or between the two; of high, low, or intermediate pitch; of the various rhythms that suit various subjects. These are the three things—volume of sound, modulation of pitch, and rhythm—that a speaker bears in mind. It is those who *do* bear them in mind who usually win prizes in the dramatic contests; and just as in drama the actors now count for more than the poets, so it is in the contests of public life, owing to the defects of our political institutions. No systematic treatise upon the rules of delivery has yet been composed; indeed, even the study of language made no progress till late in the day. Besides, delivery is—very properly—not regarded as an elevated subject of inquiry. Still, the whole business of rhetoric being concerned with appearances, we must pay attention to the subject of delivery, unworthy though it is, because we cannot do without it. The right thing in speaking really is that we should be satisfied not to annoy our hearers, without trying to delight them: we ought in fairness to fight our case with no help beyond the bare facts: nothing, therefore, should matter except the proof of those facts. Still, as has been already said, other things affect the result considerably, owing to the defects of our hearers. The arts of language cannot help having a small but real importance, whatever it is we have to expound to others: the way in which a thing is said does affect its intelligibility. Not, however, so much importance as people think. All such arts are fanciful and meant to charm the hearer. Nobody uses fine language when teaching geometry.

When the principles of delivery have been worked out, they will produce the same effect as on the stage. But only very slight attempts to deal with them have been made and by a few people, as by Thrasymachus in his 'Appeals to Pity'. Dramatic ability is a natural gift, and can hardly be systematically taught. The principles of good diction can be so taught, and therefore we have men of ability in this direction too, who win prizes in their turn, as well as those speakers who excel in delivery—speeches of the written or literary kind owe more of their effect to their diction than to their thought.

20   It was naturally the poets who first set the movement going; for 20 words represent things, and they had also the human voice at their disposal, which of all our organs can best represent other things. Thus the arts of recitation and acting were formed, and others as well. Now it was because poets seemed to win fame through their fine language when their thoughts were simple enough, that the language of oratorical prose at first took a poetical colour, e g. that of Gorgias. Even now most uneducated people think that poetical language makes the finest discourses. That is not true: the language of prose is distinct from that of poetry. This is shown by the state of things to-day, when even the language of tragedy has altered its character. Just as iambics were adopted, instead of tetrameters, because they are the most prose-like of all metres, so tragedy has given up all those words, not used in ordinary talk, which decorated the early drama and are still used by the writers of hexameter poems. It is therefore ridiculous to imitate a poetical manner which the poets themselves have dropped; and it is now plain that we have not to treat in detail the whole question of style, but may confine ourselves to that part of it which concerns our present subject, rhetoric. The other—the poetical—part of it has been discussed in the treatise on the *Art of Poetry*.[12]

[Chapter 2-12 omitted.]

13

A speech has two parts. You must state your case, and you must prove it. You cannot either state your case and omit to prove it, or prove it without having first stated it; since any proof must be a proof of something, and the only use of a preliminary statement is the proof that follows it. Of these two parts the first part is[13] called the Statement of the case, the second part the Argument, just as we distinguish[14] between Enunciation and Demonstration. The current division is absurd. For 'narration' surely is part of a forensic speech only: how in a political speech or a speech of display can there be 'narration' in the technical sense? or a reply to a forensic opponent? or an epilogue in closely-reasoned speeches? Again, introduction, comparison of conflicting arguments, and recapitulation are only found in political speeches when there is a struggle between two policies. They *may* occur then; so may even accusation and defence, often enough; but they form no essential part of a political speech. Even forensic speeches do not always need epilogues; not, for instance, a short speech, nor one in which the facts are easy to remember, the effect of an epilogue being always a reduction in the apparent length.[15] It follows, then, that the only necessary parts of a speech are the Statement and the Argument. These are the essential features of a speech; and it cannot in any case have more than Introduction, Statement, Argument, and Epilogue. 'Refutation of the Opponent' is part of the arguments: so is 'Comparison' of the opponent's case with your own, for that process is a magnifying of your own case and therefore a part of the arguments, since one who does this *proves* something. The Introduction does nothing like this; nor does the Epilogue—it merely reminds us of what has been said already. If we make such distinctions we shall end, like Theodorus and his followers, by distinguishing 'narration' proper from 'post-narration' and 'pre-narration', and 'refutation' from 'final refutation'. But we ought only to bring in a new name if it indicates a real species with distinct specific qualities; otherwise the practice is pointless and silly, like the way Licymnius invented names in his *Art of Rhetoric*—'Secundation', 'Divagation', 'Ramification'.

End Notes

1. 'Rhetoric' and 'Dialectic' may be roughly Englished as 'the art of public speaking' and 'the art of logical discussion'. Aristotle's philosophical definition of 'Rhetoric' is given at the beginning of c. 2.
2. Here, and in what follows, the English reader should understand 'judge' in a broad sense, including 'jurymen' and others who 'judge'.
3. *Topics*, i. 2, IOI[a] 30–4.
4. i. e. the right, fit, required frame of mind.
5. ii, cc. 2–II.
6. i. I. 1354[a] I.
7. Or: deliberative (advisory), legal, and epideictic—the oratory respectively of parliamentary assemblies, of law-courts, and of ceremonial occasions when there is an element of 'display', 'show', 'declamation', and the result is a 'set speech' or 'harangue'.
8. i, c. 9.
9. ii, c. 4.

10. i, c. 2.
11. i and ii.
12. *Poetics*, cc. 20–2.
13. *sc.* in rhetoric.
14. *sc.* in dialectic.
15. A good effect where a speech may seem too long; bad, where it may seem too short already

Institutes of Oratory (from his Perface)

Quintilian (c.35-95 A.D.)

1   In contrast to many authors who have made discussions of rhetoric 1
merely tedious, we . . . have not limited our books to only the
narrowest and most technical aspects of the oratorical art. But we
have indeed done the following. Our twelve books include everything
we decided would serve the education of the citizen-orator, briefly
explaining all aspects that we judge truly useful to such an education.
For if we should say as much as we might about every particular
detail, there would be no end to our discussion.

It needs to be admitted in the first place, however, that precepts
and arts are of no help without the assistance of nature. And these
instructions, therefore, are not written for the person absolutely lacking any inborn talent—any more than a manual on farming should
pretend to treat the cultivation of fields in any region of our earth
where the soil is barren. Yet having said this, we must mention the
other native strengths that most people truly have—beyond the thing
I've called talent. I mean, for example, power of voice, a robust constitution (such as can sustain enduringly patient labor), health,
courage, and grace—qualities which, if they're given to any one of us
in no more than moderate degree, may be amplified by rational guidance. Now and then, they are missing so completely that their lack
spoils all the goods of talent and study. Still, let me point up a force-
fully opposed truth. The personal advantages we have listed will, left
to themselves, come to nothing at all—unless cultivated by a learned
teacher, by dedicated study, and by persistent and continuous exercise
(that is, practice) in writing, in reading, and in study.

Let a father, then, as soon as his son is born, conceive first of all
the best possible hopes for him. . . . It is empty lamentation to complain that few—very few—possess the inner vitality to grasp what
they are taught. . . . Quite otherwise, you will find the majority of
people both quick to reason and ready to learn. Indeed reasoning
comes naturally to men—and it is as native to them from birth as is
flight to birds, speed to horses, and ferocity to wild beasts.

On Democritus and Heraclitus

Michel de Montaigne

Michel de Montaigne's De Démocritus et Héraclitus, *as edited and translated by M. A. Screech for the Penguin Classics series, is printed below. It is taken from Montaigne's three volume intellectual autobiography, his* Essais; *the last edition published in Montaigne's lifetime appeared in 1588. The essay on Democritus and Heraclitus is the fiftieth essay in Book I.*

iaugh at the world
or be mad at the world

[A]

1   Our power of judgement is a tool to be used on all subjects; it can be applied anywhere. That is why I seize on any sort of occasion for employing it in the assays I am making of it here. If it concerns a subject which I do not understand at all, that is the very reason why I assay my judgement on it; I sound out the ford from a safe distance: if I find I would be out of my depth, then I stick to the bank: the realization that I cannot get further across is one effect of its action; indeed, it is the effect that judgement is especially proud of. Sometimes, when the subject is trivial and vain, I assay whether my judgement can find anything substantial in it, anything to shore it up and support it. Sometimes I employ it on some elevated, well-trodden subject where it can discover nothing new, since the path is so well beaten that our judgement can only follow in another's tracks. In that case it plays its role by selecting what appears the best route: out of hundreds of paths it says this one or that one is the best to choose.[1]

[C] I take the first subject Fortune offers: all are equally good for me. I never plan to expound them in full for I do not see the whole of anything: neither do those who promise to help us to do so! Everything has a hundred parts and a hundred faces: I take one of them and sometimes

Reprinted from *De Democritus et Heraclitus* (1588), Penguin Classics (UK)/Penguin Books Ltd.

just touch it with the tip of my tongue or with my fingertips, and sometimes I pinch it to the bone. I jab into it, not as wide but as deep as I can; and I often prefer to catch it from some unusual angle. I might even have ventured to make a fundamental study if I did not know myself better. Scattering broadcast a word here, a word there, examples ripped from their contexts, unusual ones, with no plan and no promises, I am under no obligation to make a good job of it nor even to stick to the subject myself without varying it should it so please me; I can surrender to doubt and uncertainty and to my master-form, which is ignorance.

Anything we do reveals us. [A] The same soul of Caesar's which displayed herself in ordering and arranging the battle of Pharsalia is also displayed when arranging his idle and amorous affrays. You judge a horse not only by seeing its paces on a race-track but by seeing it walk—indeed, by seeing it in its stable.

[C] The soul has her lower functions: anyone who does not know her in those does not know her thoroughly. And you may perhaps get to know her better when she is ambling along. It is in her loftier sites that the winds of passion batter her about. Besides she throws herself wholly into every matter, and never treats more than one at a time: moreover she treats it not its way but her way.

Things external to her may have their own weight and dimension: but within inside us she gives them such measures as she wills: death is terrifying to Cicero, desirable to Cato, indifferent to Socrates. Health, consciousness, authority, knowledge, beauty and their opposites doff their garments as they enter the soul and receive new vestments, coloured with qualities of her own choosing: brown or green; light or dark; bitter or sweet, deep or shallow, as it pleases each of the individual souls, who have not agreed together on the truth of their practices, rules or ideas. Each soul is Queen in her own state. So let us no longer seek excuses from the external qualities of anything: the responsibility lies within ourselves. Our good or our bad depends on us alone. So let us make our offertories and our vows to ourselves not to Fortune: she has no power over our behaviour; on the contrary our souls drag Fortune in their train and mould her to their own idea.

Why shall I not judge Alexander chatting and drinking his fill at his table? Or if he were playing chess, what mental chord is not touched and employed in that silly childish game, which I hate and avoid because there is not enough *play* in it, feeling ashamed to give it such attention as would suffice to achieve something good: Alexander was not more preoccupied with planning his magnificent expedition into India, nor is this other man with explaining a knotty passage on which depends the salvation of the human race. Notice how our soul gives weight and depth to that silly pastime: how all her sinews are strained; how amply she provides each of us with the means of knowing himself or of judging himself aright. There is no other activity in which I can see and explore myself so thoroughly. What passion does not try us in that game: anger, vexation, hatred, impatience and an ambition to win such as carries the mind away—and that, in something where a more pardonable ambition would be to lose! For to show a rare and extraordinary excellence in frivolous pursuits is unworthy of a man of honour. And what I say in this example can also be said of all the others: every constituent of a man, each occupation, tells us about him and reveals him as well as any other.

[A] Democritus and Heraclitus were both philosophers; the former, finding our human circumstances so vain and ridiculous, never went out without a laughing and mocking look on his face: Heraclitus, feeling pity and compassion for these same circumstances of ours, wore an expression which was always sad, his eyes full of tears.

[B] *Alter*
Ridebat, quoties a limine moverat unum
Protuleratque pedem; flebat contrarius alter.

[One, whenever he put a foot over his doorstep, was laughing: the other, on the contrary, wept.][2]

[A] I prefer the former temperament, not because it is more agreeable to laugh than to weep but because it is more disdainful and condemns us men more than the other—and it seems to me that, according to our deserts, we can never be despised enough. Lamentation and compassion are mingled with some respect for the things we are lamenting: the things which we mock at are judged to be worthless. I do not think that there is so much wretchedness in us as vanity; we are not so much wicked as daft; we are not so much full of evil as of inanity; we are not so much pitiful as despicable. Thus Diogenes who frittered about all on his own trundling his barrel and cocking a snook at Alexander,[3] accounting us as no more than flies or bags of wind, was a sharper and harsher judge (and consequently, for my temperament, a juster one) than Timon who was surnamed the misanthropist. For what we hate we take to heart. Timon wished us harm; passionately desired our downfall; fled our company as dangerous, as that of evil men whose nature was depraved. Diogenes thought us worth so little that contact with us could neither trouble him nor corrupt him: he avoided our company not from fear of associating with us but from contempt. He thought us incapable of doing good or evil.

10   Statilius' reply was of a similar character when Brutus spoke to him about joining in their plot against Caesar: he thought the enterprise to be just but did not find that men were worth taking any trouble over; [C] which is in conformity with the teaching of Hegesias (who said the wise man should do nothing except for himself, since he alone is worth doing anything for) and the teaching of Theodorus, that it is unjust that the wise man should hazard his life for the good of his country, so risking his wisdom for fools.[4]

Our own specific property is to be equally laughable and able to laugh.[5]

End Notes

1.   '80: choose. *Meanwhile I leave* Fortune *to furnish me with subjects. Since* all are equally good for me, *and I do not undertake to treat them fully or to scrape the barrel; of the hundreds of features which each of them* has; I take the one *which pleases me: I grasp them preferably by some extraordinary aspect: I could well select richer, fuller ones if I had some other objective. Every act is appropriate for making ourselves known:* that same soul of Caesar's . . .

2.   Juvenal, *Satires*, X. xxviii.

3.   He asked Alexander the Great to get out of his light. On his trundling of his barrel, cf. the *Prologue* to the *Tiers Livre* of Rabelais.

4.   Plutarch, *Life of Brutus*; Diogenes Laertius, *Life of Aristippus*.

5.   Laughter is the 'property'—the specific quality—of Man. Cf. Rabelais, *Gargantua*, preliminary poem.

The Method of Scientific Investigation, 1863

Thomas Henry Huxley

From a 1863 lecture series aimed at making science under-standable to non-specialists. Extracted from Darwiniana, 1893

The method of scientific investigation is nothing but the expression of the necessary mode of working of the human mind. It is simply the mode at which all phenomena are reasoned about, rendered precise and exact. There is no more difference, but there is just the same kind of difference, between the mental operations of a man of science and those of an ordinary person, as there is between the operations and methods of a baker or of a butcher weighing out his goods in common scales, and the operations of a chemist in performing a difficult and complex analysis by means of his balance and finely graduated weights. It is not that the action of the scales in the one case, and the balance in the other, differ in the principles of their construction or manner of working; but the beam of one is set on an infinitely finer axis than the other, and of course turns by the addition of a much smaller weight.

You will understand this better, perhaps, if I give you some familiar example. You have all heard it repeated, I dare say, that men of science work by means of induction and deduction, and that by the help of these operations, they, in a sort of sense, wring from Nature certain other things, which are called natural laws, and causes, and that out of these, by some cunning skill of their own, they build up hypotheses and theories. And it is imagined by many, that the operations of the common mind can be by no means compared with these processes, and that they have to be acquired by a sort of special apprenticeship to the craft. To hear all these large words, you would think that the mind of a man of science must be constituted differently from that of his fellow men; but if you will not be frightened by terms, you will discover that you are quite wrong, and that all these terrible apparatus are being used by yourselves every day and every hour of your lives.

There is a well-known incident in one of Moliere's plays, where the author makes the hero express unbounded delight on being told that he had been talking prose during the whole of his life [*Le bourgeois gentilhomme*]. In the same way, I trust, that you will take comfort, and be delighted with yourselves, on the discovery that you have been acting on the principles of inductive and deductive philosophy during the same period. Probably there is not one here who has not in the course of the day had occasion to set in motion a complex train of reasoning, of the very same kind, as that which a scientific man goes through in tracing the causes of natural phenomena. A very trivial circumstance will serve to exemplify this. Suppose you go into a fruiterer's shop, wanting an apple,—you take up one, and, on biting it, you find it is sour; you look at it, and see that it is hard and green. You take up another one, and that too is hard, green, and sour. The shopman offers you a third; but, before biting it, you examine it, and find that it is hard and green, and you immediately say that you will not have it, as it must be sour, like those that you have already tried.

Nothing can be more simple than that, you think; but if you will take the trouble to analyse and trace out into its logical elements what has been done by the mind, you will be greatly surprised. In the first place you have performed the operation of induction. You have found that, in two experiences, hardness and greenness in apples went together with sourness. It was so in the first case, and it was confirmed by the second. True, it is a very small basis, but still it is enough to make an induction from; you generalise the facts, and you expect to find sourness in apples where you get hardness and greenness. You found upon that a general law that all hard and green apples are sour; and that, as far as it goes, is a perfect induction. Well, having got your natural law in this way, when you are offered another apple which you find is hard and green, you say, 'All hard and green apples are sour; this apple is hard and green, therefore this apple is sour.' That train of reasoning is what logicians call a syllogism, and has all its various parts and terms,—its major premiss, its minor premiss and its conclusion. And, by the help of further reasoning, which, if drawn out, would have to be exhibited in two or three other syllogisms, you arrive at your final determination, 'I will not have that apple.' 'So that, you see, you have, in the first place, established a law by induction, and upon that you have founded a deduction, and reasoned out the

*Science is accessible to all
an extension of familiar logic
- everyday instances of deduction/induction*

special particular case. Well now, suppose, having got your conclusion *(concludes)* of the law, that at some time afterwards, you are discussing the quali- *Infer-* ties of apples with a friend: you will say to him, 'It is a very curious *draw a* thing,—but I find that all hard and green apples are sour!' Your friend *conclusion* says to you, 'But how do you know that?' You at once reply, 'Oh, *as by* because I have tried them over and over again, and have always found *reasoning* them to be so.' Well, if we were talking science instead of common *(suggest)* sense, we should call that an experimental verification. And, if still *Imply-* opposed, you go further, and say, 'I have heard from the people in *indicate* Somersetshire and Devonshire, where a large number of apples are *or suggest* grown, that they have observed the same thing. It is also found to be *without* the case in Normandy, and in North America. In short, I find it to be *being* the universal experience of mankind wherever attention has been *explicity* directed to the subject.' Whereupon, your friend, unless he is a very *stated* unreasonable man, agrees with you, and is convinced that you are quite right in the conclusion you have drawn. He believes, although perhaps he does not know he believes it, that the more extensive veri- fications are,—that the more frequently experiments have been made, and the results of the same kind arrived at,—that the more varied the conditions under which the same results are attained, the more cer- tain is the ultimate conclusion. He sees that the experiment has been tried under all sorts of conditions, as to time, place, and people, with the same result; and he says with you, therefore, that the law you have laid down must be a good one, and he must believe it.

*Syllogism - an argument the conclusion of
which is supported by two premises of which
one (deductive reasoning)* → *Popper -
falsifiability*

frame/context: fear, confusion

*- apple tasting : induction
individual experience - observation
dialogue reliability - verification
- integrate/collate - generalize*

*Deductive: based on deduction from accepted premises
a process of reasoning in which a conclusion follows*

*Inductive - a form of reasoning in which the
conclusion though supported bey supported
may not follow the*

thim necessarily

The Choice Fetish: Blessings and Curses of a Market Idol

Robert B. Reich

1 Choices are supposed to be liberating. "Freedom of choice" is the economist's favorite tonic, the libertarian's ideal, the classic liberal's alternative to revolution. But are we in danger of overdoing it? Can there be such a thing as too much choice?

 My 401(k) plan offers me ten different funds, each one of them featuring several dozen permutations for allocating my savings among an array of equities, bonds, and derivatives. Yet regardless of my choice, the odds of beating a market index are very low. My HMO is competing with many others, each one providing a dizzying set of healthcare options. But basically, I'd be content with a good doctor.

 A lot of choices we face today are little more than incremental gradations of quality, based on how much you're willing or able to pay. Which is to say, the market works. Residential communities are beginning to resemble appliances or automobiles, with innumerable options and add-ons available depending on price: A pool is extra; throw in an exercise facility—it's more money. You want landscape maintenance? A security guard? There's a bigger tab.

 A young couple, new to town, asks me to which preschool they should send their four-year-old. I tell them that the quality of the attention their child will get—how caring, consistent, and stimulating—depends largely on how much they're willing to shell out. Meanwhile, many early boomers like me are making agonizing choices about caring for aging parents—assisted living; cooperative with visiting nurse; independent with home health-care aide; nursing home. Again, quality depends on money. It's agonizing when you can't afford the very best, when that's what they deserve.

Reprinted from *Civilization* (Aug/Sept 2000), Robert Reich.

5   Even the most intimate decisions are transmuting into commer-   5
cial choices. Ivy League women are selling their eggs. I saw one adver-
tisement for Ivy League sperm. Soon, there'll be Ivy League uteruses
where fetuses can thrive in a superenriched learning environment. At
later stages of development, humans can now—with increasing
ease—change their noses into almost any shape they wish, lift their
faces, reshape their corneas, put hair into balding scalps, get new hips,
and fortify their erections. In a few years, maybe you'll be able to
replace genes you don't like, and then make a perfect clone of yourself. Even choices of marriage partner are getting down to business:
One lawyer I know who specializes in prenuptial agreements tells me
business is booming. The number of "personal coaches" has doubled
each year since the early 1990s, according to Thomas Leonard,
founder of Coach University, which has already trained thousands of
them. There has also been an upsurge in online counselors, guides,
and spiritual advisors.

Blame it partly on digital technology, which is multiplying
choices. Henry Ford's assembly line lowered the cost and democra-
tized consumption of the automobile, but it did so by narrowing
choice. "Any customer can have a car painted any color that he wants
as long as it is black," he famously offered; now, you can design your
own car over the Internet. The first mass-produced shoes in America
were called "straights" because, like those that people had worn for
centuries, they didn't distinguish between left and right feet; last
Christmas, Nordstrom offered a choice of more than 20 million pairs
of shoes tailored precisely to customer specifications. A neighbor of
mine with a satellite dish atop her garage receives hundreds of television channels; it must take her days just to surf through them. At this
writing, there are more than a billion web pages. The most sophisticated search engine plumbs no more than 50 percent of them. Anyone who attempts to surf this ocean risks drowning.

When just about everything can be turned into digits and then
rearranged into an almost infinite variety, the consumer is king, or so
it's supposed. But the consumer actually becomes a day laborer,
breathlessly toiling to make sense of it all. More time and energy is
spent deciding on the best deal than enjoying the purchase itself.
Tried choosing a new computer lately? You've got to know more than
Bill Gates knew ten years ago to figure whether exactly what you
need is a 400-megahertz Pentium III with MPEG-2 digital video

full-screen playback, a 128-bit graphics accelerator, 32 megabytes of memory, and an external disk drive.

The glut of choice is also being propelled by a new prosperity that equates wealth with the ability to get exactly what you want, and by a deepening cynicism about uniform public services. "School choice" is all the rage—charter, magnet, private, schools specializing in music or science—to which upscale parents add private tutors, semesters abroad, and summer enrichment programs. Even if it is not privatized soon, Social Security has already fallen prey to widespread expectations that its contribution to the retirement income of today's workers will shrink. Coupled with the gradual disappearance of pension plans, private savings—the "third leg" of retirement income—has to bear ever more weight. That's why every big bank and securities dealer is eagerly jumping into the breach.

Public pools and parks are giving way to private health clubs that range from a simple treadmill to manicured golf courses and glass-enclosed tennis and squash courts, accompanied by small armies of personal trainers and attendants. Public roads and police departments are supplanted by gated residential communities with their own maintenance crews and security guards. The budgets of public libraries are being squeezed as the prosperous middle class buys its own books online.

10 Choices like these are sorting Americans by wealth, health, education, and age. "Public" institutions never completely leveled the field—after all, public schools were long racially segregated in the South by law, and economically segregated in the North by neighborhood—but the ideals of the public school, the public library, public police and fire departments, Social Security, and even the draft at least provided common reference points, and sometimes occasions to meet across the divides.

Even American politics is succumbing to the god of choice. We're losing public deliberation about what's good for all of us in favor of individual choices about what's best for *me*. The "public good" or "public interest" has become a quaint phrase from the era of town meetings, political parties, and democratic clubs. It's now all about opinion polls, e-voting, and ballot propositions.

Instead of liberating us, the new world of choice is making us more dependent on people who specialize in persuading us to choose this or that. A growing portion of the retirement savings we channel to Fidelity or Merrill Lynch or any other financial service goes to advertising and marketing pros who try to convince us there's a significant difference between these giants. A considerable chunk of the health-care dollars we and our employers send to health insurers and HMOs finds its way to the ad agencies that tout them. Politics is now almost completely in the hands of political consultants, lobbyists, publicists, and spin doctors, all of whom are paid large sums to convince us to choose their candidate or their cause over a competing one, even when the differences between them are so small as to be invisible to the naked eye.

I relish my freedom as much as anyone. But my freedom isn't equivalent to the breadth or quantity of my choices. You and I need freedom to make the significant choices—such as what we stand for, to what and to whom we're going to commit our lives, and what we want by way of a community and a society. Too many small choices only divert our attention from these bigger ones, robbing us of the time and energy we need to exercise true freedom. Yet the new technologies, combined with increasing middle-class prosperity and disdain for public institutions, are making fetishes out of tiny choices. Unless we choose what kinds of choices we want to be faced with— both as individuals and as a society—we will soon drown in a rising tide of inconsequential options.

III. Process

Don't You Think It's Time to Start Thinking?

Northrop Frye

Northrop Frye (1912–1991), one of Canada's most distinguished scholars, was reared in New Brunswick, and after attending school in Canada, received his MA from Oxford University, in England (1940). In 1939 Frye became a professor at the University of Toronto, where he wrote and taught until his death. His interests were literary criticism and school curriculum; his books include On Education *and* Myth and Metaphor. *The following essay insists that thinking happens only when a person writes down ideas "in the right words."*

1   A student often leaves high school today without any sense of language as a structure.

    He may also have the idea that reading and writing are elementary skills that he mastered in childhood, never having grasped the fact that there are differences in levels of reading and writing as there are in mathematics between short division and integral calculus.

    Yet, in spite of his limited verbal skills, he firmly believes that he can think, that he has ideas, and that if he is just given the opportunity to express them he will be all right. Of course, when you look at what he's written you find it doesn't make any sense. When you tell him this he is devastated.

    Part of his confusion here stems from the fact that we use the word "think" in so many bad, punning ways. Remember James Thurber's Walter Mitty who was always dreaming great dreams of glory. When his wife asked him what he was doing he would say, "Has it ever occurred to you that I might be thinking?"

5   But, of course, he wasn't thinking at all. Because we use it for every-   5
thing our minds do, worrying, remembering, daydreaming, we imagine that thinking is something that can be achieved without any training.
But again it's a matter of practice. How well we can think depends on
how much of it we have already done. Most students need to be taught,
very carefully and patiently, that there is no such thing as an inarticulate idea waiting to have the right words wrapped around it.

They have to learn that ideas do not exist until they have been
incorporated into words. Until that point you don't know whether you
are pregnant or just have gas on the stomach.

The operation of thinking is the practice of articulating ideas
until they are in the right words. And we can't think at random either.
We can only add one more idea to the body of something we have
already thought about. Most of us spend very little time doing this,
and that is why there are so few people whom we regard as having
any power to articulate at all. When such a person appears in public life, like Mr. Trudeau, we tend to regard him as possessing a gigan-
tic intellect.

A society like ours doesn't have very much interest in literacy.
It is compulsory to read and write because society must have docile
and obedient citizens. We are taught to read so that we can obey
the traffic signs and to cipher so that we can make out our income
tax, but development of verbal competency is very much left to the
individual.

And when we look at our day-to-day existence we can see that there
are strong currents at work against the development of powers of articulateness. Young adolescents today often betray a curious sense of shame
about speaking articulately, of framing a sentence with a period at the
end of it.

10   Part of the reason for this is the powerful anti-intellectual drive   10
which is constantly present in our society. Articulate speech marks you
out as an individual, and in some settings this can be rather dangerous because people are often suspicious and frightened of articulateness. So if you say as little as possible and use only stereotyped,
ready-made phrases you can hide yourself in the mass.

Then there are various epidemics sweeping over society which
use unintelligibility as a weapon to preserve the present power structure. By making things as unintelligible as possible, to as many people as possible, you can hold the present power structure together.

Understanding and articulateness lead to its destruction. This is the kind of thing that George Orwell was talking about, not just in *Nineteen Eighty-Four,* but in all his work on language. The kernel of everything reactionary and tyrannical in society is the impoverishment of the means of verbal communication.

The vast majority of things that we hear today are prejudices and clichés, simply verbal formulas that have no thought behind them but are put up as pretence of thinking. It is not until we realize these things conceal meaning, rather than reveal it, that we can begin to develop our own powers of articulateness.

The teaching of humanities is, therefore, a militant job. Teachers are faced not simply with a mass of misconceptions and unexamined assumptions. They must engage in a fight to help the student confront and reject the verbal formulas and stock responses, to convert passive acceptance into active, constructive power. It is a fight against illiteracy and for the maturation of the mental process, for the development of skills which once acquired will never become obsolete.

summary
what is the main idea?
Major evidence/logic
what's at stake/
what's the conversation   who cares?
who are they responding to   so what?

main idea
Society doesn't think when we think were thinking
* A thought is not a thought till you write down
Polemic to motivate, - hyperbole
                      - provocative

Questions on Meaning

1. Frye says that our minds can do many things besides thinking—worrying, remembering, and daydreaming, for example. Why does he say that these are not thinking?
2. What is the difference between reading to understand a traffic sign and reading to understand a play such as *Romeo and Juliet*? Why does Frye think that the distinction is so important?
3. Are the vast majority of things people say prejudices and cliches? Frye says that they are and that people in power want it that way. Why does he think that this is true? Why does he refer to the novel *1984*?

Questions on Style and Structure

1. The style of this essay is sometimes quite forceful, such as "you don't know whether you are pregnant or just have gas." Why does this kind of style make Frye's point? What do we know about his feelings on the subject?
2. In this essay, Frye argues that humanities teachers are important, but he gets to his point at the end of the essay. What effect does this structure have on the reader?
3. Frye uses a forceful style in this essay because he feels strongly about his subject and he wants teachers to see how important their job really is. Find words and phrases that show the power of his emotions, and explain those emotions.

Writing Assignments

1. Find out about George Orwell. What political and social conditions caused Orwell to write his pessimistic novel *1984*? Write about the dangers of controlling people's thoughts.
2. Interview one of your humanities (history, literature, political science, philosophy) teachers. Ask the teacher about the responsibilities of the humanities to human freedom. Write about the interview, using your own responses as well as the teacher's perspectives.
3. Frye wrote in the second half of the twentieth century. Write about examples of complacency or laziness in political or social thought in the twenty-first century. How much have things changed? How much have they remained the same?

Shitty First Drafts

Anne Lamott

Anne Lamott (1954–), a writer who writes on writing, among many other subjects, is both a creator of fiction and nonfiction and a commentator on religious subjects. She acquired her interest in writing from her father, Kenneth Lamott, the model and inspiration for her first novel, Hard Laughter *(1987).* Bird by Bird: Some Instructions on Writing and Life, *from which the following excerpt has been taken, is a much read and taught book that looks at the experiences of a writer at work. She is also known for her works on family life, including* Operating Instructions: A Journal of My Son's First Year *(1994) and* Crooked Little Heart *(1997) about the stuff that keeps a family together. Her religious works include* Traveling Mercies: Some Thoughts on Faith *(2000),* Plan B: Further Thoughts on Faith *(2005), and* Grace (Eventually): Thoughts on Faith *(2007). Lamott writes the books she would like to have discovered to read, and helps other aspiring writers to do the same.*

Most writers write terrible stuff in their first drafts, and sometimes the fear of those drafts keeps writers from writing at all. In this humorous book chapter, Lamott tells how to go right ahead and write no matter how bad the first try.

Reprinted from *Bird By Bird: Some Instructions on Writing and Life* (1995), by permission of Pantheon Books, a division of Random House, Inc.

1   **N**ow, practically even better news than that of short assign-   1
ments is the idea of shitty first drafts. All good writers write
them. This is how they end up with good second drafts and
terrific third drafts. People tend to look at successful writers, writers
who are getting their books published and maybe even doing well
financially, and think that they sit down at their desks every morning
feeling like a million dollars, feeling great about who they are and
how much talent they have and what a great story they have to tell;
that they take in a few deep breaths, push back their sleeves, roll their
necks a few times to get all the cricks out, and dive in, typing fully
formed passages as fast as a court reporter. But this is just the fantasy
of the uninitiated. I know some very great writers, writers you love
who write beautifully and have made a great deal of money, and not
one of them sits down routinely feeling wildly enthusiastic and confident. Not one of them writes elegant first drafts. All right, one of
them does, but we do not like her very much. We do not think that
she has a rich inner life or that God likes her or can even stand her.
(Although when I mentioned this to my priest friend Tom, he said
you can safely assume you've created God in your own image when it
turns out that God hates all the same people you do.)

Very few writers really know what they are doing until they've
done it. Nor do they go about their business feeling dewy and
thrilled. They do not type a few stiff warm-up sentences and then
find themselves bounding along like huskies across the snow. One
writer I know tells me that he sits down every morning and says to
himself nicely, "It's not like you don't have a choice, because you do—
you can either type or kill yourself." We all often feel like we are
pulling teeth, even those writers whose prose ends up being the most
natural and fluid. The right words and sentences just do not come
pouring out like ticker tape most of the time. Now, Muriel Spark is
said to have felt that she was taking dictation from God every morning—sitting there, one supposes, plugged into a Dictaphone, typing
away, humming. But this is a very hostile and aggressive position.
One might hope for bad things to rain down on a person like this.

For me and most of the other writers I know, writing is not rap-
turous. In fact, the only way I can get anything written at all is to
write really, really shitty first drafts.

The first draft is the child's draft, where you let it all pour out and
then let it romp all over the place, knowing that no one is going to see

it and that you can shape it later. You just let this childlike part of you channel whatever voices and visions come through and onto the page. If one of the characters wants to say, "Well, so what, Mr. Poopy Pants?," you let her. No one is going to see it. If the kid wants to get into really sentimental, weepy, emotional territory, you let him. Just get it all down on paper, because there may be something great in those six crazy pages that you would never have gotten to by more rational, grown-up means. There may be something in the very last line of the very last paragraph on page six that you just love, that is so beautiful or wild that you now know what you're supposed to be writing about, more or less, or in what direction you might go—but there was no way to get to this without first getting through the first five and a half pages.

5   I used to write food reviews for *California* Magazine before it   5
folded. (My writing food reviews had nothing to do with the magazine folding, although every single review did cause a couple of canceled subscriptions. Some readers took umbrage at my comparing mounds of vegetable puree with various ex-presidents' brains.) These reviews always took two days to write. First I'd go to a restaurant several times with a few opinionated, articulate friends in tow. I'd sit there writing down everything anyone said that was at all interesting or funny. Then on the following Monday I'd sit down at my desk with my notes, and try to write the review. Even after I'd been doing this for years, panic would set in. I'd try to write a lead, but instead I'd write a couple of dreadful sentences, XX them out, try again, XX everything out, and then feel despair and worry settle on my chest like an x-ray apron. It's over, I'd think, calmly. I'm not going to be able to get the magic to work this time. I'm ruined. I'm through. I'm toast. Maybe, I'd think, I can get my old job back as a clerk-typist. But probably not. I'd get up and study my teeth in the mirror for a while. Then I'd stop, remember to breathe, make a few phone calls, hit the kitchen and chow down. Eventually I'd go back and sit down at my desk, and sigh for the next ten minutes. Finally I would pick up my one-inch picture frame, stare into it as if for the answer, and every time the answer would come: all I had to do was to write a really shitty first draft of, say, the opening paragraph. And no one was going to see it.

So I'd start writing without reining myself in. It was almost just typing, just making my fingers move. And the writing would be *terrible*. I'd write a lead paragraph that was a whole page, even though the entire review could only be three pages long, and then I'd start writing up descriptions of the food, one dish at a time, bird by bird, and the critics would be sitting on my shoulders, commenting like cartoon characters. They'd be pretending to snore, or rolling their eyes at my overwrought descriptions, no matter how hard I tried to tone those descriptions down, no matter how conscious I was of what a friend said to me gently in my early days of restaurant reviewing. "Annie," she said, "it is just a piece of *chicken*. It is just a bit of *cake*."

But because by then I had been writing for so long, I would eventually let myself trust the process—sort of, more or less. I'd write a first draft that was maybe twice as long as it should be, with a self-indulgent and boring beginning, stupefying descriptions of the meal, lots of quotes from my black-humored friends that made them sound more like the Manson girls than food lovers, and no ending to speak of. The whole thing would be so long and incoherent and hideous that for the rest of the day I'd obsess about getting creamed by a car before I could write a decent second draft. I'd worry that people would read what I'd written and believe that the accident had really been a suicide, that I had panicked because my talent was waning and my mind was shot.

The next day, though, I'd sit down, go through it all with a colored pen, take out everything I possibly could, find a new lead somewhere on the second page, figure out a kicky place to end it, and then write a second draft. It always turned out fine, sometimes even funny and weird and helpful. I'd go over it one more time and mail it in.

Then, a month later, when it was time for another review, the whole process would start again, complete with the fears that people would find my first draft before I could rewrite it.

Almost all good writing begins with terrible first efforts. You need to start somewhere. Start by getting something—anything down on paper. A friend of mine says that the first draft is the down draft—you just get it down. The second draft is the up draft—you fix it up. You try to say what you have to say more accurately. And the third draft is the dental draft, where you check every tooth, to see if it's loose or cramped or decayed, or even, God help us, healthy.

What I've learned to do when I sit down to work on a shitty first draft is to quiet the voices in my head. First there's the vinegar-lipped Reader Lady, who says primly, "Well, *that's* not very interesting, is it?" And there's the emaciated German male who writes these Orwellian memos detailing your thought crimes. And there are your parents, agonizing over your lack of loyalty and discretion; and there's William Burroughs, dozing off or shooting up because he finds you as bold and articulate as a houseplant; and so on. And there are also the dogs: let's not forget the dogs, the dogs in their pen who will surely hurtle and snarl their way out if you ever *stop* writing, because writing is, for some of us, the latch that keeps the door of the pen closed, keeps those crazy ravenous dogs contained.

Quieting these voices is at least half the battle I fight daily. But this is better than it used to be. It used to be 87 percent. Left to its own devices, my mind spends much of its time having conversations with people who aren't there. I walk along defending myself to people, or exchanging repartee with them, or rationalizing my behavior, or seducing them with gossip, or pretending I'm on their TV talk show or whatever. I speed or run an aging yellow light or don't come to a full stop, and one nanosecond later am explaining to imaginary cops exactly why I had to do what I did, or insisting that I did not in fact do it.

I happened to mention this to a hypnotist I saw many years ago, and he looked at me very nicely. At first I thought he was feeling around on the floor for the silent alarm button, but then he gave me the following exercise, which I still use to this day.

Close your eyes and get quiet for a minute, until the chatter starts up. Then isolate one of the voices and imagine the person speaking as a mouse. Pick it up by the tail and drop it into a mason jar. Then isolate another voice, pick it up by the tail, drop it in the jar. And so on. Drop in any high-maintenance parental units, drop in any contractors, lawyers, colleagues, children, anyone who is whining in your head. Then put the lid on, and watch all these mouse people clawing at the glass, jabbering away, trying to make you feel like shit because you won't do what they want—won't give them more money, won't be more successful, won't see them more often. Then imagine that there is a volume-control button on the bottle. Turn it all the way up for a minute, and listen to the stream of angry, neglected, guilt-mongering voices. Then turn it all the way down and watch the frantic mice lunge at the glass, trying to get to you. Leave it down, and get back to your shitty first draft.

15   A writer friend of mine suggests opening the jar and shooting   15
them all in the head. But I think he's a little angry, and I'm sure nothing like this would ever occur to you.

Questions on Meaning

1. How do most writers write a first draft? What do they put into the draft, and how do they feel about beginning to write?
2. What did Lamott learn from her experience as a food columnist for a magazine that no longer exists?
3. Lamott suggests that a writer should plunge past the voices that say the work will never be any good. What does she say to do with those voices?

Questions on Rhetorical Strategy and Style

1. Lamott is funny. What does she say about the one writer she knows who writes good first drafts? How does she feel about this person, and how does her humor explain her perspective?
2. This chapter is a small narration of Lamott's processes for getting past the first draft and on to the later work of revision. How does she tell the story of her writing progress?
3. The chapter ends with an example of putting mice into a jar. What does she say about the writer friend who would just shoot the mice? Why does she end the chapter this way?

Writing Assignments

1. Write a first draft. Then write about the first draft. What did you include that you might cut later? What might you add in the next draft? Write about yourself as a first draft writer.
2. Talk to five of your friends about how they approach writing a paper. Take notes on what they do. Then write a paper comparing and contrasting their processes.
3. Choose some aspect of your life or personality that annoys or troubles you. Then devise a way of getting rid of this aspect as Lamott does the voices that tell her she cannot write. Write about the way that you would quiet the annoying aspect of your life.

Writing

William Stafford

William Stafford (1914–1993) grew up in Kansas and taught at Lewis and Clark College in Oregon. His books include Traveling Through the Dark *(1963), which received the National Book Award;* Stories That Could Be True *(1977), a collection of poems;* Writing the Australian Crawl *(1978), a collection of essays;* A Glass Face in the Rain *(1982);* You Must Revise Your Life *(1986), another collection of essays;* An Oregon Message *(1987); and* Passwords *(1991). Stafford describes a writing process that works for him—and might for you—in this timeless 1970 essay.*

1   A writer is not so much someone who has something to say as he is someone who has found a process that will bring about new things he would not have thought of if he had not started to say them. That is, he does not draw on a reservoir; instead, he engages in an activity that brings to him a whole succession of unforeseen stories, poems, essays, plays, laws, philosophies, religions, or—but wait!

     Back in school, from the first when I began to try to write things, I felt this richness. One thing would lead to another; the world would give and give. Now, after twenty years or so of trying, I live by that certain richness, an idea hard to pin, difficult to say, and perhaps offensive to some. For there are strange implications in it.

     One implication is the importance of just plain receptivity. When I write, I like to have an interval before me when I am not likely to be interrupted. For me, this means usually the early morning, before others are awake. I get pen and paper, take a glance out the window (often it is dark out there), and wait. It is like fishing. But I do not wait very long, for there is always a nibble—and this is where receptivity comes

Excerpted from "A Way of Writing.", *Field: Contemporary Poetry and Poetics*, no. 2. Published by Oberlin College Press.

in. To get started I will accept anything that occurs to me. Something always occurs, of course, to any of us. We can't keep from thinking. Maybe I have to settle for an immediate impression: it's cold, or hot, or dark, or bright, or in between! Or—well, the possibilities are endless. If I put down something, that thing will help the next thing come, and I'm off. If I let the process go on, things will occur to me that were not at all in my mind when I started. These things, odd and trivial as they may be, are somehow connected. And if I let them string out, surprising things will happen.

If I let them string out . . . Along with initial receptivity, then, there is another readiness: I must be willing to fail. If I am to keep on writing, I cannot bother to insist on high standards. I must get into action and not let anything stop me, or even slow me much. By "standards" I do not mean "correctness"—spelling, punctuation, and so on. These details become mechanical for anyone who writes for a while. I am thinking about what many people would consider "important" standards, such matters as social significance, positive values, consistency, etc. I resolutely disregard these. Something better, greater, is happening! I am following a process that leads so wildly and originally into new territory that no judgment can at the moment be made about values, significance, and so on. I am making something new, something that has not been judged before. Later others—and maybe I myself—will make judgments. Now, I am headlong to discover. Any distraction may harm the creating.

5   So, receptive, careless of failure, I spin out things on the page. And   5
a wonderful freedom comes. If something occurs to me, it is all right to accept it. It has one justification: it occurs to me. No one else can guide me. I must follow my own weak, wandering, diffident impulses.

A strange bonus happens. At times, without my insisting on it, my writings become coherent; the successive elements that occur to me are clearly related. They lead by themselves to new connections. Sometimes the language, even the syllables that happen along, may start a trend. Sometimes the materials alert me to something waiting in my mind, ready for sustained attention. At such times, I allow myself to be eloquent, or intentional, or for great swoops (treacherous! not to be trusted!) reasonable. But I do not insist on any of that; for I know that back of my activity there will be the coherence of my self, and that indulgence of my impulses will bring recurrent patterns and meanings again.

This attitude toward the process of writing creatively suggests a problem for me, in terms of what others say. They talk about "skills" in writing. Without denying that I do have experience, wide reading, automatic orthodoxies and maneuvers of various kinds, I still must insist that I am often baffled about what "skill" has to do with the precious little area of confusion when I do not know what I am going to say and then I found out what I am going to say. That precious interval I am unable to bridge by skill. What can I witness about it? It remains mysterious, just as all of us must feel puzzled about how we are so inventive as to be able to talk along through complexities with our friends, not needing to plan what we are going to say, but never stalled for long in our confident forward progress. Skill? If so, it is the skill we all have, something we must have learned before the age of three or four.

A writer is one who has become accustomed to trusting that grace, or luck, or—skill.

Yet another attitude I find necessary: most of what I write, like most of what I say in casual conversation, will not amount to much. Even I will realize, and even at the time, that it is not negotiable. It will be like practice. In conversation, I allow myself random remarks—in fact, as I recall, that is the way I learned to talk—so in writing I launch many expendable efforts. A result of this free way of writing is that I am not writing for others, mostly; they will not see the product at all unless the activity eventuates in something that later appears to be worthy. My guide is the self, and its adventuring in the language brings about communication.

10   This process-rather-than-substance view of writing invites a final,   10
dual reflection:

1. Writers may not be special—sensitive or talented in any usual sense. They are simply engaged in sustained use of a language skill we all have. Their "creations" come about through confident reliance on stray impulses that will, with trust, find occasional patterns that are satisfying.

2. But writing itself is one of the great, free human activities. There is scope for individuality, and elation, and discovery, in writing. For the person who follows with trust and forgiveness what occurs to him, the world remains always ready and deep, an inexhaustible environment, with the combined vividness of an actuality and flexibility of a dream. Working back and forth between experience and thought, writers have more than space and time can offer. They have the whole unexplored realm of human vision.

Questions on Meaning

1. Compare and contrast Stafford's thesis as it applies to fiction versus nonfiction (such as reports).
2. What does Stafford mean by not insisting on high standards? Why does he insist that writers be "willing to fail"?
3. Stafford states that writers "may not be special," but they are different. In what way do writers use "a language skill we all have"?

Questions on Rhetorical Strategy and Style

1. Find where Stafford defines what a writer is (or isn't). Compare his definition of a writer to your perception of what characterizes a writer. Describe what bests defines *you* as a writer.
2. Reread the essay and show how Stafford analyzes his writing process. Compare and contrast his rhetorical strategy of narration to a how-to list of steps. Explain which writing technique you prefer for this material.

Writing Assignments

1. Practice what Stafford preaches: At a time when you will not be disturbed, sit down and write. Afterward, assess your experience. Were you inhibited by the "substance"? Did you feel the "freedom" expressed by Stafford? Explain why his technique would or would not work for you.
2. To Stafford, "just plain receptivity" is important to successful writing. What other pursuits depend on opening your mind the way Stafford describes? Write an essay about an experience you have had—perhaps in painting, composing, or dance—in which your "receptivity" contributed to your creativity. Describe the process you used to engaged your "receptivity." What was the result? How did the experience affect subsequent creative sessions?

How I Caused That Story

Doris Kearns Goodwin

*An award-winning historian and biographer, Doris Kearns
Goodwin (1943–) was born in Brooklyn, New York and
educated at Colby College (B.A. 1961) and Harvard
University (Ph.D. 1968). After interning with the U. S.
State Department and the House of Representatives,
Goodwin became a special assistant to President Lyndon
B. Johnson in 1968. Johnson later asked her to write his
official biography, and* Lyndon Baines Johnson and the
American Dream *was published to critical acclaim in
1976. Her next book was intended to be a biography of
John F. Kennedy. But through her husband Richard's con-
nections to the Kennedy family, she was provided access to
over a hundred cartons of Joseph P. Kennedy's personal
papers, and the work ultimately grew into a chronicle of
the president's entire family.* The Fitzgeralds and the
Kennedys: An American Saga *was published in 1987.
Goodwin then turned her attention to World War II for*
No Ordinary Time: Franklin and Eleanor Roosevelt:
The Home Front in World War II, *which won the 1995
Pulitzer Prize for Biography. Her latest work,* Team of
Rivals: The Political Genius of Abraham Lincoln
*(2005), won several awards, including the Lincoln Prize
for an outstanding work about the president and/or the
American Civil War. Her only foray into personal memoir,*
Wait Till Next Year *(1997), was a best-seller but received
mixed critical reviews. Goodwin has also taught government at Harvard University and served as a political
consultant for local and national television news. In 2002
she was accused of plagiarizing passages from another*

Reprinted from *Time*, January 22, 2002, by permission of Time, Inc.

historian in her book on the Kennedys. The incident engendered a great deal of controversy, to which Goodwin responded in the Time *magazine piece below.*

1   I am a historian. With the exception of being a wife and mother, it is who I am. And there is nothing I take more seriously.

In recent days, questions have been raised about how historians go about crediting their sources, and I have been caught up in the swirl. Ironically, the more intensive and far-reaching a historian's research, the greater the difficulty of citation. As the mountain of material grows, so does the possibility of error.

Fourteen years ago, not long after the publication of my book *The Fitzgeralds and the Kennedys*, I received a communication from author Lynne McTaggart pointing out that material from her book on Kathleen Kennedy had not been properly attributed. I realized that she was right. Though my footnotes repeatedly cited Ms. McTaggart's work, I failed to provide quotation marks for phrases that I had taken verbatim, having assumed that these phrases, drawn from my notes, were my words, not hers. I made the corrections she requested, and the matter was completely laid to rest—until last week, when the *Weekly Standard* published an article reviving the issue. The larger question for those of us who write history is to understand how citation mistakes can happen.

The research and writing for this 900-page book, with its 3,500 footnotes, took place over ten years. At that time, I wrote my books and took my notes in longhand, believing I could not think well on a keyboard. Most of my sources were drawn from a multitude of primary materials: manuscript collections, private letters, diaries, oral histories, newspapers, periodicals, personal interviews. After three years of research, I discovered more than 150 cartons of materials that had been previously stored in the attic of Joe Kennedy's Hyannis Port house. These materials were a treasure trove for a historian—old report cards, thousands of family letters, movie stubs and diaries, which allowed me to cross the boundaries of time and space. It took me two additional years to read, categorize and take notes on these documents.

5   During this same period, I took handwritten notes on perhaps 300 books. Passages I wanted to quote directly were noted along with general notes on the ideas and story lines of each book. Notes on all

these sources were then arranged chronologically and kept in dozens of folders in 25 banker's boxes. Immersed in a flood of papers, I began to write the book. After each section and each chapter was completed, I returned the notes to the boxes along with notations for future foot-noting. When the manuscript was finished, I went back to all these sources to check the accuracy of attributions. As a final protection, I revisited the 300 books themselves. Somehow in this process, a few of the books were not fully rechecked. I relied instead on my notes, which combined direct quotes and paraphrased sentences. If I had had the books in front of me, rather than my notes, I would have caught mistakes in the first place and placed any borrowed phrases in direct quotes.

What made this incident particularly hard for me was the fact that I take great pride in the depth of my research and the extensive-ness of my citations. The writing of history is a rich process of build-ing on the work of the past with the hope that others will build on what you have done. Through footnotes you point the way to future historians.

The only protection as a historian is to institute a process of research and writing that minimizes the possibility of error. And that I have tried to do, aided by modern technology, which enables me, having long since moved beyond longhand, to use a computer for both organizing and taking notes. I now rely on a scanner, which reproduces the passages I want to cite, and then I keep my own com-ments on those books in a separate file so that I will never confuse the two again. But the real miracle occurred when my college-age son taught me how to use the mysterious footnote key on the computer, which makes it possible to insert the citations directly into the text while the sources are still in front of me, instead of shuffling through hundreds of folders four or five years down the line, trying desper-ately to remember from where I derived a particular statistic or quote. Still, there is no guarantee against error. Should one occur, all I can do, as I did 14 years ago, is to correct it as soon as I possibly can, for my own sake and the sake of history. In the end, I am still the same fallible person I was before I made the transition to the computer, and the process of building a lengthy work of history remains a compli-cated but honorable task.

Questions on Meaning

1. Based on your reading of this selection, how do historians "go about crediting their sources"? Why is it essential to credit sources accurately?
2. What do you think Goodwin means when she says, "Through footnotes you point the way to future historians"? How does this clarify your understanding of the purpose of footnotes and citations?
3. Why does Goodwin characterize the work of historians as "honorable"? In what ways do you consider such work honorable?

Questions on Rhetorical Strategy and Style

1. Why does Goodwin begin by identifying herself as historian, wife, and mother? What is the impact of her stating that "there is nothing I take more seriously"?
2. What, according to Goodwin, is the process that historians follow when writing a book? How has technology affected that process?
3. Why do you think Goodwin lists so many details such as the number of pages in her book, the number of footnotes, the number of boxes of materials? How do these figures affect your acceptance of her explanation?

Writing Assignments

1. Think of a time when you made a mistake that could be interpreted as deliberate wrongdoing. Using Goodwin's essay as a model, explain the mistake as you understand it, emphasizing why you believe that while you were responsible for the error, it should not reflect poorly on your character.
2. Research accounts in respected newspapers and magazines of the plagiarism controversy surrounding Goodwin's book *The Fitzgeralds and the Kennedys*. Write a report on the issue, distinguishing between fact and interpretation. Based on your research, what conclusions do you draw regarding Goodwin's explanation?

3. Consult several college handbooks and/or rhetorics, as well as several college policies, on the subject of plagiarism and appropriate citation of sources. Use this material to compose a brief guide for students on the definition of plagiarism, its significance to academic writing, and ways to ensure proper documentation of sources.

Revision Strategies of Student Writers and Experienced Adult Writers

Nancy Sommers

Nancy Sommers, formerly Director of Composition at the University of Oklahoma, is now Adjunct Assistant Professor at New York University. She has taught writing at Boston University, the Harvard Graduate School of Business Administration, and the Polaroid Corporation. An NCTE Promising Researcher for her studies of the processes of revising, she is writing a research monograph on revision.

1   Although various aspects of the writing process have been studied extensively of late, research on revision has been notably absent. The reason for this, I suspect, is that current models of the writing process have directed attention away from revision. With few exceptions, these models are linear; they separate the writing process into discrete stages. Two representative models are Gordon Rohman's suggestion that the composing process moves from prewriting to writing to rewriting and James Britton's model of the writing process as a series of stages described in metaphors of linear growth, conception—incubation—production.[1] What is striking about these theories of writing is that they model themselves on speech: Rohman defines the writer in a way that cannot distinguish him from a speaker ("A writer is a man who . . . puts [his] experience into words in his own mind"—p. 15); and Britton bases his theory of writing on what he calls (following Jakobson) the "expressiveness" of speech.[2] Moreover, Britton's study itself follows the "linear model" of the relation of thought and language in speech proposed by Vygotsky, a relationship

Reprinted from *College Composition and Communication, Vol 31, No. 4,* (Dec 1980), National Council of Teachers of English.

embodied in the linear movement "from the motive which engenders a thought to the shaping of the thought, *first* in inner speech, *then* in meanings of words, and *finally* in words" (quoted in Britton, p. 40). What this movement fails to take into account in its linear structure—"first . . . then . . . finally"—is the recursive shaping of thought by language; what it fails to take into account is *revision*. In these linear conceptions of the writing process revision is understood as a separate stage at the end of the process—a stage that comes after the completion of a first or second draft and one that is temporally distinct from the prewriting and writing stages of the process.[3]

The linear model bases itself on speech in two specific ways. First of all, it is based on traditional rhetorical models, models that were created to serve the spoken art of oratory. In whatever ways the parts of classical rhetoric are described, they offer "stages" of composition that are repeated in contemporary models of the writing process. Edward Corbett, for instance, describes the "five parts of a discourse"—*inventio, dispositio, elocutio, memoria, pronunciatio*—and, disregarding the last two parts since "after rhetoric came to be concerned mainly with written discourse, there was no further need to deal with them,"[4] he produces a model very close to Britton's conception [*inventio*], incubation [*dispositio*], production [*elocutio*]. Other rhetorics also follow this procedure, and they do so not simply because of historical accident. Rather, the process represented in the linear model is based on the irreversibility of speech. Speech, Roland Barthes says, "is irreversible":

> "A word cannot be retracted, except precisely by saying that one retracts it. To cross out here is to add: if I want to erase what I have just said, I cannot do it without showing the eraser itself (I must say: '*or rather* . . . ' '*I expressed myself badly* . . .); paradoxically, it is ephemeral speech which is indelible, not monumental writing. All that one can do in the case of a spoken utterance is to tack on another utterance."[5]

What is impossible in speech is *revision:* like the example Barthes gives, revision in speech is an afterthought. In the same way, each stage of the linear model must be exclusive (distinct from the other stages) or else it becomes trivial and counterproductive to refer to these junctures as "stages."

By staging revision after enunciation, the linear models reduce revision in writing, as in speech, to no more than an afterthought. In this way such models make the study of revision impossible. Revision, in Rohman's model, is simply the repetition of writing; or to pursue Britton's organic metaphor, revision is simply the further growth of what is already there, the "preconceived" product. The absence of research on revision, then, is a function of a theory of writing which makes revision both superfluous and redundant, a theory which does not distinguish between writing and speech.

5   What the linear models do produce is a parody of writing. Isolating revision and then disregarding it plays havoc with the experiences composition teachers have of the actual writing and rewriting of experienced writers. Why should the linear model be preferred? Why should revision be forgotten, superfluous? Why do teachers offer the linear model and students accept it? One reason, Barthes suggests, is that "there is a fundamental tie between teaching and speech," while "writing begins at the point where speech becomes *impossible.*"[6] The spoken word cannot be revised. The possibility of revision distinguishes the written text from speech. In fact, according to Barthes, this is the essential difference between writing and speaking. When we must revise, when the very idea is subject to recursive shaping by language, then speech becomes inadequate. This is a matter to which I will return, but first we should examine, theoretically, a detailed exploration of what student writers as distinguished from experienced adult writers *do* when they write and rewrite their work. Dissatisfied with both the linear model of writing and the lack of attention to the process of revision, I conducted a series of studies over the past three years which examined the revision processes of student writers and experienced writers to see what role revision played in their writing processes. In the course of my work the revision process was redefined as *a sequence of changes in a composition—changes which are initiated by cues and occur continually throughout the writing of a work.*

Methodology

I used a case study approach. The student writers were twenty freshmen at Boston University and the University of Oklahoma with SAT verbal scores ranging from 450-600 in their first semester of composition. The twenty experienced adult writers from Boston and Oklahoma City included journalists, editors, and academics. To refer to the two groups, I use the terms *student writers* and *experienced writers* because the principal difference between these two groups is the amount of experience they have had in writing.

94

Each writer wrote three essays, expressive, explanatory, and persuasive, and rewrote each essay twice, producing nine written products in draft and final form. Each writer was interviewed three times after the final revision of each essay. And each writer suggested revisions for a composition written by an anonymous author. Thus extensive written and spoken documents were obtained from each writer.

The essays were analyzed by counting and categorizing the changes made. Four revision operations were identified: deletion, substitution, addition, and reordering. And four levels of changes were identified: word, phrase, sentence, theme (the extended statement of one idea). A coding system was developed for identifying the frequency of revision by level and operation. In addition, transcripts of the interviews in which the writers interpreted their revisions were used to develop what was called a *scale of concerns* for each writer. This scale enabled me to codify what were the writer's primary concerns, secondary concerns, tertiary concerns, and whether the writers used the same scale of concerns when revising the second or third drafts as they used in revising the first draft.

Revision Strategies of Student Writers

Most of the students I studied did not use the terms *revision* or *rewriting*. In fact, they did not seem comfortable using the word *revision* and explained that revision was not a word they used, but the word their teachers used. Instead, most of the students had developed various functional terms to describe the type of changes they made. The following are samples of these definitions:

> *Scratch Out and Do Over Again:* "I say scratch out and do over, and that means what it says. Scratching out and cutting out. I read what I have written and I cross out a word and put another word in; a more decent word or a better word. Then if there is somewhere to use a sentence that I have crossed out, I will put it there."
>
> *Reviewing:* "Reviewing means just using better words and eliminating words that are not needed. I go over and change words around."
>
> *Reviewing:* "I just review every word and make sure that everything is worded right. I see if I am rambling; I see if I can put a better word in or leave one out. Usually when I

read what I have written, I say to myself, 'that word is so bland or so trite,' and then I go and get my thesaurus."

Redoing: "Redoing means cleaning up the paper and crossing out. It is looking at something and saying, no that has to go, or no, that is not right."

Marking Out: "I don't use the word rewriting because I only write one draft and the changes that I make are made on top of the draft. The changes that I make are usually just marking out words and putting different ones in."

Slashing and Throwing Out: "I throw things out and say they are not good. I like to write like Fitzgerald did by inspiration, and if I feel inspired then I don't need to slash and throw much out."

10   The predominant concern in these definitions is vocabulary. The stu-   10
dents understand the revision process as a rewording activity. They do so because they perceive words as the unit of written discourse. That is, they concentrate on particular words apart from their role in the text. Thus one student quoted above thinks in terms of dictionaries, and, following the eighteenth century theory of words parodied in *Gulliver's Travels*, he imagines a load of things carried about to be exchanged. Lexical changes are the major revision activities of the students because economy is their goal. They are governed, like the linear model itself, by the Law of Occam's razor that prohibits logically needless repetition: redundancy and superfluity. Nothing governs speech more than such superfluities; speech constantly repeats itself precisely because spoken words, as Barthes writes, are expendable in the cause of communication. The aim of revision according to the students' own description is therefore to clean up speech; the redundancy of speech is unnecessary in writing, their logic suggests, because writing, unlike speech, can be reread. Thus one student said, "Redoing means cleaning up the paper and crossing out." The remarkable contradiction of cleaning by marking might, indeed, stand for student revision as I have encountered it.

The students place a symbolic importance on their selection and rejection of words as the determiners of success or failure for their compositions. When revising, they primarily ask themselves: can I find a better word or phrase? A more impressive, not so cliched, or less hum-drum word? Am I repeating the same word or phrase too often? They approach the revision process with what could be labeled as a "thesaurus philosophy of writing"; the students consider the thesaurus a harvest of lexical substitutions and believe that most problems in their essays can be solved by rewording. What is revealed in the students' use of the thesaurus is a governing attitude toward their writing: that the meaning to be communicated is already there, already finished, already produced, ready to be communicated, and all that is necessary is a better word "rightly worded." One student defined revision as "redoing"; "redoing" meant "just using better words and eliminating words that are not needed." For the students, writing is translating: the thought to the page, the language of speech to the more formal language of prose, the word to its synonym. Whatever is translated, an original text already exists for students, one which need not be discovered or acted upon, but simply communicated.[7]

The students list repetition as one of the elements they most worry about. This cue signals to them that they need to eliminate the repetition either by substituting or deleting words or phrases. Repetition occurs, in large part, because student writing imitates—transcribes—speech: attention to repetitious words is a manner of cleaning speech. Without a sense of the developmental possibilities of revision (and writing in general) students seek, on the authority of many textbooks, simply to clean up their language and prepare to type. What is curious, however, is that students are aware of lexical repetition, but not conceptual repetition. They only notice the repetition if they can "hear" it; they do not diagnose lexical repetition as symptomatic of problems on a deeper level. By rewording their sentences to avoid the lexical repetition, the students solve the immediate problem, but blind themselves to problems on a textual level; although they are using different words, they are sometimes merely restating the same idea with different words. Such blindness, as I discovered with student writers, is the inability to "see" revision as a process: the inability to "re-view" their work again, as it were, with different eyes, and to start over.

The revision strategies described above are consistent with the students' understanding of the revision process as requiring lexical changes but not semantic changes. For the students, the extent to which they revise is a function of their level of inspiration. In fact, they use the word *inspiration* to describe the ease or difficulty with which their essay is written, and the extent to which the essay needs to be revised. If students feel inspired, if the writing comes easily, and if they don't get stuck on individual words or phrases, then they say that they cannot see any reason to revise. Because students do not see revision as an activity in which they modify and develop perspectives and ideas, they feel that if they know what they want to say, then there is little reason for making revisions.

The only modification of ideas in the students' essays occurred when they tried out two or three introductory paragraphs. This results, in part, because the students have been taught in another version of the linear model of composing to use a thesis statement as a controlling device in their introductory paragraphs. Since they write their introductions and their thesis statements even before they have really discovered what they want to say, their early close attention to the thesis statement, and more generally the linear model, function to restrict and circumscribe not only the development of their ideas, but also their ability to change the direction of these ideas.

15   Too often as composition teachers we conclude that students do 15 not willingly revise. The evidence from my research suggests that it is not that students are unwilling to revise, but rather that they do what they have been taught to do in a consistently narrow and predictable way. On every occasion when I asked students why they hadn't made any more changes, they essentially replied, "I knew something larger was wrong, but I didn't think it would help to move words around." The students have strategies for handling words and phrases and their strategies helped them on a word or sentence level. What they lack, however, is a set of strategies to help them identify the "something larger" that they sensed was wrong and work from there. The students do not have strategies for handling the whole essay. They lack procedures or heuristics to help them reorder lines of reasoning or ask questions about their purposes and readers. The students view their compositions in a linear way as a series of parts. Even such potentially useful concepts as "unity" or "form" are reduced to the rule that a composition, if it is to have form, must have an introduction, a body, and a conclusion, or the sum total of the necessary parts.

The students decide to stop revising when they decide that they have not violated any of the rules for revising. These rules, such as "Never begin a sentence with a conjunction" or "Never end a sentence with a preposition," are lexically cued and rigidly applied. In general, students will subordinate the demands of the specific problems of their text to the demands of the rules. Changes are made in compliance with abstract rules about the product, rules that quite often do not apply to the specific problems in the text. These revision strategies are teacher-based, directed towards a teacher-reader who expects compliance with rules—with pre-existing "conceptions"— and who will only examine parts of the composition (writing comments about those parts in the margins of their essays) and will cite any violations of rules in those parts. At best the students see their writing altogether passively through the eyes of former teachers or their surrogates, the textbooks, and are bound to the rules which they have been taught.

Revision Strategies of Experienced Writers

One aim of my research has been to contrast how student writers define revision with how a group of experienced writers define their revision processes. Here is a sampling of the definitions from the experienced writers:

> *Rewriting:* "It is a matter of looking at the kernel of what I have written, the content, and then thinking about it, responding to it, making decisions, and actually restructuring it."
>
> *Rewriting:* "I rewrite as I write. It is hard to tell what is a first draft because it is not determined by time. In one draft, I might cross out three pages, write two, cross out a fourth, rewrite it, and call it a draft. I am constantly writing and rewriting. I can only conceptualize so much in my first draft—only so much information can be held in my head at one time; my rewriting efforts are a reflection of how much information I can encompass at one time. There are levels and agenda which I have to attend to in each draft."
>
> *Rewriting:* "Rewriting means on one level, finding the argument, and on another level, language changes to make the argument more effective. Most of the time I feel as if I can go on rewriting forever. There is always one part of a piece that I could keep working on. It is always difficult to know at what point to abandon a piece of writing. I like this idea that a piece of writing is never finished, just abandoned."
>
> *Rewriting:* "My first draft is usually very scattered. In rewriting, I find the line of argument. After the argument is resolved, I am much more interested in word choice and phrasing."

Revising: "My cardinal rule in revising is never to fall in love with what I have written in a first or second draft. An idea, sentence, or even a phrase that looks catchy, I don't trust. Part of this idea is to wait a while. I am much more in love with something after I have written it than I am a day or two later. It is much easier to change anything with time."

Revising: "It means taking apart what I have written and putting it back together again. I ask major theoretical questions of my ideas, respond to those questions, and think of proportion and structure, and try to find a controlling metaphor. I find out which ideas can be developed and which should be dropped. I am constantly chiseling and changing as I revise."

The experienced writers describe their primary objective when revising as finding the form or shape of their argument. Although the metaphors vary, the experienced writers often use structural expressions such as "finding a framework," "a pattern," or "a design" for their argument. When questioned about this emphasis, the experienced writers responded that since their first drafts are usually scattered attempts to define their territory, their objective in the second draft is to begin observing general patterns of development and deciding what should be included and what excluded. One writer explained, "I have learned from experience that I need to keep writing a first draft until I figure out what I want to say. Then in a second draft, I begin to see the structure of an argument and how all the various sub-arguments which are buried beneath the surface of all those sentences are related." What is described here is a process in which the writer is both agent and vehicle. "Writing," says Barthes, unlike speech, "develops like a seed, not a line,"[8] and like a seed it confuses beginning and end, conception and production. Thus, the experienced writers say their drafts are "not determined by time," that rewriting is a "constant process," that they feel as if (they) "can go on forever." Revising confuses the beginning and end, the agent and vehicle; it confuses, *in order to find*, the line of argument.

After a concern for form, the experienced writers have a second objective: a concern for their readership. In this way, "production" precedes "conception." The experienced writers imagine a reader (reading their product) whose existence and whose expectations influence their revision process. They have abstracted the standards of a reader and this reader seems to be partially a reflection of themselves and functions as a critical and productive collaborator—a collaborator who has yet to love their work. The anticipation of a reader's judgment causes a feeling of dissonance when the writer recognizes incongruities between intention and execution, and requires these writers to make revisions on all levels. Such a reader gives them just what the students lacked: new eyes to "re-view" their work. The experienced writers believe that they have learned the causes and conditions, the product, which will influence their reader, and their revision strategies are geared towards creating these causes and conditions. They demonstrate a complex understanding of which examples, sentences, or phrases should be included or excluded. For example, one experienced writer decided to delete public examples and add private examples when writing about the energy crisis because "private examples would be less controversial and thus more persuasive." Another writer revised his transitional sentences because "some kinds of transitions are more easily recognized as transitions than others." These examples represent the type of strategic attempts these experienced writers use to manipulate the conventions of discourse in order to communicate to their reader.

20   But these revision strategies are a process of more than communication; they are part of the process of *discovering meaning* altogether. Here we can see the importance of dissonance; at the heart of revision is the process by which writers recognize and resolve the dissonance they sense in their writing. Ferdinand de Saussure has argued that meaning is differential or "diacritical," based on differences between terms rather than "essential" or inherent qualities of terms. "Phonemes," he said, "are characterized not, as one might think, by their own positive quality but simply by the fact that they are distinct."[9] In fact, Saussure bases his entire *Course in General Linguistics* on these differences, and such differences are dissonant; like musical dissonances which gain their significance from their relationship to the "key" of the composition which itself is determined by the whole language, specific language (parole) gains its meaning from the system of language (langue) of which it is a manifestation and part. The musical composition—a "composition" of parts—creates its "key" as in an over-all structure which determines the value (meaning) of its parts. The analogy with music is readily seen in the compositions of experienced writers: both sorts of composition are based precisely on

those structures experienced writers seek in their writing. It is this complicated relationship between the parts and the whole in the work of experienced writers which destroys the linear model; writing cannot develop "like a line" because each addition or deletion is a reordering of the whole. Explicating Saussure, Jonathan Culler asserts that "meaning depends on difference of meaning."[10] But student writers constantly struggle to bring their essays into congruence with a predefined meaning. The experienced writers do the opposite: they seek to discover (to create) meaning in the engagement with their writing, in revision. They seek to emphasize and exploit the lack of clarity, the differences of meaning, the dissonance, that writing as opposed to speech allows in the possibility of revision. Writing has spatial and temporal features not apparent in speech—words are recorded in space and fixed in time—which is why writing is susceptible to reordering and later addition. Such features make possible the dissonance that both provokes revision and promises, from itself, new meaning.

For the experienced writers the heaviest concentration of changes is on the sentence level, and the changes are predominantly by addition and deletion. But, unlike the students, experienced writers make changes on all levels and use all revision operations. Moreover, the operations the students fail to use—reordering and addition—seem to require a theory of the revision process as a totality—a theory which, in fact, encompasses the *whole* of the composition. Unlike the students, the experienced writers possess a nonlinear theory in which a sense of the whole writing both precedes and grows out of an examination of the parts. As we saw, one writer said he needed "a first draft to figure out what to say," and "a second draft to see the structure of an argument buried beneath the surface." Such a "theory" is both theoretical and strategical; once again, strategy and theory are conflated in ways that are literally impossible for the linear model. Writing appears to be more like a seed than a line.

Two elements of the experienced writers' theory of the revision process are the adoption of a holistic perspective and the perception that revision is a recursive process. The writers ask: what does my essay as a *whole* need for form, balance, rhythm, or communication. Details are added, dropped, substituted, or reordered according to their sense of what the essay needs for emphasis and proportion. This sense, however, is constantly in flux as ideas are developed and modified; it is constantly "re-viewed" in relation to the parts. As their ideas change, revision becomes an attempt to make their writing consonant with that changing vision.

The experienced writers see their revision process as a recursive process—a process with significant recurring activities—with different levels of attention and different agenda for each cycle. During the first revision cycle their attention is primarily directed towards narrowing the topic and delimiting their ideas. At this point, they are not as concerned as they are later about vocabulary and style. The experienced writers explained that they get closer to their meaning by not limiting themselves too early to lexical concerns. As one writer commented to explain her revision process, a comment inspired by the summer 1977 New York power failure: "I feel like Con Edison cutting off certain states to keep the generators going. In first and second drafts, I try to cut off as much as I can of my editing generator, and in a third draft, I try to cut off some of my idea generators, so I can make sure that I will actually finish the essay." Although the experienced writers describe their revision process as a series of different levels or cycles, it is inaccurate to assume that they have only one objective for each cycle and that each cycle can be defined by a different objective. The same objectives and sub-processes are present in each cycle, but in different proportions. Even though these experienced writers place the predominant weight upon finding the form of their argument during the first cycle, other concerns exist as well. Conversely, during the later cycles, when the experienced writers' primary attention is focused upon stylistic concerns, they are still attuned, although in a reduced way, to the form of the argument. Since writers are limited in what they can attend to during each cycle (understandings are temporal), revision strategies help balance competing demands on attention. Thus, writers can concentrate on more than one objective at a time by developing strategies to sort out and organize their different concerns in successive cycles of revision.

It is a sense of writing as discovery—a repeated process of beginning over again, starting out new—that the students failed to have. I have used the notion of dissonance because such dissonance, the incongruities between intention and execution, governs both writing and meaning. Students do not see the incongruities. They need to rely on their own internalized sense of good writing and to see their writing with their "own" eyes. Seeing in revision—seeing beyond hearing—is at the root of the word *revision* and the process itself; current dicta on revising blind our students to what is actually involved in revision. In fact, they blind them to what constitutes good writing altogether. Good writing disturbs: it creates dissonance. Students need to seek the dissonance of discovery, utilizing in their writing, as the experienced writers do, the very difference between writing and speech—the possibility of revision.

End Notes

1. D. Gordon Rohman and Albert O. Wlecke, "Pre-writing: The Construc-tion and Application of Models for Concept Formation in Writing," Coop-erative Research Project No. 2174, U.S. Office of Education, Department of Health, Education, and Welfare; James Britton, Anthony Burgess, Nancy Martin, Alex McLeod, Harold Rosen, *The Development of Writing Abilities (11-18)* (London: Macmillan Education, 1975).
2. Britton is following Roman Jakobson, "Linguistics and Poetics," in T. A. Sebeok, *Style in Language* (Cambridge, Mass: MIT Press, 1960).
3. For an extended discussion of this issue see Nancy Sommers, "The Need for Theory in Composition Research," *College Composition and Communi-cation,* 30 (February, 1979), 46-49.
4. *Classical Rhetoric for the Modern Student* (New York: Oxford University Press, 1965), p. 27.
5. Roland Barthes, "Writers, Intellectuals, Teachers," in *Image-Music-Text,* trans. Stephen Heath (New York: Hill and Wang, 1977), pp. 190-191.
6. "Writers, Intellectuals, Teachers," p. 190.
7. Nancy Sommers and Ronald Schleifer, "Means and Ends: Some Assump-tions of Student Writers," *Composition and Teaching,* II (in press).
8. *Writing Degree Zero* in *Writing Degree Zero and Elements of Semiology,* trans. Annette Lavers and Colin Smith (New York: Hill and Wang, 1968), p. 20.
9. *Course in General Linguistics,* trans. Wade Baskin (New York, 1966), p. 119.
10. Jonathan Culler, *Saussure* (Penguin Modern Masters Series; London: Pen-guin Books, 1976), p. 70.

Acknowledgment: The author wishes to express her gratitude to Professor William Smith, University of Pittsburgh, for his vital assistance with the research reported in this article and to Patrick Hays, her husband, for extensive discussions and critical editorial help.

IV. Education

The Allegory of the Cave

Plato

Plato (c. 428–347 B.C.), one of the most influential philosophers in history, was born into a wealthy, aristocratic family, presumably in Athens. A pupil of Socrates (and teacher of Aristotle), Plato left Athens for nearly 20 years after his mentor's death in 399 B.C. Upon his return in 380 B.C., he established the Academy and taught there for the remainder of his life. Much of Plato's philosophy appears in his "dialogues"—conversations between Socrates and his students. Three of these "dialogues," the Apology, *the* Crito, *and the* Phaedo, *immortalized Socrates' trial and final days. Other well-known works of Plato include the* Republic and Laws. *Plato's belief in the separate existence of the body and soul and the existence of an eternal order of Forms (the Theory of Forms) have influenced Western thought for more than 2,000 years. In "The Allegory of the Cave" (from the* Republic), *Plato argues the need to differentiate between the world of the senses and physical phenomena and the world of knowledge.*

1   *Socrates:* And now, I said, let me show in a figure how far our nature is enlightened or unenlightened:— Behold! human beings living in an underground den, which has a mouth open towards the light and reaching all along the den; here they have been from their childhood, and have their legs and necks chained so that they cannot move, and can only see before them, being prevented by the chains from turning round their heads. Above and behind them a fire is blazing at a distance, and between the fire and the prisoners there is a raised way; and you will

The den, the prisoners: the light at a distance;   1

see, if you look, a low wall built along the way, like the screen which marionette players have in front of them, over which they show the puppets.

Glaucon: I see.

And do you see, I said, men passing along the wall carrying all sorts of vessels, and statues and figures of animals made of wood and stone and various materials, which appear over the wall? Some of them are talking, others silent.

You have shown me a strange image, and they are strange prisoners.

5   Like ourselves, I replied; and they see only their own shadows, or the shadows of one another, which the fire throws on the opposite wall of the cave?

True, he said; how could they see anything but the shadows if they were never allowed to move their heads?

And of the objects which are being carried in like manner they would only see the shadows?

Yes, he said.

And if they were able to converse with one another, would they not suppose that they were naming what was actually before them?

10   Very true.

And suppose further that the prison had an echo which came from the other side, would they not be sure to fancy when one of the passersby spoke that the voice which they heard came from the passing shadow?

No question, he replied.

To them, I said, the truth would be literally nothing but the shadows of the images.

That is certain.

15   And now look again, and see what will naturally follow if the prisoners are released and disabused of their error. At first, when any of them is liberated and compelled suddenly to stand up and turn his neck round and walk and look towards the light, he will suffer sharp pains; the glare will distress him, and he will be unable to see the realities of which in his former

The low wall, and   5
*the moving figures
of which the
shadows are seen on
the opposite wall of
the den.*

The prisoners would   10
*mistake the shadows
for realities.*

And when released,   15
*they would still
persist in
maintaining the
superior truth of the
shadows.*

OED online = Oxford Dictionary allegory -
PLATO | THE ALLEGORY OF THE CAVE   structural metaphor
Essences / Ideas / Forms   or a series of
correspondences

conceptual structure

enlightment is
a form of
education - age of
reason
- we are waking
up
* In the intellectual
world the worlddue
sense is not the
real world
* Good is the source
of everything

state he had seen the shadows; and then conceive some one saying to him, that what he saw before was an illusion, but that now, when he is approaching nearer to being and his eye is turned towards more real existence, he has a clearer vision—what will be his reply? And you may further imagine that his instructor is pointing to the objects as they pass and requiring him to name them—will he not be perplexed? Will he not fancy that the shadows which he formerly saw are truer than the objects which are now shown to him?

Far truer.

And if he is compelled to look straight at the light, will he not have a pain in his eyes which will make him turn away to take refuge in the objects of vision which he can see, and which he will conceive to be in reality clearer than the things which are now being shown to him?

When dragged upwards, they would be dazzled by excess of light.

True, he said.

And suppose once more, that he is reluctantly dragged up a steep and rugged ascent, and held fast until he is forced into the presence of the sun himself, is he not likely to be pained and irritated? When he approaches the light his eyes will be dazzled, and he will not be able to see anything at all of what are now called realities.

Not all in a moment, he said.

He will require to grow accustomed to the sight of the upper world. And first he will see the shadows best, next the reflections of men and other objects in the water, and then the objects themselves; then he will gaze upon the light of the moon and the stars and the spangled heaven; and he will see the sky and the stars by night better than the sun or the light of the sun by day?

Certainly.

Last of all he will be able to see the sun, and not mere reflections of him in the water, but he will see him in his own proper place, and not in another; and he will contemplate him as he is.

At length they will see the sun and understand his nature.

20

20

Certainly.

25   He will then proceed to argue that this is he who gives the season and the years, and is the guardian of all that is in the visible world, and in a certain way the cause of all things which he and his fellows have been accustomed to behold?

Clearly, he said, he would first see the sun and then reason about him.

And when he remembered his old habitation, and the wisdom of the den and his fellow-prisoners, do you not suppose that he would felicitate himself on the change, and pity them?

They would then pity their old companions of the den.

Certainly, he would.

And if they were in the habit of conferring honours among themselves on those who were quickest to observe the passing shadows and to remark which of them went before, and which followed after, and which were together; and who were therefore best able to draw conclusions as to the future, do you think that he would care for such honors and glories, or envy the possessors of them? Would he not say with Homer, "Better to be the poor servant of a poor master," and to endure anything, rather than think as they do and live after their manner?

30   Yes, he said, I think that he would rather suffer anything than entertain those false notions and live in this miserable manner.

Imagine once more, I said, such as one coming suddenly out of the sun to be replaced in his old situation; would he not be certain to have his eyes full of darkness?

To be sure, he said.

And if there were a contest, and he had to compete in measuring the shadows with the prisoners who had never moved out of the den, while his sight was still weak, and before his eyes had become steady (and the time which would be needed to acquire this new habit of sight might be very considerable) would he not be ridiculous? Men would say of him that up

But when they returned to the den they would see much worse than those who had never left it.

he went and down he came without his eyes; and that it was better not even to think of ascending; and if any one tried to loose another and lead him up to the light, let them only catch the offender, and they would put him to death.

No question, he said.

35　　This entire allegory, I said, you may now append, dear Glaucon, to the previous argument; the prison-house is the world of sight, the light of the fire is the sun, and you will not misapprehend me if you interpret the journey upwards to be the ascent of the soul into the intellectual world according to my poor belief, which, at your desire, I have expressed—whether rightly or wrongly God knows. But, whether true or false, my opinion is that in the world of knowledge the idea of good appears last of all, and is seen only with an effort; and when seen, is also inferred to be the universal author of all things beautiful and right, parent of light and of the lord of light in this visible world, and the immediate source of reason and truth in the intellectual; and that this is the power upon which he who would act rationally either in public or private life must have his eye fixed.

I agree, he said, as far as I am able to understand you.

The prison is the world of sight, the light of the fire is the sun.　35

Questions on Meaning

1. What do the prisoners believe they are seeing as they watch the shadows on the wall? How do the echoes of the voices of the men who cast the shadows reinforce this belief?
2. What happens when a prisoner is released from the den and is "compelled to look straight at the light"? What will he see at first; what will he see as his eyes adjust? Why will he initially not accept that what he is seeing outside the cave is real? What does the prisoner see when he is returned to the cave? What does he then feel about reality? Why would the other prisoners distrust him and want to "put him to death"?

Questions on Rhetorical Strategy and Style

1. What is the thesis of Plato's allegory? How would you summarize its application to life in general?
2. The dialogue presented here is built around a narration. Find where Plato also uses description and cause and effect within his story of the prisoners.
3. What do the den (the prison), the prisoners, the shadow, the sun, and the journey out of the cave and into sunlight symbolize in Plato's allegory? Why would Plato choose to use an allegory to present his ideas?

Writing Assignments

1. Write an allegory to argue against the philosophy of a person or group with whom you disagree—such as white supremacists (race), monarchists (politics), or monopolists (business). Chose your symbolism to clarify the argument. As Plato learned from Socrates, ask rhetorical questions as you make each of your points to confirm that your reader follows—and does not disagree with—your arguments.
2. How might you apply Plato's teaching to your life? Write an essay about a time when your concept of reality was altered because of some knowledge you gained—it could be learning the truth about a friend or becoming aware of the facts about an event or situation. How did your "ascent into the intellectual world" change you? How did others respond to you once they realized that you no longer saw things as they did?

Everything Has a Name

Helen Keller

Helen Keller (1880–1968) was born in Tuscumbia, Alabama. As a result of illness, she lost her senses of sight and hearing at 19 months. Taught to speak, read, and write by Anne Sullivan, her teacher and lifelong companion, Keller graduated from Radcliffe (1904) at age 24. A symbol of personal strength and perseverance, Keller became a distinguished lecturer and writer. Her autobiography, The Story of My Life *(1902), was made into the award-winning film,* The Miracle Worker *(1959). This essay, excerpted from her autobiography, describes the moment when Keller understood the concept of language and reveals how that changed her life.*

1   The most important day I remember in all my life is the one on which my teacher, Anne Mansfield Sullivan, came to me. I am filled with wonder when I consider the immeasurable contrast between the two lives which it connects. It was the third of March, 1887, three months before I was seven years old.

On the afternoon of that eventful day, I stood on the porch, dumb, expectant. I guessed vaguely from my mother's signs and from the hurrying to and fro in the house that something unusual was about to happen, so I went to the door and waited on the steps. The afternoon sun penetrated the mass of honeysuckle that covered the porch, and fell on my upturned face. My fingers lingered almost unconsciously on the familiar leaves and blossoms which had just come forth to greet the sweet southern spring. I did not know what the future held of marvel or surprise for me. Anger and bitterness had preyed upon me continually for weeks and a deep languor had succeeded this passionate struggle.

From *The Story of My Life* published by Doubleday, a division of Bantam Double Dell Publishing Groups, Inc.

Have you ever been at sea in a dense fog, when it seemed as if a tangible white darkness shut you in, and the great ship, tense and anxious, groped her way toward the shore with plummet and sounding-line, and you waited with beating heart for something to happen? I was like that ship before my education began, only I was without compass or sounding-line, and had no way of knowing how near the harbour was. "Light! give me light!" was the wordless cry of my soul, and the light of love shone on me in that very hour.

I felt approaching footsteps. I stretched out my hand as I supposed to my mother. Some one took it, and I was caught up and held close in the arms of her who had come to reveal all things to me, and, more than all things else, to love me.

5   The morning after my teacher came she led me into her room and   5
gave me a doll. The little blind children at the Perkins Institution had sent it and Laura Bridgman [the first deaf and blind person to be educated in the United States] had dressed it; but I did not know this until afterward. When I had played with it a little while, Miss Sullivan slowly spelled into my hand the word "d-o-l-l." I was at once interested in this finger play and tried to imitate it. When I finally succeeded in making the letters correctly I was flushed with childish pleasure and pride. Running downstairs to my mother I held up my hand and made the letters for doll. I did not know that I was spelling a word or even that words existed: I was simply making my fingers go in monkey-like imitation. In the days that followed I learned to spell in this uncomprehending way a great many words, among them *pin, hat, cup,* and a few verbs like *sit, stand* and *walk.* But my teacher had been with me several weeks before I understood that everything has a name.

One day, while I was playing with my new doll, Miss Sullivan put my big rag doll into my lap also, spelled "d-o-l-l" and tried to make me understand that "d-o-l-l" applied to both. Earlier in the day we had had a tussle over the words "m-u-g" and "w-a-t-e-r." Miss Sullivan had tried to impress it upon me that "m-u-g" is *mug* and that "w-a-t-e-r" is *water,* but I persisted in confounding the two. In despair she had dropped the subject for the time, only to renew it at the first opportunity. I became impatient at her repeated attempts and, seizing the new doll, I dashed it upon the floor. I was keenly delighted when I felt the fragments of the broken doll at my feet. Neither sorrow nor regret followed my passionate outburst. I had not loved the doll. In the still, dark world in which I lived there was no strong sentiment or tenderness. I felt my teacher sweep the fragments to one side of the hearth, and I had a sense of satisfaction that the cause of my discomfort was removed. She brought me my hat, and I knew I was going out into the warm sunshine. This thought, if a wordless sensation may be called a thought, made me hop and skip with pleasure.

We walked down the path to the well-house, attracted by the fragrance of the honeysuckle with which it was covered. Some one was drawing water and my teacher placed my hand under the spout. As the cool stream gushed over one hand she spelled into the other the word *water*, first slowly, then rapidly. I stood still, my whole attention fixed upon the motions of her fingers. Suddenly I felt a misty consciousness as of something forgotten—a thrill of returning thought; and somehow the mystery of language was revealed to me. I knew then that "w-a-t-e-r" meant the wonderful cool something that was flowing over my hand. That living word awakened my soul, gave it light, hope, joy, set it free! There were barriers still, it is true, but barriers that could in time be swept away.

I left the well-house eager to learn. Everything had a name, and each name gave birth to a new thought. As we returned to the house every object which I touched seemed to quiver with life. That was because I saw everything with the strange, new sight that had come to me. On entering the door I remembered the doll I had broken. I felt my way to the hearth and picked up the pieces. I tried vainly to put them together. Then my eyes filled with tears; for I realized what I had done, and for the first time I felt repentance and sorrow.

I learned a great many new words that day. I do not remember what they all were; but I do know that *mother, father, sister, teacher* were among them—words that were to make the world blossom for me, "like Aaron's rod, with flowers." It would have been difficult to find a happier child than I was as I lay in my crib at the close of that eventful day and lived over the joys it had brought me, and for the first time longed for a new day to come.

Questions on Meaning

1. What is the significance of Keller's discovery that "everything has a name"? Why did that knowledge give her "light, hope, joy"?
2. What are "the two lives" connected by the arrival of her teacher, Anne Sullivan? If Keller could not hear or see, what clues did she have that something unusual was happening the day Sullivan arrived?
3. Why was Keller unbothered by the broken doll when she smashed it to the floor? Why did she later feel great remorse and attempt to put it back together?

Questions on Rhetorical Strategy and Style

1. Keller's narrative essay is embellished with vivid descriptions. Were you surprised at her ability to create such imagery? Compare her description of standing on the porch waiting for Sullivan to her metaphor of the ship in fog. Describe how one description reflects her personal experiences, the other her education.
2. What is the tone of Keller's essay? What does it reflect about her as a person and as a student?
3. How could Keller have reorganized the essay in some way other than the chronological? Indicate an event from during the day she describes that could have served as the lead. How would that revision affect the essay?

Writing Assignments

1. Research the Perkins Institution and Laura Bridgman to determine their historic roles in educating individuals who are deaf and blind. Find out what techniques are used today to educate individuals who are deaf and blind. How has state-of-the-art computer technology changed the way that individuals with these conditions learn?
2. Few persons have a "revelation" as significant as Keller's, but most of us do have minor awakenings during life that forever change how we see something or how we engage in an activity. Identify some such moment in your life—such as when algebra suddenly became clear, or when you finally learned to ride a bike, or when you were able to whistle. How did you respond? How did it affect the way you tackled other hurdles?

3.   Sullivan changed Keller's life. Write an essay about someone who has had a major impact on your life. Describe how this person entered your life and whether he or she was expected. Explain the effect this person had on you, comparing and contrasting the *you* before to the *you* after.

A Homemade Education

Malcolm X

Malcolm X (1925–1965), a noted political activist and writer, was born Malcolm Little in Omaha, Nebraska. The son of Earl Little, a Baptist minister who supported the back-to-Africa movement of the 1920s, Malcolm experienced as a child the violence of the Ku Klux Klan and its agencies. After his father was murdered by the Ku Klux Klan and his mother, Louise Little, was committed to a mental institution, Malcolm, in only eighth grade, quit school and drifted to the streets. Jailed for burglary in 1946, Malcolm taught himself the importance of reading and education and converted to the religion of Islam through the Black Muslim Movement led by Elijah Muhammad. When he was released from prison in 1953, Malcolm took his new name "X" signifying "the unknown" and began speaking on behalf of the Black Muslim Movement, pressing for black separatism and the use of self-defense. In 1964, following a trip to Mecca, Malcolm X began advocating for all religions and races and he founded the Organization of Afro-American Unity. A feud that developed over his desire to unify the races and free blacks in America resulted in his assassination by un-named assassins at the Audubon Ballroom in Harlem, N.Y. on February 21, 1965. Malcolm X's story was told in the early 1990s in the biographical movie by director Spike Lee. His writing includes The Autobiography of Malcolm X *(1965, written with Alex Haley),* Malcolm X Talks to Young People *(1969) and* Malcolm X on Afro-*

American Unity (1970). This essay, published in his autobiography, explains how reading in prison created his passionate thirst for education

1   It was because of my letters that I happened to stumble upon starting to acquire some kind of a homemade education.

I became increasingly frustrated at not being able to express what I wanted to convey in letters that I wrote, especially those to Mr. Elijah Muhammad. In the street, I had been the most articulate hustler out there—I had commanded attention when I said something. But now, trying to write simple English, I not only wasn't articulate, I wasn't even functional. How would I sound writing in slang, the way I would say it, something such as, "Look, daddy, let me pull your coat about a cat, Elijah Muhammad—"

Many who today hear me somewhere in person, or on television, or those who read something I've said, will think I went to school far beyond the eighth grade. This impression is due entirely to my prison studies.

It had really begun back in the Charlestown Prison, when Bimbi first made me feel envy of his stock of knowledge. Bimbi had always taken charge of any conversations he was in, and I had tried to emulate him. But every book I picked up had few sentences which didn't contain anywhere from one to nearly all of the words that might as well have been in Chinese. When I just skipped those words, of course, I really ended up with little idea of what the book said. So I had come to the Norfolk Prison Colony still going through only book-reading motions. Pretty soon, I would have quit even these motions, unless I had received the motivation that I did.

5   I saw that the best thing I could do was get hold of a dictionary—to study, to learn some words. I was lucky enough to reason also that I should try to improve my penmanship. It was sad. I couldn't even write in a straight line. It was both ideas together that moved me to request a dictionary along with some tablets and pencils from the Norfolk Prison Colony school.

I spent two days just riffling uncertainly through the dictionary's pages. I'd never realized so many words existed! I didn't know *which* words I needed to learn. Finally, just to start some kind of action, I began copying.

In my slow, painstaking, ragged handwriting, I copied into my tablet everything printed on that first page, down to the punctuation marks.

I believe it took me a day. Then, aloud, I read back, to myself, everything I'd written on the tablet. Over and over, aloud, to myself, I read my own handwriting.

I woke up the next morning, thinking about those words—immensely proud to realize that not only had I written so much at one time, but I'd written words that I never knew were in the world. Moreover, with a little effort, I also could remember what many of these words meant. I reviewed the words whose meanings I didn't remember. Funny thing, from the dictionary first page right now, that "aardvark" springs to my mind. The dictionary had a picture of it, a long-tailed, long-eared, burrowing African mammal, which lives off termites caught by sticking out its tongue as an anteater does for ants.

I was so fascinated that I went on—I copied the dictionary's next page. And the same experience came when I studied that. With every succeeding page, I also learned of people and places and events from history. Actually the dictionary is like a miniature encyclopedia. Finally the dictionary's A section had filled a whole tablet—and I went on into the B's. That was the way I started copying what eventually became the entire dictionary. It went a lot faster after so much practice helped me to pick up handwriting speed. Between what I wrote in my tablet, and writing letters, during the rest of my time in prison I would guess I wrote a million words.

I suppose it was inevitable that as my word-base broadened, I could for the first time pick up a book and read and now begin to understand what the book was saying. Anyone who has read a great deal can imagine the new world that opened. Let me tell you something: from then until I left that prison, in every free moment I had, if I was not reading in the library, I was reading on my bunk. You couldn't have gotten me out of books with a wedge. Between Mr. Muhammad's teachings, my correspondence, my visitors—usually Ella and Reginald—and my reading of books, months passed without my even thinking about being imprisoned. In fact, up to then, I never had been so truly free in my life.

The Norfolk Prison Colony's library was in the school building. A variety of classes was taught there by instructors who came from such places as Harvard and Boston universities. The weekly debates between inmate teams were also held in the school building. You would be astonished to know how worked up convict debaters and audiences would get over subjects like "Should Babies Be Fed Milk?"

Available on the prison library's shelves were books on just about every general subject. Much of the big private collection that Parkhurst had willed to the prison was still in crates and boxes in the back of the library—thousands of old books. Some of them looked ancient: covers faded; old-time parchment-looking binding. Parkhurst, I've mentioned, seemed to have been principally interested in history and religion. He had the money and the special interest to have a lot of books that you wouldn't have in general circulation. Any college library would have been lucky to get that collection.

As you can imagine, especially in a prison where there was heavy emphasis on rehabilitation, an inmate was smiled upon if he demonstrated an unusually intense interest in books. There was a sizable number of well-read inmates, especially the popular debaters. Some were said by many to be practically walking encyclopedias. They were almost celebrities. No university would ask any student to devour literature as I did when this new world opened to me, of being able to read and *understand*.

15   I read more in my room than in the library itself. An inmate who   15
was known to read a lot could check out more than the permitted maximum number of books. I preferred reading in the total isolation of my own room.

When I had progressed to really serious reading, every night at about ten P.M. I would be outraged with the "lights out." It always seemed to catch me right in the middle of something engrossing.

Fortunately, right outside my door was a corridor light that cast a glow into my room. The glow was enough to read by, once my eyes adjusted to it. So when "lights out" came, I would sit on the floor where I could continue reading in that glow.

At one-hour intervals the night guards paced past every room. Each time I heard the approaching footsteps, I jumped into bed and feigned sleep. And as soon as the guard passed, I got back out of bed onto the floor area of that light-glow, where I would read for another fifty-eight minutes—until the guard approached again. That went on until three or four every morning. Three or four hours of sleep a night was enough for me. Often in the years in the streets I had slept less than that.

The teachings of Mr. Muhammad stressed how history had been "whitened"—when white men had written history books, the black man simply had been left out. Mr. Muhammad couldn't have said anything that would have struck me much harder. I had never forgotten how when my class, me and all of those whites, had studied seventh-grade United States history back in Mason, the history of the Negro had been covered in one paragraph, and the teacher had gotten a big laugh with his joke, "Negroes' feet are so big that when they walk, they leave a hole in the ground."

This is one reason why Mr. Muhammad's teachings spread so swiftly all over the United States, among *all* Negroes, whether or not they became followers of Mr. Muhammad. The teachings ring true— to every Negro. You can hardly show me a black adult in America— or a white one, for that matter—who knows from the history books anything like the truth about the black man's role. In my own case, once I heard of the "glorious history of the black man," I took special pains to hunt in the library for books that would inform me on details about black history.

I can remember accurately the very first set of books that really impressed me. I have since bought that set of books and I have it at home for my children to read as they grow up. It's called *Wonders of the World.* It's full of pictures of archeological finds, statues that depict, usually, non-European people.

I found books like Will Durant's *Story of Civilization.* I read H.G. Wells' *Outline of History. Souls of Black Folk* by W.E.B. Du Bois gave me a glimpse into the black people's history before they came to this country. Carter G. Woodson's *Negro History* opened my eyes about black empires before the black slave was brought to the United States, and the early Negro struggles for freedom.

J.A. Rogers' three volumes of *Sex and Race* told about race-mixing before Christ's time; about Aesop being a black man who told fables; about Egypt's Pharaohs; about the great Coptic Christian Empires; about Ethiopia, the earth's oldest continuous black civilization, as China is the oldest continuous civilization.

Mr. Muhammad's teaching about how the white man had been created led me to *Findings in Genetics* by Gregor Mendel. (The dictionary's G section was where I had learned what "genetics" meant.) I really studied this book by the Austrian monk. Reading it over and over, especially certain sections, helped me to understand that if you

started with a black man, a white man could be produced; but starting with a white man, you never could produce a black man—because
the white chromosome is recessive. And since no one disputes that
there was but one Original Man, the conclusion is clear.

25   During the last year or so, in the *New York Times,* Arnold Toyn-   25
bee used the word "bleached" in describing the white man. (His words
were: "White [i.e. bleached] human beings of North European origin. . . .") Toynbee also referred to the European geographic area as
only a peninsula of Asia. He said there is no such thing as Europe. And
if you look at the globe, you will see for yourself that America is only
an extension of Asia. (But at the same time Toynbee is among those
who have helped to bleach history. He has written that Africa was the
only continent that produced no history. He won't write that again.
Every day now, the truth is coming to light.)

        I never will forget how shocked I was when I began reading about
slavery's total horror. It made such an impact upon me that it later became one of my favorite subjects when I became a minister of Mr.
Muhammad's. The world's most monstrous crime, the sin and the
blood on the white man's hands, are almost impossible to believe.
Books like the one by Frederick Olmstead opened my eyes to the horrors suffered when the slave was landed in the United States. The European woman, Fannie Kimball, who had married a Southern white
slaveowner, described how human beings were degraded. Of course I
read *Uncle Tom's Cabin.* In fact, I believe that's the only novel I have
ever read since I started serious reading.

        Parkhurst's collection also contained some bound pamphlets of
the Abolitionist Anti-Slavery Society of New England. I read descriptions of atrocities, saw those illustrations of black slave women tied up
and flogged with whips; of black mothers watching their babies being
dragged off, never to be seen by their mothers again; of dogs after
slaves, and of the fugitive slave catchers, evil white men with whips
and clubs and chains and guns. I read about the slave preacher Nat
Turner, who put the fear of God into the white slavemaster. Nat
Turner wasn't going around preaching pie-in-the-sky and "nonviolent" freedom for the black man. There in Virginia one night in 1831,
Nat and seven other slaves started out at his master's home and
through the night they went from one plantation "big house" to the
next, killing, until by the next morning 57 white people were dead
and Nat had about 70 slaves following him. White people, terrified

for their lives, fled from their homes, locked themselves up in public buildings, hid in the woods, and some even left the state. A small army of soldiers took two months to catch and hang Nat Turner. Somewhere I have read where Nat Turner's example is said to have inspired John Brown to invade Virginia and attack Harper's Ferry nearly thirty years later, with thirteen white men and five Negroes.

I read Herodotus, "the father of History," or, rather, I read about him. And I read the histories of various nations, which opened my eyes gradually, then wider and wider, to how the whole world's white men had indeed acted like devils, pillaging and raping and bleeding and draining the whole world's non-white people. I remember, for instance, books such as Will Durant's *The Story of Oriental Civilization,* and Mahatma Gandhi's accounts of the struggle to drive the British out of India.

Book after book showed me how the white man had brought upon the world's black, brown, red, and yellow peoples every variety of the sufferings of exploitation. I saw how since the sixteenth century, the so-called "Christian trader" white man began to ply the seas in his lust for Asian and African empires, and plunder, and power. I read, I saw, how the white man never has gone among the non-white peoples bearing the Cross in the true manner and spirit of Christ's teachings— meek, humble, and Christlike.

30   I perceived, as I read, how the collective white man had been   30
actually nothing but a piratical opportunist who used Faustian machinations to make his own Christianity his initial wedge in criminal conquests. First, always "religiously," he branded "heathen" and "pagan" labels upon ancient non-white cultures and civilizations. The stage thus set, he then turned upon his non-white victims his weapons of war.

I read how, entering India—half a *billion* deeply religious brown people—the British white man, by 1759, through promises, trickery and manipulations, controlled much of India through Great Britain's East India Company. The parasitical British administration kept tentacling out to half of the subcontinent. In 1857, some of the desperate people of India finally mutinied—and, excepting the African slave trade, nowhere has history recorded any more unnecessary bestial and ruthless human carnage than the British suppression of the nonwhite Indian people.

Over 115 million African blacks—close to the 1930s population of the United States—were murdered or enslaved during the slave trade. And I read how when the slave market was glutted, the cannibalistic white powers of Europe next carved up, as their colonies, the richest areas of the black continent. And Europe's chancelleries for the next century played a chess game of naked exploitation and power from Cape Horn to Cairo.

Ten guards and the warden couldn't have torn me out of those books. Not even Elijah Muhammad could have been more eloquent than those books were in providing indisputable proof that the collective white man had acted like a devil in virtually every contact he had with the world's collective non-white man. I listen today to the radio, and watch television, and read the headlines about the collective white man's fear and tension concerning China. When the white man professes ignorance about why the Chinese hate him so, my mind can't help flashing back to what I read, there in prison, about how the blood forebears of this same white man raped China at a time when China was trusting and helpless. Those original white "Christian traders" sent into China millions of pounds of opium. By 1839, so many of the Chinese were addicts that China's desperate government destroyed twenty thousand chests of opium. The first Opium War was promptly declared by the white man. Imagine! Declaring *war* upon someone who objects to being narcotized! The Chinese were severely beaten, with Chinese-invented gunpowder.

The Treaty of Nanking made China pay the British white man for the destroyed opium: forced open China's major ports to British trade; forced China to abandon Hong Kong; fixed China's import tariffs so low that cheap British articles soon flooded in, maiming China's industrial development.

After a second Opium War, the Tientsin Treaties legalized the ravaging opium trade, legalized a British-French-American control of China's customs. China tried delaying that Treaty's ratification; Peking was looted and burned.

"Kill the foreign white devils!" was the 1901 Chinese war cry in the Boxer Rebellion. Losing again, this time the Chinese were driven from Peking's choicest areas. The vicious, arrogant white man put up the famous signs, "Chinese and dogs not allowed."

Red China after World War II closed its doors to the Western white world. Massive Chinese agricultural, scientific, and industrial efforts are described in a book that *Life* magazine recently published. Some observers inside Red China have reported that the world never has known such a hate-white campaign as is now going on in this non-white country where, present birthrates continuing, in fifty more years Chinese will be half the earth's population. And it seems that some Chinese chickens will soon come home to roost, with China's recent successful nuclear tests.

Let us face reality. We can see in the United Nations a new world order being shaped, along color lines—an alliance among the non-white nations. America's U.N. Ambassador Adlai Stevenson complained not long ago that in the United Nations "a skin game" was being played. He was right. He was facing reality. A "skin game" *is* being played. But Ambassador Stevenson sounded like Jesse James accusing the marshal of carrying a gun. Because who in the world's history ever has played a worse "skin game" than the white man?

Mr. Muhammad, to whom I was writing daily, had no idea of what a new world had opened up to me through my efforts to document his teachings in books.

40 When I discovered philosophy, I tried to touch all the landmarks 40 of philosophical development. Gradually, I read most of the old philosophers, Occidental and Oriental. The Oriental philosophers were the ones I came to prefer; finally, my impression was that most Occidental philosophy had largely been borrowed from the Oriental thinkers. Socrates, for instance, traveled in Egypt. Some sources even say that Socrates was initiated into some of the Egyptian mysteries. Obviously Socrates got some of his wisdom among the East's wise men.

I have often reflected upon the new vistas that reading opened to me. I knew right there in prison that reading had changed forever the course of my life. As I see it today, the ability to read awoke inside me some long dormant craving to be mentally alive. I certainly wasn't seeking any degree, the way a college confers a status symbol upon its students. My homemade education gave me, with every additional book that I read, a little bit more sensitivity to the deafness, dumbness, and blindness that was afflicting the black race in America. Not long ago, an English writer telephoned me from London, asking questions. One was, "What's your alma mater?" I told him, "Books." You will never catch me with a free fifteen minutes in which I'm not studying something I feel might be able to help the black man.

Yesterday I spoke in London, and both ways on the plane across the Atlantic I was studying a document about how the United Nations proposes to insure the human rights of the oppressed minorities of the world. The American black man is the world's most shameful case of minority oppression. What makes the black man think of himself as only an internal United States issue is just a catch-phrase, two words, "civil rights." How is the black man going to get "civil rights" before first he wins his *human* rights? If the American black man will start thinking about his *human* rights, and then start thinking of himself as part of one of the world's great peoples, he will see he has a case for the United Nations.

I can't think of a better case! Four hundred years of black blood and sweat invested here in America, and the white man still has the black man begging for what every immigrant fresh off the ship can take for granted the minute he walks down the gangplank.

But I'm digressing. I told the Englishman that my alma mater was books, a good library. Every time I catch a plane, I have with me a book that I want to read—and that's a lot of books these days. If I weren't out here every day battling the white man, I could spend the rest of my life reading, just satisfying my curiosity—because you can hardly mention anything I'm not curious about. I don't think anybody ever got more out of going to prison than I did. In fact, prison enabled me to study far more intensively than I would have if my life had gone differently and I had attended some college. I imagine that one of the biggest troubles with colleges is there are too many distractions, too much panty-raiding, fraternities, and boola-boola and all of that. Where else but in a prison could I have attacked my ignorance by being able to study intensely sometimes as much as fifteen hours a day?

Questions on Meaning

1. What inspired Malcolm X to continue his education independently? What was he trying to accomplish? How did he teach himself?
2. Explain why Malcolm X believed that white people were "devils."
3. Which philosophical concepts most appealed to Malcolm X? Cite evidence of his philosophical bent from his writing.

Questions on Rhetorical Strategy and Style:

1. Malcolm X employs a clear narrative style in this essay. Identify places in the essay where example, description, and persuasion are also used.
2. What does Malcolm X's narrative style reveal about his character and his motivations? If he were alive today, would you be drawn to him? Explain why he would or would not be a compelling figure.

Writing Assignments:

1. Research illiteracy in the United States along race, age, and income lines. Does this information surprise you? Identify some of the aspects of today's world that make it difficult for illiterate and uneducated persons to improve their lot. What programs could be implemented to help these people?
2. Malcolm X learned from his mentor, Elijah Muhammad, how history had been whitened. In the years since Malcolm X wrote this essay, many people, people of color and whites alike, have awakened to the deceit of history. As a result, Black Studies and other programs dedicated to nonwhite ethnic groups have emerged in academia. Have these programs successfully changed the roles assigned to people of color and whites by historians? Interview two or three instructors who teach history, and then write an essay on the state of whitened history today. Use examples from current teaching materials to support your arguments.
3. Unfortunately, white supremacy still exists in many areas. Research white supremacy activities in the United States today. Do these movements have more or fewer members now than during the 1960s? Describe how Malcolm X might address white supremacy organizations and such individuals today.

4. Try to appreciate the ignorance that Malcolm X felt when he was in prison, trying to communicate on various levels of intellect in his letters, with only an eighth grade education and street slang. Go to your library, select a narrowly focused, highly technical, scientific journal from a discipline that you have no familiarity with, and read an article. Then write an essay describing the hurdles you would face if you were asked to paraphrase that article— terminology, historical perspective, background, comparative topics, controversy, etc.

Civic Engagement: The University as a Public Good

Nancy E. Cantor

Nancy Cantor (1952–) graduated from Sarah Lawrence College (1974) and Stanford University (Ph.D. 1978). She taught at Princeton where she chaired the Department of Psychology. She moved on to be dean of the graduate schools at the University of Michigan, where she led the university's defense of affirmative action in the cases Grutter v. Bollinger *and* Gratz v. Bollinger—*which were decided by the Supreme Court in 2003. She wrote several papers on the issues involved in those decisions. She then became chancellor at the University of Illinois-Urbana-Champaign (2001). She is now chancellor at Syracuse University. She is a fellow of the American Academy of Arts and Sciences and has served as chair of the board of directors of the American Association of Higher Education. Her awards include Distinguished Scientific Award for an Early Career Contribution to Psychology, awarded by the American Psychological Association (1985), and Woman of Achievement Award, given by the Anti-Defamation League (2001). She co-authored* Personality and Social Intelligence, *Century Psychology Series, (Prentice Hall, 1987) and* Personality Psychology: Recent Trends and Emerging Directions *(Springer, 1989); and she edited* Personality, Cognition, and Social Interaction *(1981).*

Civic engagement at a great public university requires many kinds of involvement, including work across colleges

*and departments and work across student boundaries. In
this speech, Cantor explains her views of civic engagement
and academic diversity.*

1   As a public good, universities have a rare and critical role to   1
play. While we educate leaders for the future, we also address
important societal issues of the day. Our discoveries can and
do change the world. We lay the groundwork for the future as we
work to preserve the culture of the past. At the same time, we try out
new ways to build community.

The university's role is "rare" because it is positioned to the side
of everyday life, unconstrained by requirements for rigid adherence to
social norms or intellectual paradigms. The university can foster an
experimental attitude—playful, if you will—that can give rise to both
intellectual discovery and social innovation.

The university takes on a "critical" role when it opens its gates far
enough to listen to the different voices in the debate over the issues of
greatest concern to society and to learn about them firsthand. The
university must face outward toward work that changes the culture of
the day.

We are at our best when we build a community of scholars and
learners who feel empowered to be both playful in examining their
world and responsible for affecting societal progress. Just as we want
to open our gates and look outward, we also want to build model
communities on campus to invite the world in as partners.

Liberal learning and civic engagement

5   As AAC&U eloquently states in its Statement on Liberal Learning: 5
"Liberal learning is society's best investment in our shared future." Likewise I would argue that the best way for society to fulfill its dreams of a
shared, productive, and harmonious future is to maintain universities as
public goods. We can do this by intertwining the playfulness of liberal
learning as a mode of thought and action with the responsibility of civic
engagement with diverse stakeholders whose voices need to matter
more in our shared future. In so doing, we will be able to educate
socially responsible citizens who will not be complacent in the face of
entrenched societal norms, but will take the initiative in shaping our
diverse democracy and its global interconnections.[1]

This can happen because, at their best, liberal education and civic engagement have much in common. Each requires vibrant and sustained exchanges of both people and ideas. Universities can offer safe havens for people from different backgrounds, races, ethnic groups, and generations to talk, argue, and reflect as equals in exchanges that can and should bridge the boundaries between the university and the wider world.

Now, just one generation away from a time when white children will be the minority in our public schools, children of different races still grow up in different neighborhoods without attending each other's birthday parties, proms, weddings, and funerals. Because they and we do not know each other, the stereotypes that result have led to great inequality and injustice in such vital areas as employment, health care, and the criminal justice system.

Mirroring our divisions at home is ethnic, religious, and intergroup conflict in virtually every corner of the globe. The result is untold human and cultural carnage. To make matters worse, we have reacted to the very real pain and losses we have suffered on our own shores by turning inward, "battening the hatches" if you will, presenting real problems for the free and vital exchanges of people and ideas that are the foundation of our democracy.

The task of universities is urgent: to build on themes of diversity, not only in admissions and in recruiting, but also in creating living and learning communities that will produce a citizenry that is both engaged and informed. It is not enough to affirmatively provide access to educational opportunity. We must also create opportunities and settings in which to pursue true integration. Universities can take a leadership role in shaping a dialogue that goes beyond differences by supporting environments in which students learn from and about each other—environments in which differences are neither privileged nor ignored. (See Patricia Gurin's discussion of Benjamin Barber's distinction between ignoring and privileging differences in *Defending Diversity*, 2004.)

Building sustained exchanges: The arts as a prototype

10 Universities can fulfill this mission by offering contexts for the   10
exchanges of people and ideas that are sustained, rather than one-shot efforts over a day, a week, or even a semester. These exchanges must

appeal to people of different expertise and backgrounds. They should allow for open-mindedness, permit the suspension of everyday norms and judgments, and give standing to everyone, across generations.

In trying to envision how such exchanges might actually work, we might look to the arts—which I would define broadly as "expressive culture" in all forms—for a natural prototype. The arts stand to the side of daily life, and they allow the expression of self and of social tensions in a safe way. They can also forge sustained connections between peoples and ideas and cultures that otherwise either simply remain invisible, unexpressed, or worse yet, clash in destructive ways.

As an example, I invite you to consider the blues, a creation of African-Americans that made its way from rural slavery to our nation's cities, to people and places all over the world with different musical traditions, to young and old, and to other art forms. It is shown in a brilliant traveling exhibition entitled "Visualizing the Blues," photographs of the Mississippi Delta collected by the Dixon Gallery and Gardens in Memphis.

In the catalog for this exhibition, which was shown at the Krannert Art Museum at the University of Illinois, Deborah Willis Kennedy (2000) writes, "The blues is a life-and-death struggle. The blues permits the living to defend life/living." To visualize the blues, one must contend with prejudice and racism, blood and spit, malice and murder.

Ernest Withers took a photograph that illustrates this point. Its title is "Boarding House Bathroom From Which James Earl Ray Shot Dr. King, 422 South Main Street, Memphis, April 1968." The photograph shows a filthy toilet, an old tub, a pockmarked wall, the open window from which a killer silenced our nation's greatest voice for peace in the twentieth century. The room is repellent. Normally, we would turn away, but as soon as we realize where we are, we stay to stare. We are at the vantage point of the assassin. The image draws us into dialogue, across history and between groups.

15 The arts often serve this way, as the medium, not just the reflection, of intergroup dialogue. They offer an escape from the silencing that tends to come in "normal" society, making it possible to face highly charged and even taboo subjects. And everyone has some "standing" in the "conversation" that ensues. In the arts, for example, it is not only diplomats who can discuss and negotiate peace. Without money, limousines, or hotel reservations, children are taking it up,

one-to-one, through a "Peace through Poetry" exchange on the Internet, sponsored by iEARN, an international educational and resource network. The sixteen schools participating in this project are located in Chicago, Lithuania, Japan, Bulgaria, Moscow, and in Urbana, a few blocks from our campus at Illinois.

"Before the war commences the end is clear," writes Rositsa Kuneva, a student from Bulgaria. "All taking part are losers, nobody wins/Never wins the one who fights against his fear/Sluicing down the earth with bloody rinse."[2]

Dialogues such as these strip away the armor that we think we need to protect our place in the world, and there is nothing quite like the voices of students when they are given standing through artistic expression. The arts demonstrate that the kinds of exchanges we need in the nation's colleges and universities are possible, but we must construct ways for these exchanges to occur.

Exchanges across the boundaries of race and ethnicity

In our increasingly multiracial democracy it is vital that universities create exchanges across the rigid boundaries of race and ethnicity, religion and culture. But the exchanges that come so naturally in the arts need something more in higher education: structures that let these exchanges happen.

Our students, faculty, and community partners need settings in which we can let down our guard, acknowledge each other's standing in the conversation, and feel able to express both discomfort and ignorance. We need to be able to do this formally and informally, on and off campus, and across the groups in which we have been socialized. Then and only then will our nation come close to realizing the educational benefits of diversity. Then and only then will we begin to more fully embrace the fifty-year-old promise of *Brown v. Board of Education*.

So, why are we in higher education still talking about race? Because our failure to discard the legacy of Jim Crow has left our nation so segregated that our students, for the most part, do not meet as equals until they arrive at our doors. I will never forget a Latina student who told me, "I've never lived with so many white people before." It is up to us to shift that perspective to: "They've never had

20

the chance to live with ME before," with all the opportunities and optimism that implies. We must create learning and living communities that will make true integration possible, and we must create ways to assess how well we're doing.

We must understand that the idea of "civic engagement" goes beyond service or volunteer work. We must immerse ourselves in environments of genuine exchange, and these can start at home, on our own campuses. Vibrant multiracial/multicultural exchanges that bring the issues of society to our doorstep are as much about civic engagement as are our programs in neighboring communities. We should also take the extra step of inviting our community neighbors onto our campuses as we build new models of community.

Experiments in exchange at Illinois

What would such communities look like? And how can we use what we know about the arts as a model? At Illinois, as on many campuses, we have been asking these questions for several years and I thought it might be useful to describe a few of our efforts, keeping in mind the analogies with the artistic exchanges I have already described.

Exchanges that eschew boundaries. One of the most powerful aspects of artistic exchanges is that they eschew the "normal" boundaries and distinctions of social life—anyone and everyone can be engaged in artistic expression, and frequently these exchanges draw diverse peoples and generations together. In a similar vein, when we created our new Center for Democracy in a Multiracial Society in 2002, we resolved that it would bring together scholars, students, and community activists to engage in conversation about the many racialized positions of different groups and individuals in our society.

The Center drew its advisory board from the leadership of all of our ethnic studies programs on campus. It invited community activists to come to campus for sabbaticals at the Center. It engaged students from different campus communities in intergroup conversations and analyses that go beyond "black and white." And it funded projects to examine the experience of democracy in daily life from these different positions.

25 Many of the Center's initiatives intentionally engage multiple 25 generations of both novices and experts. They circumvent the "silencing" that comes with power and status, and they give "standing" to

those who often are the most affected but the least heard. For example, the Center faculty have mobilized with Latino/a community activists in Illinois to address two issues of critical importance to their community—narrowing the K-12 achievement gap and lobbying for the rights of children of undocumented families. As they define what it means to "mobilize with the community," the goal is to position the families and the students to be heard.

It is the families themselves who are helping to design interventions in the schools. It is our students, many of whom have firsthand experience with being excluded by virtue of their parents' status, who are speaking to the legislators in Springfield, dialoguing at the Center with statewide leaders of the newest Freedom Rides, and learning in action as they take part in opening up educational opportunity to our fastest-growing student population in Illinois. Their voices have authenticity and power when they are finally given the stage. Listen to the words of Yesenia Sanchez, who came to our campus on a Freedom Ride:

> I am fighting for my dignity. I am an undocumented student and, just like many others, feel helpless because my dreams and goals are being snatched away. I wake up every morning and feel that my life is in limbo, nothing is certain . . . I am also here for my mother. When she was a young girl, she was only able to go up to the sixth grade because she was a woman and was supposed to be at home. She tells me how every night she dreamed about going to school. Her dreams are also mine, and I am determined to be someone.

Exchanges that take a lesson from history. We also take a lesson from the arts in trying to encourage cross-talk about race and opportunity, contrasting historical dreams and contemporary realities. At the moment, for example, we are in the middle of a year-long commemoration of the fiftieth anniversary of *Brown v. Board,* honoring those who put their lives on the line for the cause of justice, reexamining their struggle, and rededicating ourselves to their still unfulfilled dream.

At our entering student convocation last August, we began with a speech from the director of our women's studies program, Professor Kal Alston, about what *Brown v. Board* had meant to her African-American family and to her own education in predominantly white schools. We'll end the year with a commencement address by legal scholar and activist, Professor Lani Guinier. In between we have sponsored symposia, performances, book clubs, community research projects and partnerships, and dialogues. We are seeing both synergy and exchange.

30   As part of the commemoration, we invited back to campus alumni from Project 500, which in 1968 recruited African-American students from all over the nation to enroll at Illinois. As graduates, many continued the struggle for civil rights their entire lives and our current students took note of their lessons. Numbers of current students told us later they were so moved by hearing the stories of this older generation that afterwards they met as a group on their own to do some soul-searching about themselves.

In fact, that kind of storytelling and social introspection is a key component in creating new contexts for exchange on campus. The *Brown v. Board* commemoration itself, for example, is now the object of study by undergraduates participating in a new initiative we are calling The Ethnography of the University. This initiative is giving students the opportunity to examine deliberately their own and their peers' experiences of race at the university and then to report their work, their interviews, their data, and their conclusions on a Web archive for future use by other students as well as faculty, staff, and members of our larger community. As the Web archive develops, we too will be able to better assess the impact of our efforts to foster multiracial exchange.

So far, the students' research on the *Brown v. Board* commemoration indicates that a big event, such as the convocation that all first year students are expected to attend, can make a big difference. Their interviews showed that, while only some of our 38,000 students knew about *Brown,* and many did not, every single first-year student interviewed knew something about it and had something to say. A massive one-time effort can create interest that then carries over to the book clubs, symposia, performances, and other venues that offer smaller, ongoing contexts for exchange.

Understanding difference in the service of building common cause happens one person at a time, and it requires that we be able to reflect on our experience and see it in relation to the experiences of others. This, of course, is what happens frequently between artist and audience, as each critiques the other's expressions. It is also what is happening to the students who are doing the research in the Ethnography of the University initiative and we hope it is happening with other students as they gather together to reflect on *Brown*.

Living and learning together in safe havens. Of course, nothing can quite match the awakening that occurs when students come together informally as peers, and in those rare but critical moments, let down their guard, shed their protective armor, and enter into what can then become sustained dialogues about diversity.

In this light, I'd like to share a comment from a University of Michigan undergraduate who answered an e-mail request to all students from the president of the Michigan Student Assembly, to describe the impact, positive or negative, of diversity on their lives. This is what she said, in her words, in 1997:

> My roommate and I roomed blind. I had no idea whom I would end up with. In mid-August I found out all about her. She was from Detroit and black. This didn't bother me one bit. So far we have gotten along great. . . . Here is one thing that I found funny. . . . My roommate has a flat iron that she uses to straighten AND curl her hair with. She had been bugging me for a while to let her try it on my hair. This one Friday night I decided to let her give it a try. . . . So she reached for my hair with her hand so that she could grab a chunk to brush. "EEEE," she shrieked. "What is that? . . . No, nothing is wrong. I just can't believe what your hair feels like! . . . I've never felt any white girl's hair before," she said. "I had no idea it was so different." We spent the next hour discussing how we take care of our hair, how much it costs to get it done, and we also argued about what a perm is. This isn't a great educational story, but now I feel a little more "worldly" and not as sheltered as I had before. It's the little things like this that make impacts on my life. Small, but nonetheless important. Diversity helps to make the world a little smaller.

In one brief moment, two students who were already friends and even shared the same room really *saw* each other in new ways, as women with hair that was different and bad hair days that were the same. One more blind spot disappeared in the slow way things happen when real integration finally occurs, when differences can be affirmed, talked about, and shared.

So how do we foster this sense of safety to express the self and social tensions in nonjudgmental and authentic ways in both living and learning environments—and preferably at the place that living and learning intersect? Again using the insight we can get from the arts, compare the difference in the courage of expression we typically see in campus theater to the muted "politeness" of many classroom discussions.

Classroom conversations can be just as courageous, but first we must structure the context to provide just enough safety for students to try to get to know each other and experience alternative perspectives on the world. At Illinois, we are building on the work of a model developed at Michigan in our Program in Intergroup Relations, which facilitates structured dialogues across small groups to create environments in which discomfort, ignorance, and even conflict are tolerated in the service of building trust and a sense of common fate.

40   Next fall, we will take another step by opening a new living and   40 learning residence for first and second year students. It will be dedicated to Intergroup Relations and Multiracial Integration, with cultural programming, structured dialogues, and classes taught by faculty fellows from our Center for Democracy. The idea here is a simple one: Since most students have had very little, if any, experience in crossing the boundaries of race and ethnicity in their daily lives, we need to structure safe environments for integration, for learning how to do the hard work of reaching out and living and learning in a multiracial community.

We know that most students, majority and minority, will say that there are substantial racial tensions on campus. At the same time, they will also say that at college they have made, often for the first time in their lives, some very good, close relationships with persons of other races and ethnicities. It is our responsibility to foster these kinds of intergroup experiences, preparing the ground of daily life in our campus community. We want to encourage the actual reaching out, on the ground, from one person to another. And we recognize that if we want students to become engaged citizens of the world, people who can question that world and prod it to be a better place—somewhere they want to live—we must invite them to change higher education, to share it, and to make it stretch to fit them. We want our students to change our university and to make it better.

Knowing the other, shaping the self

We have a hope in this nation that we can draw on the talent, skill, insight, and imagination of all of our citizens, and higher education must help to lead the way. With a nod to Walt Whitman, the poet Langston Hughes expressed this hope—this conviction—in an equally powerful way, in a poem entitled "I, Too."[3]

I, too, sing America.

I am the darker brother.
They send me to eat in the kitchen
When company comes,
But I laugh,
And eat well,
And grow strong.

Tomorrow,
I'll be at the table
When company comes.
Nobody'll dare
Say to me,
"Eat in the kitchen,"
Then.

Besides,
They'll see how beautiful I am
And be ashamed—

I, too, am America.

To lead the way toward fulfilling this hope, we in higher education must figure out how to sit together around our table and engage with difference. It is through this social introspection, done in the company of others and informed by the clash of perspectives, that liberal learning occurs, sustained by difference and strengthened by the solidarity that follows.

End Notes

1. See the Guiding Principles for the Center for Liberal Education and Civic Engagement, a cooperative effort of AAC&U and Campus Compact.

2. www.vceducation.org/peace/schools/ukraine208.html.
3. From *The Collected Poems of Langston Hughes*, by Langston Hughes, copyright © 1994 by The Estate of Langston Hughes. Used by permission of Alfred A. Knof, a division of Random House, Inc.

Works Cited

Grutter v. Bollinger, U.S. Supreme Court, No. 02–214, June 23, 2003.

Gurin, Patricia, ed., Earl Lewis, Eric Dey, Sylvia Hurtado, Jeffrey S. Lehman. 2004. *Defending diversity: Affirmative Action at the University of Michigan*. Ann Arbor: University of Michigan Press.

Kennedy, Deborah Willis. 2000. Coda: Imagine the blues. In Wendy McDoris, *Visualizing the blues: Images of the American South*. Memphis: The Dixon Gallery and Garden.

National Advisory Commission on Civil Disorders. 1968. *Report of the National Advisory Commission on Civil Disorders*. Washington, DC: Government Printing Office, March 1.

Questions on Meaning

1. What does it mean to be engaged civically? What does a university have to do to help its students and faculty understand the demands of diversity?
2. The arts is an area where everyone has a chance to cross boundaries, especially the boundaries between people of different races and backgrounds. How can the arts help us cross these boundaries?
3. What did the university do for its freshman orientation to help students see something of the history of multicultural experiences at the school? What did the returning alumni tell the freshmen about the lessons that a liberal education had taught them?

Questions on Rhetorical Strategy and Style

1. Cantor begins by letting the audience know that the situation calls for critical change. What major change in demographics does she note? What is happening to the white majority in American culture?
2. In the body of the work, Cantor discusses the many values that come from the arts. Why is this area her main focus? What does she show by talking about different artists and different programs?
3. The speech ends by quoting the great black poet of the Harlem Renaissance, Langston Hughes. Who is he reflecting in his poem? Why does a reference to both Langston Hughes and Walt Whitman make a fitting end for the speech?

Writing Assignments

1. Choose a picture, sculpture, or poem that reflects your idea of diversity and multiculturalism. Write about the work and how it expresses your views.
2. Cantor says that the liberal arts help us to understand diverse points of view. What different perspectives does a student get by studying science, history, and the arts? How can these perspectives help to expand horizons? Give examples.
3. Cantor talks of expressing oneself in safety. Describe what you see as a safe environment. Use experiences that you have had in situations that you consider to be both safe and not safe. Compare and contrast the experiences.

The Case Against College

Caroline Bird

Caroline Bird (1915-) was born in New York City. In addition to writing about business issues affecting women, she has taught at Vassar College and worked in public relations. Her books include Born Female *(1968),* What Women Want *(1979),* The Two-Paycheck Marriage *(1982),* The Good Years: Your Life in the 21st Century *(1983), and* Lives of Our Own: Secrets of Salty Old Women *(1995). In this essay, which was excerpted from* The Case Against College *(1975), Bird questions the value of college and a college education.*

The case *for* college has been accepted without question for more than a generation. All high school graduates ought to go, says Conventional Wisdom and statistical evidence, because college will help them earn more money, become "better" people, and learn to be more responsible citizens than those who don't go.

But college has never been able to work its magic for everyone. And now that close to half our high school graduates are attending, those who don't fit the pattern are becoming more numerous, and more obvious. College graduates are selling shoes and driving taxis; college students sabotage each other's experiments and forge letters of recommendation in the intense competition for admission to graduate school. Others find no stimulation in their studies, and drop out—often encouraged by college administrators.

Some observers say the fault is with the young people themselves—they are spoiled, stoned, overindulged, and expecting too much. But that's mass character assassination, and doesn't explain all campus unhappiness. Others blame the state of the world, and they are partly right. We've been told that young people have to go to college because our economy can't absorb an army of untrained eighteen-year-olds. But disillusioned graduates are learning that it can no longer absorb an army of trained twenty-two-year-olds, either. . . .

The ultimate defense of college has always been that while it may not teach you anything vocationally useful, it will somehow make you a better person, able to do anything better, and those who make it through the process are initiated into the "fellowship of educated men and women." In a study intended to probe what graduates seven years out of college thought their colleges should have done for them, the Carnegie Commission found that most alumni expected the "development of my abilities to think and express myself." But if such respected educational psychologists as Bruner and Piaget are right, specific learning skills have to be acquired very early in life, perhaps even before formal schooling begins.

5   So, when pressed, liberal-arts defenders speak instead about something more encompassing, and more elusive. "College changed me inside," one graduate told us fervently. The authors of a Carnegie Commission report, who obviously struggled for a definition, concluded that one of the common threads in the perceptions of a liberal education is that it provides "an integrated view of the world which can serve as an inner guide." More simply, alumni say that college should have "helped me to formulate the values and goals of my life,"

In theory, a student is taught to develop these values and goals himself, but in practice, it doesn't work quite that way. All but the wayward and the saintly take their sense of the good, the true, and the beautiful from the people around them. When we speak of students acquiring "values" in college, we often mean that they will acquire the values—and sometimes that means only the tastes—of their professors. The values of professors may be "higher" than many students will encounter elsewhere, but they may not be relevant to situations in which students find themselves in college and later.

Of all the forms in which ideas are disseminated, the college professor lecturing a class is the slowest and most expensive. You don't have to go to college to read the great books or learn about the great ideas of Western Man. Today you can find them everywhere—in paperbacks, in the public libraries, in museums, in public lectures, in adult-education courses, in abridged, summarized, or adapted form in magazines, films, and television. The problem is no longer one of access to broadening ideas; the problem is the other way around: how to choose among the many courses of action proposed to us, how to edit the stimulations that pour into our eyes and ears every waking hour. A college experience that piles option on option and stimulation on stimulation merely adds to the contemporary nightmare.

What students and graduates say that they did learn on campus comes under the heading of personal, rather than intellectual, development. Again and again I was told that the real value of college is learning to get along with others, to practice social skills, to "sort out my head," and these have nothing to do with curriculum.

For whatever impact the academic experience used to have on college students, the sheer size of many undergraduate classes . . . dilutes faculty-student dialogue, and, more often than not, they are taught by teachers who were hired when colleges were faced with a shortage of qualified instructors, during their years of expansion and when the big rise in academic pay attracted the mediocre and the less than dedicated.

10 On the social side, colleges are withdrawing from responsibility 10
for feeding, housing, policing, and protecting students at a time when the environment of college may be the most important service it could render. College officials are reluctant to "intervene" in the personal lives of the students. They no longer expect to take over from parents, but often insist that students—who have, most often, never lived away from home before—take full adult responsibility for their plans, achievements, and behavior.

Most college students do not live in the plush, comfortable country-clublike surroundings their parents envisage, or, in some cases, remember. Open dorms, particularly when they are coeducational, are noisy, usually overcrowded, and often messy. Some students desert the institutional "zoos" (their own word for dorms) and move into run-down, overpriced apartments. Bulletin boards in student centers are littered with notices of apartments to share and the drift of conversation suggests that a lot of money is dissipated in scrounging for food and shelter.

Taxpayers now provide more than half of the astronomical sums that are spent on higher education. But less than half of today's high school graduates go on, raising a new question of equity: Is it fair to make all the taxpayers pay for the minority who actually go to college? We decided long ago that it is fair for childless adults to pay school taxes because everyone, parents and nonparents alike, profits by a literate population. Does the same reasoning hold true for state-supported higher education? There is no conclusive evidence on either side.

Young people cannot be expected to go to college for the general good of mankind. They may be more altruistic than their elders, but no great numbers are going to spend four years at hard intellectual labor, let alone tens of thousands of family dollars, for "the advancement of human capability in society at large," one of the many purposes invoked by the Carnegie Commission report. Nor do any considerable number of them want to go to college to beat the Russians to Jupiter, improve the national defense, increase the Gross National Product, lower the crime rate, improve automobile safety, or create a market for the arts—all of which have been suggested at one time or other as benefits taxpayers get for supporting higher education.

One sociologist said that you don't have to have a reason for going to college because it's an institution. His definition of an institution is something everyone subscribes to without question. The burden of proof is not on why you should go to college, but why anyone thinks there might be a reason for not going. The implication—and some educators express it quite frankly—is that an eighteen-year-old high school graduate is still too young and confused to know what he wants to do, let alone what is good for him.

15   Mother knows best, in other words.   15

It had always been comfortable for students to believe that authorities, like Mother, or outside specialists, like educators, could determine what was best for them. However, specialists and authorities no longer enjoy the credibility former generations accorded them. Patients talk back to doctors and are not struck suddenly dead. Clients question the lawyer's bills and sometimes get them reduced. It is no longer self-evident that all adolescents must study a fixed curriculum that was constructed at a time when all educated men could agree on precisely what it was that made them educated.

The same with college. If high school graduates don't want to continue their education, or don't want to continue it right away, they may perceive more clearly than their elders that college is not for them.

College is an ideal place for those young adults who love learning for its own sake, who would rather read than eat, and who like nothing better than writing research papers. But they are a minority, even at the prestigious colleges, which recruit and attract the intellectually oriented.

The rest of our high school graduates need to look at college more closely and critically, to examine it as a consumer product, and decide if the cost in dollars, in time, in continued dependency, and in future returns, is worth the very large investment each student—and his family—must make.

Questions on Meaning

1. What is Bird's thesis in this essay? Where does she summarize her key point?
2. Bird states that many people believe college is beneficial simply because of "conventional wisdom." What does she cite as standard reasons for going to college? How has this "conventional wisdom" changed since the mid-1970s, when Bird wrote this essay?
3. Bird states that *access* to "ideas" is not a problem, but that college is the "slowest and most expensive" way to disseminate "ideas." What *is* the problem with "ideas" according to Bird?

Questions on Rhetorical Strategy and Style

1. Bird uses a number of rhetorical strategies to support her argument. Find where she presents examples (facts, statistics, opinions, etc.) and when she uses cause and effect in building her case.
2. In the second paragraph, Bird states that "close to half" of high school graduates attend college. Later in the essay (in the paragraph beginning, "Taxpayers now provide . . . "), she states that "less than half" of high school graduates go on. What is her reason for stating the same statistic in two different ways? What is your reaction to that writing strategy?

Writing Assignments

1. Describe your decision to attend college or take college courses. What college experiences have other members of your family had? What alternatives did you explore? What would you do if you discover, part way through college, that it is not for you—would you leave or try to graduate?
2. Bird states that there is no evidence to justify state-supported higher education. What is your opinion of taxpayer subsidies for college? What benefits do you feel society gains by encouraging young people to attend college that offsets the cost?
3. Conventional wisdom drives a lot of our decisions—in addition to whether or not we attend college. We try to stay warm in the winter to keep from catching a cold—although cold temperatures per se don't cause the common cold. We assume that church-going folks have high morals and ethics, although a lot of crooks and scoundrels have sat in pews. Write an essay about some

"conventional wisdom" that you take issue with. Use facts and statistics, where possible, to argue against this dictum.

Are You Politically Incorrect?

John Taylor

John Taylor, a contributing editor for New York Magazine, *wrote this article in 1991 as a backlash was gaining
strength against civil rights, feminism, and other social reform movements whose opinions and values were lumped
under the heading of "political correctness." The apparent
cause of the anger against social reformers was a series of
speech codes that college campuses adopted to censure people who committed verbal harassment against minorities.
Once the backlash began, it gathered force from people who
claimed years of frustration in dealing with oversensitive
members of minority groups. Taylor here uses a strongly
worded condemnation to "inform" his audience of New
Yorkers, renowned for their cynicism.*

1   "Racist."
     "Racist!"
     "The man is a racist!"
     "A *racist!*"
5   Such denunciations, hissed in tones of self-righteousness and contempt, vicious and vengeful, furious, smoking with hatred—such denunciations haunted Stephan Thernstrom for weeks. Whenever he
walked through the campus that spring, down Harvard's brick paths,
under the arched gates, past the fluttering elms, he found it hard not
to imagine the pointing fingers, the whispers. Racist. There goes *the
racist*. It was hellish, this persecution. Thernstrom couldn't sleep.
His nerves were frayed, his temper raw. He was making his family

miserable. And the worst thing was that he didn't know who was calling him a racist, or why.

Thernstrom, 56, a professor at Harvard University for 25 years, is considered one of the preeminent scholars of the history of race relations in America. He has tenure. He has won prizes and published numerous articles and four books and edited the *Harvard Encyclopedia of American Ethnic Groups*. For several years, Thernstrom and another professor, Bernard Bailyn, taught an undergraduate lecture course on the history of race relations in the United States called "Peopling of America." Bailyn covered the Colonial era. Thernstrom took the class up to the present.

Both professors are regarded as very much in the academic mainstream, their views grounded in extensive research on their subject, and both have solid liberal democratic credentials. But all of a sudden, in the fall of 1987, articles began to appear in the *Harvard Crimson* accusing Thernstrom and Bailyn of "racial insensitivity" in "Peopling of America." The sources for the articles were anonymous, the charges vague, but they continued to be repeated, these ringing indictments.

Finally, through the intervention of another professor, two students from the lecture course came forward and identified themselves as the sources for the articles. When asked to explain their grievances, they presented the professors with a six-page letter. Bailyn's crime had been to read from the diary of a southern planter without giving equal time to the recollections of a slave. This, to the students, amounted to a covert defense of slavery. Bailyn, who has won two Pulitzer Prizes, had pointed out during the lecture that no journals, diaries, or letters written by slaves had ever been found. He had explained to the class that all they could do was read the planter's diary and use it to speculate about the experience of slaves. But that failed to satisfy the complaining students. Since it was impossible to give equal representation to the slaves, Bailyn ought to have dispensed with the planter's diary altogether.

Thernstrom's failures, according to the students, were almost systematic. He had, to begin with, used the word *Indians* instead of *Native Americans*. Thernstrom tried to point out that he had said very clearly in class that *Indian* was the word most Indians themselves use, but that was irrelevant to the students. They considered the word racist. Thernstrom was also accused of referring to an "Oriental religion." The word *Oriental,* with its imperialist overtones, was unacceptable. Thernstrom explained that he had used the word as an adjective, not as a noun, but the students weren't buying any wriggling, sophistic evasions like that.

10   Even worse, they continued, Thernstrom had assigned a book to   10 the class that mentioned that some people regarded affirmative action as preferential treatment. That was a racist opinion. But most egregiously, Thernstrom had endorsed, in class, Patrick Moynihan's emphasis on the breakup of the black family as a cause of persistent black poverty. That was a racist idea.

All of these words and opinions and ideas and historical approaches were racist. *Racist!* They would not be tolerated.

The semester was pretty much over by then. But during the spring, when Thernstrom sat down to plan the course for the following year, he had to think about how he would combat charges of racism should they crop up again. And they assuredly would. All it took was one militant student, one word like *Oriental* taken out of context, one objection that a professor's account of slavery was insufficiently critical or that, in discussing black poverty, he had raised the "racist" issue of welfare dependency. And a charge of racism, however unsubstantiated, leaves a lasting impression. "It's like being called a Commie in the fifties," Thernstrom says. "Whatever explanation you offer, once accused, you're always suspect."

He decided that to protect himself in case he was misquoted or had comments taken out of context, he would need to tape all his lectures. Then he decided he would have to tape his talks with students in his office. He would, in fact, have to tape everything he said on the subject of race. It would require a tape-recording system worthy of the Nixon White House. Microphones everywhere, the reels turning constantly. That was plainly ridiculous. Thernstrom instead decided it would be easier just to drop the course altogether. "Peopling of America" is no longer offered at Harvard.

The New Fundamentalism

When the Christian-fundamentalist uprising began in the late seventies, Americans on the left sneered at the Bible thumpers who tried to ban the teaching of evolution in public schools, at the troglodtyes who wanted to remove *The Catcher in the Rye* from public libraries. They heaped scorn on the evangelists who railed against secular humanism and the pious hypocrites who tried to legislate patriotism and Christianity through school prayer and the Pledge of Allegiance. This last effort was considered particularly heinous. Those right-wing demagogues were interfering with individual liberties! They were trying to indoctrinate the children! It was scandalous and outrageous, and unconstitutional too.

15   But curiously enough, in the past few years, a new sort of fundamentalism has arisen precisely among those people who were the most appalled by Christian fundamentalism. And it is just as demagogic and fanatical. The new fundamentalists are an eclectic group; they include multiculturalists, feminists, radical homosexuals, Marxists, New Historicists. What unites them—as firmly as the Christian fundamentalists are united in the belief that the Bible is the revealed word of God—is their conviction that Western culture and American society are thoroughly and hopelessly racist, sexist, oppressive. "Racism and sexism are pervasive in America and fundamentally present in all American institutions," declares a draft report on "race and gender enrichment" at Tulane University. A 1989 report by a New York State Board of Education task force was even more sweeping: "Intellectual and educational oppression . . . has characterized the culture and institutions of the United States and the European American world for centuries."

The heart of the new fundamentalists' argument is not just that, as most everyone would agree, racism and sexism historically have existed within political systems designed to promote individual liberties. They believe that the doctrine of individual liberties *itself* is inherently oppressive. At the University of Pennsylvania, an undergraduate on the "diversity education committee" wrote a memo to committee members describing her "deep regard for the individual and my desire to protect the freedoms of all members of society." The tone was earnest and sincere. The young woman clearly considered herself an idealist of the Jeffersonian persuasion. Individual freedom, she seemed to indicate, was a concept to be cherished above all else.

But in the prevailing climate, Thomas Jefferson and all the Founding Fathers are in disrepute. (The Constitution, according to the 1989 New York State report, is "the embodiment of the White Male with Property Model.") One college administrator had no patience with the young woman's naïve and bourgeois sentiments. He returned her memo with the word *individual* underlined. "This is a 'RED FLAG' phrase today, which many consider RACIST," the administrator wrote. "Arguments that champion the individual over the group ultimately privilege the 'INDIVIDUALS' belonging to the largest or dominant group."

Defenders of Western culture try to point out that other civilizations—from the Islamic and the Hindu to the Confucian and the Buddhist—are rife with racism and sexism. They find it odd that while Eastern Europeans are rushing to embrace Western democracy, while the pro-democracy movement in China actually erected a replica of the Statue of Liberty in Tiananmen Square, this peculiar intellectual cult back in the States continues to insist that Western values are the source of much of the world's evil.

But one of the marvels of the new fundamentalism is the rationale it has concocted for dismissing all dissent. Just as Christian fundamentalists attack nonbelievers as agents of Satan, so the politically correct dismiss their critics as victims of, to use the famous Marxist phrase, "false consciousness." Anyone who disagrees is simply too soaked in the oppressors' propaganda to see the truth. "Racism and sexism are subtle and, for the most part, subconscious or at least subsurface," the Tulane report continues. "It is difficult for us to see and overcome racism and sexism because we are all a product of the problem, i.e., we are all the progeny of a racist and sexist society."

20 This circular reasoning enables the new fundamentalists to attack 20 not just the opinions of their critics but the right of their critics to disagree. Alternate viewpoints are simply not allowed. Though there was little visible protest when Louis Farrakhan was invited to speak at the University of Wisconsin, students at the University of Northern Colorado practically rioted when Linda Chavez, a Hispanic member of the Reagan administration who opposes affirmative action and believes immigrants should be encouraged to learn English, was asked to talk. The invitation was withdrawn. Last February, Patrick Moynihan declared during a lecture at Vassar that America was "a model of a reasonably successful multiethnic society." Afterward, he got into an argument with a black woman who disagreed with him, and when she claimed the senator had insulted her, militant students occupied a school building until Moynihan returned his lecture fee. "The disturbing factor in the success of totalitarianism is . . . the true selflessness of its adherents," Hannah Arendt wrote in *The Origins of*

Totalitarianism. "The fanaticized members can be reached by neither experience nor argument."

It is this sort of demand for intellectual conformity, enforced with harassment and intimidation, that has led some people to compare the atmosphere in universities today to that of Germany in the thirties. "It's fascism of the left," says Camille Paglia, a professor at the University of the Arts in Philadelphia and the author of *Sexual Personae.* "These people behave like the Hitler Youth."

It reminds others of America in the fifties. "This sort of atmosphere, where a few highly mobilized radical students can intimidate everyone else, is quite new," Thernstrom says. "This is a new McCarthyism. It's more frightening than the old McCarthyism, which had no support in the academy. Now the enemy is within. There are students and faculty who have no belief in freedom of speech."

And it reminds still others of China during the Cultural Revolution of the sixties, when thought criminals were paraded through towns in dunce caps. "In certain respects, the University of Pennsylvania has become like the University of Peking," says Alan Kors, a professor of history.

Indeed, schools like Berkeley and Carleton require courses in race relations, sometimes called "oppression studies." A proposed course book for a required writing seminar at the University of Texas contains, instead of models of clarity like E. B. White, essays such as "is not so gd [*sic*] to be born a girl," by Ntozake Shange. Many schools— including Stanford, Pennsylvania, and the University of Wisconsin— have adopted codes of conduct that require students who deviate from politically correct thinking to undergo thought reform. When a student at the University of Michigan read a limerick that speculated jokingly about the homosexuality of a famous athlete, he was required to attend gay-sensitivity sessions and publish a piece of self-criticism in the student newspaper called "Learned My Lesson."

25   But is any of this so awful? In the minds of its advocates, thought   25
reform is merely a well-intentioned effort to help stop the spread of the racial tensions that have proliferated in universities in recent years. "I don't know of any institution that is saying you have to adore everyone else," says Catharine Stimpson, dean of the graduate school at Rutgers. "They are saying you have to learn to live with everyone. They are taking insulting language seriously. That's a good thing. They're not laughing off anti-Semitic and homophobic graffiti."

After all, it is said, political indoctrination of one sort or another has always taken place at universities. Now that process is simply being made overt. And anyway, all these people complaining about the loss of academic freedom and the decline in standards are only trying to disguise their own efforts to retain power. "The attack on diversity is a rhetorical strategy by neoconservatives who have their own political agenda," says Stimpson. "Under the guise of defending objectivity and intellectual rigor, which is a lot of mishmash, they are trying to pre-serve the cultural and political supremacy of white heterosexual males."

Everything Is Political

If the debate over what students should be taught has become an openly political power struggle, that is only because, to the politically correct, *everything* is political. And nothing is more political, in their view, than the humanities, where much of the recent controversy has been centered.

For most of the twentieth century, professors in the humanities modeled themselves on their counterparts in the natural sciences. They thought of themselves as specialists in the disinterested pursuit of the truth. Their job, in the words of T. S. Eliot, was "the elucida-tion of art and the correction of taste," and to do so they concentrated on what Matthew Arnold called "the best that has been thought and written."

That common sense of purpose began to fracture in the sixties. The generation of professors now acquiring prominence and power at universities—Elaine Showalter, the head of the English department at Princeton; Donna Shalala, chancellor of the University of Wisconsin; James Freedman, the president of Dartmouth—came of age during that period. They witnessed its upheavals and absorbed its political commitments.

30 And by and large, they have retained them. Which means that, 30 though much of the country subsequently rejected the political vision of the sixties, it has triumphed at the universities. "If the undergrad-uate population has moved quietly to the right in recent years, the men and women who are paid to introduce students to the great works and ideas of our civilization have by and large remained true to the emancipationist ideology of the sixties," writes Roger Kimball in

his book, *Tenured Radicals*. The professors themselves eagerly admit this. "I see my scholarship as an extension of my political activism," said Annette Kolodny, a former Berkeley radical and now the dean of the humanities faculty at the University of Arizona.

In the view of such activists, the universities were hardly the havens of academic independence they pretended to be. They had hopelessly compromised their integrity by accepting contracts from the Pentagon, but those alliances with the reviled "military-industrial Establishment" were seen as merely one symptom of a larger conspiracy by white males. Less obviously, but more insidiously, they had appointed themselves guardians of the culture and compiled the list of so-called Great Books as a propaganda exercise to reinforce the notion of white-male superiority. "The canon of great literature was created by high-Anglican ass----s to underwrite their social class," Stanley Hauerwas, a professor at Duke's Divinity School, put it recently.

Several schools of French critical theory that became fashionable during the seventies provided the jargon for this critique. Semiotics and Lacanian psychoanalysis argued that language and art conveyed subliminal cultural prejudices, power configurations, metaphoric representations of gender. Deconstruction declared that texts, to use the preferred word, had no meaning outside themselves. "There is no such thing as literal meaning . . . there is no such thing as intrinsic merit," wrote Stanley Fish, the head of Duke's English department.

That being the case, any attempt to assign meaning to art, literature, or thought, to interpret it and evaluate it, was nothing more than an exercise in political power by the individual with the authority to impose his or her view. It then followed that the only reason to require students to read certain books is not to "correct taste" or because the books were "the best that has been thought or written" but because they promoted politically correct viewpoints. That ideological emphasis also applied to scholarship generally. "If the work doesn't have a strong political thrust, I don't see how it matters," said Eve Sedgwick, a professor of English at Duke and the author of such papers as "Jane Austen and the Masturbating Girl."

This agenda can produce a rather remarkable, not to say outré, reading list. Catharine Stimpson has declared that her ideal curriculum would contain the little-known book *Stars in My Pocket Like Grains of Sand*. "Like many contemporary speculative fictions," Stimpson wrote, "*Stars in My Pocket* finds conventional heterosexuality absurd. The central characters are two men, Rat Korga and Marq Dyeth, who have a complex but ecstatic affair. Marq is also the product of a rich 'nurture stream.' His ancestry includes both humans and aliens. His genetic heritage blends differences. In a sweet scene, he sees three of his mothers."

Ethnic and Ideological Purity

35   The multicultural and ethnic-studies programs now in place at most universities tend to divide humanity into five groups—whites, blacks, Native Americans, Hispanics, and Asians. (Homosexuals and feminists are usually included on the grounds that, though they are not a distinct ethnic group, they, too, have been oppressed by the "whitemale," to use the neologism of black literature professor Houston Baker, and prevented from expressing their "otherness.") These are somewhat arbitrary categories, and, in fact, the new fundamentalists have two contradictory views about just what constitutes an ethnic group and who can belong.

On the one hand, there is a reluctance to confer ethnic status on certain groups. At the University of Washington, a student-faculty Task Force on Ethnicity denied Jews, Italians, and Irish-Americans certification as ethnic groups. Status as an oppressed ethnic group is guarded even more jealously. The Washington task force also decided that a required ethnic-studies program exploring the pervasiveness of racism in America would not take up the subject of anti-Semitism. The reason, *Commentary* quoted professor Johnnella Butler as having said, was that "anti-Semitism is not institutionalized in this country."

At the same time, the racial credentials of people aspiring to membership in the officially sanctioned ethnic categories are examined with an attention to detail associated with apartheid. Recently, a Hispanic who had been turned down for an affirmative-action promotion in the San Francisco fire department filed a complaint because the person who got the job instead was from Spain rather than Latin America. Colleges are becoming equally obsessed with such distinctions. Three years ago, the faculty at Hampshire College in Amherst began interviewing candidates for a professorship in Latin American literature. The professor, of course, needed to be Latin. *Pure* Latin. One woman who applied for the job was turned down because, though she was Argentine, she had, like many Argentines, Jewish and Italian blood, and thus her Third World ethnicity was considered insufficiently pure. Her heritage made her, in the words of one faculty member, "Eurocentric."

But even as these standards become increasingly exacting, more and more groups are clamoring for oppressed status. While supporters of American involvement in the Vietnam War were denounced as "war criminals" at the University of Michigan in the sixties, the school now counts Vietnam veterans as an oppressed group. In fact, the politically correct have concluded that virtually *any*one with *any* sort of trait, anxiety, flaw, impediment, or unusual sexual preference qualifies for membership in an oppressed group. This past fall, a handout from the Office of Student Affairs at Smith College explained that many people are *unaware* they are oppressed, though with help they are finding out: "As groups of people begin the process of realizing that they are oppressed, and why, new words tend to be created to express the concepts that the existing language cannot."

This obsessive tendency to see oppression everywhere is creating a sort of New Age caste system. The Smith handout listed various categories of oppression that ranged from "classism" and "ageism" to "ableism" (identified as "oppression of the differently abled by the temporarily able") and "lookism," which was revealed to be "the construction of a standard for beauty/attractiveness; and oppression through stereotypes and generalizations of both those who do not fit that standard and those who do." Heightism may be next. In a joke now making the rounds, short people are demanding to be known as "the vertically challenged."

40 But joking isn't allowed! Even the most harmless, lighthearted remarks can lead to virulent denunciations. In October, Roderick Nash, a professor at the University of California at Santa Barbara, pointed out during a lecture on environmental ethics that there is a movement to start referring to pets as animal companions. (Apparently, domesticated animals are offended by the word *pet*.) Nash then made some sort of off-the-cuff observation about how women who pose for *Penthouse* are still called Pets (and not *Penthouse* Animal Companions). Inevitably, several female students filed a formal sexual-harassment complaint against him. Susan Rode, one of the signers, said, "Maybe this will make more people aware in other classes and make other faculty watch what they say."

Indeed, making people *watch what they say* is the central preoccupation of politically correct students. Stephan Thernstrom is not the only professor who has been forced to give up a course on race relations. Reynolds Farley, one of the leading scholars on race relations, dropped a course he had taught for nearly ten years at the University of Michigan after he was accused of racial insensitivity for reading Malcolm X's description of himself as a pimp and a thief and for discussing the southern defense of slavery. "Given the climate at Michigan," Farley said, "I could be hassled for anything I do or don't say in that class."

Watch what you say: And it's not enough just to avoid racism. One must display absolute ideological purity. The search committee at Hampshire College also considered a highly qualified Chicano candidate for the Latin American–literature post. Unfortunately for him, in his dissertation on Chicano literature he drew parallels between Shakespeare and Mexican writers. This demonstrated dangerous "Eurocentric" tendencies. Certain faculty members, doubting the candidate's ethnic purity as well, wondered whether someone of Mexican heritage was *really* Latin American. They thought a Puerto Rican might be better. He didn't get the job.

It was finally offered to Norman Holland, who seemed both ethnically and ideologically pure. But this past summer, Holland's contract was not renewed, and Holland claims it is because he also was branded "Eurocentric." Though the school's official position is that Holland was an ineffective teacher, two of the professors who reviewed his work insinuated that he had a European bias. Holland, one professor declared, had "focused mainly on Western Europe to the exclusion of cultural issues Third World students perceive as uniquely relevant." "I suppose I committed certain kinds of sins," says Holland. "When I was teaching *One Hundred Years of Solitude,* I would talk about colonial rape, but I would also talk about how the novel originated in Europe and how García Márquez was working in that tradition and addressing ideas in Proust and Joyce. I didn't limit myself to considering it as a sociological document."

The Gender Feminists and Date Rape

"Misogynistic!"
"Patriarchal!"
"Gynophobic!"
"Phallocentric!"

Last fall, Camille Paglia attended a lecture by a "feminist theorist" from a large Ivy League university who had set out to "decode" the

45

subliminal sexual oppressiveness in fashion photography. The feminist theorist stood at the front of the room showing slides of fashion photography and cosmetics ads and exposing, in the style of Lacanian psychoanalysis, their violent sexism. She had selected a Revlon ad of a woman with a heavily made-up face who was standing up to her chin in a pool of water. When it came up on the screen, she exclaimed, "Decapitation!"

She showed a picture of a black woman who was wearing aviator goggles and had the collar of her turtleneck sweater pulled up. "Strangulation!" she shouted. "Bondage!"

50   It went on like this for the entire lecture. When it was over, Paglia, 50 who considers herself a feminist, stood up and made an impassioned speech. She declared that the fashion photography of the past 40 years is great art, that instead of decapitation she saw the birth of Venus, instead of strangulation she saw references to King Tut. But political correctness has achieved a kind of exquisitely perfect rigidity among the group known as the gender feminists, and she was greeted, she says, "with gasps of horror and angry murmuring. It's a form of psychosis, this slogan-filled machinery. The radical feminists have contempt for values other than their own, and they're inspiring in students a resentful attitude toward the world."

Indeed, the central tenet of gender feminism is that Western society is organized around a "sex/gender system." What defines the system, according to Sandra Harding, a professor of philosophy at the University of Delaware and one of its exponents, is "male dominance made possible by men's control of women's productive and reproductive labor."

The primary arena for this dominance is, of course, the family, which Alison Jaggar, a professor at the University of Cincinnati and the head of the American Philosophical Association's Committee on the Status of Women in Philosophy, sees as "a cornerstone of women's oppression." The family, in Jaggar's view, "enforces heterosexuality" and "imposes the prevailing masculine and feminine character structures on the next generation."

This position makes gender feminists, as Christina Sommers has written in an article in *Public Affairs Quarterly*, from which some of these quotes were taken, "oddly unsympathetic to the women whom they claim to represent." But that poses no problem. Women who have decided to get married and raise families, women who want to become mothers, are, naturally, victims of false consciousness. The radical feminists are fond of quoting Simone de Beauvoir, who said, "No woman should be authorized to stay at home and raise children . . . precisely because if there is such a choice, too many women will make that one."

Jaggar, for one, would like to abolish the family altogether and create a society where, with the aid of technology, "one woman could inseminate another, . . . men . . . could lactate, . . . and fertilized ova could be transferred into women's or even men's bodies." All that is preventing this, according to the gender feminists, is "phallocentric-ity" and "androcentricity," the view that society is organized around the male and his sexual organs. The feminists, ablaze with revolution-ary rhetoric, have set out to overthrow this system. "What we femi-nists are doing," the philosopher Barbara Minnich has said, "is comparable to Copernicus shattering our geocentricity, Darwin shat-tering our species-centricity. We are shattering androcentricity, and the change is as fundamental, as dangerous, as exciting."

55   But unlike the pre-Copernican view that the Earth was at the cen-   55
ter of the universe, androcentricity is not, in the view of the gender feminists, merely a flawed theory. It is a moral evil, dedicated to the enslavement of women. And since most of Western culture, according to this view, has been a testament to "male power and transcendence," it is similar to evil and must be discarded. This includes not only pa-triarchal books like the Bible and sexist subjects like traditional his-tory, with its emphasis on great men and great deeds, but also the natural sciences and even the very process of analytical thinking itself. "To know is to f—" has become a radical-feminist rallying cry. Indeed, scientific inquiry itself is seen as "the rape of nature." A project spon-sored by the state of New Jersey to integrate these views into college campuses has issued a set of "feminist scholarship guidelines" that de-clares "mind was male. Nature was female, and knowledge was created as an act of aggression—a passive nature had to be interrogated, un-clothed, penetrated, and compelled by man to reveal her secrets."

To certain women, however, this is just a veiled restatement of the old idea that women don't make good scientists. "As a liberal feminist, I encourage women to study science," says Christina Sommers. "I'm not impugning science itself as hostile to the female sensibility."

But it is not just the coldly analytical and dualistic structures of male thinking that the gender feminists find so contemptible. It is

159

males themselves, or at least heterosexual males. After all, heterosexuality is responsible for the subjugation of women, and so, in the oppressive culture of the West, any woman who goes on a date with a man is a prostitute. "Both man and woman might be outraged at the description of their candlelight dinner as prostitution," Jaggar has written. "But the radical feminist argues this outrage is simply due to the participants' failure or refusal to perceive the social context in which the dinner occurs." In other words, they are victims of—what else?—false consciousness.

This eagerness to see all women as victims, to describe all male behavior with images of rape and violation, may shed some light on the phenomenon of date rape, a legitimate issue that has been exaggerated and distorted by a small group with a specific political agenda. As with the hysteria a few years ago over the sexual abuse of children, endless talk shows, television news stories, and magazine articles have been devoted to date rape, often describing it as "an epidemic" that, as the Chicago *Tribune* put it, "makes women campus prisoners" and forces them, as at Brown, to list supposed rapists on bathroom walls.

Much of this discussion starts off with the claim that one in four female students is raped by a date. The figure seems staggeringly high, and debate tends to focus on whether actual rape or merely the reporting of rape is on the rise. But the journalist Stephanie Gutmann has pointed out in *Reason* magazine the gross statistical flaws in the survey of date rape that produced this figure. According to Gutmann, "the real story about campus date rape is not that there's been any significant increase of rape on college campuses, at least of the acquaintance type, but that the word *rape* is being stretched to encompass any type of sexual interaction."

60 In fact, rape under the new definition does not have to involve 60 physical assault at all. Andrea Parrot, a professor at Cornell who has promoted the idea of the date-rape epidemic, has declared that "any sexual intercourse without mutual desire is a form of rape." In other words, a woman is being raped if she has sex when not in the mood, even if she fails to inform her partner of that fact. As a former director of Columbia's date-rape-education program told Gutmann, "Every time you have an act of intercourse, there must be explicit consent, and if there's no explicit consent, then it's rape. . . . Stone silence throughout an entire physical encounter with someone is not explicit consent." And rape is no longer limited to actual intercourse. A training manual

at Swarthmore College states that "acquaintance rape . . . spans a spectrum of incidents and behaviors ranging from crimes legally defined as rape to verbal harassment and inappropriate innuendo."

It is no surprise then that Catherine Nye, a University of Chicago psychologist interviewed by Gutmann, found that 43 percent of the women in a widely cited rape study "had not realized they had been raped." In other words, they were victims of, yes, false consciousness. But by the definition of the radical feminists, all sexual encounters that involve any confusion or ambivalence constitute rape. "Ordinary bungled sex—the kind you regret in the morning or even during—is being classified as rape," Gutmann says. "Bad or confused feelings after sex become someone else's fault." Which is fine with the feminists. "In terms of making men nervous or worried about overstepping their bounds, I don't think that's a bad thing," Parrot said. Indeed, since it encourages a general suspicion of all men, it's a good thing. As Parrot has put it, "Since you can't tell who has the potential for rape simply by looking, be on your guard with every man."

Afrocentrism

For all their fury, the gender feminists are surpassed in ideological rage by an even more extreme wing of the politically correct: the Afrocentrists. Afrocentrists argue that not only is Western culture oppressive, it isn't even really *Western*. Key accomplishments, from mathematics and biology to architecture and medicine, were in fact the work of Africans. "Very few doctors, African-American or otherwise in America, are aware of the fact that when they take their medical oath, the hypocratic [*sic*] oath, they actually swear to Imhotep, the African God of Medicine," Asa Hilliard, a professor of Afro-American history at Georgia State, has written.

The theory that Africa was the true source of Western civilization hinges on the claim that the ancient Egyptians were black. "The first 12 dynasties plus dynasties 18 and 25 were native-black-African dynasties," Hilliard has asserted. Traditional Egyptologists generally believe that while blacks, from Nubia to the south, were active in Egyptian society, ancient Egyptians, like their contemporary counterparts, tended to be of Semitic stock. But to the Afrocentrists, that explanation is merely part of the long-running conspiracy by Western whites to deny the African contribution to civilization.

161

The conspiracy began, in the Afrocentric view, when the ancient Greeks "stole" African philosophy and science from the Egyptians. To claim European credit for these discoveries, Romans and, later, Christians burned the library of Alexandria in Egypt. The conspiracy has continued ever since. Napoleon's soldiers shot off the nose and lips of the Sphinx to obliterate its Negroid features. Beethoven and Robert Browning were actually blacks whose ethnicity has been hidden. "African history has been lost, stolen, destroyed, and suppressed," Hilliard maintains.

65   Leonard Jeffries, chairman of the black-studies department at 65
City College and one of the most extreme exponents of Afrocentrism, has worked up a sort of anthropological model to explain why Europeans have oppressed Africans. The human race, according to Jeffries, is divided into the "ice people" and the "sun people." The ethnic groups descended from the ice people are materialistic, selfish, and violent, while those descended from the sun people are nonviolent, cooperative, and spiritual. In addition, blacks are biologically superior to whites, Jeffries maintains, because they have more melanin, and melanin regulates intellect and health.

Despite the spiritual benevolence one might expect from a "sun person," Jeffries is known for making the sort of hostile denunciations that, if he were at the other end of the political spectrum, would no doubt provoke howls of indignation. According to Fred Rueckher, a white student who took his course, Jeffries attacked black males for succumbing to the "white pussy syndrome," that is, pursuing white women. He called Diana Ross an "international whore" for her involvement with white men. And he applauded the destruction of the Challenger space shuttle because it would deter white people from "spreading their filth throughout the universe."

Jeffries's wild remarks are excused by the politically correct on the grounds that to be a racist, you have to have "institutional power," and since blacks do not have "institutional power," they cannot be considered racist. The somewhat flimsy propositions of Afrocentrism are excused with equal finesse. First of all, since everything is political, there has never been disinterested scholarship, only power plays by various groups to justify their own claims. And even if there are some holes in Afrocentrism, the approach is useful because it raises the "self-esteem" of black students.

Such was the reasoning of the New York State Board of Education's Task Force on Minorities, to which Leonard Jeffries was a consultant. Its report suggested that "all curricular materials [including math and science] be prepared on the basis of multicultural contributions." As a result, the report said, children from minority cultures "will have higher self-esteem and self-respect, while children from European cultures will have a less arrogant perspective." The notion has already been put into effect in public schools in Portland, Indianapolis, and Washington, D.C., where students are taught subjects like Yoruba mathematics and ancient-Egyptian astronomy.

The idea that the "self-esteem" of students—rather than historical relevance—should be the basis for including material in textbooks does have its critics. Among the most prominent is Diane Ravitch, who has said the idea "that children can learn only from the experiences of people from the same race" represents a sort of "racial fundamentalism." The success of Chinese students in math is due not to numbers but to hard work. If the "self-esteem" model had any validity, Italian-American students—the descendants of Caesar and Michelangelo—would excel in school, but in fact they have the highest dropout rate of any white group in New York City schools. By promoting a brand of history "in which everyone is either a descendant of victims or oppressors," Ravitch has declared, "ancient hatreds are fanned and re-created in each new generation."

Ravitch naturally was branded a racist for this position. Participants at a recent Afrocentrism conference in Atlanta derided her as "Miss Daisy." She has been attacked in the *City Sun* and on black television and radio programs. As a result, she has received so many threats that when we first agreed to meet, she was afraid to tell me where she lived. "They've written saying things like 'We're going to get you, bitch. We're going to beat your white ass.' "

Moonies in the Classroom

The supreme irony of the new fundamentalism is that the generation that produced the free-speech movement in Berkeley and rebelled against the idea of *in loco parentis*—that university administrators should act as surrogate parents—is now trying to restrict speech and control the behavior of a new generation of students. The enterprise is undertaken to combat racism, of course, and it is an article of faith among the politically correct that the current climate of racial hostility can be traced to the Reagan and Bush presidencies, to

163

conservative-Republican efforts to gut civil-rights legislation and affirmative-action programs. However true that may be, scholars like Shelby Steele, a black essayist and English professor, have also argued that the separatist movements at universities—black dorms, Native-American student centers, gay-studies programs, the relentless harping on "otherness"—have heightened tensions and contributed to the culture of victimization. "If you sensitize people from day one to look at everything in terms of race and sex, eventually they will see racism and sexism at the root of everything," says Alan Kors. "But not all the problems and frustrations in life are due to race and gender."

Furthermore, they say, instead of increasing self-esteem, schools that offer an Afrocentric education will only turn out students who are more resentful, and incompetent, than ever. Indeed, while the more rabid Afrocentrics have claimed that crack and AIDS are conspiracies by whites to eliminate blacks, it could just as easily be argued that white indulgence of Afrocentric education represents a conspiracy to provide blacks with a useless education that will keep them out of the job market.

Of course, to make such a statement is invariably to provoke a charge of racism. But part of the problem with this reaction is that it trivializes the debate. In fact, it makes debate impossible. But that is just as well, according to the new fundamentalists. Debate, and the analytic thinking it requires, is oppressive. It's logocentric. It favors the articulate at the expense of the inarticulate. It forces people to make distinctions, and since racism is the result of distinctions, they should be discouraged. "I have students tell me they don't need to study philosophy because it's patriarchal and logocentric," says Christina Sommers. "They're unteachable and scary. It's like having a Moonie in the classroom."

Resistance to this sort of robotic sloganeering is beginning. "Today, routinized righteous indignation has been substituted for rigorous criticism," Henry Louis Gates, a black English professor at Duke, recently declared. Some professors are actually arguing that colleges should begin to emphasize what whites, homosexuals, minorities, and women have in common rather than dwelling constantly on "difference." In November, writing in the *Stanford Daily* about a proposal to require Stanford students to take a course in diversity, David Kennedy, chairman of American studies at Stanford and previously a champion of multiculturalism, said, "I worry that the proposal will add to the already considerable weight that Stanford culture places on racial and ethnic divisiveness, rather than shared participation. I question whether this is socially wise and, further, whether it is intellectually true to the lived experience of members of this society."

75   A few emboldened administrators are actually suggesting that it is 75 not unreasonable for Western culture to enjoy a certain prominence at American colleges. In an address to incoming Yale students in September, Donald Kagan, dean of the college, encouraged them to center their undergraduate studies around Western culture. He argued that the West "has asserted the claims of the individual against those of the state, limiting its power and creating a realm of privacy into which it cannot penetrate." The West's tradition of civil liberties has produced "a tolerance and respect for diversity unknown in most cultures."

But many of the Yale freshmen—or "freshpeople," as the *Yale Daily News* puts it—considered the dean's statements "quite disturbing." And the dean was denounced with the obligatory mind-numbing litany.

"Paternalistic!"

"Racist!"

"Fascist!"

Questions on Meaning

1. A single example can effectively illustrate a point but, unless they come in large numbers, examples don't usually prove anything. List the examples that Taylor uses and distinguish individual illustrative examples from groups of examples that help to prove a point.
2. Define eurocentric, date-rape, and afrocentric.
3. Have you ever felt that you were the victim of racial, sexual, or political harassment? What did you do?

Questions on Rhetorical Strategy and Style

1. Circular reasoning (also called begging the question and, in Latin, *petitio principi*) involves pretending to prove a point by indirectly asking your audience to accept your point without proof. Is the following statement an example of circular reasoning? "It is difficult for us to see and overcome racism and sexism because we are all a product of the problem, i.e., we are all the progeny of a racist and sexist society." What point is implied in the statement?
2. Often someone skilled at argument will choose an example that is outrageous in order to inflame the reader's emotions. The reader may then accept the writer's reasoning more readily. Find an example that seems calculated to stir up your emotions and speculate about Taylor's reasons for including that example at that point in the essay.
3. Interview some of the senior faculty and administrators at your school. Ask them their opinions about political correctness and about their own political activities when they were students. Write your findings up in an essay on the politics of the powerful.

Writing Assignments

1. Would you say that Taylor's essay serves the causes of racism and sexism? Or is he providing a balanced rational analysis? Or is he clearly arguing a case but doing so fairly? Explain.
2. Write an essay that describes the influence your gender, height, weight, age, race, or religion has had on your experience of school. Clearly explain causes and effects, and describe your actions and feelings.

Dead Men's Path

Chinua Achebe

Named Albert by his missionary parents at his birth in Ogidi, Nigeria, Achebe (1930–) later adopted the traditional name Chinua. He studied at the Church Mission Society School and the Government College and University College (B.A. 1953), where he cultivated his writing. Achebe's first novel, Things Fall Apart, *appeared in 1958. His writing, which draws on African oral traditions, reflects the tumultuous period of civil wars at home in the 1960s. He has published widely in several genres, including the novels* A Man of the People *(1966) and* Home and Exile *(2000); the short story collections* The Sacrificial Egg, and Other Stories *(1962) and* Girls at War *(1972); the essay collections* Morning Yet on Creation Day *(1975) and* The Trouble with Nigeria *(1984); and the poetry collections* Beware, Soul-Brother, and Other Poems *(1971) and* Christmas in Biafra, and Other Poems *(1973). Achebe taught at a number of colleges and universities throughout the world, including the University of Nigeria, the University of Massachusetts-Amherst, the University of California-Los Angeles, Bard College, and Cambridge University. In 1981 he founded the Association of Nigerian Authors and served as its president from 1981 to 1986. During his career Achebe received awards ranging from the Margaret Wrong Memorial Prize (1959) for* Things Fall Apart; *to the Nigerian National Trophy (1961) for* No Longer at Ease; *and the Commonwealth Poetry Prize (1972) for* Beware, Soul-Brother, and Other Poems. *He was nominated for the Booker Prize in 1987 for* Anthills of the Savannah *and for the Nobel Prize in Literature in 2000.*

Reprinted from *Girls at War and Other Stories.* Reprinted by permission of Doubleday, a division of Random House, Inc. and Emma Sweeney Agency. Copyright © 1972, 1973 by Chinua Achebe.

In 2007, Achebe was awarded the Man Booker International Prize in honor of his literary career. Among institutions that have awarded Achebe honorary degrees are Dartmouth College, the University of Nigeria, the University of Prince Edward Island, the Open University, and Georgetown University. This story, originally published in 1953 and later collected in Girls at War, *features an ambitious and progressive young headmaster of an African mission school who learns a painful lesson about respecting ancient traditions.*

1   Michael Obi's hopes were fulfilled much earlier than he had   1
expected. He was appointed headmaster of Ndume Central School in January 1949. It had always been an unprogressive school, so the Mission authorities decided to send a young and energetic man to run it. Obi accepted this responsibility with enthusiasm. He had many wonderful ideas and this was an opportunity to put them into practice. He had had sound secondary school education which designated him a "pivotal teacher" in the official records and set him apart from the other headmasters in the mission field. He was outspoken in his condemnation of the narrow views of these older and often less-educated ones.

"We shall make a good job of it, shan't we?" he asked his young wife when they first heard the joyful news of his promotion.

"We shall do our best," she replied. "We shall have such beautiful gardens and everything will be just *modern* and delightful. . . ." In their two years of married life she had become completely infected by his passion for "modern methods" and his denigration of "these old and superannuated people in the teaching field who would be better employed as traders in the Onitsha market." She began to see herself already as the admired wife of the young headmaster, the queen of the school.

The wives of the other teachers would envy her position. She would set the fashion in everything. . . . Then, suddenly, it occurred to her that there might not be other wives. Wavering between hope and fear, she asked her husband, looking anxiously at him.

5   "All our colleagues are young and unmarried," he said with enthu-   5
siasm which for once she did not share. "Which is a good thing," he continued.

"Why?"

"Why? They will give all their time and energy to the school."

Nancy was downcast. For a few minutes she became skeptical about the new school; but it was only for a few minutes. Her little personal misfortune could not blind her to her husband's happy prospects. She looked at him as he sat folded up in a chair. He was stoop-shouldered and looked frail. But he sometimes surprised people with sudden bursts of physical energy. In his present posture, however, all his bodily strength seemed to have retired behind his deep-set eyes, giving them an extraordinary power of penetration. He was only twenty-six, but looked thirty or more. On the whole, he was not unhandsome.

"A penny for your thoughts, Mike," said Nancy after a while, imitating the woman's magazine she read.

10 "I was thinking what a grand opportunity we've got at last to 10 show these people how a school should be run."

Ndume School was backward in every sense of the word. Mr. Obi put his whole life into the work, and his wife hers too. He had two aims. A high standard of teaching was insisted upon, and the school compound was to be turned into a place of beauty. Nancy's dream-gardens came to life with the coming of the rains, and blossomed. Beautiful hibiscus and allamanda hedges in brilliant red and yellow marked out the carefully tended school compound from the rank neighborhood bushes.

One evening as Obi was admiring his work he was scandalized to see an old woman from the village hobble right across the compound, through a marigold flower-bed and the hedges. On going up there he found faint signs of an almost disused path from the village across the school compound to the bush on the other side.

"It amazes me," said Obi to one of his teachers who had been three years in the school, "that you people allowed the villagers to make use of this footpath. It is simply incredible." He shook his head.

"The path," said the teacher apologetically, "appears to be very important to them. Although it is hardly used, it connects the village shrine with their place of burial."

15 "And what has that got to do with the school?" asked the headmaster. 15

"Well, I don't know," replied the other with a shrug of the shoulders. "But I remember there was a big row some time ago when we attempted to close it."

"That was some time ago. But it will not be used now," said Obi as he walked away. "What will the Government Education Officer think of this when he comes to inspect the school next week? The villagers might, for all I know, decide to use the schoolroom for a pagan ritual during the inspection."

Heavy sticks were planted closely across the path at the two places where it entered and left the school premises. These were further strengthened with barbed wire.

Three days later the village priest of *Ani* called on the headmaster. He was an old man and walked with a slight stoop. He carried a stout walking-stick which he usually tapped on the floor, by way of emphasis, each time he made a new point in his argument.

"I have heard," he said after the usual exchange of cordialities, "that our ancestral footpath was recently been closed. . . ."

"Yes," replied Mr. Obi. "We cannot allow people to make a highway of our school compound."

"Look here, my son," said the priest bringing down his walking stick, "this path was here before you were born and before your father was born. The whole life of this village depends on it. Our dead relatives depart by it and our ancestors visit us by it. But most important, it is the path of children coming in to be born. . . ."

Mr. Obi listened with a satisfied smile on his face.

"The whole purpose of our school," he said finally, "is to eradicate just such beliefs as that. Dead men do not require footpaths. The whole idea is just fantastic. Our duty is to teach your children to laugh at such ideas."

"What you say may be true," replied the priest, "but we follow the practices of our fathers. If you reopen the path we shall have nothing to quarrel about. What I always say is: let the hawk perch and let the eagle perch." He rose to go.

"I am sorry," said the young headmaster. "But the school compound cannot be a thoroughfare. It is against our regulations. I would suggest your constructing another path, skirting our premises. We can even get our boys to help in building it. I don't suppose the ancestors will find the little detour too burdensome."

"I have no more words to say," said the old priest, already outside.

Two days later a young woman in the village died in child bed. A diviner was immediately consulted and he prescribed heavy sacrifices to propitiate ancestors insulted by the fence.

Obi woke up next morning among the ruins of his work. The beautiful hedges were torn up not just near the path but right round the school, the flowers trampled to death and one of the school buildings pulled down. . . . That day, the white Supervisor came to inspect the school and wrote a nasty report on the state of the premises but more seriously about the "tribal-war situation developing between the school and the village, arising in part from the misguided zeal of the new headmaster."

Questions on Meaning

1. How does Achebe characterize Michael Obi? At what point in the story do you become aware of his shortcomings?
2. How does the village priest attempt to persuade Obi to restore the path? How does his approach distinguish him from Obi?
3. After finishing the story, how do you interpret the diviner's prescription of "heavy sacrifices"?

Questions on Rhetorical Strategy and Style

1. Achebe employs limited description in this story. Reread several descriptions of characters or settings and explain their significance to the story. How would the story's impact have been altered had the author used more elaborate description?
2. Although this story is not constructed in a traditional comparison-contrast format, the contrast between progressivism and tradition is implicit throughout. What are the distinguishing features of each? Based on your reading of the story, which does Achebe consider more important?
3. What is the impact of the ironic conclusion to the story?

Writing Assignments

1. Write an essay analyzing this story as a commentary on blind adherence to progress. Focus on character, dialogue, description, and tone.
2. Imagine that you are the supervisor who inspected the school. Compose the report the supervisor might have written, including guidelines for headmasters to follow when dealing with tribal customs and local practices.
3. Write a brief essay explaining the effects of progress on the traditions of your culture. To what extent does progress respect those traditions? To what extent do traditions suffer at the hands of progress? Do you think it is possible to strike a balance between progress and tradition?

V. Language

Politics and the English Language

George Orwell

George Orwell is the pen name used by the British author Eric Blair (1903–1950). Orwell was born in the Indian village of Motihari, near Nepal, where his father was stationed in the Civil Service. India was then part of the British Empire. From 1907 to 1922 Orwell lived in England, returning to India and Burma and a position in the Imperial Police, which he held until 1927. Thereafter he lived in England, Paris, Spain, and elsewhere, writing on a wide range of topics. He fought in the Spanish Civil War and was actively engaged in several political movements, always against totalitarianism of any kind. He is best known today for two novels of political satire: Animal Farm *(1945) and* 1984 *(1949). He was also a prolific journalist and essayist, with his essays collected in five volumes. He wrote "Politics and the English Language" shortly after the end of World War II, at a time when patriotic fervor was very strong in the Allied countries such as England the United States, while Marxist ideology was growing elsewhere. Orwell was particularly sensitive to the use of language for political purposes, which he saw as a special instance of a more general corruption of the English language. In the 50 years since this was written, many of the phrases Orwell writes about have dropped from common use, so you may have difficulty understanding some of his examples. Nonetheless, his general points will be quite clear, and you will be able to find contemporary analogues to his examples.*

1   Most people who bother with the matter at all would admit   1
that the English language is in a bad way, but it is generally
assumed that we cannot by conscious action do anything
about it. Our civilization is decadent and our language—so the argument runs—must inevitably share in the general collapse. It follows
that any struggle against the abuse of language is a sentimental archaism, like preferring candles to electric light or hansom cabs to airplanes. Underneath this lies the half-conscious belief that language is
a natural growth and not an instrument which we shape for our own
purposes.

Now, it is clear that the decline of a language must ultimately have
political and economic causes: it is not due simply to the bad influence of this or that individual writer. But an effect can become a cause,
reinforcing the original cause and producing the same effect in an in-
tensified form, and so on indefinitely. A man may take to drink because he feels himself to be a failure, and then fail all the more
completely because he drinks. It is rather the same thing that is happening to the English language. It becomes ugly and inaccurate because our thoughts are foolish, but the slovenliness of our language
makes it easier for us to have foolish thoughts. The point is that the
process is reversible. Modern English, especially written English, is full
of bad habits which spread by imitation and which can be avoided if
one is willing to take the necessary trouble. If one gets rid of these
habits one can think more clearly, and to think clearly is a necessary
first step towards political regeneration: so that the fight against bad
English is not frivolous and is not the exclusive concern of professional
writers. I will come back to this presently, and I hope that by that time
the meaning of what I have said here will have become clearer. Meanwhile, here are five specimens of the English language as it is now habitually written.

These five passages have not been picked out because they are especially bad—I could have quoted far worse if I had chosen—but because they illustrate various of the mental vices from which we now
suffer. They are a little below the average, but are fairly representative samples. I number them so that I can refer back to them when
necessary:

*"(1) I am not, indeed, sure whether it is not true to say that the
Milton who once seemed not unlike a seventeenth-century Shelley*

had not become, out of an experience ever more bitter in each year, more alien (sic) *to the founder of that Jesuit sect which nothing could induce him to tolerate."*

Professor Harold Laski (Essay in *Freedom of Expression*).

"(2) Above all, we cannot play ducks and drakes with a native battery of idioms which prescribes such egregious collocations of vocables as the Basic put up with *for* tolerate *or* put at a loss *for* bewilder."

Professor Lancelot Hogben (*Interglossa*).

"(3) On the one side we have the free personality: by definition it is not neurotic, for it has neither conflict nor dream. Its desires, such as they are, are transparent, for they are just what institutional approval keeps in the forefront of consciousness; another institutional pattern would alter their number and intensity; there is little in them that is natural, irreducible, or culturally dangerous. But on the other side, *the social bond itself is nothing but the mutual reflection of these self-secure integrities. Recall the definition of love. Is not this the very picture of a small academic? Where is there a place in this hall of mirrors for either personality or fraternity?"*

Essay on psychology in *Politics* (New York).

"(4) All the 'best people' from the gentlemen's clubs, and all the frantic fascist captains, united in common hatred of Socialism and bestial horror of the rising tide of the mass revolutionary movement, have turned to acts of provocation, to foul incendiarism, to medieval legends of poisoned wells, to legalize their own destruction of proletarian organizations, and rouse the agitated petty-bourgeoisie to chauvinistic fervor on behalf of the fight against the revolutionary way out of the crisis."

Communist pamphlet.

"(5) If a new spirit is to be infused into this old country, there is one thorny and contentious reform which must be tackled, and that is the humanization and galvanization of the B.B.C. Timidity here will bespeak cancer and atrophy of the soul. The heart of Britain may be sound and of strong beat, for instance, but the British lion's roar at present is like that of Bottom in Shakespeare's Midsummer Night's Dream—*as gentle as any sucking dove. A virile new*

Britain cannot continue indefinitely to be traduced in the eyes or rather ears, of the world by the effete languors of Langham Place, brazenly masquerading as 'standard English'. When the Voice of Britain is heard at nine o'clock, better far and infinitely less ludicrous to hear aitches honestly dropped than the present priggish, inflated, inhibited, school-ma'amish arch braying of blameless bashful mewing maidens!"

Letter in *Tribune.*

Each of these passages has faults of its own, but, quite apart from avoidable ugliness, two qualities are common to all of them. The first is staleness of imagery: the other is lack of precision. The writer either has a meaning and cannot express it, or he inadvertently says something else, or he is almost indifferent as to whether his words mean anything or not. This mixture of vagueness and sheer incompetence is the most marked characteristic of modern English prose, and especially of any kind of political writing. As soon as certain topics are raised, the concrete melts into the abstract and no one seems able to think of turns of speech that are not hackneyed: prose consists less and less of words chosen for the sake of their meaning, and more and more of phrases tacked together like the sections of a prefabricated henhouse. I list below, with notes and examples, various of the tricks by means of which the work of prose-construction is habitually dodged:

Dying Metaphors

5   A newly invented metaphor assists thought by evoking a visual image,   5
while on the other hand a metaphor which is technically "dead" (e.g. *iron resolution*) has in effect reverted to being an ordinary word and can generally be used without loss of vividness. But in between these two classes there is a huge dump of worn-out metaphors which have lost all evocative power and are merely used because they save people the trouble of inventing phrases for themselves. Examples are: *Ring the changes on, take up the cudgels for, toe the line, ride roughshod over, stand shoulder to shoulder with, play into the hands of, no axe to grind, grist to the mill, fishing in troubled waters, on the order of the day, Achilles' heel, swan song, hotbed.* Many of these are used without knowledge of their meaning (what is a "rift," for instance?), and incompatible metaphors are frequently mixed, a sure sign that the writer is not interested in

what he is saying. Some metaphors now current have been twisted out of their original meaning without those who use them even being aware of the fact. For example, *toe the line* is sometimes written *tow the line*. Another example is *the hammer and the anvil*, now always used with the implication that the anvil gets the worst of it. In real life it is always the anvil that breaks the hammer, never the other way about: a writer who stopped to think what he was saying would be aware of this, and would avoid perverting the original phrase.

Operators or Verbal False Limbs

These save the trouble of picking out appropriate verbs and nouns, and at the same time pad each sentence with extra syllables which give it an appearance of symmetry. Characteristic phrases are: *render inoperative, militate against, make contact with, be subjected to, give rise to, give grounds for, have the effect of, play a leading part (role) in, make itself felt, take effect, exhibit a tendency to, serve the purpose of,* etc., etc. The keynote is the elimination of simple verbs. Instead of being a single word, such as *break, stop, spoil, mend, kill,* a verb becomes a *phrase,* made up of a noun or adjective tacked on to some general-purposes verb such as *prove, serve, form, play, render.* In addition, the passive voice is wherever possible used in preference to the active, and noun constructions are used instead of gerunds (*by examination of* instead of *by examining*). The range of verbs is further cut down by means of the *-ize* and *de-* formation, and the banal statements are given an appearance of profundity by means of the *not un-* formation. Simple conjunctions and prepositions are replaced by such phrases as *with respect to, having regard to, the fact that, by dint of, in view of, in the interests of, on the hypothesis that;* and the ends of sentences are saved from anticlimax by such resounding commonplaces as *greatly to be desired, cannot be left out of account, a development to be expected in the near future, deserving of serious consideration, brought to a satisfactory conclusion,* and so on and so forth.

Pretentious Diction

Words like *phenomenon, element, individual* (as noun), *objective, categorical, effective, virtual, basic, primary, promote, constitute, exhibit, exploit, utilize, eliminate, liquidate,* are used to dress up simple statements and give an air of scientific impartiality to biased judgments.

Adjectives like *epoch-making, epic, historic, unforgettable, triumphant, age-old, inevitable, inexorable, veritable,* are used to dignify the sordid processes of international politics, while writing that aims at glorifying war usually takes on an archaic color, its characteristic words being: *realm, throne, chariot, mailed fist, trident, sword, shield, buckler, banner, jackboot, clarion.* Foreign words and expressions such as *cul de sac, ancien régime, deus ex machina, mutatis mutandis, status quo, gleichschaltung, weltanschauung,* are used to give an air of culture and elegance. Except for the useful abbreviations *i.e., e.g.,* and *etc.,* there is no real need for any of the hundreds of foreign phrases now current in English. Bad writers, and especially scientific, political and sociological writers, are nearly always haunted by the notion that Latin or Greek words are grander than Saxon ones, and unnecessary words like *expedite, ameliorate, predict, extraneous, deracinated, clandestine, subaqueous* and hundreds of others constantly gain ground from their Anglo-Saxon opposite numbers. The jargon peculiar to Marxist writing (*hyena, hangman, cannibal, petty bourgeois, these, gentry, lacquey, flunkey, mad dog, White Guard,* etc.) consists largely of words and phrases translated from Russian, German or French; but the normal way of coining a new word is to use a Latin or Greek root with the appropriate affix and, where necessary, the *-ize* formation. It is often easier to make up words of this kind (*deregionalize, impermissible, extramarital, non-fragmentory* and so forth) than to think up the English words that will cover one's meaning. The result, in general, is an increase in slovenliness and vagueness.

Meaningless Words

In certain kinds of writing, particularly in art criticism and literary criticism, it is normal to come across long passages which are almost completely lacking in meaning. Words like *romantic, plastic, values, human, dead, sentimental, natural, vitality,* as used in art criticism, are strictly meaningless in the sense that they not only do not point to any discoverable object, but are hardly ever expected to do so by the reader. When one critic writes, "The outstanding feature of Mr. X's work is its living quality", while another writes, "The immediately striking thing about Mr. X's work is its peculiar deadness", the reader accepts this as a simple difference of opinion. If words like *black* and *white* were involved, instead of the jargon words *dead* and *living,* he would see at once that language was being used in an improper way. Many political words are similarly abused. The word *Fascism* has now no meaning except in so far as it signifies "something not desirable." The words *democracy, socialism, freedom, patriotic, realistic, justice,* have each of them several different meanings which cannot be reconciled with one another. In the case of a word like *democracy,* not only is there no agreed definition, but the attempt to make one is resisted from all sides. It is almost universally felt that when we call a country democratic we are praising it: consequently the defenders of every kind of régime claim that it is a democracy, and fear that they might have to stop using the word if it were tied down to any one meaning. Words of this kind are often used in a consciously dishonest way. That is, the person who uses them has his own private definition, but allows his hearer to think he means something quite different. Statements like *Marshal Pétain was a true patriot, The Soviet Press is the freest in the world, The Catholic Church is opposed to persecution,* are almost always made with intent to deceive. Other words used in variable meanings, in most cases more or less dishonestly, are: *class, totalitarian, science, progressive, reactionary, bourgeois, equality.*

Now that I have made this catalogue of swindles and perversions, let me give another example of the kind of writing that they lead to. This time it must of its nature be an imaginary one. I am going to translate a passage of good English into modern English of the worst sort. Here is a well-known verse from *Ecclesiastes:*

> *"I returned and saw under the sun, that the race is not to the swift, nor the battle to the strong, neither yet bread to the wise, nor yet riches to men of understanding, nor yet favour to men of skill; but time and chance happeneth to them all."*

10 Here it is in modern English: 10

> *"Objective consideration of contemporary phenomena compels the conclusion that success or failure in competitive activities exhibits no tendency to be commensurate with innate capacity, but that a considerable element of the unpredictable must invariably be taken into account."*

This is a parody, but not a very gross one. Exhibit (3), above, for instance, contains several patches of the same kind of English. It will be seen that I have not made a full translation. The beginning and ending of the sentence follow the original meaning fairly closely, but in the middle the concrete illustrations—race, battle, bread—dissolve into the vague phrase "success or failure in competitive activities." This had to be so, because no modern writer of the kind I am discussing—no one capable of using phrases like "objective consideration of contemporary phenomena"—would ever tabulate his thoughts in that precise and detailed way. The whole tendency of modern prose is away from concreteness. Now analyze these two sentences a little more closely. The first contains forty-nine words but only sixty syllables, and all its words are those of everyday life. The second contains thirty-eight words of ninety syllables: eighteen of its words are from Latin roots, and one from Greek. The first sentence contains six vivid images, and only one phrase ("time and chance") that could be called vague. The second contains not a single fresh, arresting phrase, and in spite of its ninety syllables it gives only a shortened version of the meaning contained in the first. Yet without a doubt it is the second kind of sentence that is gaining ground in modern English. I do not want to exaggerate. This kind of writing is not yet universal, and outcrops of simplicity will occur here and there in the worst-written page. Still, if you or I were told to write a few lines on the uncertainty of human fortunes, we should probably come much nearer to my imaginary sentence than to the one from *Ecclesiastes*.

As I have tried to show, modern writing at its worst does not consist in picking out words for the sake of their meaning and inventing images in order to make the meaning clearer. It consists in gumming together long strips of words which have already been set in order by someone else, and making the results presentable by sheer humbug. The attraction of this way of writing is that it is easy. It is easier—even quicker, once you have the habit—to say *In my opinion it is a not unjustifiable assumption* that than to say *I think*. If you use ready-made phrases, you not only don't have to hunt about for words; you also don't have to bother with the rhythms of your sentences, since these phrases are generally so arranged as to be more or less euphonious. When you are composing in a hurry—when you are dictating to a stenographer, for instance, or making a public speech—it is natural to fall into a pretentious, Latinized style. Tags like *a consideration which we should do well to bear in mind* or *a conclusion to which all of us would readily assent* will save many a sentence from coming down with a bump. By using stale metaphors, similes and idioms, you save much mental effort, at the cost of leaving your meaning vague, not only for your reader but for yourself. This is the significance of mixed metaphors. The sole aim of a metaphor is to call up a visual image. When these images clash—as in *The Fascist octopus has sung its swan song, the jackboot is thrown into the melting pot*—it can't be taken as certain that the writer is not seeing a mental image of the objects he is naming; in other words he is not really thinking. Look again at the examples I gave at the beginning of this essay. Professor Laski (1) uses five negatives in fifty-three words. One of these is superfluous, making nonsense of the whole passage, and in addition there is the slip *alien* for akin, making further nonsense, and several avoidable pieces of clumsiness which increase the general vagueness. Professor Hogben (2) plays ducks and drakes with a battery which is able to write prescriptions, and, while disapproving of the everyday phrase *put up with,* is unwilling to look *egregious* up in the dictionary and see what it means. (3), if one takes an uncharitable attitude towards it, is simply meaningless: probably one could work out its intended meaning by reading the whole of the article in which it occurs. In (4), the writer knows more or less what he wants to say, but an accumulation of stale phrases chokes him like tea leaves blocking a sink. In (5), words and meaning have almost parted company. People who write in this manner usually have a general emotional meaning—they dislike one thing and want to express solidarity with another—but they are not interested in the detail of what they are saying. A scrupulous writer, in every sentence that he writes, will ask himself at least four questions, thus: What am I trying to say? What words will express it? What image or idiom will make it clearer? Is this image fresh enough to have an effect? And he will probably ask himself two more: Could I put it more shortly? Have I said anything that is avoidably ugly? But you are not obliged to go to all this trouble. You can shirk it by simply throwing your mind open and letting the ready-made phrases come crowding in. They will construct your sentences for you—even think your thoughts for you, to a certain extent—and at need they will perform the important service of partially concealing your meaning even from yourself. It is at this point that the special connection between politics and the debasement of language becomes clear.

In our time it is broadly true that political writing is bad writing. Where it is not true, it will generally be found that the writer is some kind of rebel, expressing his private opinions and not a "party line."

Orthodoxy, of whatever colour, seems to demand a lifeless, imitative style. The political dialects to be found in pamphlets, leading articles, manifestos, White Papers and the speeches of under-secretaries do, of course, vary from party to party, but they are all alike in that one almost never finds in them a fresh, vivid, home-made turn of speech. When one watches some tired hack on the platform mechanically repeating the familiar phrases—*bestial atrocities, iron heel, bloodstained tyranny, free peoples of the world, stand shoulder to shoulder*—one often has a curious feeling that one is not watching a live human being but some kind of dummy: a feeling which suddenly becomes stronger at moments when the light catches the speaker's spectacles and turns them into blank discs which seem to have no eyes behind them. And this is not altogether fanciful. A speaker who uses that kind of phraseology has gone some distance towards turning himself into a machine. The appropriate noises are coming out of his larynx, but his brain is not involved as it would be if he were choosing his words for himself. If the speech he is making is one that he is accustomed to make over and over again, he may be almost unconscious of what he is saying, as one is when one utters the responses in church. And this reduced state of consciousness, if not indispensable, is at any rate favorable to political conformity.

In our time, political speech and writing are largely the defence of the indefensible. Things like the continuance of British rule in India, the Russian purges and deportations, the dropping of the atom bombs on Japan, can indeed be defended, but only by arguments which are too brutal for most people to face, and which do not square with the professed aims of political parties. Thus political language has to consist largely of euphemism, question-begging and sheer cloudy vagueness. Defenceless villages are bombarded from the air, the inhabitants driven out into the countryside, the cattle machine-gunned, the huts set on fire with incendiary bullets: this is called *pacification*. Millions of peasants are robbed of their farms and sent trudging along the roads with no more than they can carry: this is called *transfer of population* or *rectification of frontiers*. People are imprisoned for years without trial, or shot in the back of the neck or sent to die of scurvy in Arctic lumber camps: this is called *elimination of unreliable elements*. Such phraseology is needed if one wants to name things without calling up mental pictures of them. Consider for instance some comfortable English professor defending Russian totalitarianism. He cannot say outright, "I believe in killing off your opponents when you can get good results by doing so." Probably, therefore, he will say something like this:

"While freely conceding that the Soviet régime exhibits certain features which the humanitarian may be inclined to deplore, we must, I think, agree that a certain curtailment of the right to political opposition is an unavoidable concomitant of transitional periods, and that the rigors which the Russian people have been called upon to undergo have been amply justified in the sphere of concrete achievement."

The inflated style is itself a kind of euphemism. A mass of Latin words falls upon the facts like soft snow, blurring the outlines and covering up all the details. The great enemy of clear language is insincerity. When there is a gap between one's real and one's declared aims, one turns as it were instinctively to long words and exhausted idioms, like a cuttlefish squirting out ink. In our age there is no such thing as "keeping out of politics." All issues are political issues, and politics itself is a mass of lies, evasions, folly, hatred and schizophrenia. When the general atmosphere is bad, language must suffer. I should expect to find—this is a guess which I have not sufficient knowledge to verify—that the German, Russian and Italian languages have all deteriorated in the last ten to fifteen years, as a result of dictatorship.

But if thought corrupts language, language can also corrupt thought. A bad usage can spread by tradition and imitation, even among people who should and do know better. The debased language that I have been discussing is in some ways very convenient. Phrases like *a not unjustifiable assumption, leaves much to be desired, would serve no good purpose, a consideration which we should do well to bear in mind,* are a continuous temptation, a packet of aspirins always at one's elbow. Look back through this essay, and for certain you will find that I have again and again committed the very faults I am protesting against. By this morning's post I have received a pamphlet dealing with conditions in Germany. The author tells me that he "felt impelled" to write it. I open it at random, and here is almost the first sentence that I see: "(The Allies) have an opportunity not only of achieving a radical transformation of Germany's social and political structure in such a way as to avoid a nationalistic reaction in Germany itself, but at the same time of laying the foundations of a cooperative and unified Europe." You see, he "feels impelled" to write—feels, presumably, that he has something new to say—and yet his words, like cavalry horses answering the bugle, group themselves automatically into the familiar dreary pattern. This invasion of one's mind by ready-made phrases (*lay the foundations, achieve a radical transformation*) can only be prevented if one is constantly on guard against them, and every such phrase anaesthetizes a portion of one's brain.

I said earlier that the decadence of our language is probably curable. Those who deny this would argue, if they produced an argument at all, that language merely reflects existing social conditions, and that we cannot influence its development by any direct tinkering with words and constructions. So far as the general tone or spirit of a language goes, this may be true, but it is not true in detail. Silly words and expressions have often disappeared, not through any evolutionary process but owing to the conscious action of a minority. Two recent examples were *explore every avenue* and *leave no stone unturned,* which were killed by the jeers of a few journalists. There is a long list of fly-blown metaphors which could similarly be got rid of if enough people would interest themselves in the job; and it should also be possible to laugh the *not un-* formation out of existence, to reduce the amount of Latin and Greek in the average sentence, to drive out foreign phrases and strayed scientific words, and, in general, to make pretentiousness unfashionable. But all these are minor points. The defence of the English language implies more than this, and perhaps it is best to start by saying what it does not imply.

To begin with it has nothing to do with archaism, with the salvaging of obsolete words and turns of speech, or with the setting up of a "standard English" which must never be departed from. On the contrary, it is especially concerned with the scrapping of every word or idiom which has outworn its usefulness. It has nothing to do with correct grammar and syntax, which are of no importance so long as one makes one's meaning clear, or with the avoidance of Americanisms, or with having what is called a "good prose style." On the other hand it is not concerned with fake simplicity and the attempt to make written English colloquial. Nor does it even imply in every case preferring the Saxon word to the Latin one, though it does imply using the fewest and shortest words that will cover one's meaning. What is above all needed is to let the meaning choose the word, and not the other way about. In prose, the worst thing one can do with words is to surrender to them. When you think of a concrete object, you think wordlessly, and then, if you want to describe the thing you have been visualizing you probably hunt about till you find the exact words that seem to fit. When you think of something abstract you are more inclined to use words from the start, and unless you make a conscious effort to prevent it, the existing dialect will come rushing in and do the job for you, at the expense of blurring or even changing your meaning. Probably it is better to put off using words as long as possible and get one's meaning as clear as one can through pictures or sensations. Afterwards one can choose—not simply accept—the phrases that will best cover the meaning, and then switch round and decide what impression one's words are likely to make on another person. This last effort of the mind cuts out all stale or mixed images, all prefabricated phrases, needless repetitions, and humbug and vagueness generally. But one can often be in doubt about the effect of a word or a phrase, and one needs rules that one can rely on when instinct fails. I think the following rules will cover most cases: *

(i)   Never use a metaphor, simile or other figure of speech which you are used to seeing in print.
(ii) Never use a long word where a short one will do.
(iii) If it is possible to cut a word out, always cut it out.
(iv) Never use the passive where you can use the active.
(v)   Never use a foreign phrase, a scientific word or a jargon word if you can think of an everyday English equivalent.
(vi) Break any of these rules sooner than say anything outright barbarous.

20   These rules sound elementary, and so they are, but they demand   20 a deep change of attitude in anyone who has grown used to writing in the style now fashionable. One could keep all of them and still write bad English, but one could not write the kind of stuff that I quoted in those five specimens at the beginning of this article.

I have not here been considering the literary use of language, but merely language as an instrument for expressing and not for concealing or preventing thought. Stuart Chase and others have come near to claiming that all abstract words are meaningless, and have used this as a pretext for advocating a kind of political quietism. Since you don't know what Fascism is, how can you struggle against Fascism? One need not swallow such absurdities as this, but one ought to recognize that the present political chaos is connected with the decay of language, and that one can probably bring about some improvement by starting at the verbal end. If you simplify your English, you are freed from the worst follies of orthodoxy. You cannot speak any of the necessary dialects, and when you make a stupid remark its stupidity will be obvious, even to yourself. Political language—and with variations this is true of all political parties, from Conservatives to Anarchists—is designed to make lies sound truthful and murder respectable, and to give an appearance of solidity to pure wind. One cannot change this all in a moment, but one can at least change one's own habits, and from time to time one can even, if one jeers loudly enough, send some worn-out and useless phrase—some *jackboot, Achilles' heel, hotbed, melting pot, acid test, veritable inferno* or other lump of verbal refuse—into the dustbin where it belongs.

Questions on Meaning

1. Do you think the state of the English language has changed in the five decades since Orwell wrote this essay? When you compare Orwell's examples of poor use of English to what you see yourself in your reading, what if anything seems to have changed, and how?
2. If foolish thoughts result in imprecise use of language, and imprecise use of language results in foolish thoughts, which comes first? That is, does one problem most often cause the other?
3. Why, according to Orwell, is it important that language should be used in a way that is not only clear and precise and fresh but also not ugly or "barbarous"?

Questions on Rhetorical Strategy and Style

1. Cite several of Orwell's examples of bad political speech. How do these examples clarify his contention that political speech represents some of the worst English usage of his time?
2. Orwell condemns stale or "dying" metaphors that no longer conjure up a fresh image to help make the writer's point clearer or more vivid. Orwell himself uses metaphors frequently, such as this statement about one of his examples of poor writing: "an accumulation of stale phrases chokes him like tea leaves blocking a sink." Analyze the effectiveness of Orwell's metaphor here.

Writing Assignments

1. In his discussion of meaningless words, Orwell describes the problem of the word "freedom," which he says has different meanings for different people. Do you agree? Ask five or six people to explain in as much detail as possible what they mean by a "free country." Do this before you consult a dictionary definition. Then write an essay in which you attempt to define freedom as both term and concept, analyzing whatever variations in meaning you discovered from talking with others.
2. Read the letters to the editor on the opinion or editorial pages of your local newspaper, looking for phrases that manifest the kind of weak writing Orwell is discussing. Compare the style of letters and editorials on controversial and political topics to the style in letters and editorials on less emotional topics. Is there a noticeable

difference? Based on your analysis of this writing, comment on the extent to which Orwell's observations are or are not still relevant today.

3. In the library or on the Internet, find the text of a major speech by a recent American president, such as a campaign speech or State of the Union address. Analyze this speech in Orwellian terms: though many of the sentences and phrases will sound quite good, ask what is really, precisely, being said. Does the speaker intentionally avoid clarity? Why? Write an essay explaining your findings.

4. Think of five common aphorisms such as "We'll cross that bridge when we come to it" or "You can lead a horse to water but you can't make it drink." Then rewrite each, as Orwell did with the biblical passage, in an inflated bureaucratic style to make them sound grandly important. For example, "It has been immutably established that preventative measures taken during that period of time in which their effects are most efficacious are able to preclude later potentially necessary actions of a far more significant magnitude" ("A stitch in time saves nine.") Show your new sentences to others and ask them to tell you what they mean.

We Are Our Own Metaphor

Mary Catherine Bateson

Mary Catherine Bateson is the daughter of two of the world's most famous anthropologists, Gregory Bateson and Margaret Mead, author of Coming of Age in Samoa. *An eminent anthropologist herself, she is Clarence Robinson Professor of Anthropology and English at George Mason University in Fairfax, Virginia. In the article reprinted here, she combines her expertise in language and anthropology to analyze the metaphors by which humans represent the earth, demonstrating the subtle persuasive power that language exerts on our attitudes and thereby on our behavior.*

1   The Gaia hypothesis, developed by James Lovelock and Lynn Margulis, asserts that this planet is alive. This integrates a vast amount of information in a single image: What we are talking about is life. It wiggles. It may bite. The Gaian metaphor provides a bridge from high technical specificity to all the experiences that go with direct contact with a living being.

Above all, the Gaia hypothesis evokes the powerful ancient metaphor of Mother Earth. In the early seventies, there was a poster of the Earth as seen from space, the picture that has become so familiar and beloved, and underneath was written, "Your Mother—Love Her or Leave Her!" That was a brilliant but confusing poster, because every young American male knows what he is supposed to do with his mother: grow up and leave her. After all, his entire socialization is geared to achieving independence. The poster fed right into the fantasy that if we messed up this planet we could climb into space-ships and zoom to another one or perhaps to a space platform. That poster was an invitation to believe in the possibility of leaving, in the self as separate and separable.

Since the early years of the space program, the fantasy of solving environmental problems by leaving this planet behind has faded, as has the metaphor of Earth as a spaceship, but we still may not have found the metaphor that leads to effective attention. A metaphor can obscure as well as reveal. In contemporary culture, I doubt that the best way to elicit caring and responsible behavior from adults is to re-mind them of childhood, the retrospective dumping ground of prob-lems and resentments. I may feel that having the Earth thought of as female enhances me or allows me to empathize a little more deeply, but I hate to expose the planet further to the danger of rape or evoke the ambivalence that people feel about mothers.

The use of a personal name, Gaia, suggests that the planet can evoke the attitudes we reserve for identified human individuals. Do we love Gaia? Does she love or trust in return? What does it add to understanding or confusion that Gaia is the name of a deity from an ancient and polytheistic system no longer widely worshiped, the most primitive layer of Greek religion? The original Gaia was inclined to devour her own offspring, many of whom were monsters.

Perhaps we could empathize more if the metaphor were differ-ently conceived. Because the life span of a planet is potentially so long, we might learn to think of the planet as a young child that requires care and attention but has an unknown future. Such a metaphor would underline the need to protect future possibilities, not only for our human descendants but for all life on Earth, and might make ac-cepting the limitations on knowledge and control less painful.

When we use a metaphor that is drawn from human relations, it is well to look carefully for all its hidden implications, for we run the risk of evoking human conflicts. If we are going to think of the Earth as female, it behooves us to take a good look at gender relations, be-cause gender relations of dominance and exploitation will infect, have already infected, the relationship with the planet. Images of children often do evoke protectiveness and caring, yet we have been willing to incur massive debts our children will have to pay, and all too many parents exploit or abuse children and even more feel they have a right to determine a child's future. If we are going to use family images, let us take some responsibility for constructing human families that offer metaphors of mutuality and hope.

To me, the most important thing that the Gaia hypothesis proposes that was absent from earlier metaphors like "spaceship Earth" is that we are immersed in, brought into being by, a living reality, not a mechanical one. We are completely dependent, as we would be in a spaceship, but we do not have full blueprints and we cannot expect to be in complete control.

The Gaia hypothesis demands that we are totally contained in and sustained by a single living system, in which all the parts are interconnected and everything we do resonates with the whole. Nothing is fully localized. The destruction of an ecosystem or a species is an amputation and, like the amputation of a limb, can trigger fatal shock or, at the least, require learning new ways to function. One extraneous item introduced in the wrong place in a living body can trigger pathology. The Gaia hypothesis becomes, at every level of its metaphorical evocation, a reminder that the world we live in is a biological, or if you like a biologized world, a sacred process in which we share, a community to participate in, not an object to be used.

The Gaia hypothesis pulls the data together, but it goes further by offering a metaphor for organizing awareness of the interconnections. It proposes empathy as a way of knowing and imaging connections about which we cannot yet be explicit. It cannot, however, guarantee love or respect any more than centuries of religion and philosophy have been able to end the exploitation by human beings of one another. We continue to be unable to provide adequate care either for the old, our parents, or for the young, our children, to whom we will entrust the future, so it is no wonder we mistake the planet that represents both source and destiny for a shopping mall. What would it be like to walk through the woods or the city in the presence of—aware of—Gaia? Part of that awareness can be built up by letting children look through microscopes, germinate seeds, learn about soil chemistry, but part of it comes into being through the experiences of loving and being loved, resolving quarrels, learning new ways of family life, attending patiently to things we do not understand.

10   All thought relies on metaphor, on ways of noticing similarity so   10 that what has been learned in one situation can be transferred to another. Scientists try to purge metaphor and intuition from their pub-

lications, but the speech of scientists is like all human speech and thought, full of metaphors, often unconscious and unexamined.

The solution is not to purge metaphors from speech; the solution is to take responsibility for the choice of metaphors, to savor them and ponder their suggestions, above all to live with many and take no one metaphor as absolute. There are truths to be discovered in equating one's mother with a toad; there are truths to be discovered in looking at a butchered sheep and recognizing heart and lungs and death itself as common.

Not long ago, in 1988, a group of parents in Tennessee brought a lawsuit protesting that their children were being taught the religion of "secular humanism" in the schools, and objecting to the use of fantasy and mythology in education. A picture from a reading primer that showed a little boy and a little girl sitting at a kitchen table, with the little boy putting a piece of bread into a toaster, was cited as undermining traditional concepts of the family. This may seem extreme, yet these parents were right in their understanding of how people think and learn. Not only does such a picture undermine traditional concepts of the family but it undermines traditional concepts of God, for male dominance over females has long provided a model for the relationship between God and humankind. They would also be right to resist the metaphor of the dryad, along with any other suggestion of sacred presence immanent in the natural world, as undermining the idea of God as transcendent, ruling from outside and above.

Family systems, the organization of institutions, the way we run our country, the way we respond to other cultures and races, and the uses of political and military power—all these things are based on interlocking sets of metaphors. Our many relationships are isomorphic: they have the same form. There is a pattern that connects, and it is a pattern of dominance and exploitation, taught again and again in the most ordinary human arrangements. That pattern is expressed in the fierce and ultimately self-destructive attack on this planet that we cannot rule because we are a part of it.

In effect, because knowledge and perception are so dependent on available models, they cannot be changed without a commitment to changing basic patterns of social life. This is the most significant sense in which we are our own metaphor.

Questions on Meaning

1. Explain the title of this article.
2. What is the Gaia hypothesis? What is the spaceship metaphor?

Questions on Rhetorical Strategy and Style

1. The strategy of comparison is used in an intricate way in this essay. In fact, the comparisons between the earth and other entities are themselves compared with one another. List the main comparisons that illustrate the article, and explain the points Bateson makes through the comparisons.
2. To define something is to place it in a class and then to distinguish it from other members of its class. If the earth is defined as a ship, what distinguishes it from other members of the class "ship." If the earth is defined as a person, what distinguishes it from other members of the class "person."

Writing Assignments

1. Among your friends and acquaintances, who do you think would be most likely to agree with this writer's point of view? Explain why. If you have access to the person, ask him or her to read the article and give you an opinion. Report the results.
2. Write an essay in which you explore the ways that planet Earth is like a person, a ship, an animal, or a goddess.

Two Kinds

Amy Tan

Amy Tan was born in Oakland, California in 1952, several years after her mother and father immigrated from China. She was raised in various cities in the San Francisco Bay Area. When she was eight, her essay, "What the Library Means to Me," won first prize among elementary school participants, for which Tan received a transistor radio and publication in the local newspaper. Upon the deaths of her brother and father in 1967 and 1968 from brain tumors, the family began a haphazard journey through Europe, before settling in Montreux, Switerland, where Tan graduated in her junior year in 1969.

For the next seven years, Tan attended five schools. She first went to Linfield College in McMinnville, Oregon, and there, on a blind date, met her future husband, Lou DeMattei. She followed him to San Jose, where she enrolled in San Jose City College. She next attended San Jose State University, and, while working two part-time jobs, she became an English honor's students and a President's Scholar, while carrying a semester course load of 21 units. In 1972 she graduated with honors, receiving a B.A. with a double major in English and Linguistics. She was awarded a scholarship to attend the Summer Linguistics Institute at the University of California, Santa Cruz. In 1973, she earned her M.A. in Linguistics, also from San Jose State University, and was then awarded a Graduate Minority Fellowship under the affirmative action program at the University of California, Berkeley, where she enrolled as a doctoral student in linguistics.

My mother believed you could be anything you wanted to be in America. You could open a restaurant. You could work for the government and get good retirement. You could buy a house with almost no money down. You could become rich. You could become instantly famous.

"Of course you can be prodigy, too," my mother told me when I was nine. "You can be best anything. What does Auntie Lindo know? Her daughter, she is only best tricky."

America was where all my mother's hopes lay. She had come here in 1949 after losing everything in China: her mother and father, her family home, her first husband, and two daughters, twin baby girls. But she never looked back with regret. There were so many ways for things to get better.

We didn't immediately pick the right kind of prodigy. At first my mother thought I could be a Chinese Shirley Temple. We'd watch Shirley's old movies on TV as though they were training films. My mother would poke my arm and say, *"Ni kan"*—You watch. And I would see Shirley tapping her feet, or singing a sailor song, or pursing her lips into a very round O while saying, "Oh my goodness."

"Ni kan," said my mother as Shirley's eyes flooded with tears. "You already know how. Don't need talent for crying!"

Soon after my mother got this idea about Shirley Temple, she took me to a beauty training school in the Mission district and put me in the hands of a student who could barely hold the scissors without shaking. Instead of getting big fat curls, I emerged with an uneven mass of crinkly black fuzz. My mother dragged me off to the bathroom and tried to wet down my hair.

"You look like Negro Chinese," she lamented, as if I had done this on purpose.

The instructor of the beauty training school had to lop off these soggy clumps to make my hair even again. "Peter Pan is very popular these days," the instructor assured my mother. I now had hair the length of a boy's, with straight-across bangs that hung at a slant two inches above my eyebrows. I liked the haircut and it made me actually look forward to my future fame.

In fact, in the beginning, I was just as excited as my mother, maybe even more so. I pictured this prodigy part of me as many different images, trying each one on for size. I was a dainty ballerina girl standing by the curtains, waiting to hear the right music that would send me floating on my tiptoes. I was like the Christ child lifted out of the straw manger, crying with holy indignity. I was Cinderella stepping from her pumpkin carriage with sparkly cartoon music filling the air.

10   In all of my imagingings, I was filled with a sense that I would   10
soon become *perfect*. My mother and father would adore me. I would be beyond reproach. I would never feel the need to sulk for anything.

But sometimes the prodigy in me became impatient. "If you don't hurry up and get me out of here, I'm disappearing for good," it warned. "And then you'll always be nothing."

Every night after dinner, my mother and I would sit at the Formica kitchen table. She would present new tests, taking her examples from stories of amazing children she had read in *Ripley's Believe It or Not,* or *Good Housekeeping, Reader's Digest,* and a dozen other magazines she kept in a pile in our bathroom. My mother got these magazines from people whose houses she cleaned. And since she cleaned many houses each week, we had a great assortment. She would look through them all, searching for stories about remarkable children.

The first night she brought out a story about a three-year-old boy who knew the capitals of all the states and even most of the European countries. A teacher was quoted as saying the little boy could also pronounce the names of the foreign cities correctly.

"What's the capital of Finland?" my mother asked me, looking at the magazine story.

15   All I knew was the capital of California, because Sacramento was   15
the name of the street we lived on in Chinatown. "Nairobi!" I guessed, saying the most foreign word I could think of. She checked to see if that was possibly one way to pronounce "Helsinki" before showing me the answer.

The tests got harder—multiplying numbers in my head, finding the queen of hearts in a deck of cards, trying to stand on my head without using my hands, predicting the daily temperatures in Los Angeles, New York, and London.

One night I had to look at a page from the Bible for three minutes and then report everything I could remember. "Now Jehoshaphat had riches and honor in abundance and . . . that's all I remember, Ma," I said.

And after seeing my mother's disappointed face once again, something inside of me began to die. I hated the tests, the raised hopes and failed expectations. Before going to bed that night, I looked in the mirror above the bathroom sink and when I saw only my face staring back—and that it would always be this ordinary face—I began to cry. Such a sad, ugly girl! I made high-pitched noises like a crazed animal, trying to scratch out the face in the mirror.

And then I saw what seemed to be the prodigy side of me—because I had never seen that face before. I looked at my reflection, blinking so I could see more clearly. The girl staring back at me was angry, powerful. This girl and I were the same. I had new thoughts, willful thoughts, or rather thoughts filled with lots of won'ts. I won't let her change me, I promised myself. I won't be what I'm not.

20   So now on nights when my mother presented her tests, I performed listlessly, my head propped on one arm. I pretended to be bored. And I was. I got so bored I started counting the bellows of the foghorns out on the bay while my mother drilled me in other areas. The sound was comforting and reminded me of the cow jumping over the moon. And the next day, I played a game with myself, seeing if my mother would give up on me before eight bellows. After a while I usually counted only one, maybe two bellows at most. At last she was beginning to give up hope.   20

Two or three months had gone by without any mention of my being a prodigy again. And then one day my mother was watching "The Ed Sullivan Show" on TV. The TV was old and the sound kept shorting out. Every time my mother got halfway up from the sofa to adjust the set, the sound would go back on and Ed would be talking. As soon as she sat down, Ed would go silent again. She got up, the TV broke into loud piano music. She sat down. Silence. Up and down, back and forth, quiet and loud. It was like a stiff embraceless dance between her and the TV set. Finally she stood by the set with her hand on the sound dial.

She seemed entranced by the music, a little frenzied piano piece with this mesmerizing quality, sort of quick passages and then teasing lilting ones before it returned to the quick playful parts.

"*Ni kan,*" my mother said, calling me over with hurried hand gestures. "Look here."

I could see why my mother was fascinated by the music. It was being pounded out by a little Chinese girl, about nine years old, with a Peter Pan haircut. The girl had the sauciness of a Shirley Temple. She was proudly modest like a proper Chinese child. And she also did this fancy sweep of a curtsy, so that the fluffy skirt of her white dress cascaded slowly to the floor like the petals of a large carnation.

25   In spite of these warning signs, I wasn't worried. Our family had   25
no piano and we couldn't afford to buy one, let alone reams of sheet
music and piano lessons. So I could be generous in my comments
when my mother bad-mouthed the little girl on TV.

"Play note right, but doesn't sound good! No singing sound,"
complained my mother.

"What are you picking on her for?" I said carelessly. "She's pretty
good. Maybe she's not the best, but she's trying hard." I knew almost
immediately I would be sorry I said that.

"Just like you," she said. "Not the best. Because you not trying."
She gave a little huff as she let go of the sound dial and sat down on
the sofa.

The little Chinese girl sat down also to play an encore of "Anitra's
Dance" by Grieg. I remember the song because later on I had to learn
how to play it.

30   Three days after watching "The Ed Sullivan Show," my mother   30
told me what my schedule would be for piano lessons and piano practice. She had talked to Mr. Chong, who lived on the first floor of our
apartment building. Mr. Chong was a retired piano teacher and my
mother had traded housecleaning services for weekly lessons and a
piano for me to practice on every day, two hours a day, from four
until six.

When my mother told me this, I felt as though I had been sent
to hell. I whined and then kicked my foot a little when I couldn't stand
it anymore.

"Why don't you like me the way I am? I'm *not* a genius! I can't
play the piano. And even if I could, I wouldn't go on TV if you paid
me a million dollars!" I cried.

My mother slapped me. "Who ask you be genius?" she shouted.
"Only ask you be your best. For you sake. You think I want you be
genius? Hnnh! What for! Who ask you!"

"So ungrateful," I heard her mutter in Chinese. "If she had as
much talent as she has temper, she would be famous now."

35   Mr. Chong, whom I secretly nicknamed Old Chong, was very   35
strange, always tapping his fingers to the silent music of an invisible
orchestra. He looked ancient in my eyes. He had lost most of the hair
on top of his head and he wore thick glasses and had eyes that always
looked tired and sleepy. But he must have been younger than I
thought, since he lived with his mother and was not yet married.

I met Old Lady Chong once and that was enough. She had this peculiar smell like a baby that had done something in its pants. And her fingers felt like a dead person's, like an old peach I once found in the back of the refrigerator; the skin just slid off the meat when I picked it up.

I soon found out why Old Chong had retired from teaching piano. He was deaf. "Like Beethoven!" he shouted to me. "We're both listening only in our head!" And he would start to conduct his frantic silent sonatas.

Our lessons went like this. He would open the book and point to different things, explaining their purpose: "Key! Treble! Bass! No sharps or flats! So this is C major! Listen now and play after me!"

And then he would play the C scale a few times, a simple chord, and then, as if inspired by an old, unreachable itch, he gradually added more notes and running trills and a pounding bass until the music was really something quite grand.

I would play after him, the simple scale, the simple chord and then I just played some nonsense that sounded like a cat running up and down on top of garbage cans. Old Chong smiled and applauded and then said, "Very good! But now you must learn to keep time!"

So that's how I discovered that Old Chong's eyes were too slow to keep up with the wrong notes I was playing. He went through the motions in half-time. To help me keep rhythm, he stood behind me, pushing down on my right shoulder for every beat. He balanced pennies on top of my wrists so I would keep them still as I slowly played scales and arpeggios. He had me curve my hand around an apple and keep that shape when playing chords. He marched stiffly to show me how to make each finger dance up and down, staccato like an obedient little soldier.

He taught me all these things, and that was how I also learned I could be lazy and get away with mistakes, lots of mistakes. If I hit the wrong notes because I hadn't practiced enough, I never corrected myself. I just kept playing in rhythm. And Old Chong kept conducting his own private reverie.

So maybe I never really gave myself a fair chance. I did pick up the basics pretty quickly, and I might have become a good pianist at that young age. But I was so determined not to try, not to be anybody different that I learned to play only the most ear-splitting preludes, the most discordant hymns.

Over the next year, I practiced like this, dutifully in my own way. And then one day I heard my mother and her friend Lindo Jong both talking in a loud bragging tone of voice so others could hear. It was after church, and I was leaning against the brick wall wearing a dress with stiff white petticoats. Auntie Lindo's daughter, Waverly, who was about my age, was standing farther down the wall about five feet away. We had grown up together and shared all the closeness of two sisters squabbling over crayons and dolls. In other words, for the most part, we hated each other. I thought she was snotty. Waverly Jong had gained a certain amount of fame as "Chinatown's Littlest Chinese Chess Champion."

45   "She bring home too many trophy," lamented Auntie Lindo that 45 Sunday. "All day she play chess. All day I have no time do nothing but dust off her winnings." She threw a scolding look at Waverly, who pretended not to see her.

"You lucky you don't have this problem," said Auntie Lindo with a sigh to my mother.

And my mother squared her shoulders and bragged: "Our problem worser than yours. If we ask Jing-mei wash dish, she hear nothing but music. It's like you can't stop this natural talent."

And right then, I was determined to put a stop to her foolish pride.

A few weeks later, Old Chong and my mother conspired to have me play in a talent show which would be held in the church hall. By then, my parents had saved up enough to buy me a secondhand piano, a black Wurlitzer spinet with a scarred bench. It was the showpiece of our living room.

50   For the talent show, I was to play a piece called "Pleading Child" from 50 Schumann's *Scenes from Childhood*. It was a simple, moody piece that sounded more difficult than it was. I was supposed to memorize the whole thing, playing the repeat parts twice to make the piece sound longer. But I dawdled over it, playing a few bars and then cheating, looking up to see what notes followed, I never really listened to what I was playing. I daydreamed about being somewhere else, about being someone else.

The part I liked to practice best was the fancy curtsy: right foot out, touch the rose on the carpet with a pointed foot, sweep to the side, left leg bends, look up and smile.

My parents invited all the couples from the Joy Luck Club to witness my debut. Auntie Lindo and Uncle Tin were there. Waverly and her two older brothers had also come. The first two rows were filled with children both younger and older than I was. The littlest ones got to go first. They recited simple nursery rhymes, squawked out tunes on miniature violins, twirled Hula Hoops, pranced in pink ballet tutus, and when they bowed or curtsied, the audience would sigh in unison, "Awww," and then clap enthusiastically.

When my turn came, I was very confident. I remember my childish excitement. It was as if I knew, without a doubt, that the prodigy side of me really did exist. I had no fear whatsoever, no nervousness. I remember thinking to myself, This is it! I looked out over the audience, at my mother's blank face, my father's yawn, Auntie Lindo's stiff-lipped smile, Waverly's sulky expression. I had on a white dress layered with sheets of lace, and a pink bow in my Peter Pan haircut. As I sat down I envisioned people jumping to their feet and Ed Sullivan rushing up to introduce me to everyone on TV.

And I started to play. It was so beautiful. I was so caught up in how lovely I looked that at first I didn't worry how I would sound: So it was a surprise to me when I hit the first wrong note and I realized something didn't sound quite right. And then I hit another and another followed that. A chill started at the top of my head and began to trickle down. Yet I couldn't stop playing, as though my hands were bewitched. I kept thinking my fingers would adjust themselves back, like a train switching to the right track. I played this strange jumble through two repeats, the sour notes staying with me all the way to the end.

55 When I stood up, I discovered my legs were shaking. Maybe I had 55 just been nervous and the audience, like Old Chong, had seen me go through the right motions and had not heard anything wrong at all. I swept my right foot out, went down on my knee, looked up and smiled. The room was quiet, except for Old Chong, who was beaming and shouting, "Bravo! Bravo! Well done!" But then I saw my mother's face, her stricken face. The audience clapped weakly, and as I walked back to my chair, with my whole face quivering as I tried not to cry, I heard a little boy whisper loudly to his mother, "That was awful," and the mother whispered back, "Well, she certainly tried."

And now I realized how many people were in the audience, the whole world it seemed. I was aware of eyes burning into my back. I felt the shame of my mother and father as they sat stiffly throughout the rest of the show.

We could have escaped during intermission. Pride and some strange sense of honor must have anchored my parents to their chairs.

201

And so we watched it all: the eighteen-year-old boy with a fake mustache who did a magic show and juggled flaming hoops while riding a unicycle. The breasted girl with white makeup who sang from *Madama Butterfly* and got honorable mention. And the eleven-year-old boy who won first prize playing a tricky violin song that sounded like a busy bee.

After the show, the Hsus, the Jongs, and the St. Clairs from the Joy Luck Club came up to my mother and father.

"Lots of talented kids," Auntie Lindo said vaguely, smiling broadly.

60 "That was somethin' else," said my father, and I wondered if he was referring to me in a humorous way, or whether he even remembered what I had done.

Waverly looked at me and shrugged her shoulders. "You aren't a genius like me," she said matter-of-factly. And if I hadn't felt so bad, I would have pulled her braids and punched her stomach.

But my mother's expression was what devastated me: a quiet, blank look that said she had lost everything. I felt the same way, and it seemed as if everybody were now coming up, like gawkers at the scene of an accident, to see what parts were actually missing. When we got on the bus to go home, my father was humming the busy-bee tune and my mother was silent. I kept thinking she wanted to wait until we got home before shouting at me. But when my father unlocked the door to our apartment, my mother walked in and then went to the back, into the bedroom. No accusations. No blame. And in a way, I felt disappointed. I had been waiting for her to start shouting, so I could shout back and cry and blame her for all my misery.

I assumed my talent-show fiasco meant I never had to play the piano again. But two days later, after school, my mother came out of the kitchen and saw me watching TV.

"Four clock," she reminded me as if it were any other day. I was stunned, as though she were asking me to go through the talent-show torture again. I wedged myself more tightly in front of the TV.

65 "Turn off TV," she called from the kitchen five minutes later.

I didn't budge. And then I decided. I didn't have to do what my mother said anymore. I wasn't her slave. This wasn't China. I had listened to her before and look what happened. She was the stupid one.

She came out from the kitchen and stood in the arched entryway of the living room. "Four clock," she said once again, louder.

202

"I'm not going to play anymore," I said nonchalantly. "Why should I? I'm not a genius."

She walked over and stood in front of the TV. I saw her chest was heaving up and down in an angry way.

"No!" I said, and I now felt stronger, as if my true self had finally emerged. So this was what had been inside me all along.

"No! I won't!" I screamed.

She yanked me by the arm, pulled me off the floor, snapped off the TV. She was frighteningly strong, half pulling, half carrying me toward the piano as I kicked the throw rugs under my feet. She lifted me up and onto the hard bench. I was sobbing by now, looking at her bitterly. Her chest was heaving even more and her mouth was open, smiling crazily as if she were pleased I was crying.

"You want me to be someone that I'm not!" I sobbed. "I'll never be the kind of daughter you want me to be!"

"Only two kinds of daughters," she shouted in Chinese. "Those who are obedient and those who follow their own mind! Only one kind of daughter can live in this house. Obedient daughter!"

"Then I wish I wasn't your daughter. I wish you weren't my mother," I shouted. As I said these things I got scared. I felt like worms and toads and slimy things were crawling out of my chest, but it also felt good, as if this awful side of me had surfaced, at last.

"Too late change this," said my mother shrilly.

And I could sense her anger rising to its breaking point. I wanted to see it spill over. And that's when I remembered the babies she had lost in China, the ones we never talked about. "Then I wish I'd never been born!" I shouted. "I wish I were dead! Like them."

It was as if I had said the magic words. Alakazam!—and her face went blank, her mouth closed, her arms went slack, and she backed out of the room, stunned, as if she were blowing away like a small brown leaf, thin, brittle, lifeless.

It was not the only disappointment my mother felt in me. In the years that followed, I failed her so many times, each time asserting my own will, my right to fall short of expectations. I didn't get straight A's. I didn't become class president. I didn't get into Stanford. I dropped out of college.

For unlike my mother, I did not believe I could be anything I wanted to be. I could only be me.

And for all those years, we never talked about the disaster at the recital or my terrible accusations afterward at the piano bench. All that remained unchecked, like a betrayal that was now unspeakable. So I never found a way to ask her why she had hoped for something so large that failure was inevitable.

And even worse, I never asked her what frightened me the most: Why had she given up hope?

For after our struggle at the piano, she never mentioned my playing again. The lessons stopped. The lid to the piano was closed, shutting out the dust, my misery, and her dreams.

So she surprised me. A few years ago, she offered to give me the piano, for my thirtieth birthday. I had not played in all those years. I saw the offer as a sign of forgiveness, a tremendous burden removed.

85 "Are you sure?" I asked shyly. "I mean, won't you and Dad miss it?"

'No, this your piano," she said firmly. "Always your piano. You only one can play."

"Well, I probably can't play anymore," I said. "It's been years."

"You pick up fast," said my mother, as if she knew this was certain. "You have natural talent. You could been genius if you want to."

"No I couldn't."

90 "You just not trying," said my mother. And she was neither angry nor sad. She said it as if to announce a fact that could never be disproved. "Take it," she said.

But I didn't at first. It was enough that she had offered it to me. And after that, every time I saw it in my parents' living room, standing in front of the bay windows, it made me feel proud, as if it were a shiny trophy I had won back.

Last week I sent a tuner over to my parents' apartment and had the piano reconditioned, for purely sentimental reasons. My mother had died a few months before and I had been getting things in order for my father, a little bit at a time. I put the jewelry in special silk pouches. The sweaters she had knitted in yellow, pink, bright orange—all the colors I hated—I put those in moth-proof boxes. I found some old Chinese silk dresses, the kind with little slits up the sides. I rubbed the old silk against my skin, then wrapped them in tissue and decided to take them home with me.

After I had the piano tuned, I opened the lid and touched the keys. It sounded even richer than I remembered. Really, it was a very good piano. Inside the bench were the same exercise notes with hand-written scales, the same secondhand music books with their covers held together with yellow tape.

I opened up the Schumann book to the dark little piece I had played at the recital. It was on the left-hand side of the page. "Pleading Child." It looked more difficult than I remembered. I played a few bars, surprised at how easily the notes came back to me.

95 And for the first time, or so it seemed, I noticed the piece on the 95 right-hand side. It was called "Perfectly Contented." I tried to play this one as well. It had a lighter melody but the same flowing rhythm and turned out to be quite easy. "Pleading Child" was shorter but slower; "Perfectly Contented" was longer but faster. And after I played them both a few times, I realized they were two halves of the same song.

[Handwritten annotations:]

Themes — parental/maternal pressure in individuals

plot: mother tries to make: daughter a prodigy

mother daughter relationship & coming into her own

: two kinds" – Chinese culture vs. U.S.

< traditional, close minded
  liberal, open minded

conflict

<pleading>
<contended>

Questions on Meaning

1. Why does the mother so fervently wish for her daughter to excel at something?
2. Explain the symbolic meaning of songs the narrator plays at the end of the story. What idea is suggested by the statement that "Pleading Child" and "Perfectly Contented" are two halves of the same song? Who is, or would be, perfectly contented?
3. What is the root of the disagreement between this mother and daughter? How much of it relates to cultural differences between a more traditional Chinese mother and a less traditional Chinese-American girl, and how much of it seems a universal conflict between two generations?

Questions on Rhetorical Strategy and Style

1. What does the mother mean by "prodigy"? When the daughter becomes rebellious and sees herself "angry, powerful" in the mirror, she thinks she sees "the prodigy side of me." Do they use this word to mean the same or different things? How does this word relate to a theme of the story?
2. Tan use techniques of comparison and contrast to characterize the mother and daughter. Make a list of 5 adjectives that describe the mother. Then write a list of their opposites. How many of these opposites are true of the daughter? In what specific areas of the story do we see them in sharp contrast?

Writing Assignments

1. Is being "willful" a negative characteristic in America? How does willfulness relate to the concept of the American Dream?
2. The daughter in this story feels pain because she cannot meet the high expectations of her mother. Many parents have high expectations for their children—is this always a bad thing, dooming their children to failure? Is it better to have no expectations at all and to accept any level of behavior in one's child? How should parents know where to draw a line between realistic and unrealistic expectations? Using your own upbringing as an example, write an essay in which you examine this issue from the parents' point of view.

3. The story begins with an echo of the American Dream: "you could be anything you wanted to be in America." Using that as a definition of the American Dream, write an essay in which you explore that concept. What are the origins of this dream? Why might the dream be more alive for immigrants than for those born in America? Is the American Dream still alive?

Public and Private Language

Richard Rodriguez

Richard Rodriguez (1944–) was born in San Francisco. A child of Mexican immigrants, Rodriguez spoke Spanish until he went to a Catholic school at age 6. As a youth, he delivered newspapers and worked as a gardener. Rodriguez received a B.A. from Stanford University, an M.A. from Columbia University, and a Ph.D. in English Renaissance literature from the University of California at Berkeley; he later attended the Warburg Institute in London on a Fulbright fellowship. A noted prose stylist, Rodriguez has worked as a teacher, journalist, and educational consultant, in addition to writing, lecturing, and appearing frequently on the Public Broadcast System (PBS) program, "The MacNeil-Lehrer News Hour." Rodriguez's books include Hunger of Memory: The Education of Richard Rodriguez *(1982), a collection of autobiographical essays;* Mexico's Children *(1990); and* Days of Obligation: An Argument With My Mexican Father *(1992), which was nominated for a National Book Award. In addition, he has been published in* The American Scholar, Change, College English, Harper's, Mother Jones, Reader's Digest, *and* Time. *A controversial writer, Rodriguez often speaks out against affirmative action and bilingual education. Rodriguez uses the concept of a "private language" of the family and a "public language" of the community in this essay to push his argument against bilingual education.*

1   I remember to start with that day in Sacramento—a California now   1
nearly thirty years past—when I first entered a classroom, able to
understand some fifty stray English words.

The third of four children, I had been preceded to a neighborhood
Roman Catholic school by an older brother and sister. But neither of
them had revealed very much about their classroom experiences. Each
afternoon they returned, as they left in the morning, always together,
speaking in Spanish as they climbed the five steps of the porch. And
their mysterious books, wrapped in shopping-bag paper, remained on
the table next to the door, closed firmly behind them.

An accident of geography sent me to a school where all my classmates were white, many the children of doctors and lawyers and business executives. All my classmates certainly must have been uneasy on
that first day of school—as most children are uneasy—to find themselves apart from their families in the first institution of their lives. But
I was astonished.

The nun said, in a friendly but oddly impersonal voice, "Boys and
girls, this is Richard Rodriguez." (I heard her sound out: *Rich-heard
Road-ree-guess.*) It was the first time I had heard anyone name me in
English. "Richard," the nun repeated more slowly, writing my name
down in her black leather book. Quickly I turned to see my mother's
face dissolve in a watery blur behind the pebbled glass door.

5   Many years later there is something called bilingual education—   5
a scheme proposed in the late 1960s by Hispanic-American social activists, later endorsed by a congressional vote. It is a program that seeks
to permit non-English-speaking children, many from lower-class
homes, to use their family language as the language of school. (Such
is the goal its supporters announce.) I hear them and am forced to say
no: It is not possible for a child—any child—ever to use his family's
language in school. Not to understand this is to misunderstand the
public uses of schooling and to trivialize the nature of intimate life—
a family's "language."

Memory teaches me what I know of these matters; the boy reminds the adult. I was a bilingual child, a certain kind—socially
disadvantaged—the son of working-class parents, both Mexican
immigrants.

In the early years of my boyhood, my parents coped very well in
America. My father had steady work. My mother managed at home.

They were nobody's victims. Optimism and ambition led them to a house (our home) many blocks from the Mexican south side of town. We lived among *gringos* and only a block from the biggest, whitest houses. It never occurred to my parents that they couldn't live wherever they chose. Nor was the Sacramento of the fifties bent on teaching them a contrary lesson. My mother and father were more annoyed than intimidated by those two or three neighbors who tried initially to make us unwelcome. ("Keep your brats away from my sidewalk!") But despite all they achieved, perhaps because they had so much to achieve, any deep feeling of ease, the confidence of "belonging" in public was withheld from them both. They regarded the people at work, the faces in crowds, as very distant from us. They were the others, *los gringos*. That term was interchangeable in their speech with another, even more telling, *los americanos*.

I grew up in a house where the only regular guests were my relations. For one day, enormous families of relatives would visit and there would be so many people that the noise and the bodies would spill out to the backyard and front porch. Then, for weeks, no one came by. (It was usually a salesman who rang the doorbell.) Our house stood apart. A gaudy yellow in a row of white bungalows. We were the people with the noisy dog. The people who raised pigeons and chickens. We were the foreigners on the block. A few neighbors smiled and waved. We waved back. But no one in the family knew the names of the old couple who lived next door; until I was seven years old, I did not know the names of the kids who lived across the street.

In public, my father and mother spoke a hesitant, accented, not always grammatical English. And they would have to strain—their bodies tense—to catch the sense of what was rapidly said by *los gringos*. At home they spoke Spanish. The language of their Mexican past sounded in counterpoint to the English of public society. The words would come quickly, with ease. Conveyed through those sounds was the pleasing, soothing, consoling reminder of being at home.

10 During those years when I was first conscious of hearing, my 10
mother and father addressed me only in Spanish; in Spanish I learned to reply. By contrast, English *(inglés)*, rarely heard in the house, was the language I came to associate with *gringos*. I learned my first words of English overhearing my parents speak to strangers. At five years age, I knew just enough English for my mother to trust me on errands to stores one block away. No more.

I was a listening child, careful to hear the very different sounds of Spanish and English. Wide-eyed with hearing, I'd listen to sounds more than words. First, there were English *(gringo)* sounds. So many words were still unknown that when the butcher or the lady at the drugstore said something to me, exotic polysyllabic sounds would bloom in the midst of their sentences. Often, the speech of people in public seemed to me very loud, booming with confidence. The man behind the counter would literally ask, "What can I do for you?" But by being so firm and so clear, the sound of his voice said that he was a *gringo;* he belonged in public society.

I would also hear then the high nasal notes of middle-class American speech. The air stirred with sound. Sometimes, even now, when I have been traveling abroad for several weeks, I will hear what I heard as a boy. In hotel lobbies or airports, in Turkey or Brazil, some Americans will pass, and suddenly I will hear it again—the high sound of American voices. For a few seconds I will hear it with pleasure, for it is now the sound of *my* society—a reminder of home. But inevitably— already on the flight headed for home—the sound fades with repetition. I will be unable to hear it anymore.

When I was a boy, things were different. The accent of *los gringos* was never pleasing nor was it hard to hear. Crowds at Safeway or at bus stops would be noisy with sound. And I would be forced to edge away from the chirping chatter above me.

I was unable to hear my own sounds, but I knew very well that I spoke English poorly. My words could not stretch far enough to form complete thoughts. And the words I did speak I didn't know well enough to make into distinct sounds. (Listeners would usually lower their heads, better to hear what I was trying to say.) But it was one thing for *me* to speak English with difficulty. It was more troubling for me to hear my parents speak in public: their high-whining vowels and guttural consonants; their sentences that got stuck with "ch" and "ah" sounds; the confused syntax; the hesitant rhythm of sounds so different from the way *gringos* spoke. I'd notice, moreover, that my parents' voices were softer than those of *gringos* we'd meet.

15   I am tempted now to say that none of this mattered. In adulthood   15
I am embarrassed by childhood fears. And, in a way, it didn't matter very much that my parents could not speak English with ease. Their linguistic difficulties had no serious consequences. My mother and father made themselves understood at the county hospital clinic and at

government offices. And yet, in another way, it mattered very much—it was unsettling to hear my parents struggle with English. Hearing them, I'd grow nervous, my clutching trust in their protection and power weakened.

There were many times like the night at a brightly lit gasoline station (a blaring white memory) when I stood uneasily, hearing my father. He was talking to a teenaged attendant. I do not recall what they were saying, but I cannot forget the sounds my father made as he spoke. At one point his words slid together to form one word—sounds as confused as the threads of blue and green oil in the puddle next to my shoes. His voice rushed through what he had left to say. And, toward the end, reached falsetto notes, appealing to his listener's understanding. I looked away to the lights of passing automobiles. I tried not to hear anymore. But I heard only too well the calm, easy tones in the attendant's reply. Shortly afterward, walking toward home with my father, I shivered when he put his hand on my shoulder. The very first chance that I got, I evaded his grasp and ran on ahead into the dark, skipping with feigned boyish exuberance.

But then there was Spanish. *Español:* my family's language. *Español:* the language that seemed to me a private language. I'd hear strangers on the radio and in the Mexican Catholic church across town speaking in Spanish, but I couldn't really believe that Spanish was a public language, like English. Spanish speakers, rather, seemed related to me, for I sensed that we shared—through our language—the experience of feeling apart from *los gringos*. It was thus a ghetto Spanish that I heard and I spoke. Like those whose lives are bound by a barrio, I was reminded by Spanish of my separateness from *los otros, los gringos* in power. But more intensely than for most barrio children—because I did not live in a barrio—Spanish seemed to me the language of home. (Most days it was only at home that I'd hear it.) It became the language of joyful return.

A family member would say something to me and I would feel myself specially recognized. My parents would say something to me and I would feel embraced by the sounds of their words. Those sounds said: *I am speaking with ease in Spanish. I am addressing you in words I never use with* los gringos. *I recognize you as someone special, close, like no one outside. You belong with us. In the family.*

(Ricardo.)

20   At the age of five, six, well past the time when most other children no longer easily notice the difference between sounds uttered at   20

home and words spoken in public, I had a different experience. I lived in a world magically compounded of sounds. I remained a child longer than most; I lingered too long, poised at the edge of language—often frightened by the sounds of *los gringos,* delighted by the sounds of Spanish at home. I shared with my family a language that was startlingly different from that used in the great city around us.

For me there were none of the gradations between public and private society so normal to a maturing child. Outside the house was public society; inside the house was private. Just opening or closing the screen door behind me was an important experience. I'd rarely leave home all alone or without reluctance. Walking down the sidewalk, under the canopy of tall trees, I'd warily notice the—suddenly—silent neighborhood kids who stood warily watching me. Nervously, I'd arrive at the grocery store to hear there the sounds of the *gringo*—foreign to me—reminding me that in this world so big, I was a foreigner. But then I'd return. Walking back toward our house, climbing the steps from the sidewalk, when the front door was open in summer, I'd hear voices beyond the screen door talking in Spanish. For a second or two, I'd stay, linger there, listening. Smiling, I'd hear my mother call out, saying in Spanish (words): "Is that you, Richard?" All the while her sounds would assure me: *You are home now; come closer; inside. With us.*

"Sí,' I'd reply.

Once more inside the house I would resume (assume) my place in the family. The sounds would dim, grow harder to hear. Once more at home, I would grow less aware of that fact. It required, however, no more than the blurt of the doorbell to alert me to listen to sounds all over again. The house would turn instantly still while my mother went to the door. I'd hear her hard English sounds. I'd wait to hear her voice return to soft-sounding Spanish, which assured me, as surely as did the clicking tongue of the lock on the door, that the stranger was gone.

Plainly, it is not healthy to hear such sounds so often. It is not healthy to distinguish public words from private sounds so easily. I remained cloistered by sounds, timid and shy in public, too dependent on voices at home. And yet it needs to be emphasized: I was an extremely happy child at home. I remember many nights when my father would come back from work, and I'd hear him call out to my mother in Spanish, sounding relieved. In Spanish, he'd sound light and free notes he never could manage in English. Some nights I'd jump up just at hearing his voice. With *mis hermanos* I would come running into the room where he was with my mother. Our laughing (so deep was the pleasure!) became screaming. Like others who know the pain of public alienation, we transformed the knowledge of our public separateness and made it consoling—the reminder of intimacy. *We are speaking now the way we never speak out in public. We are alone—together,* voices sounded, surrounded to tell me. Some nights, no one seemed willing to loosen the hold sounds had on us. At dinner, we invented new words. (Ours sounded Spanish, but made sense only to us.) We pieced together new words by taking, say, an English verb and giving it Spanish endings. My mother's instructions at bedtime would be lacquered with mock-urgent tones. Or a word like *sí* would become, in several notes, able to convey added measures of feeling. Tongues explored the edges of words, especially the fat vowels. And we happily sounded that military drum roll, the twirling roar of the Spanish *rr.* Family language: my family's sounds. The voices of my parents and sisters and brother. Their voices insisting: *You belong here. We are family members. Related. Special to one another. Listen!* Voices singing and sighing, rising, straining, then surging, teeming with pleasure that burst syllables into fragments of laughter. At times it seemed there was steady quiet only when, from another room, the rustling whispers of my parents faded and I moved closer to sleep.

25   Supporters of bilingual education today imply that students like me miss a great deal by not being taught in their family's language. What they seem not to recognize is that, as a socially disadvantaged child, I considered Spanish to be a private language. What I needed to learn in school was that I had the right—and the obligation—to speak the public language of *los gringos.* The odd truth is that my first-grade classmates could have become bilingual, in the conventional sense of that word, more easily than I. Had they been taught (as upper-middle-class children are often taught early) a second language like Spanish or French, they could have regarded it simply as that: another public language. In my case such bilingualism could not have been so quickly achieved. What I did not believe was that I could speak a single public language.

Without question, it would have pleased me to hear my teachers address me in Spanish when I entered the classroom. I would have felt much less afraid. I would have trusted them and responded with ease. But I would have delayed—for how long postponed?—having to learn the language of public society. I would have evaded—and for how long could I have afforded to delay?—learning the great lesson of school, that I had a public identity.

Fortunately, my teachers were unsentimental about their responsibility. What they understood was that I needed to speak a public language. So their voices would search me out, asking me questions. Each time I'd hear them, I'd look up in surprise to see a nun's face frowning at me. I'd mumble, not really meaning to answer. The nun would persist, "Richard, stand up. Don't look at the floor. Speak up. Speak to the entire class, not just to me!" But I couldn't believe that the English language was mine to use. (In part, I did not want to believe it.) I continued to mumble. I resisted the teacher's demands. (Did I somehow suspect that once I learned public language my pleasing family life would be changed?) Silent, waiting for the bell to sound, I remained dazed, diffident, afraid.

Because I wrongly imagined that English was intrinsically a public language and Spanish an intrinsically private one, I easily noted the difference between classroom language and the language of home. At school, words were directed to a general audience of listeners. ("Boys and girls.") Words were meaningfully ordered. And the point was not self-expression alone but to make oneself understood by many others. The teacher quizzed: "Boys and girls, why do we use that word in this sentence? Could we think of a better word to use there? Would the sentence change its meaning if the words were differently arranged? And wasn't there a better way of saying much the same thing?" (I couldn't say. I wouldn't try to say.)

Three months. Five. Half a year passed. Unsmiling, ever watchful, my teachers noted my silence. They began to connect my behavior with the difficult progress my older sister and brother were making. Until one Saturday morning three nuns arrived at the house to talk to our parents. Stiffly, they sat on the blue living room sofa. From the doorway of another room, spying the visitors, I noted the incongruity—the clash of two worlds, the faces and voices of school intruding upon the familiar setting of home. I overheard one voice gently wondering, "Do your children speak only Spanish at home, Mrs. Rodriguez?" While another voice added, "That Richard especially seems so timid and shy."

30   *That Rich-heard!*   30

With great tact the visitors continued, "Is it possible for you and your husband to encourage your children to practice their English when they are home?" Of course, my parents complied. What would they not do for their children's well-being? And how could they have questioned the Church's authority which those women represented? In an instant, they agreed to give up the language (the sounds) that had revealed and accentuated our family's closeness. The moment after the visitors left, the change was observed. "*Ahora,* speak to us *en inglés,*" my father and mother united to tell us.

At first, it seemed a kind of game. After dinner each night, the family gathered to practice "our" English. (It was still then *inglés,* a language foreign to us, so we felt drawn as strangers to it.) Laughing, we would try to define words we could not pronounce. We played with strange English sounds, often overanglicizing our pronunciations. And we filled the smiling gaps of our sentences with familiar Spanish sounds. But that was cheating, somebody shouted. Everyone laughed. In school, meanwhile, like my brother and sister, I was required to attend a daily tutoring session. I needed a full year of special attention. I also needed my teachers to keep my attention from straying in class by calling out, *Rich-heard*—their English voices slowly prying loose my ties to my other name, its three notes, *Ri-car-do.* Most of all I needed to hear my mother and father speak to me in a moment of seriousness in broken—suddenly heartbreaking—English. The scene was inevitable: One Saturday morning I entered the kitchen where my parents were talking in Spanish. I did not realize that they were talking in Spanish however until, at the moment they saw me, I heard their voices change to speak English. Those *gringo* sounds they uttered startled me. Pushed me away. In that moment of trivial misunderstanding and profound insight, I felt my throat twisted by unsounded grief. I turned quickly and left the room. But I had no place to escape to with Spanish. (The spell was broken.) My brother and sisters were speaking English in another part of the house.

Again and again in the days following, increasingly angry, I was obliged to hear my mother and father: "Speak to us *en inglés. (Speak.)*" Only then did I determine to learn classroom English. Weeks after, it happened: One day in school I raised my hand to volunteer an answer. I spoke out in a loud voice. And I did not think it remarkable when the entire class understood. That day, I moved very far from the disadvantaged child I had been only days earlier. The belief, the calming assurance that I belonged in public, had at last taken hold.

Shortly after, I stopped hearing the high and loud sounds Of *los gringos.* A more and more confident speaker of English, I didn't trouble to listen to *how* strangers sounded, speaking to me. And there simply were too many English-speaking people in my day for me to hear American accents anymore. Conversations quickened. Listening to persons who sounded eccentrically pitched voices, I usually noted their sounds for an initial few seconds before I concentrated on *what* they were saying. Conversations became content-full. Transparent. Hearing someone's *tone* of voice—angry or questioning or sarcastic or happy or sad—I didn't distinguish it from the words it expressed. Sound and word were thus tightly wedded. At the end of a day, I was often bemused, always relieved to realize how "silent," though crowded with words, my day in public had been. (This public silence measured and quickened the change in my life.)

35   At last, seven years old, I came to believe what had been technically true since my birth: I was an American citizen.

But the special feeling of closeness at home was diminished by then. Gone was the desperate, urgent, intense feeling of being at home; rare was the experience of feeling myself individualized by family intimates. We remained a loving family, but one greatly changed. No longer so close; no longer bound tight by the pleasing and troubling knowledge of our public separateness. Neither my older brother nor sister rushed home after school anymore. Nor did I. When I arrived home there would often be neighborhood kids in the house. Or the house would be empty of sounds.

The silence at home, however, was finally more than a literal silence. Fewer words passed between parent and child, but more profound was the silence that resulted from my inattention to sounds. At about the time I no longer bothered to listen with care to the sounds of English in public, I grew careless about listening to the sounds family members made when they spoke. Most of the time I heard someone speaking at home and didn't distinguish his sounds from the words people uttered in public. I didn't even pay much attention to my parents' accented and ungrammatical speech. At least not at home. Only when I was with them in public would I grow alert to their accents. Though, even then, their sounds caused me less and less concern. For I was increasingly confident of my own public identity.

I would have been happier about my public success had I not sometimes recalled what it had been like earlier, when my family had conveyed its intimacy through a set of conveniently private sounds. Sometimes in public, hearing a stranger, I'd hark back to my past. A Mexican farmworker approached me downtown to ask directions to somewhere. *"¿Hijito . . . ?"* he said. And his voice summoned deep longing. Another time, standing beside my mother in the visiting room of a Carmelite convent, before the dense screen which rendered the nuns shadowy figures, I heard several Spanish-speaking nuns—their busy, singsong overlapping voices—assure us that yes, yes, we were remembered, all our family was remembered in their prayers. (Their voices echoed faraway family sounds.) Another day, a dark-faced old woman—her hand light on my shoulder—steadied herself against me as she boarded a bus. She murmured something I couldn't quite comprehend. Her Spanish voice came near, like the face of a never-before-seen relative in the instant before I was kissed. Her voice, like so many of the Spanish voices I'd hear in public, recalled the golden age of my youth. Hearing Spanish then, I continued to be a careful, if sad, listener to sounds. Hearing a Spanish-speaking family walking behind me, I turned to look. I smiled for an instant, before my glance found the Hispanic-looking faces of strangers in the crowd going by.

Today I hear bilingual educators say that children lose a degree of "individuality" by becoming assimilated into public society. (Bilingual schooling was popularized in the seventies, that decade when middle-class ethnics began to resist the process of assimilation—the American melting pot.) But the bilingualists simplistically scorn the value and necessity of assimilation. They do not seem to realize that there are *two ways* a person is individualized. So they do not realize that while one suffers a diminished sense of *private* individuality by becoming assimilated into public society, such assimilation makes possible the achievement of *public* individuality.

40 The bilingualists insist that a student should be reminded of his 40 difference from others in mass society, his heritage. But they equate mere separateness with individuality. The fact is that only in private—with intimates—is separateness from the crowd a prerequisite for individuality. (An intimate draws me apart, tells me that I am unique, unlike all others.) In public, by contrast, full individuality is achieved, paradoxically, by those who are able to consider themselves members of the crowd. Thus it happened for me: Only when I was able to think of myself as an American, no longer an alien in *gringo* society, could I seek the rights and opportunities necessary for full public individuality. The social and political advantages I enjoy as a man result from the day that I came to believe that my name, indeed, is *Rich-heard*

Road-ree-guess. It is true that my public society today is often impersonal. (My public society is usually mass society.) Yet despite the anonymity of the crowd and despite the fact that the individuality I achieve in public is often tenuous—because it depends on my being one in a crowd—I celebrate the day I acquired my new name. Those middle-class ethnics who scorn assimilation seem to me filled with decadent self-pity, obsessed by the burden of public life. Dangerously, they romanticize public separateness and they trivialize the dilemma of the socially disadvantaged.

Questions on Meaning

1. Rodriguez speaks of his "family language" or "private language." What does he mean by this term? Explain why this distinct language, separate from his "public language," would or would not exist if he had grown up in a Spanish-speaking country.
2. Why did Rodriguez consider himself "socially disadvantaged"?
3. In the concluding paragraph to this essay, Rodriguez argues that "only in private is separateness from the crowd a prerequisite for individuality." Why does he feel that it is desirable to strive to *lose* one's individuality in public? What does he believe one gains from that status?

Questions on Rhetorical Strategy and Style

1. Using description, Rodriguez communicates the sounds of his youth and the impact that those sounds had on him. Locate these descriptions and compare the Hispanic sound he recalls to the *gringo* sound. What did the Hispanic sound mean to him? Why did he "edge away from the chirping chatter" of *los gringos* ?
2. Reread Rodriguez's description of the nuns visiting his home to talk to his parents about his lack of progress in school. In what ways does he compare and contrast the nuns and what they represented to his parents and his home?

Writing Assignments

1. Learn about the status of bilingual education today. Identify its opponents and its proponents. Find arguments for and against bilingual education in Rodriguez's essay.
2. Rodriguez writes that after he became assimilated, he lost his ear for the sound of language. What does this "sound" represent to him? Why did he lose his sensitivity to it? What causes it to return?
3. Identify a cultural debate that you have been involved in— perhaps over speaking a different language at home, following an ethnic or religious custom during a holiday celebration, or continuing a local tradition in your community. Write an essay describing the elements of the debate and arguing your position. Analyze the impact of the issues at hand on the different people involved in the debate.

I Think, Therefore IM

Jennifer Lee

*Jennifer Lee (1976–) was born in New York City. She grad-
uated from Harvard University in 1999 with a degree in
mathematics and economics. While at Harvard she spent a
year at Beijing University on a fellowship studying international relations. Lee has received a scholarship from the
Asian American Journalism Association and has interned at*
The Boston Globe, The New York Times, Newsday, The
Wall Street Journal, *and* The Washington Post. *She joined
the staff of* The New York Times *in 2001 as a technology
reporter and began writing for the Metro section the next
year. The following selection on instant-messaging language
originally appeared in the* Times *in September 2002.*

1   Each September Jacqueline Harding prepares a classroom presentation on the common writing mistakes she sees in her students'
work.

Ms. Harding, an eighth-grade English teacher at Viking Middle
School in Guernee, Ill., scribbles the words that have plagued generations of school children across her whiteboard:

> There. Their. They're.
> Your. You're.
> To. Too. Two.
> Its. It's.

This September, she has added a new list: u, r, ur, b4, wuz, cuz, 2.

When she asked her students how many of them used shortcuts
like them in their writing, Ms. Harding said, she was not surprised
when most of them raised their hands. This, after all, is their online

lingua franca: English adapted for the spitfire conversational style of Internet instant messaging.

Ms. Harding, who has seen such shortcuts creep into student papers over the last two years, said she gave her students a warning: "If I see this in your assignments, I will take points off."

5 "Kids should know the difference," said Ms. Harding, who decided to address this issue head-on this year. "They should know where to draw the line between formal writing and conversational writing."

As more and more teenagers socialize online, middle school and high school teachers like Ms. Harding are increasingly seeing a breezy form of Internet English jump from e-mail into schoolwork. To their dismay, teachers say that papers are being written with shortened words, improper capitalization and punctuation, and characters like &, $ and @.

Teachers have deducted points, drawn red circles and tsk-tsked at their classes. Yet the errant forms continue. "It stops being funny after you repeat yourself a couple of times," Ms. Harding said.

But teenagers, whose social life can rely as much these days on text communication as the spoken word, say that they use instant-messaging shorthand without thinking about it. They write to one another as much as they write in school, or more.

"You are so used to abbreviating things, you just start doing it unconsciously on schoolwork and reports and other things," said Eve Brecker, 15, a student at Montclair High School in New Jersey.

10 Ms. Brecker once handed in a midterm exam riddled with instant-messaging shorthand. "I had an hour to write an essay on *Romeo and Juliet*," she said. "I just wanted to finish before my time was up. I was writing fast and carelessly. I spelled 'you' 'u.'" She got a C.

Even terms that cannot be expressed verbally are making their way into papers. Melanie Weaver was stunned by some of the term papers she received from a 10th-grade class she recently taught as part of an internship. "They would be trying to make a point in a paper, they would put a smiley face in the end," said Ms. Weaver, who teaches at Alvernia College in Reading, PA. "If they were presenting an argument and they needed to present an opposite view, they would put a frown."

As Trisha Fogarty, a sixth-grade teacher at Houlton Southside School in Houlton, Maine, puts it, today's students are "Generation Text."

Almost 60 percent of the online population under age 17 uses instant messaging, according to Nielsen/NetRatings. In addition to cellphone text messaging, Weblogs and e-mail, it has become a popular means of flirting, setting up dates, asking for help with homework and keeping in contact with distant friends. The abbreviations are a natural outgrowth of this rapid-fire style of communication.

"They have a social life that centers around typed communication," said Judith S. Donath, a professor at the Massachusetts Institute of Technology's Media Lab who has studied electronic communication. "They have a writing style that has been nurtured in a teenage social milieu."

15 Some teachers see the creeping abbreviations as part of a continuing assault of technology on formal written English. Others take it more lightly, saying that it is just part of the larger arc of language evolution.

"To them it's not wrong," said Ms. Harding, who is 28. "It's acceptable because it's in their culture. It's hard enough to teach them the art of formal writing. Now we've got to overcome this new instant-messaging language."

Ms. Harding noted that in some cases the shorthand isn't even shorter. "I understand 'cuz,' but what's with the 'wuz'? It's the same amount of letters as 'was,' so what's the point?" she said.

Deborah Bova, who teaches eighth-grade English at Raymond Park Middle School in Indianapolis, thought her eyesight was failing several years ago when she saw the sentence "B4 we perform, ppl have 2 practice" on a student assignment.

"I thought, 'My God, what is this?' " Ms. Bova said. "Have they lost their minds?"

20 The student was summoned to the board to translate the sentence into standard English: "Before we perform, people have to practice." She realized that the students thought she was out of touch. "It was like 'Get with it, Bova,' " she said. Ms. Bova had a student type up a reference list of translations for common instant-messaging expressions. She posted a copy on the bulletin board by her desk and took another one home to use while grading.

Students are sometimes unrepentant.

"They were astonished when I began to point these things out to them," said Henry Assetto, a social studies teacher at Twin Valley High School in Elverson, Pa. "Because I am a history teacher, they did not

223

think a history teacher would be checking up on their grammar or their spelling," said Mr. Assetto, who has been teaching for 34 years.

But Montana Hodgen, 16, another Montclair student, said she was so accustomed to instant-messaging abbreviations that she often read right past them. She proofread a paper last year only to get it returned with the messaging abbreviations circled in red.

"I was so used to reading what my friends wrote to me on Instant Messenger that I didn't even realize that there was something wrong," she said. She said her ability to separate formal and informal English declined the more she used instant messages. "Three years ago, if I had seen that, I would have been 'What is that?' "

25   The spelling checker doesn't always help either, students say. For   25 one, Microsoft Word's squiggly red spell-check lines don't appear beneath single letters and numbers such as u, r, c, 2 and 4. Nor do they catch words which have numbers in them such as "l8r" and "b4" by default.

Teenagers have essentially developed an unconscious "accent" in their typing, Professor Donath said. "They have gotten facile at typing and they are not paying attention."

Teenagers have long pushed the boundaries of spoken language, introducing words that then become passe with adult adoption. Now teenagers are taking charge and pushing the boundaries of written language. For them, expressions like "oic" (oh I see), "nm" (not much), "jk" (just kidding) and "lol" (laughing out loud), "brb" (be right back), "ttyl" (talk to you later) are as standard as conventional English.

"There is no official English language," said Jesse Sheidlower, the North American editor of the *Oxford English Dictionary*. "Language is spread not because anyone dictates any one thing to happen. The decisions are made by the language and the people who use the language."

Some teachers find the new writing style alarming. "First of all, it's very rude, and it's very careless," said Lois Moran, a middle school English teacher at St. Nicholas School in Jersey City.

30   "They should be careful to write properly and not to put these little   30 codes in that they are in such a habit of writing to each other," said Ms. Moran, who has lectured her eighth-grade class on such mistakes.

Others say that the instant-messaging style might simply be a fad, something that students will grow out of. Or they see it as an opportunity to teach students about the evolution of language.

"I turn it into a very positive teachable moment for kids in the class," said Erika V. Karres, an assistant professor at the University of North Carolina at Chapel Hill who trains student teachers. She shows students how English has evolved since Shakespeare's time. "Imagine Langston Hughes's writing in quick texting instead of 'Langston writing,'" she said. "It makes teaching and learning so exciting."

Other teachers encourage students to use messaging shorthand to spark their thinking processes. "When my children are writing first drafts, I don't care how they spell anything, as long as they are writing," said Ms. Fogarty, the sixth-grade teacher from Houlton, Maine. "If this lingo gets their thoughts and ideas onto paper quicker, the more power to them." But during editing and revising, she expects her students to switch to standard English.

Ms. Bova shares the view that instant-messaging language can help free up their creativity. With the help of students, she does not even need the cheat sheet to read the shorthand anymore.

35 "I think it's a plus," she said. "And I would say that with a + sign." 35

Questions on Meaning

1. What are the social and technological conditions that have shaped cyberlingo vocabulary and its uses?
2. What does the term "lingua franca" mean? How does it capture the full significance of the text messaging style of young people?
3. Why, in your opinion, are adults frequently appalled when students use an informal or unconventional style in their writing?

Questions on Rhetorical Strategy and Style

1. Why does Lee open her article with the words Ms. Harding puts on the board each September? What is she trying to suggest to her readers?
2. How does the article adhere to the conventions of the newspaper journalism? Does the writer remain balanced and objective? Explain how.
3. Why does the writer quote the editor of the *Oxford English Dictionary?*

Writing Assignments

1. Why do teachers often seem fussy, and even offended, by their students' use of language? Why are they so insistent about the conventions of standard, edited English? Write an essay that explains to your teachers your experience trying to learn these conventions, and why your language is necessary to your sense of identity.
2. Try the exercise used by Erika Karres, the teacher at the University of North Carolina. Take a poem or any piece of writing and translate it into a quick text version. How does the meaning of it change?

From Silence to Words: Writing as Struggle

Min-zhan Lu

[handwritten annotations: (Richard Rodriguez, Amy Tan, Seeing England) discourse - language that shapes perception/exp — values + beliefs — logic system — identity mixed cultural multiple racial ethnic]

Min-zhan Lu (1946–) was born in China. Lu, who grew up speaking English as well as a number of Chinese dialects, has taught composition and literary criticism at Drake University. She has published both academic articles related to composition issues and articles about her life in China. This article, published in College English *in 1987, relates Lu's challenges acquiring literacy in both China and the United States and how those challenges have affected her writing and teaching.*

Imagine that you enter a parlor. You come late. When you arrive, others have long preceded you, and they are engaged in a heated discussion. . . .You listen for a while, until you decide that you have caught the tenor of the argument; then you put in your oar. Someone answers; you answer him; another comes to your defense; another aligns himself against you, to either the embarrassment or gratification of your opponent, depending upon the quality of your ally's assistance. However, the discussion is interminable. The hour grows late, you must depart. And you do depart, with the discussion still vigorously in progress.

—*Kenneth Burke,* The Philosophy of Literary Form

Men are not built in silence, but in word, in work, in action-reflection.

—*Paulo Freire,* Pedagogy of the Oppressed

From *College English*, April, 1987. Copyright © 1987 by the National Council of Teachers of English.

[handwritten annotations: What are the sort of different ways you describe the world, or what you ex. religious communities work - the way you use your language public/professional classroom political/parties]

227

1   My mother withdrew into silence two months before she   1
died. A few nights before she fell silent, she told me she re-
gretted the way she had raised me and my sisters. I knew
she was referring to the way we had been brought up in the midst of
two conflicting worlds—the world of home, dominated by the ideology of the Western humanistic tradition, and the world of a society
dominated by Mao Tse-tung's Marxism. My mother had devoted her
life to our education, an education she knew had made us suffer political persecution during the Cultural Revolution. I wanted to find a
way to convince her that, in spite of the persecution, I had benefited
from the education she had worked so hard to give me. But I was
silent. My understanding of my education was so dominated by memories of confusion and frustration that I was unable to reflect on what
I could have gained from it.

This paper is my attempt to fill up that silence with words, words
I didn't have then, words that I have since come to by reflecting on
my earlier experience as a student in China and on my recent experience as a composition teacher in the United States. For in spite of the
frustration and confusion I experienced growing up caught between
two conflicting worlds, the conflict ultimately helped me to grow as a
reader and writer. Constantly having to switch back and forth between
the discourse of home and that of school made me sensitive and self-
conscious about the struggle I experienced every time I tried to read,
write, or think in either discourse. Eventually, it led me to search for
constructive uses for such struggle.

From early childhood, I had identified the differences between
home and the outside world by the different languages I used in each.
My parents had wanted my sisters and me to get the best education
they could conceive of—Cambridge. They had hired a live-in tutor, a
Scot, to make us bilingual. I learned to speak English with my parents, my tutor, and my sisters. I was allowed to speak Shanghai dialect
only with the servants. When I was four (the year after the Communist Revolution of 1949), my parents sent me to a local private school
where I learned to speak, read, and write in a new language—Standard
Chinese, the official written language of New China.

In those days I moved from home to school, from English to Standard Chinese to Shanghai dialect, with no apparent friction. I spoke
each language with those who spoke the language. All seemed quite
"natural"—servants spoke only Shanghai dialect because they were

servants; teachers spoke Standard Chinese because they were teachers; languages had different words because they were different languages. I thought of English as my family language, comparable to the many strange dialects I didn't speak but had often heard some of my classmates speak with their families. While I was happy to have a special family language, until second grade I didn't feel that my family language was any different than some of my classmates' family dialects.

5   My second grade homeroom teacher was a young graduate from a missionary school. When she found out I spoke English, she began to practice her English on me. One day she used English when asking me to run an errand for her. As I turned to close the door behind me, I noticed the puzzled faces of my classmates. I had the same sensation I had often experienced when some stranger in a crowd would turn on hearing me speak English. I was more intensely pleased on this occasion, however, because suddenly I felt that my family language had been singled out from the family languages of my classmates. Since we were not allowed to speak any dialect other than Standard Chinese in the classroom, having my teacher speak English to me in class made English an official language of the classroom. I began to take pride in my ability to speak it.

This incident confirmed in my mind what my parents had always told me about the importance of English to one's life. Time and again they had told me of how my paternal grandfather, who was well versed in classic Chinese, kept losing good-paying jobs because he couldn't speak English. My grandmother reminisced constantly about how she had slaved and saved to send my father to a first-rate missionary school. And we were made to understand that it was my father's fluent English that had opened the door to his success. Even though my family had always stressed the importance of English for my future, I used to complain bitterly about the extra English lessons we had to take after school. It was only after my homeroom teacher had "sanctified" English that I began to connect English with my education. I became a much more eager student in my tutorials.

What I learned from my tutorials seemed to enhance and reinforce what I was learning in my classroom. In those days each word had one meaning. One day I would be making a sentence at school: "The national flag of China is red." The next day I would recite at home, "My love is like a red, red rose." There seemed to be an agreement between the Chinese "red" and the English "red," and both corresponded to the patch of color printed next to the word. "Love" was my love for my mother at home and my love for my "motherland" at school; both "loves" meant how I felt about my mother. Having two loads of homework forced me to develop a quick memory for words and a sensitivity to form and style. What I learned in one language carried over to the other. I made sentences such as, "I saw a red, red rose among the green leaves," with both the English lyric and the classic Chinese lyric—red flower among green leaves—running through my mind, and I was praised by both teacher and tutor for being a good student.

Although my elementary schooling took place during the fifties, I was almost oblivious to the great political and social changes happening around me. Years later, I read in my history and political philosophy textbooks that the fifties were a time when "China was making a transition from a semi-feudal, semi-capitalist, and semi-colonial country into a socialist country," a period in which "the Proletarians were breaking into the educational territory dominated by Bourgeois Intellectuals." While people all over the country were being officially classified into Proletarians, Petty-bourgeois, National-bourgeois, Poor-peasants, and Intellectuals, and were trying to adjust to their new social identities, my parents were allowed to continue the upper middle-class life they had established before the 1949 Revolution because of my father's affiliation with British firms. I had always felt that my family was different from the families of my classmates, but I didn't perceive society's view of my family until the summer vacation before I entered high school.

First, my aunt was caught by her colleagues talking to her husband over the phone in English. Because of it, she was criticized and almost labeled a Rightist. (This was the year of the Anti-Rightist movement, a movement in which the Intellectuals became the target of the "socialist class-struggle.") I had heard others telling my mother that she was foolish to teach us English when Russian had replaced English as the "official" foreign language. I had also learned at school that the American and British Imperialists were the arch-enemies of New China. Yet I had made no connection between the arch-enemies and the English our family spoke. What happened to my aunt forced the connection on me. I began to see my parents' choice of a family language as an anti-Revolutionary act and was alarmed that I had participated in such an act. From then on, I took care not to use English outside home and to conceal my knowledge of English from my new classmates.

10   Certain words began to play important roles in my new life at the   10
junior high. On the first day of school, we were handed forms to fill out with our parents' class, job, and income. Being one of the few people not employed by the government, my father had never been officially classified. Since he was a medical doctor, he told me to put him down as an Intellectual. My homeroom teacher called me into the office a couple of days afterwards and told me that my father couldn't be an Intellectual if his income far exceeded that of a Capitalist. He also told me that since my father worked for Foreign Imperialists, my father should be classified as an Imperialist Lackey. The teacher looked nonplussed when I told him that my father couldn't be an Imperialist Lackey because he was a medical doctor. But I could tell from the way he took notes on my form that my father's job had put me in an unfavorable position in his eyes.

The Standard Chinese term "class" was not a new word for me. Since first grade, I had been taught sentences such as, "The Working class are the masters of New China." I had always known that it was good to be a worker, but until then, I had never felt threatened for not being one. That fall, "class" began to take on a new meaning for me. I noticed a group of Working-class students and teachers at school. I was made to understand that because of my class background, I was excluded from that group.

Another word that became important was "consciousness." One of the slogans posted in the school building read, "Turn our students into future Proletarians with socialist consciousness and education!" For several weeks we studied this slogan in our political philosophy course, a subject I had never had in elementary school. I still remember the definition of "socialist consciousness" that we were repeatedly tested on through the years: "Socialist consciousness is a person's political soul. It is the consciousness of the Proletarians represented by Marxist Mao Tse-tung thought. It takes expression in one's action, language, and lifestyle. It is the task of every Chinese student to grow up into a Proletarian with a socialist consciousness so that he can serve the people and the motherland." To make the abstract concept accessible to us, our teacher pointed out that the immediate task for students from Working-class families was to strengthen their socialist consciousnesses. For those of us who were from other class backgrounds, the task was to turn ourselves into Workers with social-ist consciousnesses. The teacher never explained exactly how we were supposed to "turn" into Workers. Instead, we were given samples of the ritualistic annual plans we had to write at the beginning of each term. In these plans, we performed "self-criticism" on our conscious-nesses and made vows to turn ourselves into Workers with socialist consciousnesses. The teacher's division between those who did and those who didn't have a socialist consciousness led me to reify the no-tion of "consciousness" into a thing one possesses. I equated this in-tangible "thing" with a concrete way of dressing, speaking, and writing. For instance, I never doubted that my political philosophy teacher had a socialist consciousness because she was from a steel-worker's family (she announced this the first day of class) and was a party member who wore grey cadre suits and talked like a philosophy textbook. I noticed other things about her. She had beautiful eyes and spoke Standard Chinese with such a pure accent that I thought she should be a film star. But I was embarrassed that I had noticed things that ought not to have been associated with her. I blamed my obser-vation on my Bourgeois consciousness.

At the same time, the way reading and writing were taught through memorization and imitation also encouraged me to reduce concepts and ideas to simple definitions. In literature and political philosophy classes, we were taught a large number of quotations from Marx, Lenin, and Mao Tse-tung. Each concept that appeared in these quotations came with a definition. We were required to memorize the definitions of the words along with the quotations. Every time I mem-orized a definition, I felt I had learned a word: "The national red flag symbolizes the blood shed by Revolutionary ancestors for our social-ist cause"; "New China rises like a red sun over the eastern horizon." As I memorized these sentences, I reduced their metaphors to dictio-nary meanings: "red" meant "Revolution" and "red sun" meant "New China" in the "language" of the Working class. I learned mechanically but eagerly. I soon became quite fluent in this new language.

As school began to define me as a political subject, my parents tried to build up my resistance to the "communist poisoning" by ex-posing me to the "great books"—novels by Charles Dickens, Nathaniel Hawthorne, Emily Brontë, Jane Austen, and writers from around the turn of the century. My parents implied that these writers represented how I, their child, should read and write. My parents replaced the word "Bourgeois" with the word "cultured." They reminded me that I was in school only to learn math and science. I needed to pass the other courses to stay in school, but I was not to let the "Red doctrines" corrupt my mind. Gone were the days when I could innocently write, "I saw the red, red rose among the green leaves," collapsing, as I did, English and Chinese cultural traditions. "Red" came to mean Revolution at school, "the Commies" at home, and adultery in *The Scarlet Letter.* Since I took these symbols and metaphors as meanings natural to people of the same class, I abandoned my earlier definitions of English and Standard Chinese as the language of home and the language of school. I now defined English as the language of the Bourgeois and Standard Chinese as the language of the Working class. I thought of the language of the Working class as someone else's language and the language of the Bourgeois as my language. But I also believed that, although the language of the Bourgeois was my real language, I could and would adopt the language of the Working class when I was at school. I began to put on and take off my Working class language in the same way I put on and took off my school clothes to avoid being criticized for wearing Bourgeois clothes.

15   In my literature classes, I learned the Working-class formula for reading. Each work in the textbook had a short "Author's Biography": "X X X, born in 19—in the province of X X X, is from a Worker's family. He joined the Revolution in 19—. He is a Revolutionary realist with a passionate love for the Party and Chinese Revolution. His work expresses the thoughts and emotions of the masses and sings praise to the prosperous socialist construction on all fronts of China." The teacher used the "Author's Biography" as a yardstick to measure the texts. We were taught to locate details in the texts that illustrated these summaries, such as words that expressed Workers' thoughts and emotions or events that illustrated the Workers' lives.

I learned a formula for Working-class writing in the composition classes. We were given sample essays and told to imitate them. The theme was always about how the collective taught the individual a lesson. I would write papers about labor-learning experiences or school-cleaning days, depending on the occasion of the collective activity closest to the assignment. To make each paper look different, I dressed it up with details about the date, the weather, the environment, or the appearance of the Master-worker who had taught me "the lesson." But as I became more and more fluent in the generic voice of the Working-class Student, I also became more and more self-conscious about the language we used at home.

For instance, in senior high we began to have English classes ("to study English for the Revolution," as the slogan on the cover of the textbook said), and I was given my first Chinese-English dictionary. There I discovered the English version of the term "class-struggle." (The Chinese characters for a school "class" and for a social "class" are different.) I had often used the English word "class" at home in sentences such as, "So and so has class," but I had not connected this sense of "class" with "class-struggle." Once the connection was made, I heard a second layer of meaning every time someone at home said a person had "class." The expression began to mean the person had the style and sophistication characteristic of the bourgeoisie. The word lost its innocence. I was uneasy about hearing that second layer of meaning because I was sure my parents did not hear the word that way. I felt that therefore I should not be hearing it that way either. Hearing the second layer of meaning made me wonder if I was losing my English.

My suspicion deepened when I noticed myself unconsciously merging and switching between the "reading" of home and the "reading" of school. Once I had to write a report on *The Revolutionary Family*, a book about an illiterate woman's awakening and growth as a Revolutionary through the deaths of her husband and all her children for the cause of the Revolution. In one scene the woman deliberated over whether or not she should encourage her youngest son to join the Revolution. Her memory of her husband's death made her afraid to encourage her son. Yet she also remembered her earlier married life and the first time her husband tried to explain the meaning of the Revolution to her. These memories made her feel she should encourage her son to continue the cause his father had begun.

I was moved by this scene. "Moved" was a word my mother and sisters used a lot when we discussed books. Our favorite moments in novels were moments of what I would now call internal conflict, moments which we said "moved" us. I remember that we were "moved" by Jane Eyre when she was torn between her sense of ethics, which compelled her to leave the man she loved, and her impulse to stay with the only man who had ever loved her. We were also moved by Agnes in *David Copperfield* because of the way she restrained her love for

David so that he could live happily with the woman he loved. My standard method of doing a book report was to model it on the review by the Publishing Bureau and to dress it up with detailed quotations from the book. The review of *The Revolutionary Family* emphasized the woman's Revolutionary spirit. I decided to use the scene that had moved me to illustrate this point. I wrote the report the night before it was due. When I had finished, I realized I couldn't possibly hand it in. Instead of illustrating her Revolutionary spirit, I had dwelled on her internal conflict, which could be seen as a moment of weak sentimentality that I should never have emphasized in a Revolutionary heroine. I wrote another report, taking care to illustrate the grandeur of her Revolutionary spirit by expanding on a quotation in which she decided that if the life of her son could change the lives of millions of sons, she should not begrudge his life for the cause of Revolution. I handed in my second version but kept the first in my desk.

20   I never showed it to anyone. I could never show it to people outside my family, because it had deviated so much from the reading enacted by the jacket review. Neither could I show it to my mother or sisters, because I was ashamed to have been so moved by such a "Revolutionary" book. My parents would have been shocked to learn that I could like such a book in the same way they liked Dickens. Writing this book report increased my fear that I was losing the command over both the "language of home" and the "language of school" that I had worked so hard to gain. I tried to remind myself that, if I could still tell when my reading or writing sounded incorrect, then I had retained my command over both languages. Yet I could no longer be confident of my command over either language because I had discovered that when I was not careful—or even when I was—my reading and writing often surprised me with its impurity. To prevent such impurity, I became very suspicious of my thoughts when I read or wrote. I was always asking myself why I was using this word, how I was using it, always afraid that I wasn't reading or writing correctly. What confused and frustrated me most was that I could not figure out why I was no longer able to read or write correctly without such painful deliberation.

I continued to read only because reading allowed me to keep my thoughts and confusion private. I hoped that somehow, if I watched myself carefully, I would figure out from the way I read whether I had really mastered the "languages." But writing became a dreadful chore. When I tried to keep a diary, I was so afraid that the voice of school might slip in that I could only list my daily activities. When I wrote for school, I worried that my Bourgeois sensibilities would betray me.

The more suspicious I became about the way I read and wrote, the more guilty I felt for losing the spontaneity with which I had learned to "use" these "languages." Writing the book report made me feel that my reading and writing in the "language" of either home or school could not be free of the interference of the other. But I was unable to acknowledge, grasp, or grapple with what I was experiencing, for both my parents and my teachers had suggested that, if I were a good student, such interference would and should not take place. I assumed that once I had "acquired" a discourse, I could simply switch it on and off every time I read and wrote as I would some electronic tool. Furthermore, I expected my readings and writings to come out in their correct forms whenever I switched the proper discourse on. I still regarded the discourse of home as natural and the discourse of school alien, but I never had doubted before that I could acquire both and switch them on and off according to the occasion.

When my experience in writing conflicted with what I thought should happen when I used each discourse, I rejected my experience because it contradicted what my parents and teachers had taught me. I shied away from writing to avoid what I assumed I should not experience. But trying to avoid what should not happen did not keep it from recurring whenever I had to write. Eventually my confusion and frustration over these recurring experiences compelled me to search for an explanation: how and why had I failed to learn what my parents and teachers had worked so hard to teach me?

I now think of the internal scene for my reading and writing about *The Revolutionary Family* as a heated discussion between myself, the voices of home, and those of school. The review on the back of the book, the sample student papers I came across in my composition classes, my philosophy teacher—these I heard as voices of one group. My parents and my home readings were the voices of an opposing group. But the conversation between these opposing voices in the internal scene of my writing was not as polite and respectful as the parlor scene Kenneth Burke has portrayed (see epigraph). Rather, these voices struggled to dominate the discussion, constantly incorporating, dismissing, or suppressing the arguments of each other, like the battles between the hegemonic and counter-hegemonic forces described in Raymond Williams' *Marxism and Literature* (108–14).

25   When I read *The Revolutionary Family* and wrote the first version   25
of my report, I began with a quotation from the review. The voices of
both home and school answered, clamoring to be heard. I tried to listen to one group and turn a deaf ear to the other. Both persisted. I negotiated my way through these conflicting voices, now agreeing with
one, now agreeing with the other. I formed a reading out of my interaction with both. Yet I was afraid to have done so because both
home and school had implied that I should speak in unison with only
one of these groups and stand away from the discussion rather than
participate in it.

My teachers and parents had persistently called my attention to
the intensity of the discussion taking place on the external social scene.
The story of my grandfather's failure and my father's success had from
my early childhood made me aware of the conflict between Western
and traditional Chinese cultures. My political education at school
added another dimension to the conflict; the war of Marxist-Maoism
against them both. Yet when my parents and teachers called my attention to the conflict, they stressed the anxiety of having to live
through China's transformation from a semi-feudal, semi-capitalist,
and semi-colonial society to a socialist one. Acquiring the discourse of
the dominant group was, to them, a means of seeking alliance with
that group and thus of surviving the whirlpool of cultural currents
around them. As a result, they modeled their pedagogical practices on
this utilitarian view of language. Being the eager student, I adopted
this view of language as a tool for survival. It came to dominate my
understanding of the discussion on the social and historical scene and
to restrict my ability to participate in that discussion.

To begin with, the metaphor of language as a tool for survival led
me to be passive in my use of discourse, to be a bystander in the discussion. In Burke's "parlor," everyone is involved in the discussion. As
it goes on through history, what we call "communal discourses"—arguments specific to particular political, social, economic, ethnic, sexual, and family groups—form, re-form and transform. To use a
discourse in such a scene is to participate in the argument and to contribute to the formation of the discourse. But when I was growing up,
I could not take on the burden of such an active role in the discussion. For both home and school presented the existent conventions of
the discourse each taught me as absolute laws for my action. They
turned verbal action into a tool, a set of conventions produced and

shaped prior to and outside of my own verbal acts. Because I saw language as a tool, I separated the process of producing the tool from the process of using it. The tool was made by someone else and was then acquired and used by me. How the others made it before I acquired it determined and guaranteed what it produced when I used it. I imagined that the more experienced and powerful members of the community were the ones responsible for making the tool. They were the ones who participated in the discussion and fought with opponents. When I used what they made, their labor and accomplishments would ensure the quality of my reading and writing. By using it, I could survive the heated discussion. When my immediate experience in writing the book report suggested that knowing the conventions of school did not guarantee the form and content of my report, when it suggested that I had to write the report with the work and responsibility I had assigned to those who wrote book reviews in the Publishing bureau, I thought I had lost the tool I had earlier acquired.

Another reason I could not take up an active role in the argument was that my parents and teachers contrived to provide a scene free of conflict for practicing my various languages. It was as if their experience had made them aware of the conflict between their discourse and other discourses and of the struggle involved in reproducing the conventions of any discourse on a scene where more than one discourse exists. They seemed convinced that such conflict and struggle would overwhelm someone still learning the discourse. Home and school each contrived a purified space where only one discourse was spoken and heard. In their choice of textbooks, in the way they spoke, and in the way they required me to speak, each jealously silenced any voice that threatened to break the unison of the scene. The homogeneity of home and of school implied that only one discourse could and should be relevant in each place. It led me to believe I should leave behind, turn a deaf ear to, or forget the discourse of the other when I crossed the boundary dividing them. I expected myself to set down one discourse whenever I took up another just as I would take off or put on a particular set of clothes for school or home.

Despite my parents' and teachers' attempts to keep home and school discrete, the internal conflict between the two discourses continued whenever I read or wrote. Although I tried to suppress the voice of one discourse in the name of the other, having to speak aloud in the voice I had just silenced each time I crossed the boundary kept both voices active in my mind. Every "I think . . . " from the voice of home or school brought forth a "However . . . " or a "But. . ." from the voice of the opponents. To identify with the voice of home or school, I had to negotiate through the conflicting voices of both by re-stating, taking back, qualifying my thoughts. I was unconsciously doing so when I did my book report. But I could not use the interaction comfortably and constructively. Both my parents and my teachers had implied that my job was to prevent that interaction from happening. My sense of having failed to accomplish what they had taught silenced me.

30 To use the interaction between the discourses of home and school 30 constructively, I would have to have seen reading or writing as a process in which I worked my way towards a stance through a dialectical process of identification and division. To identify with an ally, I would have to have grasped the distance between where he or she stood and where I was positioning myself. In taking a stance against an opponent, I would have to have grasped where my stance identified with the stance of my allies. Teetering along the "wavering line of pressure and counter-pressure" from both allies and opponents, I might have worked my way towards a stance of my own (Burke, *A Rhetoric of Motives,* 23). Moreover, I would have to have understood that the voices in my mind, like the participants in the parlor scene, were in constant flux. As I came into contact with new and different groups of people or read different books, voices entered and left. Each time I read or wrote, the stance I negotiated out of these voices would always be at some distance from the stances I worked out in my previous and my later readings or writings.

I could not conceive such a form of action for myself because I saw reading and writing as an expression of an established stance. In delineating the conventions of a discourse, my parents and teachers had synthesized the stance they saw as typical for a representative member of the community. Burke calls this the stance of a "god" or the "prototype"; Williams calls it the "official" or "possible" stance of the community. Through the metaphor of the survival tool, my parents and teachers had led me to assume I could automatically reproduce the official stance of the discourse I used. Therefore, when I did my book report on *The Revolutionary Family,* I expected my knowledge of the official stance set by the book review to ensure the actual stance of my report. As it happened, I began by trying to take the official stance of the review. Other voices interrupted. I answered back. In the process, I worked out a stance approximate but not identical to the official stance I began with. Yet the experience of having to labor to realize my knowledge of the official stance or to prevent myself from wandering away from it frustrated and confused me. For even though I had been actually reading and writing in a Burkean scene, I was afraid to participate actively in the discussion. I assumed it was my role to survive by staying out of it.

Not long ago, my daughter told me that it bothered her to hear her friend "talk wrong." Having come to the United States from China with little English, my daughter has become sensitive to the way English, as spoken by her teachers, operates. As a result, she has amazed her teachers with her success in picking up the language and in adapting to life at school. Her concern to speak the English taught in the classroom "correctly" makes her uncomfortable when she hears people using "ain't" or double negatives, which her teacher considers "improper." I see in her the me that had eagerly learned and used the discourse of the Working class at school. Yet while I was torn between the two conflicting worlds of school and home, she moves with seeming ease from the conversations she hears over the dinner table to her teacher's words in the classroom. My husband and I are proud of the good work she does at school. We are glad she is spared the kinds of conflict between home and school I experienced at her age. Yet as we watch her becoming more and more fluent in the language of the classroom, we wonder if, by enabling her to "survive" school, her very fluency will silence her when the scene of her reading and writing expands beyond that of the composition classroom.

For when I listen to my daughter, to students, and to some composition teachers talking about the teaching and learning of writing, I am often alarmed by the degree to which the metaphor of a survival tool dominates their understanding of language as it once dominated my own. I am especially concerned with the way some composition classes focus on turning the classroom into a monological scene for the students' reading and writing. Most of our students live in a world similar to my daughter's, somewhere between the purified world of the classroom and the complex world of my adolescence. When composition classes encourage these students to ignore those voices that seem irrelevant to the purified world of the classroom, most students are often able to do so without much struggle. Some of them are so adept at doing it that the whole process has for them become automatic.

However, beyond the classroom and beyond the limited range of these students' immediate lives lies a much more complex and dynamic social and historical scene. To help these students become actors in such a scene, perhaps we need to call their attention to voices that may seem irrelevant to the discourse we teach rather than encourage them to shut them out. For example, we might intentionally complicate the classroom scene by bringing into it discourses that stand at varying distances from the one we teach. We might encourage students to explore ways of practicing the conventions of the discourse they are learning by negotiating through these conflicting voices. We could also encourage them to see themselves as responsible for forming or transforming as well as preserving the discourse they are learning.

35   As I think about what we might do to complicate the external and internal scenes of our students' writing, I hear my parents and teachers saying: "Not now. Keep them from the wrangle of the marketplace until they have acquired the discourse and are skilled at using it." And I answer: "Don't teach them to 'survive' the whirlpool of crosscurrents by avoiding it. Use the classroom to moderate the currents. Moderate the currents, but teach them from the beginning to struggle." When I think of the ways in which the teaching of reading and writing as classroom activities can frustrate the development of students, I am almost grateful for the overwhelming complexity of the circumstances in which I grew up. For it was this complexity that kept me from losing sight of the effort and choice involved in reading or writing with and through a discourse.

References

Burke, Kenneth. *The Philosophy of Literary Form: Studies in Symbolic Action.* 2nd ed. Baton Rouge: Louisiana State UP, 1967.

———. *A Rhetoric of Motives.* Berkeley: U of California P, 1969.

Freire, Paulo. *Pedagogy of the Oppressed.* Trans. M. B. Ramos. New York: Continuum, 1970.

Williams, Raymond. *Marxism and Literature.* New York: Oxford UP, 1977.

Questions on Meaning

1. What were the two conflicting worlds in which Lu grew up? What were the "two discourses" of these worlds? How did these "two discourses" create tension in her life? Why did her mother regret bringing her up in these conflicting worlds?
2. What did Lu consider her "family language"? How did her perception of her "family language" change as she learned more about *class* in her society? Why did she become alarmed at her family's use of that language?
3. How did the metaphor of "language as a tool" cause Lu to become passive in her discourse?
4. Reread the section where Lu compares and contrasts her first and second versions of her book review of *The Revolutionary Family*. Why did her first version trouble her so? Why could she not show it to anyone outside her family? How did this experience affect her reading and writing—notably her writing in her diary?

Questions on Rhetorical Strategy and Style

1. How does Lu use a cause and effect writing strategy to relate the two worlds in which she lived as a child to her development as a reader and writer? What was the effect of the two loads of homework Lu carried, one from her English tutor, one from her Chinese teachers? What was the effect of her Chinese teachers' requirement that she learn reading and writing through memorization and imitation?
2. Lu uses the words "class" and "consciousness" as examples of words that "began to play important roles in my new life at the junior high." How did the word "class" make her feel different? Why did the word "consciousness" create confusion in her life?

Writing Assignments

1. Describe a time when you were afraid to reveal something you had written because it deviated from what was expected. What made it unacceptable? Why had you written it? Ultimately, what did you do with it?
2. Learn more about Kenneth Burke. Why are his theories important to Lu's argument? Why did she become a "bystander" in his "parlor"?

3. Write an essay about a time when you used language as a tool, such as through word choice, diction, and maybe even accent. (Perhaps you were putting on airs to impress someone, trying to sound like a regular Joe to hide your education, or talking slowly and methodically to someone who does not have strong command of English.) Who was the audience? What was the result of your use of language as a tool? Explain why language is or is not an effective communications tool for you.

VI. Challenges

The Meaning of July Fourth for The Negro

Frederick Douglass

THE MEANING OF JULY FOURTH FOR
THE NEGRO, SPEECH AT ROCHESTER,
NEW YORK, JULY 5, 1852

Mr. President, Friends and Fellow Citizens:

He who could address this audience without a quailing sensation has stronger nerves than I have. I do not remember ever to have appeared as a speaker before any assembly more shrinkingly, nor with greater distrust of my ability, than I do this day. A feeling has crept over me quite unfavorable to the exercise of my limited powers of speech. The task before me is one which requires much previous thought and study for its proper performance. I know that apologies of this sort are generally considered flat and unmeaning. I trust, however, that mine will not be so considered. Should I seem at ease, my appearance would much misrepresent me. The little experience I have had in addressing public meetings, in country school houses, avails me nothing on the present occasion.

The papers and placards say that I am to deliver a Fourth of July Oration. This certainly sounds large, and out of the common way, for me. It is true that I have often had the privilege to speak in this beautiful Hall, and to address many who now honor me with their presence. But neither their familiar faces, nor the perfect gage I think I have of Corinthian Hall seems to free me from embarrassment.

The fact is, ladies and gentlemen, the distance between this platform and the slave plantation, from which I escaped, is considerable—and the difficulties to be overcome in getting from the latter to the former are by no means slight. That I am here to-day is, to me, a matter of astonishment as well as of gratitude. You will not, therefore, be

Reprinted from *The Life and Writings of Frederick Douglass, Pre-Civil War Decade, 1850–1860*, Volume II, edited by Philip S. Foner (1950).

surprised, if in what I have to say I evince no elaborate preparation, nor grace my speech with any high sounding exordium. With little experience and with less learning, I have been able to throw my thoughts hastily and imperfectly together; and trusting to your patient and generous indulgence, I will proceed to lay them before you.

This, for the purpose of this celebration, is the Fourth of July. It is the birthday of your National Independence, and of your political freedom. This, to you, is what the Passover was to the emancipated people of God. It carries your minds back to the day, and to the act of your great deliverance; and to the signs, and to the wonders, associated with that act, and that day. This celebration also marks the beginning of another year of your national life; and reminds you that the Republic of America is now 76 years old. I am glad, fellow-citizens, that your nation is so young. Seventy-six years, though a good old age for a man, is but a mere speck in the life of a nation. Three score years and ten is the allotted time for individual men; but nations number their years by thousands. According to this fact, you are, even now, only in the beginning of your national career, still lingering in the period of childhood. I repeat, I am glad this is so. There is hope in the thought, and hope is much needed, under the dark clouds which lower above the horizon. The eye of the reformer is met with angry flashes, portending disastrous times; but his heart may well beat lighter at the thought that America is young, and that she is still in the impressible stage of her existence. May he not hope that high lessons of wisdom, of justice and of truth, will yet give direction to her destiny? Were the nation older, the patriot's heart might be sadder, and the reformer's brow heavier. Its future might be shrouded in gloom, and the hope of its prophets go out in sorrow. There is consolation in the thought that America is young.—Great streams are not easily turned from channels, worn deep in the course of ages. They may sometimes rise in quiet and stately majesty, and inundate the land, refreshing and fertilizing the earth with their mysterious properties. They may also rise in wrath and fury, and bear away, on their angry waves, the accumulated wealth of years of toil and hardship. They, however, gradually flow back to the same old channel, and flow on as serenely as ever. But, while the river may not be turned aside, it may dry up, and leave nothing behind but the withered branch, and the unsightly rock, to howl in the abyss-sweeping wind, the sad tale of departed glory. As with rivers so with nations.

5   Fellow-citizens, I shall not presume to dwell at length on the   5
associations that cluster about this day. The simple story of it is, that,
76 years ago, the people of this country were British subjects. The
style and title of your "sovereign people" (in which you now glory)
was not then born. You were under the British Crown. Your fathers
esteemed the English Government as the home government; and
England as the fatherland. This home government, you know,
although a considerable distance from your home, did, in the exercise
of its parental prerogatives, impose upon its colonial children, such
restraints, burdens and limitations, as, in its mature judgment, it
deemed wise, right and proper.

But your fathers, who had not adopted the fashionable idea of
this day, of the infallibility of government, and the absolute character
of its acts, presumed to differ from the home government in respect
to the wisdom and the justice of some of those burdens and restraints.
They went so far in their excitement as to pronounce the measures of
government unjust, unreasonable, and oppressive, and altogether
such as ought not to be quietly submitted to. I scarcely need say,
fellow-citizens, that my opinion of those measures fully accords with
that of your fathers. Such a declaration of agreement on my part
would not be worth much to anybody. It would certainly prove nothing as to what part I might have taken had I lived during the great
controversy of 1776. To say now that America was right, and England
wrong, is exceedingly easy. Everybody can say it; the dastard, not less
than the noble brave, can flippantly discant on the tyranny of England
towards the American Colonies. It is fashionable to do so; but there
was a time when, to pronounce against England, and in favor of the
cause of the colonies, tried men's souls. They who did so were
accounted in their day plotters of mischief, agitators and rebels, dangerous men. To side with the right against the wrong, with the weak
against the strong, and with the oppressed against the oppressor! here
lies the merit, and the one which, of all others, seems unfashionable
in our day. The cause of liberty may be stabbed by the men who glory
in the deeds of your fathers. But, to proceed.

Feeling themselves harshly and unjustly treated, by the home
government, your fathers, like men of honesty, and men of spirit,
earnestly sought redress. They petitioned and remonstrated; they did
so in a decorous, respectful, and loyal manner. Their conduct was
wholly unexceptionable. This, however, did not answer the purpose.

They saw themselves treated with sovereign indifference, coldness and scorn. Yet they persevered. They were not the men to look back.

As the sheet anchor takes a firmer hold, when the ship is tossed by the storm, so did the cause of your fathers grow stronger as it breasted the chilling blasts of kingly displeasure. The greatest and best of British statesmen admitted its justice, and the loftiest eloquence of the British Senate came to its support. But, with that blindness which seems to be the unvarying characteristic of tyrants, since Pharaoh and his hosts were drowned in the Red Sea, the British Government persisted in the exactions complained of.

The madness of this course, we believe, is admitted now, even by England; but we fear the lesson is wholly lost on our present rulers.

10   Oppression makes a wise man mad. Your fathers were wise men,   10
and if they did not go mad, they became restive under this treatment. They felt themselves the victims of grievous wrongs, wholly incurable in their colonial capacity. With brave men there is always a remedy for oppression. Just here, the idea of a total separation of the colonies from the crown was born! It was a startling idea, much more so than we, at this distance of time, regard it. The timid and the prudent (as has been intimated) of that day were, of course, shocked and alarmed by it.

Such people lived then, had lived before, and will, probably, ever have a place on this planet; and their course, in respect to any great change (no matter how great the good to be attained, or the wrong to be redressed by it), may be calculated with as much precision as can be the course of the stars. They hate all changes, but silver, gold and copper change! Of this sort of change they are always strongly in favor.

These people were called Tories in the days of your fathers; and the appellation, probably, conveyed the same idea that is meant by a more modern, though a somewhat less euphonious term, which we often find in our papers, applied to some of our old politicians.

Their opposition to the then dangerous thought was earnest and powerful; but, amid all their terror and affrighted vociferations against it, the alarming and revolutionary idea moved on, and the country with it.

On the 2d of July, 1776, the old Continental Congress, to the dismay of the lovers of ease, and the worshipers of property, clothed that dreadful idea with all the authority of national sanction. They did so in the form of a resolution; and as we seldom hit upon resolutions, drawn up in our day, whose transparency is at all equal to this, it may refresh your minds and help my story if I read it.

> "Resolved, That these united colonies are, and of right, ought to be free and Independent States; that they are absolved from all allegiance to the British Crown; and that all political connection between them and the State of Great Britain is, and ought to be, dissolved."

15   Citizens, your fathers made good that resolution. They suc- 15
ceeded; and to-day you reap the fruits of their success. The freedom gained is yours; and you, therefore, may properly celebrate this anniversary. The 4th of July is the first great fact in your nation's history—the very ringbolt in the chain of your yet undeveloped destiny.

Pride and patriotism, not less than gratitude, prompt you to celebrate and to hold it in perpetual remembrance. I have said that the Declaration of Independence is the ringbolt to the chain of your nation's destiny; so, indeed, I regard it. The principles contained in that instrument are saving principles. Stand by those principles, be true to them on all occasions, in all places, against all foes, and at whatever cost.

From the round top of your ship of state, dark and threatening clouds may be seen. Heavy billows, like mountains in the distance, disclose to the leeward huge forms of flinty rocks! That bolt drawn, that chain broken, and all is lost. Cling to this day—cling to it, and to its principles, with the grasp of a storm-tossed mariner to a spar at midnight.

The coming into being of a nation, in any circumstances, is an interesting event. But, besides general considerations, there were peculiar circumstances which make the advent of this republic an event of special attractiveness.

The whole scene, as I look back to it, was simple, dignified and sublime. The population of the country, at the time, stood at the insignificant number of three millions. The country was poor in the munitions of war. The population was weak and scattered, and the country a wilderness unsubdued. There were then no means of concert and combination, such as exist now. Neither steam nor lightning had then been reduced to order and discipline. From the Potomac to the Delaware was a journey of many days. Under these, and innumerable other disadvantages, your fathers declared for liberty and independence and triumphed.

20   Fellow-citizens, I am not wanting in respect for the fathers of this 20 republic. The signers of the Declaration of Independence were brave men. They were great men, too—great enough to give frame to a great age. It does not often happen to a nation to raise, at one time, such a number of truly great men. The point from which I am compelled to view them is not, certainly, the most favorable; and yet I cannot contemplate their great deeds with less than admiration. They were statesmen, patriots and heroes, and for the good they did, and the principles they contended for, I will unite with you to honor their memory.

They loved their country better than their own private interests; and, though this is not the highest form of human excellence, all will concede that it is a rare virtue, and that when it is exhibited it ought to command respect. He who will, intelligently, lay down his life for his country is a man whom it is not in human nature to despise. Your fathers staked their lives, their fortunes, and their sacred honor, on the cause of their country. In their admiration of liberty, they lost sight of all other interests.

They were peace men; but they preferred revolution to peaceful submission to bondage. They were quiet men; but they did not shrink from agitating against oppression. They showed forbearance; but that they knew its limits. They believed in order; but not in the order of tyranny. With them, nothing was "settled" that was not right. With them, justice, liberty and humanity were "final"; not slavery and oppression. You may well cherish the memory of such men. They were great in their day and generation. Their solid manhood stands out the more as we contrast it with these degenerate times.

How circumspect, exact and proportionate were all their movements! How unlike the politicians of an hour! Their statesmanship looked beyond the passing moment, and stretched away in strength into the distant future. They seized upon eternal principles, and set a glorious example in their defence. Mark them!

Fully appreciating the hardships to be encountered, firmly believing in the right of their cause, honorably inviting the scrutiny of an on-looking world, reverently appealing to heaven to attest their sincerity, soundly comprehending the solemn responsibility they were about to assume, wisely measuring the terrible odds against them, your fathers, the fathers of this republic, did, most deliberately, under the inspiration of a glorious patriotism, and with a sublime faith in the great principles of justice and freedom, lay deep, the corner-stone of the national super-structure, which has risen and still rises in grandeur around you.

Of this fundamental work, this day is the anniversary. Our eyes are met with demonstrations of joyous enthusiasm. Banners and pennants wave exultingly on the breeze. The din of business, too, is hushed. Even mammon seems to have quitted his grasp on this day. The ear-piercing fife and the stirring drum unite their accents with the ascending peal of a thousand church bells. Prayers are made, hymns are sung, and sermons are preached in honor of this day; while the quick martial tramp of a great and multitudinous nation, echoed back by all the hills, valleys and mountains of a vast continent, bespeak the occasion one of thrilling and universal interest—a nation's jubilee.

Friends and citizens, I need not enter further into the causes which led to this anniversary. Many of you understand them better than I do. You could instruct me in regard to them. That is a branch of knowledge in which you feel, perhaps, a much deeper interest than your speaker. The causes which led to the separation of the colonies from the British Crown have never lacked for a tongue. They have all been taught in your common schools, narrated at your firesides, unfolded from your pulpits, and thundered from your legislative halls, and are as familiar to you as household words. They form the staple of your national poetry and eloquence.

I remember, also, that, as a people, Americans are remarkably familiar with all facts which make in their own favor. This is esteemed by some as a national trait—perhaps a national weakness. It is a fact, that whatever makes for the wealth or for the reputation of Americans and can be had cheap! will be found by Americans. I shall not be charged with slandering Americans if I say I think the American side of any question may be safely left in American hands.

I leave, therefore, the great deeds of your fathers to other gentlemen whose claim to have been regularly descended will be less likely to be disputed than mine!

My business, if I have any here to-day, is with the present. The accepted time with God and His cause is the ever-living now.

Trust no future, however pleasant,
Let the dead past bury its dead;
Act, act in the living present,
Heart within, and God overhead.

30 We have to do with the past only as we can make it useful to the present 30
and to the future. To all inspiring motives, to noble deeds which can be
gained from the past, we are welcome. But now is the time, the important
time. Your fathers have lived, died, and have done their work, and have done
much of it well. You live and must die, and you must do your work. You
have no right to enjoy a child's share in the labor of your fathers, unless your
children are to be blest by your labors. You have no right to wear out and
waste the hard-earned fame of your fathers to cover your indolence. Sydney
Smith tells us that men seldom eulogize the wisdom and virtues of their
fathers, but to excuse some folly or wickedness of their own. This truth is not
a doubtful one. There are illustrations of it near and remote, ancient and
modern. It was fashionable, hundreds of years ago, for the children of Jacob
to boast, we have "Abraham to our father," when they had long lost Abraham's faith and spirit. That people contented themselves under the shadow
of Abraham's great name, while they repudiated the deeds which made his
name great. Need I remind you that a similar thing is being done all over this
country to-day? Need I tell you that the Jews are not the only people who
built the tombs of the prophets, and garnished the sepulchers of the righteous? Washington could not die till he had broken the chains of his slaves.
Yet his monument is built up by the price of human blood, and the traders
in the bodies and souls of men shout—"We have Washington to *our*
father."—Alas! that it should be so; yet so it is.

The evil that men do, lives after them,
The good is oft interred with their bones.

Fellow-citizens, pardon me, allow me to ask, why am I called
upon to speak here to-day? What have I, or those I represent, to do
with your national independence? Are the great principles of political
freedom and of natural justice, embodied in that Declaration of Independence, extended to us? and am I, therefore, called upon to bring
our humble offering to the national altar, and to confess the benefits
and express devout gratitude for the blessings resulting from your
independence to us?

Would to God, both for your sakes and ours, that an affirmative answer could be truthfully returned to these questions! Then would my task be light, and my burden easy and delightful. For *who* is there so cold, that a nation's sympathy could not warm him? Who so obdurate and dead to the claims of gratitude, that would not thankfully acknowledge such priceless benefits? Who so stolid and selfish, that would not give his voice to swell the hallelujahs of a nation's jubilee, when the chains of servitude had been torn from his limbs? I am not that man. In a case like that, the dumb might eloquently speak, and the "lame man leap as an hart."

But such is not the state of the case. I say it with a sad sense of the disparity between us. I am not included within the pale of this glorious anniversary! Your high independence only reveals the immeasurable distance between us. The blessings in which you, this day, rejoice, are not enjoyed in common.—The rich inheritance of justice, liberty, prosperity and independence, bequeathed by your fathers, is shared by you, not by me. The sunlight that brought light and healing to you, has brought stripes and death to me. This Fourth of July is *yours*, not *mine. You* may rejoice, *I* must mourn. To drag a man in fetters into the grand illuminated temple of liberty, and call upon him to join you in joyous anthems, were inhuman mockery and sacrilegious irony. Do you mean, citizens, to mock me, by asking me to speak to-day? If so, there is a parallel to your conduct. And let me warn you that it is dangerous to copy the example of a nation whose crimes, towering up to heaven, were thrown down by the breath of the Almighty, burying that nation in irrevocable ruin! I can to-day take up the plaintive lament of a peeled and woe-smitten people!

"By the rivers of Babylon, there we sat down. Yea! we wept when we remembered Zion. We hanged our harps upon the willows in the midst thereof. For there, they that carried us away captive, required of us a song; and they who wasted us required of us mirth, saying, Sing us one of the songs of Zion. How can we sing the Lord's song in a strange land? If I forget thee, O Jerusalem, let my right hand forget her cunning. If I do not remember thee, let my tongue cleave to the roof of my mouth."

Fellow-citizens, above your national, tumultuous joy, I hear the mournful wail of millions! whose chains, heavy and grievous yesterday, are, to-day, rendered more intolerable by the jubilee shouts that reach them. If I do forget, if I do not faithfully remember those bleeding children of sorrow this day, "may my right hand forget her cunning, and may my tongue cleave to the roof of my mouth!" To forget them, to pass lightly over their wrongs, and to chime in with the popular theme, would be treason most scandalous and shocking, and would make me a reproach before God and the world. My subject, then, fellow-citizens, is American slavery. I shall see this day and its popular characteristics from the slave's point of view. Standing there identified with the American bondman, making his wrongs mine, I do not hesitate to declare, with all my soul, that the character and conduct of this nation never looked blacker to me than on this 4th of July! Whether we turn to the declarations of the past, or to the professions of the present, the conduct of the nation seems equally hideous and revolting. America is false to the past, false to the present, and solemnly binds herself to be false to the future. Standing with God and the crushed and bleeding slave on this occasion, I will, in the name of humanity which is outraged, in the name of liberty which is fettered, in the name of the constitution and the Bible which are disregarded and trampled upon, dare to call in question and to denounce, with all the emphasis I can command, everything that serves to perpetuate slavery—the great sin and shame of America! "I will not equivocate; I will not excuse"; I will use the severest language I can command; and yet not one word shall escape me that any man, whose judgment is not blinded by prejudice, or who is not at heart a slaveholder, shall not confess to be right and just.

But I fancy I hear some one of my audience say, "It is just in this circumstance that you and your brother abolitionists fail to make a favorable impression on the public mind. Would you argue more, and denounce less; would you persuade more, and rebuke less; your cause would be much more likely to succeed." But, I submit, where all is plain there is nothing to be argued. What point in the anti-slavery creed would you have me argue? On what branch of the subject do the people of this country need light? Must I undertake to prove that the slave is a man? That point is conceded already. Nobody doubts it. The slaveholders themselves acknowledge it in the enactment of laws for their government. They acknowledge it when they punish disobedience on the part of the slave. There are seventy-two crimes in the State of Virginia which, if committed by a black man (no matter how ignorant he be), subject him to the punishment of death; while only two of the same crimes will subject a white man to the like punishment. What is this but the acknowledgment that the slave is a moral, intellectual, and responsible being? The manhood of the slave is conceded. It is admitted in the fact that Southern statute books are covered with enactments forbidding, under severe fines and penalties, the teaching of the slave to read or to write. When you can point to any such laws in reference to the beasts of the field, then I may consent to argue the manhood of the slave. When the dogs in your streets, when the fowls of the air, when the cattle on your hills, when the fish of the sea, and the reptiles that crawl, shall be unable to distinguish the slave from a brute, *then* will I argue with you that the slave is a man!

For the present, it is enough to affirm the equal manhood of the Negro race. Is it not astonishing that, while we are ploughing, planting, and reaping, using all kinds of mechanical tools, erecting houses, constructing bridges, building ships, working in metals of brass, iron, copper, silver and gold; that, while we are reading, writing and ciphering, acting as clerks, merchants and secretaries, having among us lawyers, doctors, ministers, poets, authors, editors, orators and teachers; that, while we are engaged in all manner of enterprises common to other men, digging gold in California, capturing the whale in the Pacific, feeding sheep and cattle on the hill-side, living, moving, acting, thinking, planning, living in families as husbands, wives and children, and, above all, confessing and worshipping the Christian's God, and looking hopefully for life and immortality beyond the grave, we are called upon to prove that we are men!

Would you have me argue that man is entitled to liberty? that he is the rightful owner of his own body? You have already declared it. M... I argue the wrongfulness of s...

sticks, to flay their flesh with the lash, to load their limbs with irons, to hunt them with dogs, to sell them at auction, to sunder their families, to knock out their teeth, to burn their flesh, to starve them into obedience and submission to their masters? Must I argue that a system thus marked with blood, and stained with pollution, is *wrong?* No! I will not. I have better employment for my time and strength than such arguments would imply.

40   What, then, remains to be argued? Is it that slavery is not divine;   40
that God did not establish it; that our doctors of divinity are mistaken? There is blasphemy in the thought. That which is inhuman, cannot be divine! *Who* can reason on such a proposition? They that can, may; I cannot. The time for such argument is passed.

At a time like this, scorching irony, not convincing argument, is needed. O! had I the ability, and could reach the nation's ear, I would, to-day, pour out a fiery stream of biting ridicule, blasting reproach, withering sarcasm, and stern rebuke. For it is not light that is needed, but fire; it is not the gentle shower, but thunder. We need the storm, the whirlwind, and the earthquake. The feeling of the nation must be quickened; the conscience of the nation must be roused; the propriety of the nation must be startled; the hypocrisy of the nation must be exposed; and its crimes against God and man must be proclaimed and denounced.

What, to the American slave, is your 4th of July? I answer; a day that reveals to him, more than all other days in the year, the gross injustice and cruelty to which he is the constant victim. To him, your celebration is a sham; your boasted liberty, an unholy license; your national greatness, swelling vanity; your sounds of rejoicing are empty and heartless; your denunciation of tyrants, brass-fronted impudence; your shouts of liberty and equality, hollow mockery; your prayers and hymns, your sermons and thanksgivings, with all your religious parade and solemnity, are, to Him, mere bombast, fraud, deception, impiety, and hypocrisy—a thin veil to cover up crimes which would disgrace a nation of savages. There is not a nation on the earth guilty of practices more shocking and bloody than are the people of the United States, at this very hour.

Go where you may, search where you will, roam through all the monarchies and despotisms of the Old World, travel through South America, search out every abuse, and when you have found the last, lay your facts by the side of the everyday practices of this nation, and you will say with me, that, for revolting barbarity and shameless hypocrisy, American reigns without a rival.

Take the American slave-trade, which we are told by the papers, is especially prosperous just now. Ex-Senator Benton tells us that the price of men was never higher than now. He mentions the fact to show that slavery is in no danger. This trade is one of the peculiarities of American institutions. It is carried on in all the large towns and cities in one-half of this confederacy; and millions are pocketed every year by dealers in this horrid traffic. In several states this trade is a chief source of wealth. It is called (in contradistinction to the foreign slave-trade) *the internal slave-trade.* It is, probably, called so, too, in order to divert from it the horror with which the foreign slave-trade is contemplated. That trade has long since been denounced by this government as piracy. It has been denounced with burning words from the high places of the nation as an execrable traffic. To arrest it, to put an end to it, this nation keeps a squadron, at immense cost, on the coast of Africa. Everywhere, in this country, it is safe to speak of this foreign slave-trade as a most inhuman traffic, opposed alike to the laws of God and of man. The duty to extirpate and destroy it, is admitted even by our doctors of divinity. In order to put an end to it, some of these last have consented that their colored brethren (nominally free) should leave this country, and establish themselves on the western coast of Africa! It is, however, a notable fact that, while so much execration is poured out by Americans upon all those engaged in the foreign slave-trade, the men engaged in the slave-trade between the states pass without condemnation, and their business is deemed honorable.

45   Behold the practical operation of this internal slave-trade, the   45 American slave-trade, sustained by American politics and American religion. Here you will see men and women reared like swine for the market. You know what is a swine-drover? I will show you a man-drover. They inhabit all our Southern States. They perambulate the country, and crowd the highways of the nation, with droves of human stock. You will see one of these human flesh jobbers, armed with pistol, whip, and bowie-knife, driving a company of a hundred men, women, and children, from the Potomac to the slave market at New Orleans. These wretched people are to be sold singly, or in lots, to suit purchasers. They are food for the cotton-field and the deadly sugar-mill. Mark the sad procession, as it moves wearily along, and the

inhuman wretch who drives them. Hear his savage yells and his blood-curdling oaths, as he hurries on his affrighted captives! There, see the old man with locks thinned and gray. Cast one glance, if you please, upon that young mother, whose shoulders are bare to the scorching sun, her briny tears falling on the brow of the babe in her arms. See, too, that girl of thirteen, weeping, *yes!* weeping, as she thinks of the mother from whom she has been torn! The drove moves tardily. Heat and sorrow have nearly consumed their strength; suddenly you hear a quick snap, like the discharge of a rifle; the fetters clank, and the chain rattles simultaneously; your ears are saluted with a scream, that seems to have torn its way to the centre of your soul! The crack you heard was the sound of the slave-whip; the scream you heard was from the woman you saw with the babe. Her speed had faltered under the weight of her child and her chains! that gash on her shoulder tells her to move on. Follow this drive to New Orleans. Attend the auction; see men examined like horses; see the forms of women rudely and brutally exposed to the shocking gaze of American slave-buyers. See this drove sold and separated forever; and never forget the deep, sad sobs that arose from that scattered multitude. Tell me, citizens, where, under the sun, you can witness a spectacle more fiendish and shocking. Yet this is but a glance at the American slave-trade, as it exists, at this moment, in the ruling part of the United States.

I was born amid such sights and scenes. To me the American slave-trade is a terrible reality. When a child, my soul was often pierced with a sense of its horrors. I lived on Philpot Street, Fell's Point, Baltimore, and have watched from the wharves the slave ships in the Basin, anchored from the shore, with their cargoes of human flesh, waiting for favorable winds to waft them down the Chesapeake. There was, at that time, a grand slave mart kept at the head of Pratt Street, by Austin Woldfolk. His agents were sent into every town and county in Maryland, announcing their arrival, through the papers, and on flaming "*hand-bills*," headed cash for Negroes. These men were generally well dressed men, and very captivating in their manners; ever ready to drink, to treat, and to gamble. The fate of many a slave has depended upon the turn of a single card; and many a child has been snatched from the arms of its mother by bargains arranged in a state of brutal drunkenness.

The flesh-mongers gather up their victims by dozens, and drive them, chained, to the general depot at Baltimore. When a sufficient number has been collected here, a ship is chartered for the purpose of conveying the forlorn crew to Mobile, or to New Orleans. From the slave prison to the ship, they are usually driven in the darkness of night; for since the anti-slavery agitation, a certain caution is observed.

In the deep, still darkness of midnight, I have been often aroused by the dead, heavy footsteps, and the piteous cries of the chained gangs that passed our door. The anguish of my boyish heart was intense; and I was often consoled, when speaking to my mistress in the morning, to hear her say that the custom was very wicked; that she hated to hear the rattle of the chains and the heart-rending cries. I was glad to find one who sympathized with me in my horror.

Fellow-citizens, this murderous traffic is, to-day, in active operation in this boasted republic. In the solitude of my spirit I see clouds of dust raised on the highways of the South; I see the bleeding footsteps; I hear the doleful wail of fettered humanity on the way to the slave-markets, where the victims are to be sold like *horses, sheep,* and *swine,* knocked off to the highest bidder. There I see the tenderest ties ruthlessly broken, to gratify the lust, caprice and rapacity of the buyers and sellers of men. My soul sickens at the sight.

> *Is this the land your Fathers loved,*
> *The freedom which they toiled to win?*
> *Is this the earth whereon they moved?*
> *Are these the graves they slumber in?*

50 But a still more inhuman, disgraceful, and scandalous state of 50 things remains to be presented. By an act of the American Congress, not yet two years old, slavery has been nationalized in its most horrible and revolting form. By that act, Mason and Dixon's line has been obliterated; New York has become as Virginia; and the power to hold, hunt, and sell men, women and children, as slaves, remains no longer a mere state institution, but is now an institution of the whole United States. The power is co-extensive with the star-spangled banner, and American Christianity. Where these go, may also go the merciless slave-hunter. Where these are, man is not sacred. He is a bird for the sportsman's gun. By that most foul and fiendish of all human decrees, the liberty and person of every man are put in peril. Your broad republican domain is hunting ground for *men. Not* for

thieves and robbers, enemies of society, merely, but for men guilty of no crime. Your law-makers have commanded all good citizens to engage in this hellish sport. Your President, your Secretary of State, your *lords, nobles*, and ecclesiastics enforce, as a duty you owe to your free and glorious country, and to your God, that you do this accursed thing. Not fewer than forty Americans have, with in the past two years, been hunted down and, without a moment's warning, hurried away in chains, and consigned to slavery and excruciating torture. Some of these have had wives and children, dependent on them for bread; but of this, no account was made. The right of the hunter to his prey stands superior to the right of marriage, and to *all* rights in this republic, the rights of God included! For black men there is neither law nor justice, humanity nor religion. The Fugitive Slave *Law* makes mercy to them a crime; and bribes the judge who tries them. An American judge gets ten dollars for every victim he consigns to slavery, and five, when he fails to do so. The oath of any two villains is sufficient, under this hell-black enactment, to send the most pious and exemplary black man into the remorseless jaws of slavery! His own testimony is nothing. He can bring no witnesses for himself. The minister of American justice is bound by the law to hear but *one* side; and *that* side is the side of the oppressor. Let this damning fact be perpetually told. Let it be thundered around the world that in tyrant-killing, king-hating, people-loving, democratic, Christian America the seats of justice are filled with judges who hold their offices under an open and palpable *bribe*, and are bound, in deciding the case of a man's liberty, *to hear only his accusers!*

In glaring violation of justice, in shameless disregard of the forms of administering law, in cunning arrangement to entrap the defence-less, and in diabolical intent this Fugitive Slave Law stands alone in the annals of tyrannical legislation. I doubt if there be another nation on the globe having the brass and the baseness to put such a law on the statute-book. If any man in this assembly thinks differently from me in this matter, and feels able to disprove my statements, I will gladly confront him at any suitable time and place he may select.

I take this law to be one of the grossest infringements of Christian Liberty, and, if the churches and ministers of our country were not stupidly blind, or most wickedly indifferent, they, too, would so regard it.

At the very moment that they are thanking God for the enjoyment of civil and religious liberty, and for the right to worship God according to the dictates of their own consciences, they are utterly silent in respect to a law which robs religion of its chief significance and makes it utterly worthless to a world lying in wickedness. Did this law concern the *"mint, anise, and cummin"*—abridge the right to sing psalms, to partake of the sacrament, or to engage in any of the ceremonies of religion, it would be smitten by the thunder of a thousand pulpits. A general shout would go up from the church demanding *repeal, repeal, instant repeal!*—And it would go hard with that politician who presumed to solicit the votes of the people without inscribing this motto on his banner. Further, if this demand were not complied with, another Scotland would be added to the history of religious liberty, and the stern old covenanters would be thrown into the shade. A John Knox* would be seen at every church door and heard from every pulpit, and Fillmore† would have no more quarter than was shown by Knox to the beautiful, but treacherous, Queen Mary of Scotland.‡ The fact that the church of our country (with fractional exceptions) does not esteem "the Fugitive Slave Law"* as a declaration of war against religious liberty, implies that that church regards religion simply as a form of worship, an empty ceremony, and *not* a vital principle, requiring active benevolence, justice,

---

*John Knox (1513–1572) was leader of the reformation (the separation of the Protestant church from the Catholic church) in Scotland. He set the austere moral tone of the Church of Scotland and shaped its democratic form of government. Thus Douglass's reference to "another Scotland" in the previous sentence is a reference to national movements in favor of freedom and opposed to tyranny.

†Millard Fillmore (1800–1874) was president of the United States at the time of Douglass's address. Fillmore was vice president under Zachary Taylor and completed Taylor's term when Taylor died in 1850. He was defeated for the presidency in his own right in 1852. Fillmore signed the new Fugitive Slave Law of 1850, thus alienating abolitionists.

‡Mary Stuart (1542–1587) was the Catholic queen of Scotland who wished to return Scotland to Catholicism, but was forced by the nation's Protestant partisans to abdicate the throne in favor of her Protestant son, who later became both king of Scotland as James VI and of England as James I. Knox was one of Mary's principal opponents.

*The Fugitive Slave Law was first enacted by Congress in 1793 and mandated the right of a slaveowner to recover a runaway slave. This law made it illegal for those who opposed slavery, even in nonslavery states, to interfere with a slaveowner's attempts to remove runaway slaves from northern refuges and return them to southern slavery. A new Fugitive Slave Act passed by Congress and signed by President Fillmore in 1850 strengthened the act of 1793 and was bitterly opposed by abolitionists.

love, and good will towards man. It esteems sacrifice above mercy; psalm-singing above right doing; solemn meetings above practical righteousness. A worship that can be conducted by persons who refuse to give shelter to the houseless, to give bread to the hungry, clothing to the naked, and who enjoin obedience to a law forbidding these acts of mercy is a curse, not a blessing to mankind. The Bible addresses all such persons as "scribes, pharisees, hypocrites, who pay tithe of *mint, anise,* and *cummin,* and have omitted the weightier matters of the law, judgment, mercy, and faith."

But the church of this country is not only indifferent to the wrongs of the slave, it actually takes sides with the oppressors. It has made itself the bulwark of American slavery, and the shield of American slave-hunters. Many of its most eloquent Divines, who stand as the very lights of the church, have shamelessly given the sanction of religion and the Bible to the whole slave system. They have taught that man may, properly, be a slave; that the relation of master and slave is ordained of God; that to send back an escaped bondman to his master is clearly the duty of all the followers of the Lord Jesus Christ; and this horrible blasphemy is palmed off upon the world for Christianity.

55   For my part, I would say, welcome infidelity! welcome atheism! welcome anything! in preference to the gospel, *as preached by those Divines!*   55
They convert the very name of religion into an engine of tyranny and barbarous cruelty, and serve to confirm more infidels, in this age, than all the infidel writings of Thomas Paine, Voltaire, and Bolingbroke[†] put together have done! These ministers make religion a cold and flinty-hearted thing, having neither principles of right action nor bowels of compassion. They strip the love of God of its beauty and leave the throne of religion a huge, horrible, repulsive form. It is a religion for oppressors, tyrants, man-stealers, and *thugs.* It is not that *"pure and undefiled religion"* which is from above, and which is *"first pure, then peaceable, easy to be entreated,* full of mercy and good fruits, *without partiality, and without hypocrisy."* But a religion which favors the rich against the poor; which exalts the proud above the humble; which divides mankind into two classes, tyrants and slaves; which says to the

---

[†]Thomas Paine (1737–1809), American political philosopher; Francois-Marie Arouet, "Voltaire" (1694–1778), French philopher and athiest; and Henry St. John, 1st Viscount Bolingbroke (1678–1751), English politician and writer, were eighteenth-century figures all noted for their religious skepticism and hostility toward churches.

man in chains, *stay there;* and to the oppressor, *oppress on;* it is a religion which may be professed and enjoyed by all the robbers and enslavers of mankind; it makes God a respecter of persons, denies his fatherhood of the race, and tramples in the dust the great truth of the brotherhood of man. All this we affirm to be true of the popular church, and the popular worship of our land and nation—a religion, a church, and a worship which, on the authority of inspired wisdom, we pronounce to be an abomination in the sight of God. In the language of Isaiah, the American church might be well addressed, "Bring no more vain oblations; incense is an abomination unto me: the new moons and Sabbaths, the calling of assemblies, I cannot away with; it is iniquity, even the solemn meeting. Your new moons, and your appointed feasts my soul hateth. They are a trouble to me; I am weary to bear them; and when ye spread forth your hands I will hide mine eyes from you. Yea! when ye make many prayers, I will not hear. Your hands are full of blood; cease to do evil, learn to do well; seek judgment; relieve the oppressed; judge for the fatherless; plead for the widow."

The American church is guilty, when viewed in connection with what it is doing to uphold slavery; but it is superlatively guilty when viewed in its connection with its ability to abolish slavery.

The sin of which it is guilty is one of omission as well as of commission. Albert Barnes but uttered what the common sense of every man at all observant of the actual state of the case will receive as truth, when he declared that "There is no power out of the church that could sustain slavery an hour, if it were not sustained in it."

Let the religious press, the pulpit, the Sunday School, the conference meeting, the great ecclesiastical, missionary, Bible and tract associations of the land array their immense powers against slavery, and slave-holding; and the whole system of crime and blood would be scattered to the winds, and that they do not do this involves them in the most awful responsibility of which the mind can conceive.

In prosecuting the anti-slavery enterprise, we have been asked to spare the church, to spare the ministry; but *how,* we ask, could such a thing be done? We are met on the threshold of our efforts for the redemption of the slave, by the church and ministry of the country, in battle arrayed against us; and we are compelled to fight or flee. From *what* quarter, I beg to know, has proceeded a fire so deadly upon our ranks, during the last two years, as from the Northern pulpit? As the champions of oppressors, the chosen men of American theology have appeared—men honored for their so-called piety, and their real learning. The Lords of Buffalo, the Springs of New York, the Lathrops of Auburn, the Coxes and Spencers of Brooklyn, the Gannets and Sharps of Boston, the Deweys of Washington, and other great religious lights of the land have, in utter denial of the authority of *Him* by whom they professed to be called to the ministry, deliberately taught us, against the example of the Hebrews, and against the remonstrance of the Apostles, *that we ought to obey man's law before the law of God.*

60 My spirit wearies of such blasphemy; and how such men can be 60 supported, as the "standing types and representatives of Jesus Christ," is a mystery which I leave others to penetrate. In speaking of the American church, however, let it be distinctly understood that I mean the *great mass* of the religious organizations of our land. There are exceptions, and I thank God that there are. Noble men may be found, scattered all over these Northern States, of whom Henry Ward Beecher, of Brooklyn; Samuel J. May, of Syracuse; and my esteemed friend (Rev. R. R. Raymond) on the platform, are shining examples; and let me say further, that, upon these men lies the duty to inspire our ranks with high religious faith and zeal, and to cheer us on in the great mission of the slave's redemption from his chains.

One is struck with the difference between the attitude of the American church towards the anti-slavery movement, and that occupied by the churches in England towards a similar movement in that country. There, the church, true to its mission of ameliorating, elevating and improving the condition of mankind, came forward promptly, bound up the wounds of the West Indian slave, and restored him to his liberty. There, the question of emancipation was a high religious question. It was demanded in the name of humanity, and according to the law of the living God. The Sharps, the Clarksons, the Wilberforces, the Buxtons, the Burchells, and the Knibbs were alike famous for their piety and for their philanthropy. The anti-slavery movement *there* was not an anti-church movement, for the reason that the church took its full share in prosecuting that movement: and the antislavery movement in this country will cease to be an anti-church movement, when the church of this country shall assume a favorable instead of a hostile position towards that movement.

Americans! your republican politics, not less than your republican religion, are flagrantly inconsistent. You boast of your love of liberty, your superior civilization, and your pure Christianity, while the whole political power of the nation (as embodied in the two great political parties) is solemnly pledged to support and perpetuate the enslavement of three millions of your countrymen. You hurl your anathemas at the crowned headed tyrants of Russia and Austria and pride yourselves on your Democratic institutions, while you yourselves consent to be the mere *tools* and *body-guards* of the tyrants of Virginia and Carolina. You invite to your shores fugitives of oppression from abroad, honor them with banquets, greet them with ovations, cheer them, toast them, salute them, protect them, and pour out your money to them like water; but the fugitives from your own land you advertise, hunt, arrest, shoot, and kill. You glory in your refinement and your universal education; yet you maintain a system as barbarous and dreadful as ever stained the character of a nation—a system begun in avarice, supported in pride, and perpetuated in cruelty. You shed tears over fallen Hungary, and make the sad story of her wrongs the theme of your poets, statesmen, and orators, till your gallant sons are ready to fly to arms to vindicate her cause against the oppressor; but, in regard to the ten thousand wrongs of the American slave, you would enforce the strictest silence, and would hail him as an enemy of the nation who dares to make those wrongs the subject of public discourse! You are all on fire at the mention of liberty for France or for Ireland; but are as cold as an iceberg at the thought of liberty for the enslaved of America. You discourse eloquently on the dignity of labor; yet you sustain a system which, in its very essence, casts a stigma upon labor. You can bare your bosom to the storm of British artillery to throw off a three-penny tax on tea; and yet wring the last hard earned farthing from the grasp of the black laborers of your country. You profess to believe "that, of one blood, God made all nations of men to dwell on the face of all the earth," and hath commanded all men, everywhere, to love one another; yet you notoriously hate (and glory in your hatred) all men whose skins are not colored like your own. You declare before the world, and are understood by the world to declare that you *"hold these truths to be self-evident, that all men are created equal; and are endowed by their Creator with certain inalienable rights; and that among these are, life, liberty, and the pursuit of happiness;* and yet, you hold securely, in a bondage which, according to your own Thomas Jefferson, *"is worse than ages of that which your fathers rose in rebellion to oppose,"* a seventh* part of the inhabitants of your country.

Fellow-citizens, I will not enlarge further on your national inconsistencies. The existence of slavery in this country brands your republicanism as a sham, your humanity as a base pretense, and your Christianity as a lie. It destroys your moral power abroad: it corrupts your politicians at home. It saps the foundation of religion; it makes your name a hissing and a bye-word to a mocking earth. It is the antagonistic force in your government, the only thing that seriously disturbs and endangers your *Union*. It fetters your progress; it is the enemy of improvement; the deadly foe of education; it fosters pride; it breeds insolence; it promotes vice; it shelters crime; it is a curse to the earth that supports it; and yet you cling to it as if it were the sheet anchor of all your hopes. Oh! be warned! be warned! a horrible reptile is coiled up in your nation's bosom; the venomous creature is nursing at the tender breast of your youthful republic; *for the love of God, tear away*, and fling from you the hideous monster, and *let the weight of twenty millions crush and destroy it forever!*

But it is answered in reply to all this, that precisely what I have now denounced is, in fact, guaranteed and sanctioned by the Constitution of the United States; that, the right to hold, and to hunt slaves is a part of that Constitution framed by the illustrious Fathers of this Republic.

65 Then, I dare to affirm, notwithstanding all I have said before, 65 your fathers stooped, basely stooped

> *To palter with us in a double sense:*
> *And keep the word of promise to the dear,*
> *But break it to the heart.*

And instead of being the honest men I have before declared them to be, they were the veriest impostors that ever practised on mankind. This is the inevitable conclusion, and from it there is no escape; but I differ from those who charge this baseness on the framers of the Constitution of the United States. It is a slander upon their memory, at least, so I believe. There is not time now to argue the constitutional question at length; nor have I the ability to discuss it as it ought to be discussed. The subject has been handled with masterly power by Lysander Spooner, Esq., by William Goodell, by Samuel E. Sewall, Esq., and last, though not least, by Gerrit Smith, Esq. These gentlemen have, as I think, fully and clearly vindicated the Constitution from any design to support slavery for an hour.

Fellow-citizens! there is no matter in respect to which the people of the North have allowed themselves to be so ruinously imposed upon as that of the pro-slavery character of the Constitution. In that instrument I hold there is neither warrant, license, nor sanction of the hateful thing; but interpreted, as it ought to be interpreted, the Constitution is a glorious liberty document. Read its preamble, consider its purposes. Is slavery among them? Is it at the gateway? or is it in the temple? it is neither. While I do not intend to argue this question on the present occasion, let me ask, if it be not somewhat singular that, if the Constitution were intended to be, by its framers and adopters, a slaveholding instrument, why neither slavery, slaveholding, nor slave can anywhere be found in it. What would be thought of an instrument, drawn up, legally drawn up, for the purpose of entitling the city of Rochester to a tract of land, in which no mention of land was made? Now, there are certain rules of interpretation for the proper understanding of all legal instruments. These rules are well established. They are plain, common-sense rules, such as you and I, and all of us, can understand and apply, without having passed years in the study of law. I scout the idea that the question of the constitutionality, or unconstitutionality of slavery, is not a question for the people. I hold that every American citizen has a right to form an opinion of the constitution, and to propagate that opinion, and to use all honorable means to make his opinion the prevailing one. Without this right, the liberty of an American citizen would be as insecure as that of a Frenchman. Ex-Vice-President Dallas tells us that the constitution is an object to which no American mind can be too attentive, and no American heart too devoted. He further says, the Constitution, in its words, is plain and intelligible, and is meant for the home-bred, unsophisticated understandings of our fellow-citizens. Senator Berrien tells us that the Constitution is the fundamental law, that which controls all others. The charter of our liberties, which every citizen has a personal interest in understanding thoroughly. The testimony of Senator Breese, Lewis Cass, and many others that might be named, who are everywhere esteemed as sound lawyers, so regard the constitution. I take it, therefore, that it is not presumption in a private citizen to form an opinion of that instrument.

Now, take the Constitution according to its plain reading, and I defy the presentation of a single pro-slavery clause in it. On the other hand, it will be found to contain principles and purposes, entirely hostile to the existence of slavery.

I have detained my audience entirely too long already. At some future period I will gladly avail myself of an opportunity to give this subject a full and fair discussion.

70   Allow me to say, in conclusion, notwithstanding the dark picture   70
I have this day presented, of the state of the nation, I do not despair of this country. There are forces in operation which must inevitably work the downfall of slavery. "The arm of the Lord is not shortened," and the doom of slavery is certain. I, therefore, leave off where I began, with hope. While drawing encouragement from "the Declaration of Independence," the great principles it contains, and the genius of American Institutions, my spirit is also cheered by the obvious tendencies of the age. Nations do not now stand in the same relation to each other that they did ages ago. No nation can now shut itself up from the surrounding world and trot round in the same old path of its fathers without interference. The time was when such could be done. Long established customs of hurtful character could formerly fence themselves in, and do their evil work with social impunity. Knowledge was then confined and enjoyed by the privileged few, and the multitude walked on in mental darkness. But a change has now come over the affairs of mankind. Walled cities and empires have become unfashionable. The arm of commerce has borne away the gates of the strong city. Intelligence is penetrating the darkest corners of the globe. It makes its pathway over and under the sea, as well as on the earth. Wind, steam, and lightning are its chartered agents. Oceans no longer divide, but link nations together. From Boston to London is now a holiday excursion. Space is comparatively annihilated.—Thoughts expressed on one side of the Atlantic are distinctly heard on the other.

The far off and almost fabulous Pacific rolls in grandeur at our feet. The Celestial Empire, the mystery of ages, is being solved. The fiat of the Almighty, "Let there be Light," has not yet spent its force. No abuse, no outrage whether in taste, sport or avarice, can now hide itself from the all-pervading light. The iron shoe, and crippled foot of China must be seen in contrast with nature. Africa must rise and put on her yet unwoven garment. "Ethiopia shall stretch out her hand unto God."* In the fervent aspirations of William Lloyd Garrison, I say, and let every heart join in saying it:

---

*Douglass's general point about light is that oppressive abuses, in a day of international travel, cannot be hidden as before and will cry for redress. The "crippled foot of China" is a reference to foot binding and "Ethiopia" is here used as a term for all African people.

God speed the year of jubilee
The wide world o'er!
When from their galling chains set free,
Th' oppress'd shall vilely bend the knee,
And wear the yoke of tyranny
Like brutes no more.
That year will come, and freedom's reign,
To man his plundered rights again
Restore.

God speed the day when human blood
Shall cease to flow!
In every clime be understood,
The claims of human brotherhood,
And each return for evil, good,
Not blow for blow;
That day will come all feuds to end,
And change into a faithful friend
Each foe.

God speed the hour, the glorious hour,
When none on earth
Shall exercise a lordly power,
Nor in a tyrant's presence cower;
But to all manhood's stature tower,
By equal birth!
That hour will come, to each, to all,
And from his prison-house, to thrall
Go forth.

Until that year, day, hour, arrive,
With head, and heart, and hand I'll strive,
To break the rod, and rend the gyve,
The spoiler of his prey deprive—
So witness Heaven!
And never from my chosen post,
Whate'er the peril or the cost,
Be driven.

How It Feels to Be Colored Me

Zora Neale Hurston

Zora Neale Hurston (1891–1960) was born in a small town in Alabama, from which her family moved to all-black Eatonville, Florida, when she was still an infant. After her mother's death in 1904, Zora left home to work and attend school elsewhere. She attended Howard University, received her degree from Barnard College, and did graduate work at Columbia University. She studied folklore and anthropology. In 1921 she published her first short story, beginning a lifelong literary career. She worked as a domestic, teacher, a librarian, and a journalist at different times while she was writing. She published five books in her lifetime, including Mules and Men *(1935) and* Their Eyes Were Watching God *(1937), considered by many her finest novel. Much of her later writing was rejected by publishers but published after her death. In the late 1960s Hurston was "rediscovered" and is now recognized as an important American author, praised by critics and writers alike. The essay "How It Feels to Be Colored Me" is an early work, first printed in a magazine in 1928. In it Hurston looks back at an important moment as she came of age as an African-American woman in America.*

1   I am colored but I offer nothing in the way of extenuating circumstances except the fact that I am the only Negro in the United States whose grandfather on the mother's side was *not* an Indian chief.

I remember the very day that I became colored. Up to my thirteenth year I lived in the little Negro town of Eatonville, Florida. It is

From *The World Tomorrow* 11 (May, 1928). Copyright © 1929 by Zora Neale Hurston, renewed 1956 by John C. Hurston.

exclusively a colored town. The only white people I knew passed through the town going to or coming from Orlando. The native whites rode dusty horses, the Northern tourists chugged down the sandy village road in automobiles. The town knew the Southerners and never stopped cane chewing when they passed. But the Northerners were something else again. They were peered at cautiously from behind curtains by the timid. The more venturesome would come out on the porch to watch them go past and got just as much pleasure out of the tourists as the tourists got out of the village.

The front porch might seem a daring place for the rest of the town, but it was a gallery seat to me. My favorite place was atop the gate-post. Proscenium box for a born first-nighter. Not only did I enjoy the show, but I didn't mind the actors knowing that I liked it. I usually spoke to them in passing. I'd wave at them and when they returned my salute, I would say something like this: "Howdy-do-well-I-thank-you-where-you-goin'?" Usually the automobile or the horse paused at this, and after a queer exchange of compliments, I would probably "go a piece of the way" with them, as we say in farthest Florida. If one of my family happened to come to the front in time to see me, of course negotiations would be rudely broken off. But even so, it is clear that I was the first "welcome-to-our-state" Floridian, and I hope the Miami Chamber of Commerce will please take notice.

During this period, white people differed from colored to me only in that they rode through town and never lived there. They liked to hear me "speak pieces" and sing and wanted to see me dance the parse-me-la, and gave me generously of their small silver for doing these things, which seemed strange to me for I wanted to do them so much that I needed bribing to stop. Only they didn't know it. The colored people gave no dimes. They deplored any joyful tendencies in me, but I was their Zora nevertheless. I belonged to them, to the nearby hotels, to the county—everybody's Zora.

5   But changes came in the family when I was thirteen, and I was   5
sent to school in Jacksonville. I left Eatonville, the town of the olean-ders, as Zora. When I disembarked from the river-boat at Jacksonville, she was no more. It seemed that I had suffered a sea change. I was not Zora of Orange County any more, I was now a little colored girl. I found it out in certain ways. In my heart as well as in the mirror, I became a fast brown—warranted not to rub nor run.

But I am not tragically colored. There is no great sorrow dammed up in my soul, nor lurking behind my eyes. I do not mind at all. I do not belong to the sobbing school of Negrohood who hold that nature somehow has given them a lowdown dirty deal and whose feelings are all hurt about it. Even in the helter-skelter skirmish that is my life, I have seen that the world is to the strong regardless of a little pigmentation more or less. No, I do not weep at the world—I am too busy sharpening my oyster knife.

Someone is always at my elbow reminding me that I am the granddaughter of slaves. It fails to register depression with me. Slavery is sixty years in the past. The operation was successful and the patient is doing well, thank you. The terrible struggle that made me an American out of a potential slave said "On the line!" The Reconstruction said "Get set!"; and the generation before said "Go!" I am off to a flying start and I must not halt in the stretch to look behind and weep. Slavery is the price I paid for civilization, and the choice was not with me. It is a bully adventure and worth all that I have paid through my ancestors for it. No one on earth ever had a greater chance for glory. The world to be won and nothing to be lost. It is thrilling to think—to know that for any act of mine, I shall get twice as much praise or twice as much blame. It is quite exciting to hold the center of the national stage, with the spectators not knowing whether to laugh or to weep.

The position of my white neighbor is much more difficult. No brown specter pulls up a chair beside me when I sit down to eat. No dark ghost thrusts its leg against mine in bed. The game of keeping what one has is never so exciting as the game of getting.

I do not always feel colored. Even now I often achieve the unconscious Zora of Eatonville before the Hegira. I feel most colored when I am thrown against a sharp white background.

10 For instance at Barnard. "Beside the waters of the Hudson" I feel 10 my race. Among the thousand white persons, I am a dark rock surged upon, overswept by a creamy sea. I am surged upon and overswept, but through it all, I remain myself. When covered by the waters, I am; and the ebb but reveals me again.

Sometimes it is the other way around. A white person is set down in our midst, but the contrast is just as sharp for me. For instance, when I sit in the drafty basement that is The New World Cabaret with a white person, my color comes. We enter chatting about any little nothing that we have in common and are seated by the jazz waiters. In the abrupt way that jazz orchestras have, this one plunges into a number. It loses no time in circumlocutions, but gets right down to business. It constricts the thorax and splits the heart with its tempo and narcotic harmonies. This orchestra grows rambunctious, rears on its hind legs and attacks the tonal veil with primitive fury, rending it, clawing it until it breaks through to the jungle beyond. I follow those heathen—follow them exultingly. I dance wildly inside myself; I yell within, I whoop; I shake my assegai above my head, I hurl it true to the mark *yeeeeooww!* I am in the jungle and living in the jungle way. My face is painted red and yellow and my body is painted blue. My pulse is throbbing like a war drum. I want to slaughter something— give pain, give death to what, I do not know. But the piece ends. The men of the orchestra wipe their lips and rest their fingers. I creep back slowly to the veneer we call civilization with the last tone and find the white friend sitting motionless in his seat, smoking calmly.

"Good music they have here," he remarks, drumming the table with his fingertips.

Music! The great blobs of purple and red emotion have not touched him. He has only heard what I felt. He is far away and I see him but dimly across the ocean and the continent that have fallen between us. He is so pale with his whiteness then and I am *so* colored.

At certain times I have no race, I am *me*. When I set my hat at a certain angle and saunter down Seventh Avenue, Harlem City, feeling as snooty as the lions in front of the Forty-Second Street Library, for instance. So far as my feelings are concerned, Peggy Hopkins Joyce on the Boule Mich with her gorgeous raiment, stately carriage, knees knocking together in a most aristocratic manner, has nothing on me. The cosmic Zora emerges. I belong to no race nor time. I am the eternal feminine with its string of beads.

15 I have no separate feeling about being an American citizen and 15 colored. I am merely a fragment of the Great Soul that surges within the boundaries. My country, right or wrong.

Sometimes, I feel discriminated against, but it does not make me angry. It merely astonishes me. How *can* any deny themselves the pleasure of my company! It's beyond me.

But in the main, I feel like a brown bag of miscellany propped against a wall. Against a wall in company with other bags, white, red and yellow. Pour out the contents, and there is discovered a jumble of small things priceless and worthless. A first-water diamond, an empty spool, bits of broken glass, lengths of string, a key to a door long since crumbled away, a rusty knifeblade, old shoes saved for a road that never was and never will be, a nail bent under the weight of things too heavy for any nail, a dried flower or two, still a little fragrant. In your hand is the brown bag. On the ground before you is the jumble it held—so much like the jumble in the bags, could they be emptied, that all might be dumped in a single heap and the bags refilled without altering the content of any greatly. A bit of colored glass more or less would not matter. Perhaps that is how the Great Stuffer of Bags filled them in the first place—who knows?

Questions on Meaning

1.   What does the author mean when she writes, "No, I do not weep at the world—I am too busy sharpening my oyster knife"?
2.   Why did Zora the young girl not feel "colored"? What does it mean, later in her life, to feel colored?
3.   Hurston seems to dismiss the issue of discrimination in one brief paragraph. What attitude about racial prejudice and discrimination might be inferred from this and the essay as a whole?

Questions on Rhetorical Strategy and Style

1.   Hurston's writing is characterized by vivid figurative language, particularly in the "brown bag of miscellany" metaphor in the ending paragraph. Reread that passage and explain what that expanded metaphor reveals about her attitude toward racial differences.
2.   The essay is invigorating and life-affirming in part as a result of Hurston's buoyant style. Reread the essay and mark several passages that simply make you feel positive and upbeat when you read them. Then look more carefully at these passages and try to identify what characteristics in the writing give you this feeling.

Writing Assignments

1.   Analyze the passage in this essay in which Hurston describes sitting in the jazz club with a white man. How does this story demonstrate a major theme of the essay? Some people might say that this episode stereotypes differences between the races—how would you answer that?
2.   Some 70 years ago Hurston found it "thrilling to think—to know that for any act of mine, I shall get twice as much praise or twice as much blame." What does she mean by this? Is this still a common attitude today? Contrast this with the opposite view that "twice as much blame" is unfair and discriminatory.
3.   Take a good long view of yourself as an outsider might see you, for example, from the point of view of someone living in another country with a very different culture. Use your imagination to see yourself in that person's eyes. Write a narrative essay describing what you seem to be like from that perspective after a casual meeting.

Size 6: The Western Women's Harem

Fatema Mernissi

Fatema Mernissi (1940–), a Moroccan feminist writer and sociologist, was born in Fez and studied at the Sorbonne in Paris. Her doctorate is from Brandeis University in the United States. She has published widely in the United States and won the 2003 Prince of Asturias Award for Letters (along with Susan Sontag). She now lives and works in Rabat, Morocco where she is a lecturer at the Mohammed V University of Rabat and a research scholar at the University Institute for Scientific Research. Her publications include Beyond the Veil: Male/Female Dynamics in Modern Muslim Society *(1975);* The Veil and the Male Elite: A Feminist Interpretation of Women's Rights in Islam *(1988);* Forgotten Queens of Islam *(1990);* Islam and Democracy: Fear of the Modern World *(1992); and* Scheherazade Goes West: Different Cultures, Different Harems *(2002).*

Moroccan women must hide their faces and live in a harem, but Western women have male domination inscribed into their flesh by the demands of a "size 6" world. The fashion industry is run by men who dictate that all women must look like adolescent girls. The author thanks God that she is not a Western woman but a Muslim who can eat what she wants.

¹ It was during my unsuccessful attempt to buy a cotton skirt in an ¹
American department store that I was told my hips were too large
to fit into a size 6. That distressing experience made me realize
how the image of beauty in the West can hurt and humiliate a woman
as much as the veil does when enforced by the state police in extremist nations such as Iran, Afghanistan, or Saudi Arabia. Yes, that day I
stumbled onto one of the keys to the enigma of passive beauty in
Western harem fantasies. The elegant saleslady in the American store
looked at me without moving from her desk and said that she had no
skirt my size. "In this whole big store, there is no skirt for me?" I said.
"You are joking." I felt very suspicious and thought that she just
might be too tired to help me. I could understand that. But then the
saleswoman added a condescending judgment, which sounded to me
like an imam's fatwa. It left no room for discussion:

"You are too big!" she said.

"I am too big compared to what?" I asked, looking at her intently,
because I realized that I was facing a critical cultural gap here.

"Compared to a size 6," came the saleslady's reply.

5   Her voice had a clear-cut edge to it that is typical of those who   5
enforce religious laws. "Size 4 and 6 are the norm," she went on,
encouraged by my bewildered look. "Deviant sizes such as the one
you need can be bought in special stores."

That was the first time that I had ever heard such nonsense about
my size. In the Moroccan streets, men's flattering comments regarding
my particularly generous hips have for decades led me to believe that
the entire planet shared their convictions. It is true that with advancing age, I have been hearing fewer and fewer flattering comments
when walking in the medina, and sometimes the silence around me in
the bazaars is deafening. But since my face has never met with the
local beauty standards, and I have often had to defend myself against
remarks such as *zirafa* (giraffe), because of my long neck, I learned
long ago not to rely too much on the outside world for my sense of
self-worth. In fact, paradoxically, as I discovered when I went to
Rabat as a student, it was the self-reliance that I had developed
to protect myself against "beauty blackmail" that made me attractive
to others. My male fellow students could not believe that I did not
give a damn about what they thought about my body. "You know, my
dear," I would say in response to one of them, "all I need to survive is

bread, olives, and sardines. That you think my neck is too long is your problem, not mine."

In any case, when it comes to beauty and compliments, nothing is too serious or definite in the medina, where everything can be negotiated. But things seemed to be different in that American department store. In fact, I have to confess that I lost my usual self-confidence in that New York environment. Not that I am always sure of myself, but I don't walk around the Moroccan streets or down the university corridors wondering what people are thinking about me. Of course, when I hear a compliment, my ego expands like a cheese soufflé, but on the whole, I don't expect to hear much from others. Some mornings, I feel ugly because I am sick or tired; others, I feel wonderful because it is sunny out or I have written a good paragraph. But suddenly, in that peaceful American store that I had entered so triumphantly, as a sovereign consumer ready to spend money, I felt savagely attacked. My hips, until then the sign of a relaxed and uninhibited maturity, were suddenly being condemned as a deformity. . . .

"And who says that everyone must be a size 6?" I joked to the saleslady that day, deliberately neglecting to mention size 4, which is the size of my skinny twelve-year-old niece.

At that point, the saleslady suddenly gave me an anxious look. "The norm is everywhere, my dear," she said. "It's all over, in the magazines, on television, in the ads. You can't escape it. There is Calvin Klein, Ralph Lauren, Gianni Versace, Giorgio Armani, Mario Valentino, Salvatore Ferragamo, Christian Dior, Yves Saint-Laurent, Christian Lacroix, and Jean-Paul Gaultier. Big department stores go by the norm." She paused and then concluded, "If they sold size 14 or 16, which is probably what you need, they would go bankrupt."

She stopped for a minute and then stared at me, intrigued. "Where on earth do you come from? I am sorry I can't help you. Really, I am." And she looked it too. She seemed, all of a sudden, interested, and brushed off another woman who was seeking her attention with a cutting, "Get someone else to help you, I'm busy." Only then did I notice that she was probably my age, in her late fifties. But unlike me, she had the thin body of an adolescent girl. Her knee-length, navy blue, Chanel dress had a white silk collar reminiscent of the subdued elegance of aristocratic French Catholic schoolgirls at the turn of the century. A pearl-studded belt emphasized the

278

slimness of her waist. With her meticulously styled short hair and sophisticated makeup, she looked half my age at first glance.

"I come from a country where there is no size for women's clothes," I told her. "I buy my own material and the neighborhood seamstress or craftsman makes me the silk or leather skirt I want. They just take my measurements each time I see them. Neither the seamstress nor I know exactly what size my new skirt is. We discover it together in the making. No one cares about my size in Morocco as long as I pay taxes on time. Actually, I don't know what my size is, to tell you the truth."

The saleswoman laughed merrily and said that I should advertise my country as a paradise for stressed working women. "You mean you don't watch your weight?" she inquired, with a tinge of disbelief in her voice. And then, after a brief moment of silence, she added in a lower register, as if talking to herself: "Many women working in highly paid fashion-related jobs could lose their positions if they didn't keep to a strict diet."

Her words sounded so simple, but the threat they implied was so cruel that I realized for the first time that maybe "size 6" is a more violent restriction imposed on women than is the Muslim veil. Quickly I said good-bye so as not to make any more demands on the saleslady's time or involve her in any more unwelcome, confidential exchanges about age-discriminating salary cuts. A surveillance camera was probably watching us both.

Yes, I thought as I wandered off, I have finally found the answer to my harem enigma. Unlike the Muslim man, who uses space to establish male domination by excluding women from the public arena, the Western man manipulates time and light. He declares that in order to be beautiful, a woman must look fourteen years old. If she dares to look fifty, or worse, sixty, she is beyond the pale. By putting the spotlight on the female child and framing her as the ideal of beauty, he condemns the mature woman to invisibility. In fact, the modern Western man enforces Immanuel Kant's nineteenth-century theories: To be beautiful, women have to appear childish and brainless. When a woman looks mature and self-assertive, or allows her hips to expand, she is condemned as ugly. Thus, the walls of the European harem separate youthful beauty from ugly maturity.

15 These Western attitudes, I thought, are even more dangerous and 15 cunning than the Muslim ones because the weapon used against women is time. Time is less visible, more fluid than space. The Western man uses

images and spotlights to freeze female beauty within an idealized childhood, and forces women to perceive aging—that normal unfolding of the years—as a shameful devaluation. "Here I am, transformed into a dinosaur," I caught myself saying aloud as I went up and down the rows of skirts in the store, hoping to prove the saleslady wrong—to no avail. This Western time-defined veil is even crazier than the space-defined one enforced by the ayatollahs.

The violence embodied in the Western harem is less visible than in the Eastern harem because aging is not attacked directly, but rather masked as an aesthetic choice. Yes, I suddenly felt not only very ugly but also quite useless in that store, where, if you had big hips, you were simply out of the picture. You drifted into the fringes of nothingness. By putting the spotlight on the prepubescent female, the Western man veils the older, more mature woman, wrapping her in shrouds of ugliness. This idea gives me the chills because it tattoos the invisible harem directly onto a woman's skin. Chinese foot-binding worked the same way: Men declared beautiful only those women who had small, child-like feet. Chinese men did not force women to bandage their feet to keep them from developing normally—all they did was to define the beauty ideal. In feudal China, a beautiful woman was the one who voluntarily sacrificed her right to unhindered physical movement by mutilating her own feet, and thereby proving that her main goal in life was to please men. Similarly, in the Western world, I was expected to shrink my hips into a size 6 if I wanted to find a decent skirt tailored for a beautiful woman. We Muslim women have only one month of fasting, Ramadan, but the poor Western woman who diets has to fast twelve months out of the year. "*Quelle horreur,*" I kept repeating to myself, while looking around at the American women shopping. All those my age looked like youthful teenagers. . . .

Now, at last, the mystery of my Western harem made sense. Framing youth as beauty and condemning maturity is the weapon used against women in the West just as limiting access to public space is the weapon used in the East. The objective remains identical in both cultures: to make women feel unwelcome, inadequate, and ugly. The power of the Western man resides in dictating what women should wear and how they should look. He controls the whole fashion industry, from cosmetics to underwear. The West, I realized, was the only part of the world where women's fashion is a man's business. In places like Morocco, where you design your own clothes and discuss them with craftsmen and -women, fashion is your own business. Not so in the West. . . .

But how does the system function? I wondered. Why do women accept it?

Of all the possible explanations, I like that of the French sociologist Pierre Bourdieu the best. In his latest book, *La Domination Masculine*, he proposes something he calls *"la violence symbolique"*: "Symbolic violence is a form of power which is hammered directly on the body, and as if by magic, without any apparent physical constraint. But this magic operates only because it activates the codes pounded in the deepest layers of the body." Reading Bourdieu, I had the impression that I finally understood Western man's psyche better. The cosmetic and fashion industries are only the tip of the iceberg, he states, which is why women are so ready to adhere to their dictates. Something else is going on on a far deeper level. Otherwise, why would women belittle themselves spontaneously? Why, argues Bourdieu, would women make their lives more difficult, for example, by preferring men who are taller or older than they are? "The majority of French women wish to have a husband who is older and also, which seems consistent, bigger as far as size is concerned," writes Bourdieu. Caught in the enchanted submission characteristic of the symbolic violence inscribed in the mysterious layers of the flesh, women relinquish what he calls "les signes ordinaires de la hiérarchie sexuelle," the ordinary signs of sexual hierarchy, such as old age and a larger body. By so doing, explains Bourdieu, women spontaneously accept the subservient position. It is this spontaneity Bourdieu describes as magic enchantment.

Once I understood how this magic submission worked, I became very happy that the conservative ayatollahs do not know about it yet. If they did, they would readily switch to its sophisticated methods, because they are so much more effective. To deprive me of food is definitely the best way to paralyze my thinking capabilities. . . .

"I thank you, Allah, for sparing me the tyranny of the 'size 6 harem,'" I repeatedly said to myself while seated on the Paris-Casablanca flight, on my way back home at last. "I am so happy that the conservative male elite does not know about it. Imagine the fundamentalists switching from the veil to forcing women to fit size 6."

How can you stage a credible political demonstration and shout in the streets that your human rights have been violated when you cannot find the right skirt?

Questions on Meaning

1. Mernissi argues that the Western world represses women even more than does the Muslim world. What experience leads her to this conclusion, and what does she decide about her treatment in the department store?
2. Who defines fashion in the Western world, and who agrees to follow the rules of fashion? What effect does fashion have on women who are not pencil thin? How do women tend to feel about themselves in the Western world?
3. How do women get their clothes in the Muslim world? Why are the women indifferent to men's opinions about their body shapes?

Questions on Rhetorical Strategy and Style

1. The essay begins with a humiliating experience in which the narrator is told that she cannot buy clothes in a store because she is too fat. Why does this story seem so shocking? Or is it shocking? Are Westerners so accustomed to the rules of fashion that the event in the store seems natural? Why does the narrator compare religious law to the the saleswoman's pronouncements?
2. Mernissi discusses the Western fashion industry as if it were planned as an attack on women. Does this discussion at the center of her essay carry more force than if she had begun with the charge? Does her personal and intimate tone lead the reader to agree with her?
3. The essay ends with a humorous prayer that religious leaders will not discover the dictates of Western fashion because these dictates are far worse than being locked in a harem. What is so effective about ending on this personal note? Why is it so powerful to compare Western fashion to the thing in the Muslim world that women find so unbelievable and unbearable?

Writing Assignments

1. Spend some time in a public place such as the quad or dining hall of your school. Observe what women wear and note women's sizes. Write about the kinds of clothing women wear and how

much the women appear to weigh. Is Mernissi right according to your observations?

2. Gather some fashion magazines. Estimate the average weight of the models. Look carefully at the advertisements. Note the messages being sent about, for example, hair, eyes, waists, and feet. Write about the messages that the reader receives from the magazine.

3. We understand our own culture best by looking at another culture. Mernissi's technique of using a despised quality in Muslim culture to expose Western culture is a common approach in writing. Choose something in another culture that you do not understand or dislike. Then look carefully at your own culture to discover what parallels you can find. Write about the comparisons you discover.

From: On Seeing England for the First Time

Jamaica Kincaid

Born Elaine Potter Richardson in St. John's Antigua, in the West Indies, Jamaica Kincaid (1949–) left Antigua for New York when she was seventeen, fifteen years before the island became independent from England in 1981. She took classes at a community college, studied photography at the New School for Social Research, and attended Franconia College. She has been a staff writer for the New Yorker *and has published her work in* Rolling Stone, The Village Voice, *and* The Paris Review. *Her first book,* At the Bottom of the River *(1983) won an award from the American Academy and Institute of Arts and Letters. Her more recent works include* The Autobiography of My Mother *(1996) and* My Brother *(1997). The following is an excerpt from an essay in which Kincaid realizes her geographical position within Mother England's overarching cultural empire.*

1   When I saw England for the first time, I was a child in school sitting at a desk. The England I was looking at was laid out on a map gently, beautifully, delicately, a very special jewel; it lay on a bed of sky blue—the background of the map—its yellow form mysterious, because though it looked like a leg of mutton, it could not really look like anything so familiar as a leg of mutton because it was England—which shadings of pink and green unlike any shadings of pink and green I had seen before, squiggly veins of red running in every direction. England was a special jewel all right, and only special people got to wear it. The people who got to wear Eng-

"Excerpt from "On Seeing England for the First Time," by Jamaica Kincaid, 1981, Wylie Aitken, and Stone.

land were English people. They wore it well and they wore it everywhere: in jungles, in deserts, on plains, on top of the highest mountains, on all the oceans, on all the seas, in places where they were not
welcome, in places they should not have been. When my teacher had
pinned this map up on the blackboard, she said, "This is England"—
and she said it with authority, seriousness, and adoration, and we all
sat up. It was as if she had said, "This is Jerusalem, the place you will
go to when you die but only if you have been good." We understood
then—we were meant to understand then—that England was to be
our source myth and the source from which we got our sense of reality, our sense of what was meaningful, our sense of what was meaningless—and much about our own lives and much about the very idea
of us headed that last list.

At the time I was a child sitting at my desk seeing England for the
first time, I was already very familiar with the greatness of it. Each
morning before I left for school, I ate a breakfast of half a grapefruit,
an egg, bread and butter and a slice of cheese, and a cup of cocoa; or
half a grapefruit, a bowl of oat porridge, bread and butter and a slice
of cheese, and a cup of cocoa. The can of cocoa was often left on the
table in front of me. It had written on it the name of the company,
the year the company was established, and the words, "Made in England." Those words, "Made in England," were written on the box the
oats came in too. They would also have been written on the box the
shoes I was wearing came in; a bolt of gray linen cloth lying on the
shelf of a store from which my mother had brought three yards to
make the uniform that I was wearing had written along its edge those
three words. The shoes I wore were made in England; so were my
socks and cotton undergarments and the satin ribbons I wore tied at
the end of two plaits of my hair. My father, who might have sat next
to me at breakfast, was a carpenter and cabinet maker. The shoes he
wore to work would have been made in England, as were his khaki
shirt and trousers, his underpants and undershirt, his socks and brown
felt hat. Felt was not the proper material from which a hat that was
expected to provide shade from the hot sun should be made, but my
father must have seen and admired a picture of an Englishman wearing such a hat in England, and this picture that he saw must have been
so compelling that it caused him to wear the wrong hat for a hot climate most of his long life. And this hat—a brown felt hat—became
so central to his character that it was the first thing he put on in the

morning as he stepped out of bed and the last thing he took off before he stepped back into bed at night. As we sat at breakfast a car might go by. The car, a Hillman or a Zephyr, was made in England. The very idea of the meal itself, of breakfast, and its substantial quality and quantity was an idea from England; we somehow knew that in England they began the day with this meal called breakfast and a proper breakfast was a big breakfast. No one I knew liked eating so much food so early in the day; it made us feel sleepy, tired. But this breakfast business was Made in England like almost everything else that surrounded us, the exceptions being the sea, the sky, and the air we breathed.

At the time I saw this map—seeing England for the first time—I did not say to myself, "Ah, so that's what it looks like," because there was no longing in me to put a shape to those three words that ran through every part of my life, no matter how small; for me to have had such a longing would have meant that I lived in a certain atmosphere, an atmosphere in which those three words were felt as a burden. But I did not live in such an atmosphere. My father's brown felt hat would develop a hole in its crown, the lining would separate from the hat itself, and six weeks before he thought that he could not be seen wearing it—he was a very vain man—he would order another hat from England. And my mother taught me to eat my food in the English way: the knife in the right hand, the fork in the left, my elbows still held close to my side, the food carefully balanced on my fork and then brought up to my mouth. When I had finally mastered it, I overheard her saying to a friend, "Did you see how nicely she can eat?" But I knew then that I enjoyed my food more when I ate it with my bare hands, and I continued to do so when she wasn't looking. And when my teacher showed us the map, she asked us to study it carefully, because no test we would ever take would be complete without this statement: "Draw a map of England."

I did not know then that the statement "Draw a map of England" was something far worse than a declaration of war, for in fact, a flat-out declaration of war would have put me on alert, and again in fact, there was no need for war—I had long ago been conquered. I did not know then that this statement was part of a process that would result in my erasure, not my physical erasure, by my erasure all the same. I did not know then that this statement was meant to make me feel in awe and small whenever I heard the word "England": awe at its existence, small because I was not from it. I did not know very much of anything then—certainly not what a blessing it was that I was unable to draw a map of England correctly.

Questions on Meaning

1. How does Kincaid use everyday life items, such as clothing and eating utensils, to emphasize the power of England in the lives and hearts of its colonial subjects?
2. Kincaid says that England was a special jewel that only special people got to wear. What does she mean by calling England a jewel?
3. What does the map of England symbolize in this essay?

Questions on Rhetorical Strategy and Style

1. The essay begins with seeming praise of England, moves to a critique of colonial life, then ends by approving of the inability to draw a map of England. Why is the essay structured in this way? How does the structure draw the reader into the intention of the writer?
2. Kincaid says that England was meant to be her "source of myth." What does she mean by that phrase?
3. Why does Kincaid call herself "conquered"? Who conquered her? What images does the word evoke, and what do you think she hopes to achieve by evoking those images?

Writing Assignments

1. Draw a map of your state. What is the effect of tracing the outline? Write about your relationship to your state. Were you born there? Were your ancestors born there?
2. Interview your parents or early caregivers. Ask them what they remember about your early years. What toys did you have? What was your house like? Draw a map of your house; then write about spots on the map.
3. Read about the history of England's rule of Jamaica. Write a paper on the history, either defending or critiquing the English approach to the island's government.

Class in America—2006

Gregory Mantsios

Gregory Mantsios is director of worker education at Queens College, City University of New York. His assignments at Queens College also include working for the Labor Education & Advancement Program. He formerly taught sociology at William Paterson University. He published "Media Magic: Making Class Invisible" (in Race, Class, and Gender in the United States: An Integrated Study, *3/e, St. Martin's Press, 1995) and edited* A New Labor Movement for the New Century *(Monthly Review Press, 1998).*

In this selection, which appeared in Race Class, and Gender in the United States: An Integrated Study, *7/e, Mantsios discusses the myths surrounding class in the U.S.—the first being that we live in a "classless" society—and the realities of class domination.*

1   People in the United States don't like to talk about class. Or so it   1
would seem. We don't speak about class privileges, or class
oppression, or the class nature of society. These terms are not
part of our everyday vocabulary, and in most circles they are associated
with the language of the rhetorical fringe. Unlike people in most other
parts of the world, we shrink from using words that classify along economic lines or that point to class distinctions: phrases like "working
class," "upper class," and "ruling class" are rarely uttered by Americans.

For the most part, avoidance of class-laden vocabulary crosses
class boundaries. There are few among the poor who speak of themselves as lower class; instead, they refer to their race, ethnic group, or
geographic location. Workers are more likely to identify with their
employer, industry, or occupational group than with other workers,
or with the working class.[1]

Neither are those at the other end of the economic spectrum likely to use the word "class." In her study of thirty-eight wealthy and socially prominent women, Susan Ostrander asked participants if they considered themselves members of the upper class. One participant responded, "I hate to use the word 'class.' We are responsible, fortunate people, old families, the people who have something."

Another said, "I hate [the term] upper class. It is so non-upper class to use it. I just call it 'all of us,' those who are wellborn."[2]

5   It is not that Americans, rich or poor, aren't keenly aware of class differences—those quoted above obviously are; it is that class is not in the domain of public discourse. Class is not discussed or debated in public because class identity has been stripped from popular culture. The institutions that shape mass culture and define the parameters of public debate have avoided class issues. In politics, in primary and secondary education, and in the mass media, formulating issues in terms of class is unacceptable, perhaps even un-American. See my paper, "Media Magic: Making Class Invisible," Selection 7 in Part VIII of this volume.

There are, however, two notable exceptions to this phenomenon. First, it is acceptable in the United States to talk about "the middle class." Interestingly enough, such references appear to be acceptable precisely because they mute class differences. References to the middle class by politicians, for example, are designed to encompass and attract the broadest possible constituency. Not only do references to the middle class gloss over differences, but these references also avoid any suggestion of conflict or injustice.

This leads us to the second exception to the class-avoidance phenomenon. We are, on occasion, presented with glimpses of the upper class and the lower class (the language used is "the wealthy" and "the poor"). In the media, these presentations are designed to satisfy some real or imagined voyeuristic need of "the ordinary person." As curiosities, the ground-level view of street life and the inside look at the rich and the famous serve as unique models, one to avoid and one to aspire to. In either case, the two models are presented without causal relation to each other: one is not rich because the other is poor.

Similarly, when social commentators or liberal politicians draw attention to the plight of the poor, they do so in a manner that obscures the class structure and denies any sense of exploitation. Wealth and poverty are viewed as one of several natural and inevitable states of being: differences are only differences. One may even say differences are the American way, a reflection of American social diversity.

We are left with one of two possibilities: either talking about class and recognizing class distinctions are not relevant to U.S. society, or we mistakenly hold a set of beliefs that obscure the reality of class differences and their impact on people's lives.

10   Let us look at four common, albeit contradictory, beliefs about   10 the United States.

Myth 1: The United States is fundamentally a classless society. Class distinctions are largely irrelevant today, and whatever differences do exist in economic standing, they are—for the most part—insignificant. Rich or poor, we are all equal in the eyes of the law, and such basic needs as health care and education are provided to all regardless of economic standing.

Myth 2: We are, essentially, a middle-class nation. Despite some variations in economic status, most Americans have achieved relative affluence in what is widely recognized as a consumer society.

Myth 3: We are all getting richer. The American public as a whole is steadily moving up the economic ladder, and each generation propels itself to greater economic well-being. Despite some fluctuations, the U.S. position in the global economy has brought previously unknown prosperity to most, if not all, Americans.

Myth 4: Everyone has an equal chance to succeed. Success in the United States requires no more than hard work, sacrifice, and perseverance: "In America, anyone can become a millionaire; it's just a matter of being in the right place at the right time."

In trying to assess the legitimacy of these beliefs, we want to ask several important questions. Are there significant class differences among Americans? If these differences do exist, are they getting bigger or smaller, and do these differences have a significant impact on the way we live? Finally, does everyone in the United States really have an equal opportunity to succeed?

The Economic Spectrum

Let's begin by looking at difference. An examination of available data reveals that variations in economic well-being are, in fact, immense. Consider the following:

- The wealthiest 1 percent of the American population holds 34 percent of the total national wealth. That is, they own over one-third of all the consumer durables (such as houses, cars, and stereos) and financial assets (such as stocks, bonds, property, and savings accounts). The richest 20 percent of Americans hold nearly 85 percent of the total household wealth in the country.[3]

- Approximately 183,000 Americans, or approximately three-quarters of 1 percent of the adult population, earn more than $1 million **annually**.[4] There are nearly 400 billionaires in the U.S today, more than three dozen of them worth more than $10 billion each. It would take the average American (earning $35,672 and spending absolutely nothing at all) a total of 28,033 years (or approximately 400 lifetimes) to earn just $1 billion.

Affluence and prosperity are clearly alive and well in certain segments of the U.S. population. However, this abundance is in contrast to the poverty and despair that is also prevalent in the United States. At the other end of the spectrum:

- Approximately 13 percent of the American population—that is, nearly one of every eight people in this country—live below the official poverty line (calculated in 2004 at $9,645 for an individual and $19,307 for a family of four).[5] An estimated 3.5 million people —of whom nearly 1.4 million are children—experience homelessness in any given year.[6]
- Approximately one out of every five children (4.4 million) in the United States under the age of six lives in poverty.[7]

The contrast between rich and poor is sharp, and with nearly one-third of the American population living at one extreme or the other, it is difficult to argue that we live in a classless society. Big-payoff reality shows, celebrity salaries, and multimillion dollar lotteries notwithstanding, evidence suggests that the level of inequality in the United States is getting higher. Census data show the gap between the rich and the poor to be the widest since the government began collecting information in 1947[8] and that this gap is continuing to grow. In 2004 alone, the average real income of 99 percent of the U.S. population grew by little more than 1 percent, while the real income of the richest 1 percent saw their income rise by 12 percent in the same year.[9]

15   Nor is such a gap between rich and poor representative of the rest   15 of the industrialized world. In fact, the United States has by far the most unequal distribution of household income.[10] The income gap between rich and poor in the United States (measured as the percent-

age of total income held by the wealthiest 20 percent of the population versus the poorest 20 percent) is approximately 12 to 1, one of the highest ratios in the industrialized world. The ratio in Japan and Germany, by contrast, is 4 to 1.[11]

Reality 1: There are enormous differences in the economic standing of American citizens. A sizable proportion of the U.S. population occupies opposite ends of the economic spectrum. In the middle range of the economic spectrum:

- Sixty percent of the American population holds less than 6 percent of the nation's wealth.[12]
- While the real income of the top 1 percent of U.S. families skyrocketed by more than 180 percent between 1979 and 2000, the income of the middle fifth of the population grew only slightly (12.4 percent over that same 21-year period) and its share of income (15 percent of the total compared to 48 percent of the total for the wealthiest fifth) actually declined during this period.[13]
- Regressive changes in governmental tax policies and the weakening of labor unions over the last quarter century have led to a significant rise in the level of inequality between the rich and the middle class. Between 1979 and 2000, the gap in household income between the top fifth and middle fifth of the population rose by 31 percent.[14] During the economic boom of the 1990s, the top fifth of the nation's population saw their share of net worth increase (from 59 to 63 percent) while four out of five Americans saw their share of net worth decline.[15] One prominent economist described economic growth in the United States as a "spectator sport for the majority of American families."[16] Economic decline, on the other hand, is much more "inclusive," with layoffs impacting hardest on middle-and lower-income families—those with fewer resources to fall back on.

The level of inequality is sometimes difficult to comprehend fully by looking at dollar figures and percentages. To help his students visualize the distribution of income, the well-known economist Paul Samuelson asked them to picture an income pyramid made of children's blocks, with each layer of blocks representing $1,000. If we were to construct Samuelson's pyramid today, the peak of the pyramid would be much higher than the Eiffel Tower, yet almost all of us would be within six feet of the ground.[17] In other words, the distribution of income is heavily skewed; a small minority of families take the lion's share of national income, and the remaining income is distributed among the vast majority of middle-income and low-income families. Keep in mind that Samuelson's pyramid represents the distribution of income, not wealth. The distribution of wealth is skewed even further.

Reality 2: The middle class in the United States holds a very small share of the nation's wealth and that share is declining steadily. The gap between rich and poor and between rich and the middle class is larger than it has ever been.

American Life-Styles

At last count, nearly 37 million Americans across the nation lived in unrelenting poverty.[18] Yet, as political scientist Michael Harrington once commented, "America has the best dressed poverty the world has ever known."[19] Clothing disguises much of the poverty in the United States, and this may explain, in part, its middle-class image. With increased mass marketing of "designer" clothing and with shifts in the nation's economy from blue-collar (and often better-paying) manufacturing jobs to white-collar and pink-collar jobs in the service sector, it is becoming increasingly difficult to distinguish class differences based on appearance.[20] The dress-down environment prevalent in the high-tech industry (what one author refers to as the "no-collars movement") has reduced superficial distinctions even further.[21]

Beneath the surface, there is another reality. Let's look at some "typical" and not-so-typical life-styles.

American Profile

Name:	Harold S. Browning
Father:	manufacturer, industrialist
Mother:	prominent social figure in the community
Principal child-rearer:	governess
Primary education:	an exclusive private school on Manhattan's Upper East Side
	Note: a small, well-respected primary school where teachers and administrators have a reputation for nurturing student creativity and for providing the finest educational preparation
	Ambition: "to become President"
Supplemental tutoring:	tutors in French and mathematics

Summer camp: sleep-away camp in northern Connecticut

Note: camp provides instruction in the creative arts, athletics, and the natural sciences

Secondary education: a prestigious preparatory school in Westchester County

Note: classmates included the sons of ambassadors, doctors, attorneys, television personalities, and well-known business leaders

Supplemental education: private SAT tutor
After-school activities: private riding lessons
Ambition: "to take over my father's business"
High-school graduation gift: BMW

Family activities: theater, recitals, museums, summer vacations in Europe, occasional winter trips to the Caribbean

Note: as members of and donors to the local art museum, the Brownings and their children attend private receptions and exhibit openings at the invitation of the museum director

Higher education: an Ivy League liberal arts college in Massachusetts

Major: economics and political science
After-class activities: debating club, college newspaper, swim team
Ambition: "to become a leader in business"

First full-time job (age 23): assistant manager of operations, Browning Tool and Die, Inc. (family enterprise)

Subsequent employment: *3 years*—executive assistant to the president, Browning Tool and Die

Responsibilities included: purchasing (materials and equipment), personnel, and distribution networks
4 years—advertising manager, Lackheed Manufacturing (home appliances)
3 years—director of marketing and sales, Comerex, Inc. (business machines)

Present employment (age 38): executive vice president, SmithBond and Co. (digital instruments)

Typical daily activities: review financial reports and computer printouts, dictate memoranda, lunch with clients, initiate conference calls, meet with assistants, plan business trips, meet with associates

Transportation to and from work: chauffeured com
pany limousine *Annual salary:* $324,000
Ambition: "to become chief executive officer of
the firm, or one like it, within the next five to ten
years"

Present residence: eighteenth-floor condominium on Manhattan's
Upper West Side, eleven rooms, including five
spacious bedrooms and terrace overlooking river
Interior: professionally decorated and accented
with elegant furnishings, valuable antiques, and
expensive artwork
Note: building management provides doorman
and elevator attendant; family employs au pair
for children and maid for other domestic chores

Second residence: farm in northwestern Connecticut, used for
weekend retreats and for horse breeding (invest-
ment/hobby)
Note: to maintain the farm and cater to the family
when they are there, the Brownings employ a
part-time maid, groundskeeper, and horse breeder

Harold Browning was born into a world of nurses, maids, and
governesses. His world today is one of airplanes and limousines, five-
star restaurants, and luxurious living accommodations. The life and
life-style of Harold Browning is in sharp contrast to that of Bob
Farrell.

American Profile

Name: Bob Farrell

Father: machinist

Mother: retail clerk

Principal child-rearer: mother and sitter

Primary education: a medium-size public school in Queens, New
York, characterized by large class size, outmoded
physical facilities, and an educational philosophy
emphasizing basic skills and student discipline
Ambition: "to become President"

Supplemental tutoring: none

Summer camp: YMCA day camp
Note: emphasis on team sports, arts and crafts

Secondary education: large regional high school in Queens

Note: classmates included the sons and daughters of carpenters, postal clerks, teachers, nurses, shopkeepers, mechanics, bus drivers, police officers, salespersons
Supplemental education: SAT prep course offered by national chain
After-school activities: basketball and handball in school park *Ambition:* "to make it through college"
High-school graduation gift: $500 savings bond

Family activities: family gatherings around television set, softball, an occasional trip to the movie theater, summer Sundays at the public beach

Higher education: a two-year community college with a technical orientation

Major: electrical technology

After-school activities: employed as a part-time bagger in local supermarket
Ambition: "to become an electrical engineer"

First full-time job (age 19): service-station attendant
Note: continued to take college classes in the evening

Subsequent employment: mail clerk at large insurance firm; manager trainee, large retail chain

Present employment (age 38): assistant sales manager, building supply firm
Typical daily activities: demonstrate products, write up product orders, handle customer complaints, check inventory

Transportation to and from work: city subway

Annual salary: $45,261

Ambition: "to open up my own business"
Additional income: $6,100 in commissions from evening and weekend work as salesman in local men's clothing store

Present residence: the Farrells own their own home in a working-class neighborhood in Queens, New York

[20]   Bob Farrell and Harold Browning live very differently: the life-   [20]
style of one is privileged; that of the other is not so privileged. The

differences are class differences, and these differences have a profound impact on the way they live. They are differences between playing a game of handball in the park and taking riding lessons at a private stable; watching a movie on television and going to the theater; and taking the subway to work and being driven in a limousine. More important, the difference in class determines where they live, who their friends are, how well they are educated, what they do for a living, and what they come to expect from life.

Yet, as dissimilar as their life-styles are, Harold Browning and Bob Farrell have some things in common; they live in the same city, they work long hours, and they are highly motivated. More important, they are both white males.

Let's look at someone else who works long and hard and is highly motivated. This person, however, is black and female.

American Profile

Name:	Cheryl Mitchell
Father:	janitor
Mother:	waitress
Principal child-rearer:	grandmother
Primary education:	large public school in Ocean Hill-Brownsville, Brooklyn, New York
	Note: rote teaching of basic skills and emphasis on conveying the importance of good attendance, good manners, and good work habits; school patrolled by security guards
	Ambition: "to be a teacher"
Supplemental tutoring:	none
Summer camp:	none
Secondary education:	large public school in Ocean Hill-Brownsville
	Note: classmates included sons and daughters of hairdressers, groundskeepers, painters, dressmakers, dishwashers, domestics
	Supplemental education: none
	After-school activities: domestic chores, part-time employment as babysitter and housekeeper
	Ambition: "to be a social worker"
	High-school graduation gift: corsage
Family activities:	church-sponsored socials
Higher education:	one semester of local community college

Note: dropped out of school for financial reasons

First full-time job (age 17): counter clerk, local bakery

Subsequent employment: file clerk with temporary-service agency, supermarket checker

Present employment (age 38): nurse's aide at a municipal hospital

Typical daily activities: make up hospital beds, clean out bedpans, weigh patients and assist them to the bathroom, take temperature readings, pass out and collect food trays, feed patients who need help, bathe patients, and change dressings

Annual salary: $15,820

Ambition: "to get out of the ghetto"

Present residence: three-room apartment in the South Bronx, needs painting, has poor ventilation, is in a high-crime area

Note: Cheryl Mitchell lives with her four-year-old son and her elderly mother

When we look at the lives of Cheryl Mitchell, Bob Farrell, and Harold Browning, we see life-styles that are very different. We are not looking, however, at economic extremes. Cheryl Mitchell's income as a nurse's aide puts her above the government's official poverty line.[22] Below her on the income pyramid are 37 million poverty-stricken Americans. Far from being poor, Bob Farrell has an annual income as an assistant sales manager that puts him well above the median income level—that is, more than 50 percent of the U.S. population earns less money than Bob Farrell.[23] And while Harold Browning's income puts him in a high-income bracket, he stands only a fraction of the way up Samuelson's income pyramid. Well above him are the 183,000 individuals whose annual salary exceeds $1 million. Yet Harold Browning spends more money on his horses than Cheryl Mitchell earns in a year.

Reality 3: Even ignoring the extreme poles of the economic spectrum, we find enormous class differences in the life-styles among the haves, the have-nots, and the have-littles.

Class affects more than life-style and material well-being. It has a significant impact on our physical and mental well-being as well.

25   Researchers have found an inverse relationship between social   25
class and health. Lower-class standing is correlated to higher rates of
infant mortality, eye and ear disease, arthritis, physical disability, dia-
betes, nutritional deficiency, respiratory disease, mental illness, and
heart disease.[24] In all areas of health, poor people do not share the
same life chances as those in the social class above them. Furthermore,
lower-class standing is correlated with a lower quality of treatment for
illness and disease. The results of poor health and poor treatment are
borne out in the life expectancy rates within each class. Researchers
have found that the higher your class standing, the higher your life
expectancy. Conversely, they have also found that within each age
group, the lower one's class standing, the higher the death rate; in
some age groups, the figures are as much as two and three times as
high.[25]

Reality 4: From cradle to grave, class standing has a significant
impact on our chances for survival.

The lower one's class standing, the more difficult it is to secure
appropriate housing, the more time is spent on the routine tasks of
everyday life, the greater is the percentage of income that goes to pay
for food and other basic necessities, and the greater is the likelihood
of crime victimization.[26] Class can accurately predict chances for
both survival and success.

Class and Educational Attainment

School performance (grades and test scores) and educational attainment (level of schooling completed) also correlate strongly with economic class. Furthermore, despite some efforts to make testing fairer
and schooling more accessible, current data suggest that the level of
inequity is staying the same or getting worse.

In his study for the Carnegie Council on Children nearly thirty
years ago, Richard De Lone examined the test scores of over half a
million students who took the College Board exams (SATs). His
findings were consistent with earlier studies that showed a relationship between class and scores on standardized tests; his conclusion:
"the higher the student's social status, the higher the probability that
he or she will get higher grades."[27] Almost thirty years after the
release of the Carnegie report, College Board surveys reveal data that
are no different: test scores still correlate strongly with family
income.

Average Combined Scores by Income
(400 to 1600 scale)[28]

Family Income	Median Score
More than $100,000	1119
$80,000 to $100,000	1063
$70,000 to $80,000	1039
$60,000 to $70,000	1026
$50,000 to $60,000	1014
$40,000 to $50,000	996
$30,000 to $40,000	967
$20,000 to $30,000	937
$10,000 to $20,000	906
less than $10,000	884

These figures are based on the test results of 987,584 SAT takers in 2005.

A little more than thirty years ago, researcher William Sewell showed a positive correlation between class and overall educational achievement. In comparing the top quartile (25 percent) of his sample to the bottom quartile, he found that students from upper-class families were twice as likely to obtain training beyond high school and four times as likely to attain a postgraduate degree. Sewell concluded: "Socioeconomic background . . . operates independently of academic ability at every stage in the process of educational attainment."[29]

Today, the pattern persists. There are, however, two significant changes. On the one hand, the odds of getting into college have improved for the bottom quartile of the population, although they still remain relatively low compared to the top. On the other hand, the chances of completing a college degree have deteriorated markedly for the bottom quartile. Researchers estimate the chances of completing a four-year college degree (by age 24) to be nineteen times as great for the top 25 percent of the population as it is for the bottom 25 percent.[30]

Reality 5: Class standing has a significant impact on chances for educational achievement.

Class standing, and consequently life chances, are largely determined at birth. Although examples of individuals who have gone from rags to riches abound in the mass media, statistics on class mobility show these leaps to be extremely rare. In fact, dramatic advances in class standing are relatively infrequent. One study showed that fewer than one in five men surpass the economic status of their fathers.[31] For those whose annual income is in six figures, economic success is due in large part to the wealth and privileges bestowed on them at birth. Over 66 percent of the consumer units with incomes of $100,000 or more have inherited assets. Of these units, over 86 percent reported that inheritances constituted a substantial portion of their total assets.[32]

Economist Harold Wachtel likens inheritance to a series of Monopoly games in which the winner of the first game refuses to relinquish his or her cash and commercial property for the second game. "After all," argues the winner, "I accumulated my wealth and income by my own wits." With such an arrangement, it is not difficult to predict the outcome of subsequent games.[33]

Reality 6: All Americans do not have an equal opportunity to succeed. Inheritance laws ensure a greater likelihood of success for the offspring of the wealthy.

Spheres of Power and Oppression

When we look at society and try to determine what it is that keeps most people down—what holds them back from realizing their potential as healthy, creative, productive individuals—we find institutional forces that are largely beyond individual control. Class domination is one of these forces. People do not choose to be poor or working class; instead, they are limited and confined by the opportunities afforded or denied them by a social and economic system. The class structure in the United States is a function of its economic system: capitalism, a system that is based on private rather than public ownership and control of commercial enterprises. Under capitalism, these enterprises are governed by the need to produce a profit for the owners, rather than to fulfill societal needs. Class divisions arise from the differences between those who own and control corporate enterprise and those who do not.

Racial and gender domination are other forces that hold people down. Although there are significant differences in the way capitalism, racism, and sexism affect our lives, there are also a multitude of parallels. And although class, race, and gender act independently of each other, they are at the same time very much interrelated.

On the one hand, issues of race and gender cut across class lines. Women experience the effects of sexism whether they are well-paid

302

professionals or poorly paid clerks. As women, they are not only sub-jected to catcalls and stereotyping, but face discrimination and are denied opportunities and privileges that men have. Similarly, a wealthy black man faces racial oppression, is subjected to racial slurs, and is denied opportunities because of his color. Regardless of their class standing, women and members of minority races are constantly dealing with institutional forces that are holding them down precisely because of their gender, the color of their skin, or both.

On the other hand, the experiences of women and minorities are differentiated along class lines. Although they are in subordi-nate positions vis-à-vis white men, the particular issues that con-front women and people of color may be quite different depending on their position in the class structure.

Power is incremental, and class privileges can accrue to individual women and to individual members of a racial minority. While power is incremental, oppression is cumulative, and those who are poor, black, and female are often subject to all of the forces of class, race, and gender discrimination simultaneously. This cumulative situation is what is meant by the double and triple jeopardy of women and minorities.

Furthermore, oppression in one sphere is related to the likelihood of oppression in another. If you are black and female, for example, you are much more likely to be poor or working class than you would be as a white male. Census figures show that the incidence of poverty varies greatly by race and gender.

Chances of Being Poor in America[34]

White male/ female	White female head*	Hispanic male/ female	Hispanic female head*	Black male/ female	Black female head*
1 in 10	1 in 5	1 in 5	1 in 3	1 in 4	1 in 3

*Persons in families with female householder, no husband present.

In other words, being female and being nonwhite are attributes in our society that increase the chances of poverty and of lower-class standing.

Reality 7: Racism and sexism significantly compound the effects of class in society.

40 None of this makes for a very pretty picture of our country. 40
Despite what we like to think about ourselves as a nation, the truth is

that opportunity for success and life itself are highly circumscribed by our race, our gender, and the class we are born into. As individuals, we feel hurt and anger when someone is treating us unfairly; yet as a society we tolerate unconscionable injustice. A more just society will require a radical redistribution of wealth and power. We can start by reversing the current trends that further polarize us as a people and adapt policies and practices that narrow the gaps in income, wealth, and privilege

End Notes

1. See Jay MacLead, *Ain't No Makin' It: Aspirations and Attainment in a Lower-Income Neighborhood* (Boulder, CO: Westview Press, 1995); Benjamin DeMott, *The Imperial Middle* (New York: Morrow, 1990); Ira Katznelson, *City Trenches: Urban Politics and Patterning of Class in the United States* (New York: Pantheon Books, 1981); Charles W. Tucker, "A Comparative Analysis of Subjective Social Class: 1945–1963," *Social Forces*, no. 46, June 1968, pp. 508–514; Robert Nisbet, "The Decline and Fall of Social Class," *Pacific Sociological Review*, vol. 2, Spring 1959, pp. 11–17; and Oscar Glantz, "Class Consciousness and Political Solidarity," *American Sociological Review*, vol. 23, August 1958, pp. 375–382.
2. Susan Ostander, "Upper-Class Women: Class Consciousness as Conduct and Meaning," in G. William Domhoff, *Power Structure Research* (Beverly Hills, CA: Sage Publications, 1980), pp. 78–79. Also see Stephen Birmingham, *America's Secret Aristocracy* (Boston: Little Brown, 1987).
3. Lawrence Mishel, Jared Bernstein, and Sylvia Allegretto, *The State of Working America: 2004–2005* (Ithaca: ILR Press, Cornell University Press, 2005), p. 282.
4. The number of individuals filing tax returns showing a gross adjusted income of $1 million or more in 2003 was 182, 932 (Tax Stats at a Glance, Internal Revenue Service, U.S. Treasury Department, available at http://www.irs.gov/taxstats/article/0,,id=102886,00.html).
5. Carmen DeNavas-Walt, Bernadette D. Proctor, and Cheryl Hill Lee, U.S. Census Bureau, Current Population Reports, P60-229, *Income, Poverty, and Health Insurance in the United States: 2004* (Washington, DC: U.S. Government Printing Office, 2005), pp. 9, 45.
6. National Coalition for the Homeless "How many people experience homelessness?" NCH Fact Sheet #2 (June 2006), citing a 2004 National Law Center on Homelessness and Poverty study. Available at http://www.nationalhomeless.org/publications/facts/How_Many.pdf
7. Mishel et al., op. cit., pp. 318–319.
8. Lawrence Mishel, Jared Bernstein, and Heather Boushey, *The State of Working America: 2002–2003* (Ithaca: ILR Press, Cornell University Press, 2003), p. 53.
9. Paul Krugman, "Left Behind Economics" *New York Times*, July 14, 2006.

10. Based on a comparison of 19 industrialized states: Mishel et al., *2004–2005*, pp. 399–401.

11. Mishel et al., ibid, p. 64.

12. Derived from Mishel et al., 2002–2003, p. 281.

13. Mishel et al., 2004–2005, ibid, pp. 62–63.

14. Mishel et al. 2002–2003 ibid, p. 70.

15. Mishel et al., ibid, p. 280.

16. Alan Blinder, quoted by Paul Krugman, in "Disparity and Despair," *U.S. News and World Report*, March 23, 1992, p. 54.

17. Paul Samuelson, *Economics*, 10th ed. (New York: McGraw-Hill, 1976), p. 84.

18. DeNavas-Walt et al., op. cit., p. 9.

19. Michael Harrington, *The Other America* (New York: Macmillan, 1962), pp. 12–13.

20. Stuart Ewen and Elizabeth Ewen, *Channels of Desire: Mass Images and the Shaping of American Consciousness* (New York: McGraw-Hill, 1982).

21. Andrew Ross, *No-Collar: The Humane Work Place and Its Hidden Costs* (New York: Basic Books, 2002).

22. Based on a poverty threshold for a three-person household in 2004 of $15,205. DeNavas et al., op. cit., p. 45.

23. The median income in 2004 was $40,798 for men, $31,223 for women, and $44,389 for households. DeNavas-Walt et al., op. cit., pp. 3–5.

24. E. Pamuk, D. Makuc, K. Heck, C. Reuben, and K. Lochner, *Socioeconomic Status and Health Chartbook, Health, United States, 1998* (Hyattsville, MD: National Center for Health Statistics, 1998), pp. 145–159; Vincente Navarro "Class, Race, and Health Care in the United States," in Bersh Berberoglu, *Critical Perspectives in Sociology*, 2nd ed. (Dubuque, IA: Kendall/Hunt, 1993), pp. 148–156; Melvin Krasner, *Poverty and Health in New York City* (New York: United Hospital Fund of New York, 1989). See also U.S. Dept. of Health and Human Services, *Health Status of Minorities and Low Income Groups*, 1985; and Dan Hughes, Kay Johnson, Sara Rosenbaum, Elizabeth Butler, and Janet Simons, *The Health of America's Children* (The Children's Defense Fund, 1988).

25. E. Pamuk et al., op. cit.; Kenneth Neubeck and Davita Glassberg, *Sociology; A Critical Approach* (New York: McGraw-Hill, 1996), pp. 436–438; Aaron Antonovsky, "Social Class, Life Expectancy, and Overall Mortality," in *The Impact of Social Class* (New York: Thomas Crowell, 1972), pp. 467–491. See also Harriet Duleep, "Measuring the Effect of Income on Adult Mortality Using Longitudinal Administrative Record Data," *Journal of Human Resources*, vol. 21, no. 2, Spring 1986. See also Paul Farmer, *Pathologies of Power: Health, Human Rights, and the New War on the Poor*, (Berkeley: University of California Press, 2005).

26. E. Pamuk et al., op. cit., fig. 20; Dennis W. Roncek, "Dangerous Places: Crime and Residential Environment," *Social Forces*, vol. 60, no. 1, September 1981, pp. 74–96.

27. Richard De Lone, *Small Futures* (New York: Harcourt Brace Jovanovich, 1978), pp. 14–19.

28. Derived from "2005 College-Bound Seniors, Total Group Profile," *College Board*, p. 7, available at http://www.collegeboard.com/prod_downloads/about/news_info/cbsenior/yr2005/2005-college-bound-seniors.pdf.

29. William H. Sewell, "Inequality of Opportunity for Higher Education," *American Sociological Review*, vol. 36, no. 5, 1971, pp. 793–809.

30. The Mortenson Report on Public Policy Analysis of Opportunity for Postsecondary Education, "Postsecondary Education Opportunity" (Iowa City, IA: September 1993, no. 16).

31. De Lone, op. cit., pp. 14–19.

32. Howard Tuchman, *Economics of the Rich* (New York: Random House, 1973), p. 15. For more information on inheritance see, Sam Bowles and Herbert Gintis, "The Inheritance of Inequality," *The Journal of Economic Perspectives*, vol. 16, no. 3 (summer, 2002) pp. 2–30 and Tom Hertz, *Understanding Mobility in America*, Center for American Progress, http://www.americanprogress.org/site/pp.asp?c=biJRJ8OVF&b=1579981.

33. Howard Wachtel, *Labor and the Economy* (Orlando, FL: Academic Press, 1984), pp. 161–162.

34. Derived from DeNavas et al., op. cit., pp. 46–51.

Questions on Meaning

1. Summarize the four myths Mantsios identifies in his article. Which ones do you believe most people subscribe to and why? Where are these myths reflected as part of our belief system? How do they relate to what is called the "meritocracy"?
2. What is the difference between the real income percentage increases among the wealthy as opposed to those among the middle class? What do these statistics reveal about "the economic standing of American citizens"?
3. Summarize the seven realities Mantsios offers in response to the myths about class in the U.S. Offer a brief comment on each one. According to the author, they present a very grim picture of class, race, and sexism in this country. How do they have the incremental and cumulative effects he asserts?

Questions on Rhetorical Strategy and Style

1. What is the purpose of the three profiles? Why has the author organized them to appear like resumes?
2. Why does the author rely upon visuals—charts and various text design features—to convey his points? In what ways do these elements address the needs of the reader and change the way in which you may read and reread the text?
3. What does the author assume about his readers and their level of knowledge on the topic? What features of the article—the diction, tone, evidence—reveal the author's sense of his audience?

Writing Assignments

1. As someone once said during a political campaign, "Are you better off now than you were four years ago?" Write an essay responding to this question. How might our reading selection help you to frame your response?
2. A critical claim in the essay is that class distinctions in U.S. culture have become less distinct, perhaps even invisible. Try testing the author's claim yourself as it pertains to the media. For example, how do the most popular television shows represent, or fail to represent, images and representation of class? Write an essay in which you analyze these programs.

The Human Cost of an Illiterate Society

Jonathan Kozol

PRECAUTIONS. READ BEFORE USING.
Poison: Contains sodium hydroxide (caustic soda-lye).
Corrosive: Causes severe eye and skin damage, may cause blindness.
Harmful or fatal if swallowed.
If swallowed, give large quantities of milk or water.

Do not induce vomiting.
Important: Keep water out of can at all times to prevent contents from
violently erupting . . .

—warning on a can of Drano

1   Questions of literacy, in Socrates' belief, must at length be judged   1
as matters of morality. Socrates could not have had in mind the moral
compromise peculiar to a nation like our own. Some of our Founding
Fathers did, however, have this question in their minds. One of the
wisest of those Founding Fathers (one who may not have been most
compassionate but surely was more prescient than some of his peers)
recognized the special dangers that illiteracy would pose to basic equity in the political construction that he helped to shape.

"A people who mean to be their own governors," James Madison
wrote, "must arm themselves with the power knowledge gives. A popular government without popular information or the means of acquiring it, is but a prologue to a farce or a tragedy, or perhaps both."

Tragedy looms larger than farce in the United States today. Illiterate citizens seldom vote. Those who do are forced to cast a vote of
questionable worth. They cannot make informed decisions based on
serious print information. Sometimes they can be alerted to their interests by aggressive voter education. More frequently, they vote for a
face, a smile, or a style, not for a mind or character or body of beliefs.

The number of illiterate adults exceeds by 16 million the entire
vote cast for the winner in the 1980 presidential contest. If even one
third of all illiterates could vote, and read enough and do sufficient
math to vote in their self-interest, Ronald Reagan would not likely
have been chosen president. There is, of course, no way to know for
sure. We do know this: Democracy is a mendacious term when used
by those who are prepared to countenance the forced exclusion of one
third of our electorate. So long as 60 million people are denied significant participation, the government is neither of, nor for, nor by,
the people. It is a government, at best, of those two thirds whose
wealth, skin color, or parental privilege allows them opportunity to
profit from the provocation and instruction of the written word.

5   The undermining of democracy in the United States is one "ex-   5
pense" that sensitive Americans can easily deplore because it represents
a contradiction that endangers citizens of all political positions. The
human price is not so obvious at first.

Since I first immersed myself within this work I have often had the following dream: I find that I am in a railroad station or a large department store within a city that is utterly unknown to me and where I cannot understand the printed words. None of the signs or symbols is familiar. Everything looks strange: like mirror writing of some kind. Gradually I understand that I am in the Soviet Union. All the letters on the walls around me are Cyrillic. I look for my pocket dictionary but I find that it has been mislaid. Where have I left it? Then I recall that I forgot to bring it with me when I packed my bags in Boston. I struggle to remember the name of my hotel. I try to ask somebody for directions. One person stops and looks at me in a peculiar way. I lose the nerve to ask. At last I reach into my wallet for an ID card. The card is missing. Have I lost it? Then I remember that my card was confiscated for some reason, many years before. Around this point, I wake up in a panic.

This panic is not so different from the misery that millions of adult illiterates experience each day within the course of their routine existence in the U.S.A.

Illiterates cannot read the menu in a restaurant.

They cannot read the cost of items on the menu in the *window* of the restaurant before they enter.

10 Illiterates cannot read the letters that their children bring home 10 from their teachers. They cannot study school department circulars that tell them of the courses that their children must be taking if they hope to pass the SAT exams. They cannot help with homework. They cannot write a letter to the teacher. They are afraid to visit in the classroom. They do not want to humiliate their child or themselves.

Illiterates cannot read instructions on a bottle of prescription medicine. They cannot find out when a medicine is past the year of safe consumption; nor can they read of allergenic risks, warnings to diabetics, or the potential sedative effect of certain kinds of nonprescription pills. They cannot observe preventive health care admonitions. They cannot read about "the seven warning signs of cancer" or the indications of blood-sugar fluctuations or the risks of eating certain foods that aggravate the likelihood of cardiac arrest.

Illiterates live, in more than literal ways, an uninsured existence. They cannot understand the written details on a health insurance form. They cannot read the waivers that they sign preceding surgical procedures. Several women I have known in Boston have entered a slum hospital with the intention of obtaining a tubal ligation and have emerged a few days later after having been subjected to a hysterectomy. Unaware of their rights, incognizant of jargon, intimidated by the unfamiliar air of fear and atmosphere of ether that so many of us find oppressive in the confines even of the most attractive and expensive medical facilities, they have signed their names to documents they could not read and which nobody, in the hectic situation that prevails so often in those overcrowded hospitals that serve the urban poor, had even bothered to explain.

Childbirth might seem to be the last inalienable right of any female citizen within a civilized society. Illiterate mothers, as we shall see, already have been cheated of the power to protect their progeny against the likelihood of demolition in deficient public schools and, as a result, against the verbal servitude within which they themselves exist. Surgical denial of the right to bear that child in the first place represents an ultimate denial, an unspeakable metaphor, a final darkness that denies even the twilight gleamings of our own humanity. What greater violation of our biological, our biblical, our spiritual humanity could possibly exist than that which takes place nightly, perhaps hourly these days, within such over-burdened and benighted institutions as the Boston City Hospital? Illiteracy has many costs; few are so irreversible as this.

Even the roof above one's head, the gas or other fuel for heating that protects the residents of northern city slums against the threat of illness in the winter months become uncertain guarantees. Illiterates cannot read the lease that they must sign to live in an apartment which, too often, they cannot afford. They cannot manage check accounts and therefore seldom pay for anything by mail. Hours and entire days of difficult travel (and the cost of bus or other public transit) must be added to the real cost of whatever they consume. Loss of interest on the check accounts they do not have, and could not manage if they did, must be regarded as another of the excess costs paid by the citizen who is excluded from the common instruments of commerce in a numerate society.

15 "I couldn't understand the bills," a woman in Washington, D.C., 15 reports, "and then I couldn't write the checks to pay them. We signed things we didn't know what they were."

Illiterates cannot read the notices that they receive from welfare offices or from the IRS. They must depend on word-of-mouth instruction from the welfare worker—or from other persons whom they have good reason to mistrust. They do not know what rights they have, what deadlines and requirements they face, what options they might choose to exercise. They are half-citizens. Their rights exist in print but not in fact.

Illiterates cannot look up numbers in a telephone directory. Even if they can find the names of friends, few possess the sorting skills to make use of the yellow pages; categories are bewildering and trade names are beyond decoding capabilities for millions of nonreaders. Even the emergency numbers listed on the first page of the phone book—"Ambulance," "Police," and "Fire"—are too frequently beyond the recognition of nonreaders.

Many illiterates cannot read the admonition on a pack of cigarettes. Neither the Surgeon General's warning nor its reproduction on the package can alert them to the risks. Although most people learn by word of mouth that smoking is related to a number of grave physical disorders, they do not get the chance to read the detailed stories which can document this danger with the vividness that turns concern into determination to resist. They can see the handsome cowboy or the slim Virginia lady lighting up a filter cigarette; they cannot heed the words that tell them that this product is (not "may be") dangerous to their health. Sixty million men and women are condemned to be the unalerted, high-risk candidates for cancer.

Illiterates do not buy "no-name" products in the supermarkets. They must depend on photographs or the familiar logos that are printed on the packages of brand-name groceries. The poorest people, therefore, are denied the benefits of the least costly products.

20   Illiterates depend almost entirely upon label recognition. Many 20 labels, however, are not easy to distinguish. Dozens of different kinds of Campbell's soup appear identical to the nonreaders The purchaser who cannot read and does not dare to ask for help, out of the fear of being stigmatized (a fear which is unfortunately realistic), frequently comes home with something which she never wanted and her family never tasted.

Illiterates cannot read instructions on a pack of frozen food. Packages sometimes provide an illustration to explain the cooking preparations; but illustrations are of little help to someone who must "boil water, drop the food—*within* its plastic wrapper—in the boiling water, wait for it to simmer, instantly remove."

Even when labels are seemingly clear, they may be easily mistaken. A woman in Detroit brought home a gallon of Crisco for her children's dinner. She thought that she had bought the chicken that was pictured on the label. She had enough Crisco now to last a year—but no more money to go back and buy the food for dinner.

Recipes provided on the packages of certain staples sometimes tempt a semiliterate person to prepare a meal her children have not tasted. The longing to vary the uniform and often starchy content of low-budget meals provided to the family that relies on food stamps commonly leads to ruinous results. Scarce funds have been wasted and the food must be thrown out. The same applies to distribution of food-surplus produce in emergency conditions. Government inducements to poor people to "explore the ways" by which to make a tasty meal from tasteless noodles, surplus cheese, and powdered milk are useless to nonreaders. Intended as benevolent advice, such recommendations mock reality and foster deeper feelings of resentment and of inability to cope. (Those, on the other hand, who cautiously refrain from "innovative" recipes in preparation of their children's meals must suffer the opprobrium of "laziness," "lack of imagination. . . .")

Illiterates cannot travel freely. When they attempt to do so, they encounter risks that few of us can dream of. They cannot read traffic signs and, while they often learn to recognize and to decipher symbols, they cannot manage street names which they haven't seen before. The same is true for bus and subway stops. While ingenuity can sometimes help a man or woman to discern directions from familiar landmarks, buildings, cemeteries, churches, and the like, most illiterates are virtually immobilized. They seldom wander past the streets and neighborhoods they know. Geographical paralysis becomes a bitter metaphor for their entire existence. They are immobilized in almost every sense we can imagine. They can't move up. They can't move out. They cannot see beyond. Illiterates may take an oral test for drivers' permits in most sections of America. It is a questionable concession. Where will they go? How will they get there? How will they get home? Could it be that some of us might like it better if they stayed where they belong?

25   Travel is only one of many instances of circumscribed existence.   25
Choice, in almost all its facets, is diminished in the life of an illiterate adult. Even the printed TV schedule, which provides most people with the luxury of preselection, does not belong within the arsenal of options in illiterate existence. One consequence is that the viewer watches only what appears at moments when he happens to have time to turn the switch. Another consequence, a lot more common, is that the TV set remains in operation night and day. Whatever the program offered at the hour when he walks into the room will be the nutriment

that he accepts and swallows. Thus, to passivity, is added frequency—indeed, almost uninterrupted continuity. Freedom to select is no more possible here than in the choice of home or surgery or food.

"You don't choose," said one illiterate woman. "You take your wishes from somebody else." Whether in perusal of a menu, selection of highways, purchase of groceries, or determination of affordable enjoyment, illiterate Americans must trust somebody else: a friend, a relative, a stranger on the street, a grocery clerk, a TV copywriter.

"All of our mail we get, it's hard for her to read. Settin' down and writing a letter, she can't do it. Like if we get a bill . . . we take it over to my sister-in-law . . . My sister-in-law reads it."

Billing agencies harass poor people for the payment of the bills for purchases that might have taken place six months before. Utility companies offer an agreement for a staggered payment schedule on a bill past due. "You have to trust them," one man said. Precisely for this reason, you end up by trusting no one and suspecting everyone of possible deceit. A submerged sense of distrust becomes the corollary to a constant need to trust. "They are cheating me . . . I have been tricked . . . I do not know . . ."

Not knowing: This is a familiar theme. Not knowing the right word for the right thing at the right time is one form of subjugation. Not knowing the world that lies concealed behind those words is a more terrifying feeling. The longitude and latitude of one's existence are beyond all easy apprehension. Even the hard, cold stars within the firmament above one's head begin to mock the possibilities for self-location. Where am I? Where did I come from? Where will I go?

"I've lost a lot of jobs," one man explains. "Today, even if you're a janitor, there's still reading and writing . . . They leave a note saying, 'Go to room so-and-so . . .' You can't do it. You can't read it. You don't know."

"The hardest thing about it is that I've been places where I didn't know where I was. You don't know where you are . . . You're lost."

"Like I said: I have two kids. What do I do if one of my kids starts choking? I go running to the phone . . . I can't look up the hospital phone number. That's if we're at home. Out on the street, I can't read the sign. I get to a pay phone. 'Okay, tell us where you are. We'll send an ambulance.' I look at the street sign. Right there, I can't tell you what it says. I'd have to spell it out, letter for letter. By that time, one of my kids would be dead . . . These are the kinds of fears you go with, every single day . . ."

"Reading directions, I suffer with. I work with chemicals . . . That's scary to begin with . . . "

"You sit down. They throw the menu in front of you. Where do you go from there? Nine times out of ten you say, 'Go ahead. Pick out something for the both of us.' I've eaten some weird things, let me tell you!"

35   Menus. Chemicals. A child choking while his mother searches for   35 a word she does not know to find assistance that will come too late. Another mother speaks about the inability to help her kids to read: "I can't read to them. Of course that's leaving them out of something they should have. Oh, it matters. You believe it matters! I ordered all these books. The kids belong to a book club. Donny wanted me to read a book to him. I told Donny: 'I can't read,' He said: 'Mommy, you sit down. I'll read it to you.' I tried it one day, reading from the pictures. Donny looked at me. He said, 'Mommy, that's not right.' He's only five. He knew I couldn't read . . .'"

A landlord tells a woman that her lease allows him to evict her if her baby cries and causes inconvenience to her neighbors. The consequence of challenging his words conveys a danger which appears, unlikely as it seems, even more alarming than the danger of eviction. Once she admits that she can't read, in the desire to maneuver for the time in which to call a friend, she will have defined herself in terms of an explicit impotence that she cannot endure. Capitulation in this case is preferable to self-humiliation. Resisting the definition of oneself in terms of what one cannot do, what others take for granted, represents a need so great that other imperatives (even one so urgent as the need to keep one's home in winter's cold) evaporate and fall away in face of fear. Even the loss of home and shelter, in this case, is not so terrifying as the loss of self.

"I come out of school. I was sixteen. They had their meetings. The directors meet. They said that I was wasting their school paper. I was wasting pencils . . ."

Another illiterate, looking back, believes she was not worthy of her teacher's time. She believes that it was wrong of her to take up space within her school. She believes that it was right to leave in order that somebody more deserving could receive her place.

Children choke. Their mother chokes another way: on more than chicken bones.

40   People eat what others order, know what others tell them, strug-   40 gle not to see themselves as they believe the world perceives them. A

man in California speaks about his own loss of identity, of self-location, definition:

"I stood at the bottom of the ramp. My car had broke down on the freeway. There was a phone. I asked for the police. They was nice. They said to tell them where I was. I looked up at the signs. There was one that I had seen before. I read it to them: ONE WAY STREET. They thought it was a joke. I told them I couldn't read. There was other signs above the ramp. They told me to try. I looked around for somebody to help. All the cars was going by real fast. I couldn't make them understand that I was lost. The cop was nice. He told me: 'Try once more,' I did my best. I couldn't read. I only knew the sign above my head. The cop was trying to be nice. He knew that I was trapped. 'I can't send out a car to you if you can't tell me where you are.' I felt afraid. I nearly cried. I'm forty-eight years old. I only said: 'I'm on a one-way street . . .'"

The legal problems and the courtroom complications that confront illiterate adults have been discussed above. The anguish that may underlie such matters was brought home to me this year while I was working on this book. I have spoken, in the introduction, of a sudden phone call from one of my former students, now in prison for a criminal offense. Stephen is not a boy today. He is twenty-eight years old. He called to ask me to assist him in his trial, which comes up next fall. He will be on trial for murder. He has just knifed and killed a man who first enticed him to his home, then cheated him, and then insulted him—as "an illiterate subhuman."

Stephen now faces twenty years to life. Stephen's mother was illiterate. His grandparents were illiterate as well. What parental curse did not destroy was killed off finally by the schools. Silent violence is repaid with interest. It will cost us $25,000 yearly to maintain this broken soul in prison. But what is the price that has been paid by Stephen's victim? What is the price that will be paid by Stephen?

Perhaps we might slow down a moment here and look at the realities described above. This is the nation that we live in. This is a society that most of us did not create but which our President and other leaders have been willing to sustain by virtue of malign neglect. Do we possess the character and courage to address a problem which so many nations, poorer than our own, have found it natural to correct?

45   The answers to these questions represent a reasonable test of our   45
belief in the democracy to which we have been asked in public school to swear allegiance.

Questions on Meaning

1. Define what Kozol means by "human cost." You might start your thinking by considering how this cost is different from the literal monetary costs that are also described at different points in the essay.
2. Kozol relates illiteracy to the concept of subjugation. Brainstorm what your think he means by this. Who are the subjugators? What is their motivation for subjugating illiterate people?
3. In a sentence or two, express the primary theme of this essay.

Questions on Rhetorical Strategy and Style

1. One characteristic of Kozol's style is passages that link concrete examples with larger abstractions or generalizations. For example, in paragraph 24, in the context of the difficulties of an illiterate person traveling, Kozol writes, "Geographical paralysis becomes a bitter metaphor for their entire existence. They are immobilized in almost every sense we can imagine." Another example occurs in paragraphs 12 and 13, where Kozol speaks of women given a hysterectomy without being informed of the meaning of this surgery as "a final darkness that denies even the twilight gleamings of our own humanity." Analyze this passage and explain why Kozol calls this the "ultimate denial."
2. Kozol frequently uses description as a rhetorical device for developing the essay. Read back through the essay and identify at least three examples of illiterate people whose problem Kozol describes in detail. How does each of these examples contribute to the effectiveness of the essay overall?
3. How successful is Kozol in building his argument about the costs of illiteracy? What specific characteristics of the essay contribute to your evaluation?

Writing Assignments

1. To better understand the difficulty illiterates face in many types of communication, use your imagination to solve the following problem. You are the director of a new program at your college or university for teaching reading at no cost to adult illiterates in the community. You have funding to hire teachers and pay for classrooms and materials, but very little money left over to publicize the

program. How do you inform illiterates in the community about your reading classes? How do you give them basic information such as where to come and what times and how to get there? Brainstorm with others to reach the most effective solution that overcomes the problems of communication.

2. Kozol says our political leaders sustain the problem of illiteracy through "malign neglect." What does he mean by this phrase? Why is this neglect "malign"? Consider other social problems, such as homelessness or lack of good health care for people in poverty. Do you see "malign neglect" with these problems too? Write an essay in which you explore the reasons why leaders might be neglectful in these ways.

3. In paragraph 3 Kozol states that illiterate persons can only "cast a vote of questionable worth" because their decision is not based on "serious print information" but on "a face, a smile, or a style." Some social critics would say the same is true of many people who can read: that they vote based on television images and sound bytes rather than careful reading of the issues. If true, this only heightens the resulting national tragedy to which Kozol refers. What do you think about this idea? Do most people take the time to study the issues in depth before voting? Ask a few other people about how much they read before the last election. Think about what you learn from their comments, and formulate your own thesis about what really happens in an election and what you think *should* happen. Write a persuasive essay that develops your thesis.

Letter to Bank Trustee, William Yaeger

Margie Brauer

Margie Brauer was one of many people devastated by President Jimmy Carter's 1979 grain embargo against the Soviet Union. Because so many U.S. farmers relied on such exports to remain solvent, the embargo spawned foreclosures on numerous family farms. Farmers' financial problems were worsened with the continuing economic problems of the country in general. In certain areas, these troubles led to conditions that had not been witnessed since the Great Depression of the 1930s. In her letter to William Yaeger, a bank trustee, Brauer seeks to put a human face on the farmer's economic plight.

Mr. William L. Yaeger
Durham, N.C.
Re: Case No. B-86-00887C-7

Dear Mr. Yaeger,

1   I suppose that bankruptcy is intended to be a "cut and dried"   1
business decision, and in the final analysis perhaps that is the end
result. However, with first hand knowledge, I do know there is a
far greater involvement, especially the emotional traumas of seeing the
upheaval and disposal of a lifetime of very hard work.
   My husband and I are from farm families of many generations.
Except for brief periods of our lives, we have always farmed and know
little of any other way of life. Ernie, at 69 years of age, was off the

farm during the years of 1939–1945 while he was in service during World War 11 with 30 months overseas. When he returned in 1945 we were promptly married, having known each other for many years. In early 1946 we bargained for a very run-down piece of land on which we spent $800 to build a two-room cottage without the amenities of plumbing or electricity on a rural unpaved road. Conditions eventually improved—the road was paved and we did get electricity and running water, but no bath facility for 16 years.

Our two daughters were born while we lived in that little house— one was nine years old and the other three when we moved into our modest FHA-financed home. The intervening years were good because we loved the work of clearing those rolling hills and turning red clay into beautiful green pastures and fields—grabbing up roots and stumps and hauling off endless rocks. It should have mattered that we never had any money at the end of the year, but we always felt the promise and the hope of a better year next year. I worked off the farm at a local bank, an insurance company, a truck line (some of the time at two jobs) along with canning and freezing fruits and vegetables to make ends meet. I sewed for the children and if I needed new curtains or a bedspread, I made them. So much of what we made from the farm went back into the farm, but we didn't require a lot for family living and we simply plowed everything back to the farm.

Out of it all, we raised two very special girls—not extremely beautiful or extremely intellectual, but attractive and smart—pretty stable and altogether satisfactory. Through work-study programs, loans, and scholarships, they both acquired a fairly good basic education. One teaches, the other is a health educator with our local health department. Both have apparently solid and satisfactory marriages. The older one has two little girls, the younger has a new little daughter.

5   I am not sure why I am writing you this except that perhaps I   5 need to reaffirm to myself that our dilemma is not the result of high and riotous living—that we are and have always been a plain, hard-working farm family. We've had a few health problems, none of which were very expensive, three or four really bad drought years that really set us back, perhaps some bad business decisions and maybe some management weakness. Actually we were not in bad shape until the years with the terrible interest rates and the grain embargo—it

seems in retrospect that was the real beginning of a long, painful decline to this sorry state of affairs.

I think I want to tell you that, faced with the certainty of Federal land bank and Farmers Home foreclosure, we came to the conclusion that Chapter 7, with its inherent finality, seemed the preferred route out of the morass of worry and debt. We are trying to maintain our self-respect and a degree of dignity (all honor & pride have gone by the way), trying to get through this most difficult of times with our sanity intact and see what we can do to maintain a livelihood so that we need not resort to public assistance or dependence on our children. At Ernie's age, it will be difficult to find work; his knees are worn out, too; but his Social Security of $296 monthly will help. I was able to get work at a nearby hospital at $4.10 hourly as a ward clerk—completely out of my past experience of book-keeping and accounting but it will pay routine bills, if we are very, very frugal.

Mr. Yaeger, we are very ignorant about bankruptcy, never having had anyone in either of our families or any of our associates involved in bankruptcy. We believe that when this is over, we will be relieved of all our holdings and of all our debts in their entirety and we will be left with our household goods and clothing. I would like to know if it would be possible for me to get a new pair of glasses (mine have not been changed in four or five years and the bifocal is no longer right for my vision). This would probably cost one half of a cow or about $130. I also have two teeth badly in need of repair—one needs a cap in order to save it and the other is in pretty bad shape also—will probably cost two cows or about $500. Also electric bills are continuing for the poultry house and will need to be paid soon. How will the auctioneer be paid? How will you be paid? Is there any way we can come out of this with even a few hundred dollars? We have nothing. We have acquired and accumulated nothing—with the 40 productive years of our life down the drain. How long can we remain in our house?

Our oldest daughter and her husband own a mobile home into which we will move. This has to be relocated since it now is located on a part of the bankruptcy property. Would it be possible or reasonable to request that we be allowed to live in our house perhaps as long as 60 days from probable discharge or until late September or October?

If you do not have the time to dictate a letter answering these questions, perhaps you can call me. Thank you for your time in reading this rather long letter. Perhaps it will establish that we are real flesh and blood people with very real problems and not merely a case number. I pray that the agonizing we have done in order to accept the inevitability of this decision has been the worst part of it and we will greatly appreciate anything you can do to ease the finalizing technicalities and to enable us to pick up the fragments of our lives.

Sincerely,
Margie M. Brauer

Questions on Meaning

1. What do you consider the primary purpose of Brauer's letter? Where in the letter does that purpose become clear to you?
2. What does Brauer mean when she says, "all honor & pride have gone by the way"? After reading this letter, do you agree with this statement? Why or why not?

Questions on Rhetorical Strategy and Style

1. Effective narration often depends on vivid images created in the reader's mind. Cite several such images in Brauer's letter and explain their impact on you as a reader.
2. Brauer provides several examples of her family's financial condition. In your view, what is her primary purpose in offering these examples? What other purpose might the examples serve?
3. Why is it important to Brauer to clarify the cause of her and her husband's bankruptcy? What does she want Yaeger to understand regarding the cause?

Writing Assignments

1. Yaeger did reply sympathetically to Brauer, and she and her husband were able to remain in their home despite the loss of their farm. Write your own reply to her, explaining the impact of her letter on you.
2. On your own behalf or on behalf of someone close to you, write a letter to a corporation or government agency, in which you put a human face on a social or financial problem. Try to use the nonconfrontational tone of Brauer's letter.
3. Many U.S. farmers were hurt by President Carter's 1979 grain embargo against the Soviet Union. Research the embargo. Then write an essay explaining the embargo's purpose and its impact on farmers.

The Toughest Indian in the World

Sherman Alexie

Sherman Alexie (1966–) was born on a Spokane Indian Reservation in Wellprint, Washington. His mother was Spokane while his father Coeur d'Alene. Though his life began with medical difficulties, he learned to read at three and became a star high school athlete. He graduated from Washington State University-Pullman in American Studies. In addition to writing, he has participated in the Museum of Tolerance project; appeared on the Lehrer News Hour (with President Clinton); recorded albums; performed as a standup comedian; and written and produced a film. He was awarded a Washington State Arts Commission Poetry Fellowship in 1991, and the National Endowment for the Arts Poetry Fellowship in 1992. Other awards include the PEN/Hemingway Award, the Lila Wallace Reader's Digest Writers' Award, the Before Columbus Foundation's American Book Award, and The Filmmakers Trophy. His works include The Lone Ranger and Tonto Fistfight in Heaven *(1994),* Reservation Blues *(1996), and* The First Indian on the Moon *(2004).*

1   Being a Spokane Indian, I only pick up Indian hitchhikers. I learned this particular ceremony from my father, a Coeur d'Aléne, who always stopped for those twentieth-century aboriginal nomads who refused to believe the salmon were gone. I don't know what they believed in exactly, but they wore hope like a bright shirt. My father never taught me about hope. From an early age, I was told that our salmon would never come back, and though

such lessons may seem cruel, I learned to cover my heart in a crowd of white people.

"They'll kill you if they get the chance," my father said. "Love you or hate you, white people will shoot you in the heart. Even after all these years, they'll still smell the salmon on you, the dead salmon, and that will make white people dangerous."

All of us, Indian and white, are haunted by salmon.

When I was a boy, I leaned over the edge of one dam or another—perhaps Long Lake or Little Falls or the great gray dragon known at the Grand Coulee—and watched the ghosts of salmon rise from the water to the sky and become constellations. Believe me, for most Indians stars are nothing more than white tombstones scattered across a dark graveyard.

5   But the Indian hitchhikers my father picked up refused to admit the existence of sky, let alone the possibility that salmon might be stars. They were common people who believed only in the thumb and the foot. My father envied those simple Indian hitchhikers. He wanted to change their minds about salmon; he wanted to break open their hearts and see the future in their blood, because he loved them.

Driving along one highway or another, my father would point out a hitchhiker standing beside the road a mile or two in the distance.

"Indian," he would say, and he was never wrong, though I could never tell if the distant figure was male or female, let alone Indian or not.

If that distant figure happened to be white, my father would drive by without comment. That was how I learned to be silent in the presence of white people. The silence is not about hate or pain or fear. Indians just like to believe that white people will vanish, perhaps explode into smoke, if they are ignored enough times. Perhaps a thousand white families are still waiting for their sons and daughters to return home, and can't recognize them when they float back as morning fog.

"Indian," my father would say again as we approached one of those dream filled hitchhikers. Hell, those hitchhikers' faces grew red and puffy with the weight of their dreams.

10   "We better stop," my mother would say from the passenger seat. She was one of those Spokane women who always wore a purple bandanna tied tightly around their heads. These days, her bandanna is usually red. There are reasons, motives, traditions behind the choice of color, but my mother keeps them secret.

"Make room," my father would say to my siblings and me as we stat on the floor in the cavernous passenger area of our blue van. We sat on carpet samples because my father had torn out the seats in a sober rage not long after he bought the van from a crazy white man.

I have three brothers and three sisters now. Back then, I had four of each. I missed one of the funerals and cried myself sick during the other one.

"Make room," my father would say again—he said everything twice and only then would we scramble to make space for the Indian hitchhiker.

Of course, it was easy enough to make room for one hitchhiker, but Indians usually travel in packs. Once or twice, we picked up entire all-Indian basketball teams, along with their coaches, girlfriends, and cousins. Fifteen, twenty Indian strangers squeezed into the back of a blue van with nine wide-eyed Indian kids.

Back in those days, I loved the smell of Indians, and of Indian hitchhikers in particular. They were usually in some stage of drunkenness, often in need of soap and towel, and always ready to sing.

Oh, the songs! Indian blues bellowed at the highest volumes. We called them "49s," those cross-cultural songs that combined Indian lyrics and rhythms with country-and-Western and blues melodies. It seemed that every Indian knew all the lyrics to every Hank Williams song ever recorded. Hank was our Jesus, Patsy Cline was our Madonna, and Freddy Fender, George Jones, Conway Twitty, Loretta Lynn, Tammy Wynette, Charlie Pride, Ronnie Milsap, Tanya Tucker, Marty Robbins, Johnny Horton, Donna Fargo, and Charlie Rich were our disciples.

We all know that nostalgia is dangerous, but I remember those days with a clear conscience. We live in different days now, and there aren't as many Indian hitchhikers as there used to be.

Today, I drive my own car, a 1998 Toyota Camry, the best-selling automobile in the United States, and therefore the one most often stolen. *Consumer Reports* has named it the most reliable family sedan for sixteen years running, and I believe them.

With my Camry I pick up three or four Indian hitchhikers a week. Mostly men. They're usually headed home, back to their reservations or somewhere close to their reservations. Indians hardly ever travel in a straight line, so a Crow Indian might hitchhike west when his reservation is back east in Montana. He has some people to see in Seattle, he might explain if I ever asked him. But I never ask Indians their reasons for hitchhiking. They were Indian, walking, raising a thumb, and I was there to pick them up.

20   At the newspaper where I work, my fellow reporters think I'm crazy to pick up hitchhikers. They're all white and never stop to pick up anybody, let alone an Indian. After all, we're the ones who write the stories and headlines: "HITCHHIKER KILLS HUSBAND AND WIFE," "MISSING GIRL'S BODY FOUND," "RAPIST STRIKES AGAIN." If I really tried, maybe I could explain to them why I pick up any Indian, but who wants to try? Instead, if they ask I just give them a smile and turn back to my computer. My coworkers smile back and laugh loudly. They're always laughing loudly at me, at one another, at themselves, at goofy typos in the newspaper, at the idea of hitchhikers.

I dated one of them for a few months. Cindy. She covered the local courts: speeding tickets and divorces, drunk driving and embezzlement. Cindy firmly believed in the who-what-where-when-why-and-how of journalism. In daily conversation, she talked like she was writing the lead of her latest story. Hell, she talked like that in bed.

"How does that feel?" I would ask, quite possibly becoming the only Indian man who has ever asked that question.

"I love it when you touch me there," she would answer. "But it would help if you rubbed it about thirty percent lighter and with your thumb instead of your middle finger. And could you maybe turn the radio to a different station? KYZY would be good. I feel like soft jazz will work better for me right now. A minor chord, a C or G flat, or something like that. O.K., honey?"

During lovemaking, I would get so exhausted by the size of her vocabulary that I would fall asleep before my orgasm, continue pumping away as if I were awake, and then regain consciousness with a sudden start when I finally did come, more out of reflex than passion.

25   Don't get me wrong. Cindy was a good one, cute and smart, funny as hell, a good catch no matter how you define it, but she was also one of those white women who only date brown-skinned guys, Indians like me, black dudes, Mexicans, even a few Iranians. I started to feel like a trophy, or like one of those entries in a personal ad. I asked Cindy why she never dated pale boys.

"White guys bore me," she said. "All they want to talk about is their fathers."

327

"What do brown guys talk about?" I asked her.

"Their mothers," she said and laughed, then promptly left me for a public defender who was half Japanese and half African—a combination that left Cindy dizzy with the interracial possibilities.

Since Cindy, I haven't dated anyone. I live in my studio apartment with the ghosts of two dogs. Felix and Oscar, and a laptop computer stuffed with bad poems, the aborted halves of three novels, and some three-paragraph personality pieces I wrote for the newspaper.

30 I'm a features writer, and an Indian at that, so I get all the shit jobs. Not the dangerous shit jobs or the monotonous shit jobs. No, I get to write the articles designed to please the eye, ear, and heart. And there is no journalism more soul-endangering to write than journalism that aims to please.

So it was with reluctance that I hopped into my car last week and headed down Highway 2 to write some damn pleasant story about some damn pleasant people. Then I saw the Indian hitchhiker standing beside the road. He looked the way Indian hitchhikers usually look. Long, straggly black hair. Brown eyes and skin. Missing a couple of teeth. Bad complexion. Crooked nose that had been broken more than once. Big, misshapen ears. A few whiskers masquerading as a mustache. Even before he climbed into my car, I could tell he was tough. He has some serious muscles that threatened to rip through his blue jeans and denim jacket. When he was in the car, I could see his hands up close and they told the whole story. His fingers were twisted into weird shapes, and his knuckles were covered with layers of scar tissue.

"Jeez," I said. "You're a fighter, enit?"

The hitchhiker looked down at his hands, flexed them into fists. I could tell it hurt him to do that.

"Yeah," he said.

35 I pulled back onto the highway, looking over my shoulder to check my blind spot.

"What tribe are you?" I asked him.

"Lummi," he said. "What about you?"

"Spokane."

"I know some Spokanes. Haven't seen them in a long time."

40 He clutched his backpack in his lap like he didn't want to let it go for nothing. He reached inside a pocket and pulled out a piece of deer jerky. I recognized it by the smell.

"Want some?" he asked.

"Sure."

It had been a long time since I'd eaten jerky. The salt, the gamy taste. I felt as Indian as Indian gets, driving down the road in a fast car, chewing on jerky, talking to an indigenous fighter.

"Where you headed?" I asked.

45 "Home. Back to the rez."

I nodded my head as I passed a big truck. The driver gave us a smile as we went by. I tooted the horn.

"Big truck," said the fighter.

I haven't lived on my reservation for years. But I live in Spokane, which is only an hour's drive from the rez. Still, I hardly ever go there. I don't know why not. I don't think about it much, I guess, but my mom and dad still live in the same house where I grew up. My brothers and sisters, too. The ghosts of my two dead siblings share an apartment in the converted high school. Believe me. It's just a local call from Spokane to the rez, so I talk to all of them once or twice a week. Smoke signals courtesy of the U.S. West Communications. Sometimes they call me up to talk about the stories they've seen that I write for the newspaper. Pet pigs and support groups and science fairs. Once in a while, I used to fill in for the obituaries writer when she was sick. Then she died, and I had to write her obituary.

"How far you going?" asked the fighter, meaning how much closer was he going to get to his reservation than he was now.

50 "Up to Wenatchee," I said. "I've got some people to interview 50 there."

"Interview? What for?"

"I'm a reporter. I work for the newspaper."

"No," said the fighter, looking at me like I was stupid for thinking he was stupid. "I mean, what's the story about?"

"Oh, not much. There's two sets of twins who work for the fire department. Human interest stuff, you know?"

55 "Two sets of twins, enit? That's weird." 55

He offered me more deer jerky, but I was too thirsty from the salty meat, so I offered him a Pepsi instead. It's a little known fact that Indians can be broken up into two distinct groups: Pepsi tribes and Coke tribes.

"Don't mind if I do," he said. He was obviously a member of a Pepsi tribe.

"They're in the cooler on the back seat," I said. "Grab me one, too."

He maneuvered his backpack carefully and found room enough to reach into the back seat for the soda pop. He opened my can first and handed it to me. I took a big mouthful and hiccupped loudly.

60 "That always happens to me when I drink cold things," he said. 60

We sipped slowly after that. I kept my eyes on the road while he stared out his window into the wheat fields. We were quiet for many miles.

"Who do you fight?" I asked as we passed through another anonymous small town.

"Mostly Indians," he said. "Money fights, you know? I go from rez to rez, fighting the best they have. Winner takes all."

"Jeez, I never heard of that."

65 "Yeah, I guess it's illegal." 65

He rubbed his hands together. I could see fresh wounds.

"Man," I said. "Those fights must be rough."

The fighter stared out the window. I watched him for a little too long and almost drove off the road. Car horns sounded all around us.

"Jeez," the fighter said. "Close one, enit?"

70 "Close enough," I said. 70

He pulled his backpack closer to him, using it as a barrier between his chest and the dashboard. An Indian hitchhiker's version of a passenger-side air bag.

"Who'd you fight last?" I asked, trying to concentrate on the road.

"Some Flathead kid," he said. "In Arlee. He was supposed to be the toughest Indian the world."

"Was he?"

75 "Nah, no way. Wasn't even close. Wasn't even tougher than me." 75

He told me how big the Flathead kid was, way over six feet tall and two hundred and some pounds. Big buck Indian. Had hands as big as this and arms as big as that. Had a chin like a damn buffalo. The fighter told me that he hit the Flathead kid harder than he ever hit anybody before.

"I hit him like he was a white man," the fighter said. "I hit him like he was two or three white men rolled into one."

But the Flathead kid would not go down, even though his face swelled up so bad that he looked like the Elephant Man. There were no referees, no judge, no bells to signal the end of the round. The winner was the Indian still standing. Punch after punch, man, and the kid would not go down.

"I was so tired after a while," said the fighter, "that I just took a step back and watched the kid. He stood there with his arms down, swaying from side to side like some toy, you know? Head bobbing on his neck like there was no bone at all. You couldn't even see his eyes no more. He was all messed up."

80 "What'd you do?" I asked. 80

"Ah, hell, I couldn't fight him no more. That kid was planning to die before he ever went down. So I just sat on the ground while they counted me out. Dumb Flathead kid didn't even know what was happening. I just sat on the ground while they raised his hand. While all the winners collected their money and all the losers cussed me out. I just sat there, man."

"Jeez," I said. "What happened next?"

"Not much. I sat there until everybody was gone. Then I stood up and headed for home. I'm tired of this shit. I just want to go home for a while. I got enough money to last me a long time. I'm a rich Indian, you hear? I'm a rich Indian."

The fighter finished his Pepsi with one last swallow, rolled down his window, and pitched the can out. I almost protested, but decided against it. I kept my empty can wedged between my legs.

85 "That's a hell of a story," I said. 85

"Ain't no story," he said. "It's what happened."

"Jeez," I said. "You would've been a warrior in the old days, enit? You would've been a killer. You would've stolen everybody's goddamn horses. That would've been you. You would've been it."

I was excited. I wanted the fighter to know how much I thought of him. He didn't even look at me.

"A killer," he said. "Sure."

90 We didn't talk much after that. I pulled into Wenatchee just before 90 sundown, and the fighter seemed happy to be leaving me.

"Thanks for the ride, cousin," he said as he climbed out. Indians always call each other cousin, especially if they're strangers.

"Wait," I said.

He looked at me, waiting impatiently.

I wanted to know if he had a place to sleep that night. It was supposed to get cold. There was a mountain range between Wenatchee and his reservation. Big mountains that used to be volcanoes. Big mountains that were still volcanoes. It could all blow up at any time. We wrote about it once in the newspaper. Things can change so quickly. So many emergencies and disasters that we can barely keep track. I wanted to tell him how much I cared about my job, even if I had to write about small town firemen. I wanted to tell the fighter that I always picked up every Indian hitchhiker, young and old, men and women. Believe me, I pick them up and get them all a little closer to home, even if I can't get them all the way. I wanted to tell him that the night sky was a graveyard. I wanted to know if he was the toughest Indian in the world.

95   "It's late," I finally said. "You can crash with me, if you want."   95

He studied my face and then looked down the long road toward his reservation.

"O.K.," he said. "That sounds good."

We got a room at the Pony Soldier Motel, and both of us laughed at the irony of it all. Inside the room, in a generic watercolor hanging above the bed, the U.S. Cavalry was kicking the crap out of a band of renegade Indians.

"What tribe you think they are?" I asked the fighter.

100   "All of them," he said.   100

The fighter crashed on the floor while I curled up in the uncomfortable bed. I couldn't sleep for the longest time. I listened to the fighter talk in his sleep. I stared up at the water-stained ceiling. I don't know what time it was when I finally drifted off, and I don't know what time it was when the fighter got into bed with me. He was naked and his penis was hard. I could feel it press against my back as he snuggled up close to me, reached inside my underwear, and took my penis in his hand. Neither of us said a word. He just continued to stroke me as he rubbed himself against my back. That went on for a long time. I had never been that close to another man, but the fighter's callused fingers felt better than I would have imagined if I had ever allowed myself to imagine such things.

"This isn't working," he whispered. "I can't come."

Without thinking, I reached out and took the fighter's penis in my hand. He was surprisingly small.

"No," he said. "I want to be inside you."

105   "I don't know," I said. "I've never done this before."   105
"It's O.K.," he said. "I'll be careful. I have rubbers."

Without waiting for my answer, he released me and got up from the bed. I turned to look at him. He was beautiful and scarred. So much brown skin marked with bruises, badly healed wounds, and tattoos. His long black hair was unbraided and hung down to his thin waist. My slacks and dress shirt were carefully folded and draped over the chair near the window. My shoes were sitting on the table. Blue light filled the room. The fighter bent down to his pack and searched for his condoms. For reasons I could not explain and cannot explain now, I kicked off my underwear and rolled over on my stomach. I could not see him, but I could hear him breathing heavily as he found the condoms, tore open a package, and rolled one over his penis. He crawled onto the bed, between my legs, and slid a pillow beneath my belly.

"Are you ready?" he asked.

"I'm not gay," I said.

110   "Sure," he said as he pushed himself into me. He was small but it 110 hurt more than I expected, and I knew I would be sore for days afterward. But I wanted him to save me. He didn't say anything. He just pumped into me for a few minutes, came with a loud sigh, and then pulled out. Believe me. I wanted him to save me. I quickly rolled off the bed and went into the bathroom. I locked the door behind me and stood there in the dark. I smelled like salmon.

"Hey," the fighter said through the door. "Are you O.K.?"

"Yes," I said. "I'm fine."

A long silence.

"Hey," he said. "Would you mind if I slept in the bed with you?"

115   I had no answer to that.   115

"Listen," I said. "That Flathead boy you fought? You know, the one you really beat up? The one who wouldn't fall down?"

In my mind, I could see the fighter pummeling that boy. Punch after punch. The boy too beaten to fight back but too strong to fall down.

"Yeah, what about him?" asked the fighter.

"What was his name?"

120   "His name?"   120

"Yeah, his name."

"Elmer something or other."

"Did he have an Indian name?"

"I have no idea. How the hell would I know that?"

I stood there in the dark for a long time. I was chilled. I wanted
to get into bed and fall asleep.

"Hey," I said. "I think, I think maybe—well, I think you should
leave now."

"Yeah," the fighter said. He was not surprised. I could hear him
softly singing as he dressed and stuffed all of his belongings into his
pack. I couldn't tell what he was singing, but I wanted to know. I
opened the bathroom door just as he was opening the door to leave.
He stopped, looked back at me, and smiled.

"Hey, tough guy," he said. "You were good."

The fighter walked out the door then, leaving it open, and walked
away. I stood in the doorway and watched him continue his walk
down the highway, past the city limits. I watched him rise from earth
to sky and become a new constellation. I closed the door and wondered what was going to happen next. Feeling uncomfortable and
cold, I went back into the bathroom. I ran the shower with the hottest
water possible. I stared at myself in the mirror. Steam quickly filled
the room. I threw a few shadow punches. Feeling stronger, I got in the
shower and searched my body for changes. A middle-aged man needs
to look for tumors. I dried myself with a towel too small for the job.
Then I crawled naked into bed. I wondered if I was a warrior in this
life and if I had been a warrior in a previous life. Lonely and laughing,
I fell asleep. I didn't dream at all, not one bit. Or perhaps I did dream,
but I can't remember any of it. Instead, I woke early the next morning, before sunrise, and went out into the world. I walked past my
car. I stepped onto the pavement, still warm from the previous day's
sun. I started walking. In bare feet, I traveled upriver toward the place
where I was born and will someday die. Believe me. At that moment,
if you had broken open my heart you could have looked inside and
seen the thin white skeletons of a thousand salmon.

Questions on Meaning

1. Is the toughest Indian in the world the fighter who the narrator picks up, or is it someone else? What does it mean to be tough in the narrator's world?

2. The story works through a variety of sexual undercurrents, using the salmon as symbols and icons of lost Indian life. Why does the narrator think he himself smells of salmon after the encounter with the Indian?

3. What does fighting mean for men? Why do they fight for money and power? What is the narrator implying about the nature of these fights?

Questions on Rhetorical Strategy and Style

1. The essay begins with ominous undertones about the dangers of picking up hitchhikers and about his family tradition of picking up Indian hitchhikers? How does this introduction set the tone for the essay?

2. The pivotal point of the story seems to be the episode in which the fighter fights with the Dumb Flathead Kid who will not be beaten. What is the old fighter saying about himself? What has he lost and what has he found?

3. In the final episode of the story, the narrator declares that he is not gay. Why is this declaration important to the mood and tone of the story? Why does the narrator talk about ghosts of dogs and siblings? Who has died and why?

Writing Assignments

1. How do the people you know define you? What does your choice of friends tell about you as a person? Write an essay in which you introduce yourself by talking about the friends you have chosen.

2. Read newspaper headlines about scary things that happen to people who travel. Then write about your imagined fears of being on the road.

3. What do scars tell us about people? The narrator in the story thinks he understands the fighter because of the old and new wounds on the man's hands. Write about scars you have and about what those scars mean to you.

Ambivalent Communities: How Americans Understand Their Localities

Claude S. Fischer

According to community sociologist Claude S. Fischer, Americans are a society of joiners but are ambivalent about community. As Fischer explains, we have mixed feelings about community because we value the friendships that community encourages, but we do not want it to infringe on our individual freedom. As you read this article, think about your own community and the values it promotes.

Americans of the Left and of the Right esteem the local community. It rests in the pantheon of American civil religion paradoxically close to that supreme value, individualism. In our ideology, the locality is, following the family, the premier locus for "community," in the fullest sense of solidarity, commitment, and intimacy. Thus, activists of all political hues seek to restore, empower, and mobilize the locality . . . . Over the years, Americans have become more committed, in practical ways, to their localities, even while enjoying access to ever-widening social horizons. This localism has served most individual American families well, but the political role of the locality exacts severe costs to the national community.

Contrasting Visions of Community

Americans' affections for "community" are ironic, for much of American history and ideology undercut traditional local solidarity.

Reprinted from *America at Century's End*, edited by Alan Wolfe (1991), Regents of the University of California.

Unlike Europe, the United States lacks the feudal experience of closed, corporate communities; its founders resisted hierarchy; marketplace liberalism undergirds its economics and politics; its settlers were linguistically, religiously, and culturally diverse; its people have always been mobile; its once-dominant farmers usually lived in isolated homesteads; and in all, unlike Europe, Americans have been, consensus has it, intensely individualistic.[1]

In spite—or perhaps because—of these conditions, Americans have glorified and sought the local community. From before Tocqueville to beyond Riesman, observers have described us as inveterate joiners, people in quest of fellowship. The quest has been for the locally based association as much or more than any other. Although American culture esteems the wilderness as an escape from society, as for Thoreau, it simultaneously values the small, rural community as the locus of intimate society, as in Brook Farm. Most Americans believe that small communities preserve morality. Politicians' rhetoric celebrates the virtues of the small, local community. (Recall Geraldine Ferraro's claim in 1984 that her corner of Queens, New York City, was *really* just a small town—like Mondale's Elmore, Minnesota, and Reagan's Dixon, Illinois—and by being that, entitled her to the same halo of grassroots innocence that the others claimed.) And local political autonomy has long been entrenched in strong home rule, dispersed authority, and checks against central government. Americans continue to subscribe to "community ideologies," beliefs about the inherent connection between place and *persona,* theories that where we live partly determines who we are, and most often that the best people are to be found in the smallest, most localized places.

This contradiction between individualism and the pursuit of fellowship has yielded paradoxical forms of "voluntary community" in the United States. The classic old-world village, nowadays viewed through pastel prisms, was a place of constraint. Confined together by barriers of geography, poverty, illness, ignorance, law, prejudice, and custom, most old-world people lived out their lives in a small group, shared a common fate, and knew one another intimately. This familiarity, by the way, did not necessarily mean affection. In contrast, Americans have more typically found their fellowship in voluntary associations, be it clubs, churches, or neighborhoods. They have also joined or left those associations as each individual deemed appropriate.[2] We can see this voluntarism in the American approach to caring for the unfortunate, well expressed in George

Bush's "thousand points of light" rhetoric. And so with our neighborhoods. They are, as Morris Janowitz termed them, "communities of limited liability," associations in which we invest our families, wealth, and concern—but we guiltlessly leave them for larger houses, more rewarding jobs, or finer amenities.[3]

5   With minor exceptions, Americans founded their towns as business ventures. Developers platted the land and advertised its bountiful future. Settlers came and then left in search of a higher standard of living. Indeed, they left in vast numbers, making for a great churning of population in nineteenth-century America, through the big cities and small towns alike. Despite sentiment, then, we have for the most part long treated our residential communities as "easy come, easy go," rather than as social worlds that envelop us.

Is Ours a "Rootless" Society?

How has the connection of Americans to their localities changed over the years? Many believe that ours has become an ever more "rootless" society; sage commentators diagnose "placelessness" as the source of modern America's ills. The facts are more complex. In several ways, Americans have become more "rooted" to their localities, and in several ways, less rooted. To simplify these complexities, I will argue that, in net, several historical changes have *increased* Americans' commitments to their localities, *decreased* their dependence on the locality for sociability, but *increased* their political—and thus, social—significance.

We cannot directly judge how people of earlier periods felt about their localities and compare them to people of today, but we can examine several changes that, logically, should have affected Americans' attachments to place. Several historical changes probably increased how much Americans care about and invest themselves in their localities.

Reduced residential mobility is one such change. Americans are more mobile than other Western peoples, and they have always been highly mobile. But this mobility has been declining. Historians, by comparing lists of town residents from one year to another, have found that Americans in the nineteenth century were at least as geographically mobile and perhaps twice as much so as contemporary Americans. Since World War II, Census Bureau evidence shows the total rate of moving from one house to another generally dropped . . . .

Among those who moved, proportionately more crossed county lines recently, a change attributable to suburbanization and thus implying that these movers remained in the same urban area. The year-to-year fluctuations can be tied to oscillations in the job and housing markets. But the general picture is one of modestly increasing residential *stability.*

In cross-national perspective, however, Americans remain nobly more footloose than Europeans, although only a little more so than the other continental Anglophone countries, Canada and Australia.[4] The reasons are probably structural (our many dispersed metropolises), historical (our open-door immigration until 1924), and cultural (our famed individualism). What has probably changed over the years is a modest shift from "push" to "pull" mobility. Some pushes on the nineteenth-century Americans to move—such as land shortages, job losses, disasters, and poverty—weakened in the twentieth century, while pulls—such as retirement communities, climate, college, and job opportunities—expanded.

10   Americans' greater residential stability has probably increased   10 their attachment to their localities. Studies have repeatedly shown that the longer people live in a place the stronger their emotional and social commitments to it.

Another secular change that, in net, probably increased local commitment is the dispersal of the urban population. Despite the popular image of the ever more crowded city, over the last century, American metropolises have been spreading and thinning out. As a result, proportionally more Americans live in suburban single-family houses, located in small, autonomous, suburban municipalities. For about a generation now more Americans have lived in suburbs than in either center cities or non-metropolitan areas. These, low-density housing and suburban governments, in turn, tend to encourage local commitments.

(What about the great migration from farm to city in this century? In that area, one of rural Americans' chronic problems was their difficulty in forming communities—in organizing associations, mobilizing politically, or seeing one another socially. For former homesteaders, the move to town probably increased local involvement.)

A third change, one connected to the growth of urban sprawl, has been the evolution of class-homogeneous neighborhoods. At least until the early streetcar era in the 1880s, all but the affluent lived close to their jobs. The elite had their suburban enclaves but different classes mixed in city neighborhoods, although residents were sometimes well separated by ethnicity. Today, neighborhoods are less segregated by ethnicity—greatly excepting black ghettos—but more finely differentiated by income level. Greater local homogeneity also reinforces neighboring and attachment to the neighborhood.

The great exception of the black ghettos in fact gives emphasis to the general increase in local homogeneity. During the twentieth century, blacks, at least those in the North, became more segregated from whites, even as white ethnic groups, and for that matter Asians and Hispanics, became less segregated from one another. This racial divide has provided to whites neighborhoods devoid of what many find to be the unsettling presence of blacks. It has largely confined blacks, including many in the middle class, to districts with other blacks, including the very poor. Analyses by Douglas Massey and his colleagues suggest that there may have been some small breaches in racial walls recently, but for poor blacks, geographic isolation increased through the 1970s.

15   A fourth trend is increasing home ownership. Over the century,   15 most American families came to own their homes, with the fastest increase occurring between 1940 and 1960 . . . . The most dramatic change was among the young. In the 1940s the median age of male homeowner was forty-one, but in 1970 it was 28.[5] Home ownership has stagnated in the last fifteen to twenty years of housing inflation and economic doldrums, but remained historically high. (These data do not consider any increase in homelessness.)

Although Americans have long vested their dwellings with important moral qualities—a proper house both reflects and nurtures noble values—in the nineteenth century, Americans did not esteem ownership as they do now. Many middle-class families were content to be renters. The connection between property and propriety apparently arose around the turn of the century, when increasing affordability, suburbanization, and ideologies of domesticity combined to make ownership easier and socially correct. Then, in the twentieth century, rising affluence, new mortgage instruments, government subsidies, tax breaks, and in the 1950s the family boom spurred home ownership to its current levels.

Today, home ownership, preferably of a single, detached house, is the American ideal, despite the financial hurdles involved. In a 1985 poll, for example, 76 percent of respondents agreed that people who do not own their homes are "missing out on an important part of the

American dream."[6] Being a renter is stigmatizing unless the person is in a transitional stage, a young single, or elderly.

Growth in home ownership has slowed and even declined slightly in the late 1980s. A sense of crisis about middle-class housing arose. In historical perspective, still, the decline has been mild. Demographic changes in the last thirty years—aging of the baby-boomers, more divorce, delayed marriage and child rearing—should have led to home ownership sagging much more than it did. The big drop in ownership during the 1980s was precisely among Americans under thirty, who were increasingly putting off marriage and childbearing. Still, income losses, housing speculation, and financing changes strained many families, forcing some to rely on two incomes when they would have preferred one, and pushing some home-seekers out of the market. Other would-be owners turned to condominiums or, in rural areas, mobile homes.[7] The proportion of available housing that is single detached units has dropped since the 1960s.[8] This shift to condos or trailers also contributes to a sense of crisis, since the American dream is so closely tied to the single-family house. Altogether, much of the concern arises from a comparison to the late 1960s, when, with boom times, owning a detached house was easier than now and seemed so normal.

Despite fluctuations owing to changes in demographics and economics, the general increase in home ownership during the twentieth century is unlikely to be soon reversed.

20 These conditions—urban sprawl, segregation, and home ownership— 20 distinguish America from most European societies. David Popenoe credits them for creating a higher level of neighborhood involvement in the United States than he observed in either Sweden or the United Kingdom.[9] Changes in these conditions over the last few generations, along with declining mobility, would all seem to have helped Americans further attach themselves to their neighborhoods and towns. Besides, most Americans have enjoyed increasing freedom of choice in where they live. Freedom can mean lack of commitment and transiency; but it seems here to have made it easier for most people to find and stay in places they most prefer.

Yet, other changes in the twentieth century may have reduced commitment to the locality. One such change has been the increasing separation of home and workplace. Although some commentators have exaggerated the extent to which home and work were entwined in the past—most people in days gone by were *not* independent craftsmen working in their homes—the distance between where people live and where they work expanded, particularly with the coming of streetcars in the 1880s. Working outside one's home area probably detracts not only from the time people spend in the neighborhood but also from their subjective feeling of commitment to it.

A second such change is the increasing participation of married women in the labor force. In 1900, 6 percent of married women worked for pay; by 1987, 56 percent did. (The rates for divorced women, a growing fraction of all women, were much higher.)[10] Though married women's employment has typically been part-time, it does mean that fewer American households have a "traditional" homemaker at home all day, the same homemaker who critically connected the family to the neighborhood.

Third, households shrank. With the virtual disappearance of servants, boarders, and lodgers, with later marriage, more divorce, and fewer children, the size of the median American household shrank from 4.8 people in 1900 to 2.7 in 1987.[11] We can assume that, generally, the fewer people at home, the less attached the household is to the locality.

Thus, in the complex weave of twentieth-century social changes, some drew Americans closer to and some pulled them from their neighborhoods and towns. As it stands, the changes that more tightly bound people to places probably outweighed those that weakened the bonds, and the best estimate is that, contrary to convention, Americans are more "rooted," practically and sentimentally, to their communities than ever before.

The Fate of Local Ties

25 On another dimension, however, Americans have probably become 25
less rooted to their residential communities: social ties. Although this evidence is also indirect, probably fewer of Americans' relatives, friends, and associates live near them than was true in earlier generations. (I am not referring here to "neighboring," defined as causal interaction with people living nearby. Americans are often "neighborly" but rarely socially close to their neighbors.) In one study, fewer than a third of respondents' important relations were with people living within a five-minute drive. This dispersion was even greater for the middle class. The neighborhood provides proportionately few of middle-class Americans' important ties.

. . .

The best guess is that there has been a historical change, that Americans' social ties are today less localized than they were a century ago. The more striking conclusion, however, is that the change may not have been as great as we imagine.

. . .

The Place of Place

Peter Rossi has pointed out that "the world has become increasingly cosmopolitan, but the daily lives of most people are contained within local communities."[12] Place still matters. The variations in house prices between and within regions, for example, mock economists' models and futurists' projections that the nation is leveling out into a uniform, placeless realm. How important place will be in the future we can only speculate. Will "cocooning," a media buzzword of the 1980s, typify the next decades, or will there be increasing cosmopolitanism? Much will depend on economic changes and demographic shifts. Unless the economy fails, American wealth should help sustain residential stability and home ownership. As baby-boomers move beyond child rearing and then retire, they will increase geographical mobility, but they will also release more single-family housing for their grandchildren. Spots of inner-city gentrification notwithstanding, the sprawling of the metropolises continues, augmenting suburbanization and "exurbanization" beyond the suburbs. That trend suggests yet more homogeneity, low-density housing, and autonomous political localities.

Most Americans would, in all likelihood, applaud those trends. Raising a family in a detached house, in a homogeneously middle-class, suburban locality, governed by people much like oneself, seems almost ideal. As with other equity issues, even Americans who lack this privilege would preserve it. Experts may criticize localism for its "collective irrationalities" costly to residents themselves—traffic congestion, governmental paralysis, unbalanced growth, domination by business interests, and so on—and for its "externalities" costly to the wider community—ghettoization of the poor, abandonment of the great cities, unjust tax burdens, and so on. No matter. In America, the free pursuit of the private good is the public good. Localism is, as much as ever an instrument to that good.

Herein lies a seeming contradiction: an inconsistency between the locality's communal role and its role as a vehicle for individual interest. American ideologies of community paint the locality, especially the small one, as a site for fellowship, in contrast to the atomism of the wider, especially the urban, world. Many Americans value and enjoy the congeniality of a local community. They often resist that same local community, yet, when it constrains their interests, be they constraints in taxes, behavioral codes, or infringements of private property. Neighborhood organizations, for example, typically awaken when outsiders threaten residents' safety or wealth. Otherwise, the energy that drives them usually rests dormant. Neighborhood groups rarely act as local governments. Other evidence of the priority of the individual comes in negotiations within condominium complexes, where collective needs and rules run up against assertions of home owners' rights. While Americans value the locality as solidarity, it takes second place to individual freedom.

. . . . The reality is that Americans generally resist government at all levels, but give more grudging preference to local rule by like-minded neighbors as the lesser evil.

30   National action, piecemeal as it is, also occurs in response to 30
translocal coalitions. That was one lesson, for example, of the Civil Rights struggle, which as movement and as legislation ran roughshod over local autonomy. The environmental movement is a more complex example. In some ways, it too imposed national concerns over local ones, for example, threatening local jobs for old trees or peculiar fish. (In other ways, though, it reinforced the NIMBY* pattern of localism, legitimating a "draw up the drawbridge" style of conservatism.) Although local events—Love Canal, for one—dramatized the environmental agenda, the movement's power still appears to rest on coalitions of interests that are translocal.

A strategy to move the nation in a progressive direction would in a similar way involve rethinking the ideology of locality, an ideology really more attuned to privilege than to reform. Thomas Bender has pointed out the dangers of confusing values attached to "community" with the needs of the public, political sphere. To insist, for example, on personal knowledge of political candidates may mean selecting the lesser rather than the better candidate. Or, to cry for "local control" for a community wealthier in needs than in resources

---

*Eds. Note—Not in my back yard.

may end by perpetuating disadvantage.[13] It is important to look clear-eyed at the consequences of America's localism, not with romanticized nostalgia.

End Notes

1. The notable exceptions to many of these descriptions are the early puritan villages, which only goes to show how atypical they were, their ideological legacy notwithstanding.
2. This pattern is the sort of thing treated by Robert N. Bellah and his colleagues in *Habits of the Heart* (Berkeley and Los Angeles: University of California Press, 1985).
3. Janowitz, M. (1967). *The community press in an urban setting.* (2nd ed.). Chicago: University of Chicago Press.
4. Long & Boertlein, *Geographical mobility;* Long, *Migration and residential mobility,* 253–282.
5. Chevan, A. (1989). The growth of home ownership: 1940–1980. *Demography, 26,* 255.
6. *New York Times* (1985, February 28), 17.
7. Chevan, Growth of home ownership; Home Ownership, *New York Times;* Adams, *Housing America.*
8. U.S. Bureau of the Census. (1975). *Historical statistics of the United States, colonial times to 1970.* Washington, DC: Government Printing Office, 639, 683.
9. Popenoe, D. (1985). *Private pleasure, public plight: American metropolitan community life in comparative perspective.* New Brunswick, NJ: Transaction.
10. U.S. Bureau of the Census. *Historical Statistics,* 133; idem., *Statistical Abstract: 1988,* 374.
11. U.S. Bureau of the Census, *Historical Statistics,* 41; idem, *Statistical Abstract: 1988,* 43.
12. Rossi, P. (1972). Community social indicators. In A. Campbell & P. E. Converse (Eds.), *The human meaning of social change* (p. 87). New York: Russell Sage Foundation.
13. Bender, *Community and social change,* chapter 5.

The basic conflict of the American.
Community <———> individual
belonging   autonomy
"community"   "society"
less diverse in communitey by class

Questions

1. Fischer argues that Americans subscribe to "community ideologies." Explain what he means by this, and give an example to illustrate.
2. What are some of the things that have increased Americans' commitment to community? What changes have decreased our commitment to community?
3. Fischer argues that "while Americans value the locality as solidarity, it takes second place to individual freedom." Explain what he means by this, and provide an example to illustrate.
4. What does NIMBY mean? Give an example of this philosophy from your community.

VII. Resolutions

The *Crito*

Plato

Translated by Benjamin Jowett, revised by Peter White

Plato (c.428–347 B.C.*), one of the most influential philosophers in history, was born into a wealthy, aristocratic family, presumably in Athens. A pupil of Socrates (and teacher of Aristotle), Plato left Athens for nearly 20 years after his mentor's death in 399* B.C. *Upon his return, he established the Academy and taught there for the remainder of his life. Much of Plato's philosophy appears in his "dialogues"—conversations between Socrates and his students. Three of these "dialogues,"* the Apology, *the* Crito, *and the* Phaedo, *immortalized Socrates' trial and final days. Other well-known works of Plato include the* Republic *and* Laws. *Plato's belief in the separate existence of the body and soul and the existence of an eternal order of Forms (the Theory of Forms) have influenced Western thought for more than 2,000 years. In the* Crito, *Plato presents Socrates' argument to his friend, Crito, who wants Socrates to escape, explaining why his respect for the law and his own integrity demand that he meet his fate with dignity.*

1 SOCRATES: Why have you come at this hour, Crito? It must be quite early?

CRITO: Yes, certainly.

SOCRATES: What is the exact time?

CRITO: The dawn is breaking.

5 SOCRATES: I wonder that the keeper of the prison would let you in.

From *The Dialogues of Plato,* translated by Benjamin Jowett (4th ed., 1953). Published by Oxford University Press.

CRITO: He knows me, because I often come, Socrates; moreover, I have done him a kindness.

SOCRATES: And are you only just arrived?

CRITO: I came some time ago.

SOCRATES: Then why did you sit and say nothing instead of at once awakening me?

10 CRITO: That I could never have done, Socrates. I only wish I were not so sleepless and distressed myself. I have been looking at you, wondering how you can sleep so comfortably, and I didn't wake you on purpose, so that you could go on sleeping in perfect comfort. All through your life, I have often thought you were favored with a good disposition, but I have never been so impressed as in the present misfortune, seeing how easily and tranquilly you bear it.

SOCRATES: Why, Crito, when a man has reached my age he ought not to be repining at the approach of death.

CRITO: And yet other old men find themselves in similar misfortunes, and age does not prevent them from repining.

SOCRATES: That is true. But you have not told me why you come at this early hour.

CRITO: I come with a message which is painful—not, I expect, to you, but painful and oppressive for me and all your friends, and I think it weighs most heavily of all on me.

15 SOCRATES: What? Has the ship come from Delos, on the arrival of which I am to die?*

CRITO: No, the ship has not actually arrived, but she will probably be here today, as persons who have come from Sunium tell me that they left her there; and therefore tomorrow, Socrates, will be the last day of your life.

SOCRATES: Very well, Crito; if such is the will of the gods, I am willing; but my belief is that there will be a day's delay.

CRITO: Why do you think so?

---

*Once every year Athens sent a state ship on a ceremonial pilgrimage to the island of Delos; no executions could be carried out between its departure and return.

SOCRATES: I will tell you. I am to die on the day after the arrival of the ship.

CRITO: Yes; that is what the authorities say.

SOCRATES: But I do not think that the ship will be here until to-morrow; this I infer from a vision which I had last night, or rather only just now, when you fortunately allowed me to sleep.

CRITO: And what was the nature of the vision?

SOCRATES: There appeared to me the likeness of a woman, fair and comely, clothed in bright raiment, who called to me and said: O Socrates,

"The third day hence to fertile Phthia shalt thou come."†

CRITO: What a singular dream, Socrates!

SOCRATES: There can be no doubt about the meaning, Crito, I think.

CRITO: Yes; the meaning is only too clear. But, oh! my beloved Socrates, let me entreat you once more to take my advice and escape. For if you die, I shall not only lose a friend who can never be replaced, but there is another evil: people who do not know you and me will believe that I might have saved you if I had been willing to give money but that I did not care. Now, can there be a worse disgrace than this—that I should be thought to value money more than the life of a friend? For the many will not be persuaded that I wanted you to escape and that you refused.

SOCRATES: But why, my dear Crito, should we care about the opinion of the many? Good men, and they are the only persons who are worth considering, will think of these things truly as they occurred.

CRITO: But you see, Socrates, that the opinion of the many must be regarded, for what is now happening shows that they can do the greatest evil to anyone who has lost their good opinion.

SOCRATES: I only wish it were so, Crito, and that the many could do the greatest evil; for then they would also be able to do the greatest good—and what a fine thing this would be! But in reality they

---

†The apparition borrows the words in which Achilles contemplated a return from Troy to his home, *Iliad* 9.363.

can do neither; for they cannot make a man either wise or fool-ish, and whatever result they produce is the result of chance.

30 CRITO: Well, I will not dispute with you; but please tell me, 30 Socrates, whether you are not acting out of regard to me and your other friends: Are you not afraid that, if you escape from prison, we may get into trouble with the informers for having stolen you away and lose either the whole or a great part of our property— or that even a worse evil may happen to us? Now, if you fear on our account, be at ease; for in order to save you, we ought surely to run this or even a greater risk; be persuaded, then, and do as I say.

SOCRATES: Yes, Crito, that is one fear which you mention, but by no means the only one.

CRITO: Fear not—there are persons who are willing to get you out of prison at no great cost; and as for the informers, they are far from being exorbitant in their demands—a little money will sat-isfy them. My means, which are certainly ample, are at your ser-vice; and if, out of solicitude about me, you hesitate to use mine, there are non-Athenians here who will give you the use of theirs; and one of them, Simmias the Theban, has brought a large sum of money for this very purpose; and Cebes and many others are prepared to spend their money in helping you to escape. There-fore do not hesitate to save yourself because you are worried about this, and do not say, as you did in the court, that you will have difficulty in knowing what to do with yourself anywhere else. For men will love you in other places to which you may go, and not in Athens only; there are friends of mine in Thessaly, if you would like to go to them, who will value and protect you, and no Thes-salian will give you any trouble. Nor can I think that you are at all justified, Socrates, in betraying your own life when you might be saved. You are only working to bring about what your enemies, who want to destroy you, would and did in fact work to accom-plish. And further, I should say that you are deserting your own children; for you might bring them up and educate them, instead of which you go away and leave them, and they will have to take their chances; and if they do not meet with the usual fate of or-phans, there will be small thanks to you. No man should bring children into the world who is unwilling to persevere to the end in their nurture and education. But you appear to be choosing the easier part, not the better and manlier, which would have been more becoming in one who has professed a life-long concern for virtue, like yourself. And indeed, I am ashamed not only of you but of us, who are your friends, when I reflect that the whole business will be attributed entirely to our want of courage. The trial need never have come on or might have been managed differently. And now it may seem that we have made a ridiculous bungle of this last chance, thanks to our lack of toughness and courage, since we failed to save you and you failed to save yourself, even though it was possible and practicable if we were good for anything at all. So, Socrates, you must not let this turn into a disgrace as well as a tragedy for yourself and us. Make up your mind then, or rather have your mind already made up; for the time of deliberation is over, and there is only one thing to be done, which must be done this very night, and, if we delay at all, it will be no longer practicable or possible; I beseech you therefore, Socrates, be persuaded by me, and do not be contrary.

SOCRATES: My dear Crito, your solicitude is invaluable if it is rightly directed, but otherwise, the more intense, the more difficult it is to deal with. And so we should consider whether I ought to follow this course or not. You know it has always been true that I paid no heed to any consideration I was aware of except that argument which, on reflection, seemed best to me. I cannot throw over the arguments I used to make in times past just because this situation has arisen: they look the same to me as before, and I respect and honor them as much as ever. You must therefore understand that if, on the present occasion, we cannot make better arguments, I will not yield to you—not even if the power of the people conjures up the bugaboos of imprisonment and death and confiscation, as though we could be scared like little children. What will be the fairest way of considering the question? Shall I return to your old argument about the opinions of men? We were saying that some of them are to be regarded, and others not. Now were we right in maintaining this before I was condemned? And has the argument which was once good now proved to be talk for the sake of talking—mere childish nonsense? That is what I want to consider with your help, Crito: whether, under my present circumstances, the argument will appear to be in any way different or not, and whether we shall subscribe to it or let it go. That argument, which, as I believe, is maintained by many persons of authority, was to the effect, as I was saying, that the opinions of some men are to be regarded, and of other men not to be regarded. Now you, Crito, are not going to die tomorrow—at least, there is no human probability of this—and therefore you are disinterested and not liable to be deceived by the circumstances in which you are placed. Tell me, then, whether I am right in saying that some opinions, and the opinions of some men only, are to be valued and that other opinions, and the opinions of other men, are not to be valued. I ask you whether I was right in maintaining this?

CRITO: Certainly.

35 SOCRATES: The good opinions are to be regarded, and not the bad?   35

CRITO: Yes.

SOCRATES: And the opinions of the wise are good, and the opinions of the unwise are bad?

CRITO: Certainly.

SOCRATES: Now what was the argument about this: does the serious athlete attend to the praise and blame and opinion of every man or of one man only—his physician or trainer, whoever he may be?

40 CRITO: Of one man only.   40

SOCRATES: And he ought to fear the censure and welcome the praise of that one only, and not of the many?

CRITO: Clearly so.

SOCRATES: And he ought to act and train and eat and drink in the way which seems good to his single master, who has understanding, rather than according to the opinion of all other men put together?

CRITO: True.

45 SOCRATES: And if he disobeys and disregards the opinion and approval of the one, and regards the opinion of the many who have no understanding, will he not suffer harm?   45

CRITO: Certainly he will.

SOCRATES: And what will the harm be: where will it be localized, and what part of the disobedient person will it affect?

CRITO: Clearly, it will affect the body; that is what is destroyed.

SOCRATES: Very good, and is not this true, Crito, of other things, which we need not separately enumerate? In questions of just and unjust, fair and foul, good and evil, which are the subjects of our present consultation, ought we to follow the opinion of the many, and to fear them, or the opinion of the one man who has understanding? Ought we not to fear and reverence him more than all the rest of the world, and, if we desert him, shall we not ruin and mutilate that principle in us which is improved by justice and deteriorated by injustice—there is such a principle?

50   CRITO: Certainly there is, Socrates.   50

SOCRATES: Take a parallel instance: if, ignoring the advice of those who have understanding, we destroy that which is improved by health and is deteriorated by disease, would life be worth having? and that which has been destroyed is—the body?

CRITO: Yes.

SOCRATES: Would life be worth living with an evil and corrupted body?

CRITO: Certainly not.

55   SOCRATES: And will life be worth living if that faculty which injus-   55
tice damages and justice improves is ruined? Do we suppose that principle—whatever it may be in man which has to do with justice and injustice—to be inferior to the body?

CRITO: Certainly not.

SOCRATES: More honorable than the body?

CRITO: Far more.

SOCRATES: Then, my friend, we must not regard what the many say of us but what he, the one man who has understanding of just and unjust, will say and what the truth will say. And therefore you begin in error when you advise that we should regard the opinion of the many about just and unjust, good and evil, honorable and dishonorable. "Well," someone will say, "but the many can kill us."

60   CRITO: That is plain, and a person might well say so. You are right,   60
Socrates.

SOCRATES: But dear Crito, the argument which we have gone over still seems as valid as before. And I should like to know whether

I may say the same of another proposition—that not life, but a good life, is to be chiefly valued?

CRITO: Yes, that also remains unshaken.

SOCRATES: And a good life is equivalent to an honorable and just one—that holds also?

CRITO: Yes, it does.

65 SOCRATES: From these premises I proceed to argue the question whether I am justified in trying to escape without the consent of the Athenians; and if I am clearly right in escaping, then I will make the attempt, but, if not, I will abstain. The other considerations which you mention—of money and loss of character and the duty of educating one's children—are, I fear, only the doctrines of the multitude, who, if they could, would restore people to life as readily as they put them to death—and with as little reason. But since we have been forced this far by the logic of our argument, the only question which remains to be considered is whether we shall do right in giving money and thanks to those who will rescue me, and in taking a direct role in the rescue ourselves, or whether in fact we will be doing wrong. And if it appears that we will be doing wrong, then neither death nor any other calamity that follows from staying and doing nothing must be judged more important than that.

CRITO: I think that you are right, Socrates. How then shall we proceed?

SOCRATES: Let us consider the matter together, and you, either refute me if you can, and I will be convinced, or else cease, my dear friend, from repeating to me that I ought to escape against the wishes of the Athenians. It is most important to me that I act with your assent and not against your will. And now please consider whether my starting point is adequately stated, and also try to answer my questions as you think best.

CRITO: I will.

SOCRATES: Are we to say that we are never intentionally to do wrong, or that in one way we ought and in another we ought not to do wrong? Or is doing wrong always evil and dishonorable, as we often concluded in times past? Or have all those past conclusions been thrown overboard during the last few days? And have we, at our age, been earnestly discoursing with one another all our life long only to discover that we are no better than children? Or, in spite of the opinion of the many, and in spite of consequences, whether better or worse, shall we insist on the truth of what was then said, that injustice is always an evil and a dishonor to him who acts unjustly? Shall we say so or not?

70 CRITO: Yes.

SOCRATES: Then we must do no wrong?

CRITO: Certainly not.

SOCRATES: Nor, when injured, injure in return, as the many imagine; for we must injure no one at all?

CRITO: Clearly not.

75 SOCRATES: Again, Crito, may we do evil?

CRITO: Surely not, Socrates.

SOCRATES: And what of doing evil in return for evil, which is the morality of the many—is that just or not?

CRITO: Not just.

SOCRATES: For doing evil to another is the same as injuring him?

80 CRITO: Very true.

SOCRATES: Then we ought not to retaliate or render evil for evil to anyone, whatever evil we may have suffered from him. But I would have you consider, Crito, whether you really mean what you are saying. For this opinion has never been held, and never will be held, by any considerable number of persons; and those who are agreed and those who are not agreed upon this point have no common ground and can only despise one another when they see how widely they differ. Tell me, then, whether you agree with and assent to my first principle, that neither injury nor retaliation nor warding off evil by evil is ever right. And shall that be the premise of our argument? Or do you decline and dissent from this? For so I have ever thought, and continue to think; but, if you are of another opinion, let me hear what you have to say. If, however, you remain of the same mind as formerly, I will proceed to the next step.

CRITO: You may proceed, for I have not changed my mind.

SOCRATES: The next thing I have to say, or, rather, my next question, is this: Ought a man to do what he admits to be right, or ought he to betray the right?

CRITO: He ought to do what he thinks right.

85 SOCRATES: In light of that, tell me whether or not there is some 85 victim—a particularly undeserving victim—who is hurt if I go away without persuading the city. And do we abide by what we agree was just or not?

CRITO: I cannot answer your question, Socrates, because I do not see what you are getting at.

SOCRATES: Then consider the matter in this way: imagine that I am about to run away (you may call the proceeding by any name which you like), and the laws and the government come and interrogate me: "Tell us, Socrates," they say; "what are you up to? are you not going by an act of yours to destroy us—the laws, and the whole state—as far as in you lies? Do you imagine that a state can subsist and not be overthrown in which the decisions of law have no power but are set aside and trampled upon by individuals?" What will be our answer, Crito, to questions like these? Anyone, and especially a rhetorician, would have a good deal to say against abrogation of the law that requires a sentence to be carried out. He will argue that this law should not be set aside. Or shall we retort, "Yes; but the state has injured us and given an unjust sentence." Suppose I say that?

CRITO: Very good, Socrates.

SOCRATES: "And was that our agreement with you?" the laws would answer; "or were you to abide by the sentence of the state?" And if I were to express my astonishment at their talking this way, they would probably add: "Take control of your astonishment and answer, Socrates—you are in the habit of asking and answering questions. Tell us: What complaint have you to make against us which justifies you in attempting to destroy us and the state? In the first place, did we not bring you into existence? Your father married your mother by our aid and brought you into the world. Say whether you have any objection to urge against those of us who regulate marriage." None, I should reply. "Or against those of us who after birth regulate the nurture and education of children, in which you also were trained? Were not the laws, which have the charge of education, right in commanding your father to train you in music and athletics?" Right, I should reply. "Well then, since you were brought into the world and nurtured and educated by us, can you deny in the first place that you are our child and slave, as your fathers were before you? And if this is true, do you really think you have the same rights as we do and that you are entitled to do to us whatever we do to you? Would you have any right to strike or revile or do any other evil to your father or your master, if you had one, because you had been struck or reviled by him or received some other evil at his hands?—you would not say this? And because we think it right to destroy you, do you think that you have any right to destroy us in return, and your country, as far as in you lies? Will you, O professor of true virtue, pretend that you are justified in this? Has a philosopher like you failed to discover that our country is more to be valued and higher and holier far more than mother or father or any ancestor, and more to be regarded in the eyes of the gods and of men of understanding? Also to be soothed and gently and reverently entreated when angry, even more than a father, and either to be persuaded or, if not persuaded, to be obeyed? And when we are punished by her, whether with imprisonment or beatings, the punishment is to be endured in silence; and if she leads us to wounds or death in battle, there we follow as is right; neither may anyone yield or retreat or leave his rank, but whether in battle, or in a court of law, or in any other place, he must do what his city and his country order him, or he must change their view of what is just; and if he may do no violence to his father or mother, much less may he do violence to his country." What answer shall we make to this, Crito? Do the laws speak truly, or do they not?

90 CRITO: I think that they do.   90

SOCRATES: Then the laws will say, "Consider, Socrates, if we are speaking truly that in your present attempt you are going to do us an injury. For, having brought you into the world, and nurtured and educated you, and given you and every other citizen a share in every good which we had to give, we further proclaim to any Athenian, by the liberty which we allow him, that if he does not like us when he has come of age and has seen the ways of the city and made our acquaintance, he may go where he pleases and take his goods with him. None of us laws will stand in the way if any of you who are dissatisfied with us and the city want to go to a colony or to move anywhere else. None of us forbids anyone to go where he likes, taking his property with him. But he who has experience of the manner in which we order justice and administer the state, and still remains, has entered into an implied contract that he will do as we command him. And he who disobeys us is, as we maintain, thrice wrong: first, because in disobeying us he is disobeying his parents; secondly, because we are the authors of his education; thirdly, because he has made an agreement with us that he will duly obey our commands, but he neither obeys them nor convinces us that our commands are unjust. We show flexibility. We do not brutally demand his compliance but offer him the choice of obeying or persuading us; yet he does neither.

"These are the sorts of accusations to which, as we were saying, you, Socrates, will be exposed if you accomplish your intentions; you, above all other Athenians." Suppose now I ask, why I rather than anybody else? They might reasonably take me to task because I above all other men have acknowledged the agreement. "There is clear proof," they will say, "Socrates, that we and the city were not displeasing to you. Of all Athenians you have been the most constant resident in the city, which, as you never leave it, you may be supposed to love. For you never went out of the city either to see the games, except once, when you went to the Isthmus, or to any other place unless when you were on military service; nor did you travel as other men do. Nor had you any curiosity to know other states or their laws: your affections did not go beyond us and our state; we were your special favorites, and you acquiesced in our government of you; and here in this city you had your children, which is a proof of your satisfaction. Moreover, you might in the course of the trial, if you had liked, have fixed the penalty at banishment, and then you could have done with the city's consent what you now attempt against its will. But you pretended that you preferred death to exile and that you were not unwilling to die. And now you do not blush at the thought of your old arguments and pay no respect to us, the laws, of whom you are the destroyer, and are doing what only a miserable slave would do, running away and turning your back on the compacts and agreements by which you agreed to act as a citizen. And, first of all, answer this very question: Are we right in saying that by your actions if not in words you agreed to our terms of citizenship? Is that true or not?" How shall we answer, Crito? Must we not assent?

CRITO: We cannot help it, Socrates.

SOCRATES: Then will they not say: "You, Socrates, are breaking the covenants and agreements which you made with us. You were not compelled to agree, or tricked, or forced to make up your mind in a moment, but had a period of seventy years during which you were free to depart if you were dissatisfied with us and the agreements did not seem fair. You did not pick Sparta or Crete, whose fine government you take every opportunity to praise, or any other state of the Greek or non-Greek world. You spent less time out of Athens than men who are crippled or blind or otherwise handicapped. That shows how much more than other Athenians you valued the city and us too, its laws (for who would value a city without laws?). And will you not now abide by your agreements? You will if you listen to us, Socrates, and you will not make yourself ridiculous by leaving the city.

95   "For just consider: if you transgress and err in this sort of way,   95 what good will you do either to yourself or to your friends? That your friends will be driven into exile and deprived of citizenship or will lose their property is tolerably certain. And you yourself, if you go to one of the neighboring cities, like Thebes or Megara (both being well-ordered states, of course), will come as an enemy of their government, and all patriotic citizens will eye you suspiciously as a subverter of the laws, and you will confirm in the minds of the judges the justice of their own condemnation of you. For he who is a corrupter of the laws is more than likely to be a corrupter of the young and foolish portion of mankind. Will you then flee from well-ordered cities and law-abiding men? And will life be worth living if you do that? Or will you approach them and discourse unashamedly about—about what, Socrates? Will you discourse as you did here, about how virtue and justice and institutions and laws are the best things among men? Don't you think that such behavior coming from Socrates will seem disgusting? Surely one must think so. But if you go away from well-governed states to Crito's friends in Thessaly, where there is great disorder and license, they will be charmed to hear the tale of your escape from prison, set off with ludicrous particulars of the manner in which you were wrapped in a goatskin or some other disguise and metamorphosed in the usual manner of runaways. But will there be no one to comment that in your old age, when in all probability you had only a little time left to live, you were not ashamed to violate the most sacred laws from the greedy desire of a little more

life? Perhaps not, if you keep them in good temper; but if they are out of temper, you will hear many degrading things. You will live as the flatterer and slave of all men, achieving what else but the chance to feast in Thessaly, as though you had gone abroad in order to get a meal? And where will the old arguments be, about justice and virtue? Say that you wish to live for the sake of your children—you want to bring them up and educate them—will you take them into Thessaly and deprive them of Athenian citizenship? Is this the benefit which you will confer upon them? Or are you under the impression that they will be better cared for and educated here if you are still alive, although absent from them; for your friends will take care of them? Do you fancy that, if you move to Thessaly, they will take care of them but that, if you move into the other world, they will not take care of them? No, if those who call themselves friends are good for anything, they will—to be sure, they will.

"Listen, then, Socrates, to us who have brought you up. Think not of life and children first and of justice afterwards but of justice first, so that you may defend your conduct to the rulers of the world below. For neither will you nor any that belong to you be happier or holier or juster in this life, or happier in another, if you do as Crito bids. Now you depart in innocence, a sufferer and not a doer of evil; a victim, not of the laws but of men. But if you escape, returning evil for evil and injury for injury, breaking the covenants and agreements which you have made with us and wronging those you ought least of all to wrong—that is to say, yourself, your friends, your country, and us—we shall be angry with you while you live, and our brethren, the laws in the world below, will receive you in no kindly spirit; for they will know that you have done your best to destroy us. Listen, then, to us and not to Crito."

This, dear Crito, is the voice I seem to hear murmuring in my ears, like the sound of the flute in the ears of the mystic; that voice, I say, is humming in my ears and prevents me from hearing any other. You must realize that you will be wasting your time if you speak against the convictions I hold at the moment. But if you think you will get anywhere, go ahead.

CRITO: No, Socrates, I have nothing to say.

SOCRATES: Then be resigned, Crito, and let us follow this course, since this is the way the god points out.

Questions on Meaning

1. Summarize Socrates' argument against escape, as presented by Plato in this dialogue. Why must Socrates reject the proposed escape if he is to preserve his integrity?
2. What are the arguments Crito uses to justify Socrates' escape? In general, do these arguments reflect the feelings, opinions, and reactions of few or many individuals?
3. What does Socrates say to the suggestion that changed circumstances (his death sentence) justify his disregard for the law (his escape)? Why does he state that escape would be "returning evil for evil and injury for injury"?

Questions on Rhetorical Strategy and Style

1. Argumentation has three primary elements: logos, pathos, and ethos. Which predominates in the writing strategy of persuasion in this dialogue? Explain why the other factors are less forceful.
2. Find where Socrates personifies the "laws and the government." How did you react to this strategy? How could Socrates have made his argument without affording the "laws and government" a character role in the dialogue?
3. Plato uses definition to establish the basis for Socrates' argument against escape. What is the definition of a "good life"? Why is that definition important?

Writing Assignments

1. How could you apply Socrates' argument in this dialogue to an unpopular regulation or law that affects your life? Perhaps it is a city ordinance against walking through a park after sundown, a dormitory regulation against noise, or a landlord's rule about packaging your trash. What are you to gain, what are you to lose, by violating this ordinance? What does your willful violation of it say about you as a person, about your integrity?
2. Socrates' strict adherence to the law appears to contradict the beliefs of advocates of civil disobedience. Research the philosophies of noted proponents of civil disobedience: Henry David Thoreau, Mohandas (Mahatma) Gandhi, and Martin Luther King. Why do you think they would agree or disagree with Socrates' decision?

3. Write an essay presenting your view on Socrates' "first principle," that "neither injury, nor retaliation nor warding off evil by evil is ever right." Use example and cause and effect to support your argument. If appropriate, include the opinions of philosophers, jurists, and politicians you are familiar with.

The Ethic of Compassion
The Dalai Lama

His Holiness the Dalai Lama (1935–) was born a peasant in Taktser, Tibet under the birth name of Lhamo Dhondrub. He is the fourteenth Dalai Lama (spiritual leader of Tibet, reincarnation of the thirteenth Dalai Lama, and an incarnation of the Buddha of Compassion). He lives in Dharamsala, India. He was recognized at age two as the Dalai Lama and was enthroned on February 22, 1940. He completed the Geshe Lharampa Degree (equivalent to a Doctorate of Buddhist Philosophy) in 1959 and became head of Tibet—but was driven out by a Chinese invasion. He has worked on behalf of Tibet from India, asking the United Nations for help and working to bring Buddhist beliefs back to the country. He received the Albert Schweitzer Humanitarian Award (1987); Raoul Wallenberg Congressional Human Rights Award (1989); the Nobel Peace Prize (1989); Franklin D. Roosevelt Freedom Medal (1994); and the Hessian Peace Prize (2005). His books include Kindness, Clarity and Insight *(Snow Lion, 1984);* Compassion and the Individual *(Wisdom Publications, 1991); and* The Power of Compassion *(Harper Collins, 1995).*

Compassion is good when first considered, for it is easy to feel compassion for one who suffers. Compassion is harder to muster for wealthy and powerful people and even harder to feel when true compassion leads to a career change or an even greater life upheaval.

W^e noted earlier that all the world's major religions stress the importance of cultivating love and compassion. In the Buddhist philosophical tradition, different levels of attainment

Reprinted from *Ethics for the New Millennium,* by permission of Riverhead Books, an imprint of Penguin Group (USA) Inc. and The Wylie Agency. Copyright © 1999, 2001 by Kyabje Tenzin Gyatso, 14th Dalai Lama of Tibet.

are described. At a basic level, compassion (*nying je*) is understood mainly in terms of empathy—our ability to enter into and, to some extent, share others' suffering. But Buddhist—and perhaps others— believe that this can be developed to such a degree that not only does our compassion arise without any effort, but it is unconditional, undifferentiated, and universal in scope. A feeling of intimacy toward all other sentient beings, including of course those who would harm us, is generated, which is likened in the literature to the love a mother has for her only child.

But this sense of equanimity toward all others is not seen as an end in itself. Rather, it is seen as the springboard to a love still greater. Because our capacity for empathy is innate, and because the ability to reason is also an innate faculty, compassion shares the characteristics of consciousness itself. The potential we have to develop it is therefore stable and continuous. It is not a resource which can be used up—as water is used up when we boil it. And though it can be described in terms of activity, it is not like a physical activity which we train for, like jumping, where once we reach a certain height we can go no further. On the contrary, when we enhance our sensitivity toward others' suffering through deliberately opening ourselves up to it, it is believed that we can gradually extend out compassion to the point where the individual feels so moved by even the subtlest suffering of others that they come to have an over-whelming sense of responsibility toward those others. This causes the one who is compassionate to dedicate themselves entirely to helping others overcome both their suffering and the causes of their suffering. In Tibetan, this ultimate level of attainment is called *nying je chenmo*, literally "great compassion."

Now I am not suggesting that each individual must attain these advanced states of spiritual development in order to lead an ethically wholesome life. I have described *nying je chenmo* not because it is a precondition of ethical conduct but rather because I believe that pushing the logic of compassion to the highest level can act as a powerful inspiration. If we can just keep the aspiration to develop *nying je chenmo*, or great compassion, as an ideal, it will naturally have a significant impact on our outlook. Based on the simple recognition that, just as I do, so do all others desire to be happy and not to suffer, it will serve as a constant reminder against selfishness and partiality. It will remind us that there is little to be gained from being kind and generous because we hope to win something in return. It will remind us that actions motivated by the desire to create a good name for our-selves are still selfish, however much they may appear to be acts of kindness. It will also remind us that there is nothing exceptional about acts of charity toward those we already feel close to. And it will help us to recognize that the bias we naturally feel toward our families and friends is actually a highly unreliable thing on which to base ethi-cal conduct. If we reserve ethical conduct for those whom we feel close to, the danger is that we will neglect our responsibilities toward those outside this circle.

Why is this? So long as the individuals in question continue to meet our expectations, all is well. But should they fail to do so, some-one we consider a dear friend one day can become our sworn enemy the next. As we saw earlier, we have a tendency to react badly to all who threaten fulfillment of our cherished desires, though they may be our closest relations. For this reason, compassion and mutual respect offer a much more solid basis for our relations with others. This is also true of partnerships. If our love for someone is based largely on attraction, whether it be their looks or some other superficial charac-teristic, our feelings for that person are liable, over time, to evaporate. When they lose the quality we found alluring, or when we find our-selves no longer satisfied by it, the situation can change completely, this despite their being the same person. This is why relationships based purely on attraction are almost always unstable. On the other hand, when we begin to perfect our compassion, neither the other's appearance nor their behavior affects our underlying attitude.

Consider, too, that habitually our feelings toward others depend very much on their circumstances. Most people, when they see some-one who is handicapped, feel sympathetic toward that person. But then when they see others who are wealthier, or better educated, or better placed socially, they immediately feel envious and competitive toward them. Our negative feelings prevent us from seeing the same-ness of ourselves and all others. We forget that just like us, whether fortunate or unfortunate, distant or near, they desire to be happy and not to suffer.

The struggle is thus to overcome these feelings of partiality. Cer-tainly, developing genuine compassion for our loved ones is the obvi-ous and appropriate place to start. The impact our actions have on our close ones will generally be much greater than on others, and therefore our responsibilities toward them are greater. Yet we need to recognize that, ultimately, there are no grounds for discriminating in their favor. In this sense, we are all in the same position as a doctor confronted by ten patients suffering the same serious illness. They are each equally deserving of treatment. The reader should not suppose that what is being advocated here is a state of detached indifference, however. The further essential challenge, as we begin to extend our compassion toward all others, is to maintain the same level of intimacy as we feel toward those closest to us. In other words, what is being suggested is that we need to strive for even-handedness in our approach toward all others, a level ground into which we can plant the seed of *nying je chenmo,* of great love and compassion.

If we can begin to relate to others on the basis of such equanimity, our compassion will not depend on the fact that so and so is my husband, my wife, my relative, my friend. Rather, a feeling of closeness toward all others can be developed based on the simple recognition that, just like myself, all wish to be happy and to avoid suffering. In other words, we will start to relate to others on the basis of their sentient nature. Again, we can think of this in terms of an ideal, one which it is immensely difficult to attain. But, for myself, I find it one which is profoundly inspiring and helpful.

Let us now consider the role of compassionate love and kindheartedness in our daily lives. Does the ideal of developing it to the point where it is unconditional mean that we must abandon our own interests entirely? Not at all. In fact, it is the best way of serving them—indeed, it could even be said to constitute the wisest course for fulfilling self-interest. For if it is correct that those qualities such as love, patience, tolerance, and forgiveness are what happiness consists in, and if it is also correct that *nying je,* or compassion, as I have defined it, is both the source and the fruit of these qualities, then the more we are compassionate, the more we provide for our own happiness. Thus, any idea that concern for others, though a noble quality, is a matter for our private lives only, is simply short-sighted. Compassion belongs to every sphere of activity, including, of course, the workplace.

Here, though, I must acknowledge the existence of a perception—shared by many, it seems—that compassion is, if not actually an impediment, at least irrelevant to professional life. Personally, I would argue that not only is it relevant, but that when compassion is lacking, our activities are in danger of becoming destructive. This is because when we ignore the question of the impact our actions have on others' well-being, inevitably we end up hurting them. The ethic of compassion helps provide the necessary foundation and motivation for both restraint and the cultivation of virtue. When we begin to develop a genuine appreciation of the value of compassion, our outlook on others begins automatically to change. This alone can serve as a powerful influence on the conduct of our lives. When, for example, the temptation to deceive others arises, our compassion for them will prevent us from entertaining the idea. And when we realize that our work itself is in danger of being exploited to the detriment of others, compassion will cause us to disengage from it. So to take an imaginary case of a scientist whose research seems likely to be a source of suffering, they will recognize this and act accordingly, even if this means abandoning the project.

I do not deny that genuine problems can arise when we dedicate ourselves to the ideal of compassion. In the case of a scientist who felt unable to continue in the direction their work was taking them, this could have profound consequences both for themselves and for their families. Likewise, those engaged in the caring professions—in medicine, counseling, social work, and so on—or even those looking after someone at home may sometimes become so exhausted by their duties that they feel overwhelmed. Constant exposure to suffering, coupled occasionally with a feeling of being taken for granted, can induce feelings of helplessness and even despair. Or it can happen that individuals may find themselves performing outwardly generous actions merely for the sake of it—simply going through the motions, as it were. Of course this is better than nothing. But when left unchecked, this can lead to insensitivity toward others' suffering. If this starts to happen, it is best to disengage for a short while and make a deliberate effort to reawaken that sensitivity. In this it can be helpful to remember that despair is never a solution. It is, rather, the ultimate failure. Therefore, as the Tibetan expression has it, even if the rope breaks nine times, we must splice it back together a tenth time. In this way, even if ultimately we do fail, at least there will be no feelings of regret. And when we combine this insight with a clear appreciation of our potential to benefit others, we find that we can begin to restore our hope and confidence.

Some people may object to this ideal on the grounds that by entering into others' suffering, we bring suffering on ourselves. To an extent, this is true. But I suggest that there is an important qualitative distinction to be made between experiencing one's own suffering and experiencing suffering in the course of sharing in others'. In the case of one's own suffering, given that it is involuntary, there is a sense of oppression: it seems to come from outside us. By contrast, sharing in someone else's suffering must at some level involve a degree of voluntariness, which itself is indicative of a certain inner strength. For this reason, the disturbance it may cause is considerably less likely to paralyze us than our own suffering.

Of course, even as an ideal, the notion of developing unconditional compassion is daunting. Most people, including myself, must struggle even to reach the point where putting others' interests on a par with our own becomes easy. We should not allow this to put us off, however. And while undoubtedly there will be obstacles on the way to developing a genuinely warm heart, there is the deep consolation of knowing that in doing so we are creating the conditions for our own happiness. As I mentioned earlier, the more we truly desire to benefit others, the greater the strength and confidence we develop and the greater the peace and happiness we experience. If this still seems unlikely, it is worth asking ourselves how else we are to do so. With violence and aggression? Of course not. With money? Perhaps up to a point, but no further. But with love, by sharing in others' suffering, by recognizing ourselves clearly in all others—especially those who are disadvantaged and those whose rights are not respected—by helping them to, be happy: yes. Through love, through kindness, through compassion we establish understanding between ourselves and others. This is how we forge unity and harmony.

Compassion and love are not mere luxuries. As the source both of inner and external peace, they are fundamental to the continued survival of our species. On the one hand, they constitute non-violence in action. On the other, they are the source of all spiritual qualities: of forgiveness, tolerance, and all the virtues. Moreover, they are the very thing that gives meaning to our activities and makes them constructive. There is nothing amazing about being highly educated; there is nothing amazing about being rich. Only when the individual has a warm heart do these attributes become worthwhile.

So to those who say that the Dalai Lama is being unrealistic in advocating this ideal of unconditional love, I urge them to experiment with it nonetheless. They will discover that when we reach beyond the confines of narrow self-interest, our hearts become filled with strength. Peace and joy become our constant companion. It breaks down barriers of every kind and in the end destroys the notion of my interest as independent from others' interest. But most important, so far as ethics is concerned, where love of one's neighbor, affection, kindness, and compassion live, we find that ethical conduct is automatic. Ethically wholesome actions arise naturally in the context of compassion.

Questions on Meaning

1. Compassion means to empathize with another, to feel that person's joy, pain, and hope. Why does the author say that feeling compassion for the disabled or the poor is easy? Why is it hard to feel sympathy for those we envy?

2. What would happen to our ordinary, selfish lives if we were to start feeling real compassion? Would we be able to use the environment and the rest of the world as we do now? What would we have to change?

3. What does the individual gain by feeling compassion? Is the kind of peace and love that are described in this essay really what people want? Why do most of us live lives that are aimed at making money and winning, rather than loving?

Questions on Rhetorical Strategy and Style

1. The tone of this essay is very gentle and kind, but the message is quite tough. How does the author warn the reader in the introduction that the essay is going to be demanding and maybe a bit disturbing?

2. The essay moves to a cause and effect structure: If one feels true compassion, the feeling may cause one to have to change one's life. The feeling, though a good one, may lead to uncomfortable results. How does this causality affect the reader of the essay? Is a reader likely to change behavior in light of this cause and effect explanation?

3. The end of the essay promises that great good can come from feeling compassion. How does the writer hope to persuade the reader that these benefits are worthwhile? Does this ending promise better things for the world if many readers are persuaded? Is it even possible?

Writing Assignments

1. A wise person once said that we should feel compassion rather than guilt, for we will act from compassion, but we will merely suffer from guilt. Think of someone you know whom you consider compassionate. Write about what that person does with life. What kind of work does the person do? What kind of entertainment and leisure activities does that person pursue?

2. Write about a world leader whom you consider compassionate. Show how this feeling is displayed in the person's actions. What would happen to world politics if everyone acted with compassion?
3. Consider a world conflict, either one occurring now or one in history. Write about how the events could be or would have been different had the parties shown more compassion and less aggression.

On Liberty (1859)

John Stuart Mill

John Stuart Mill (1806–1873) was an English philosopher and social reformer. A leading nineteenth-century intellectual, he was leader of the Benthamite utilitarian movement and helped form the Utilitarian Society. His major works include A System of Logic (1843), On Liberty (1859), Utilitarianism (1863) and Three Essays on Religion (1874). He was also elected to parliament, where he was a leading advocate for women's suffrage and liberalism.

Under what conditions does the government have a legitimate right to limit liberty? Classical liberals (people who support a free market economy and limited, representative government) want to maximize economic and political liberty because they believe freedom is essential to the health and vitality of society. British philosopher John Stuart Mill, a leading classical liberal, has been called the "Einstein of the nineteenth century." In his essay On Liberty, *the most famous work ever written on this subject, he asserts "that the sole end for which mankind are warranted, individually or collectively in interfering with the liberty of action of any of their number, is self-protection." Mill specifically denies that advancing the welfare of some is sufficient grounds for limiting the freedom of others. Freedom of speech is especially important because only when speech is unrestricted will we be able to discover the truth.*

1   The subject of this Essay is not the so-called Liberty of the Will, so   1
unfortunately opposed to the misnamed doctrine of Philosophical Necessity; but Civil, or Social Liberty: the nature and limits
of the power which can be legitimately exercised by society over the

---

(1859).

individual. A question seldom stated, and hardly ever discussed, in general terms, but which profoundly influences the practical controversies of the age by its latent presence, and is likely soon to make itself recognized as the vital question of the future. It is so far from being new, that, in a certain sense, it has divided mankind, almost from the remotest ages; but in the stage of progress into which the more civilized portions of the species have now entered, it presents itself under new conditions, and requires a different and more fundamental treatment.

The struggle between Liberty and Authority is the most conspicuous feature in the portions of history with which we are earliest familiar, particularly in that of Greece, Rome, and England. But in old times this contest was between subjects, or some classes of subjects, and the government. By liberty, was meant protection against the tyranny of the political rulers. The rulers were conceived (except in some of the popular governments of Greece) as in a necessarily antagonistic position to the people whom they ruled. They consisted of a governing One, or a governing tribe or caste, who derived their authority from inheritance or conquest, who, at all events, did not hold it at the pleasure of the governed, and whose supremacy men did not venture, perhaps did not desire, to contest, whatever precautions might be taken against its oppressive exercise. Their power was regarded as necessary, but also as highly dangerous; as a weapon which they would attempt to use against their subjects, no less than against external enemies. To prevent the weaker members of the community from being preyed upon by innumerable vultures, it was needful that there should be an animal of prey stronger than the rest, commissioned to keep them down. But as the king of the vultures would be no less bent upon preying upon the flock than any of the minor harpies, it was indispensable to be in a perpetual attitude of defense against his beak and claws. The aim, therefore, of patriots, was to set limits to the power which the ruler should be suffered to exercise over the community; and this limitation was what they meant by liberty. It was attempted in two ways. First, by obtaining a recognition of certain immunities, called political liberties or rights, (which it was to be regarded as a breach of duty in the ruler to infringe, and which, if he did infringe, specific resistance, or general rebellion, was held to be justifiable). A second, and generally a later expedient, was the establishment of constitutional checks, (by which the consent of the community, or of a body of some sort supposed to represent its interests, was made a necessary condition to some of the more important acts of the governing power). To the first of these modes of limitation, the ruling power, in most European countries, was compelled, more or less, to submit. It was not so with the second; and, to attain this, or when already in some degree possessed, to attain it more completely, became everywhere the principal object of the lovers of liberty. And so long as mankind were content to combat one enemy by another, and to be ruled by a master, on condition of being guaranteed more or less efficaciously against his tyranny, they did not carry their aspirations beyond this point.

A time, however, came in the progress of human affairs, when men ceased to think it a necessity of nature that their governors should be an independent power, opposed in interest to themselves. It appeared to them much better that the various magistrates of the State should be their tenants or delegates, revocable at their pleasure. In that way alone, it seemed, could they have complete security that the powers of government would never be abused to their disadvantage. By degrees, this new demand for elective and temporary rulers became the prominent object of the exertions of the popular party, wherever any such party existed; and superseded, to a considerable extent, the previous efforts to limit the power of rulers. As the struggle proceeded for making the ruling power emanate from the periodical choice of the ruled, some persons began to think that too much importance had been attached to the limitation of the power itself. *That* (it might seem) was a resource against rulers whose interests were habitually opposed to those of the people. What was now wanted was that the rulers should be identified with the people; that their interest and will should be the interest and will of the nation. The nation did not need to be protected against its own will. There was no fear of its tyrannizing over itself. Let the rulers be effectually responsible to it, promptly removable by it, and it could afford to trust them with power of which it could itself dictate the use to be made. Their power was but the nation's own power, concentrated, and in a form convenient for exercise. This mode of thought, or rather perhaps of feeling, was common among the last generation of European liberalism, in the Continental section of which it still apparently predominates. Those who admit any limit to what a government may do, except in the case of such governments as they think ought not to exist, stand out as brilliant exceptions among the political thinkers of the Continent. A similar tone of sentiment might by this time have been prevalent in our own country, if the circumstances which for a time encouraged it, had continued unaltered.

But, in political and philosophical theories, as well as in persons, success discloses faults and infirmities which failure might have concealed from observation. The notion, that the people have no need to limit their power over themselves, might seem axiomatic when popular government was a thing only dreamed about, or read of as having existed at some distant period of the past. Neither was that notion necessarily disturbed by such temporary aberrations as those of the French Revolution, the worst of which were the work of an usurping few, and which, in any case, belonged, not to the permanent working of popular institutions, but to a sudden and convulsive outbreak against monarchical and aristocratic despotism. In time, however, a democratic republic came to occupy a large portion of the earth's surface, and made itself felt as one of the most powerful members of the community of nations; and elective and responsible government became subject to the observations and criticisms which wait upon a great existing fact. It was now perceived that such phrases as "self-government," and "the power of the people over themselves," do not express the true state of the case. The "people" who exercise the power, are not always the same people with those over whom it is exercised; and the "self-government" spoken of is not the government of each by himself, but of each by all the rest. The will of the people, moreover, practically means the will of the most numerous or the most active *part* of the people: the majority, or those who succeed in making themselves accepted as the majority; the people, consequently, *may* desire to oppress a part of their number; and precautions are as much needed against this as against any other abuse of power. The limitation, therefore, of the power of government over individuals loses none of its importance when the holders of power are regularly accountable to the community, that is, to the strongest party therein. This view of things, recommending itself equally to the intelligence of thinkers and to the inclination of those important classes in European society to whose real or supposed interests democracy is adverse, has had no difficulty in establishing itself; and in political speculations "the tyranny of the majority" is now generally included among the evils against which society requires to be on its guard.

5 Like other tyrannies, the tyranny of the majority was at first, and is 5 still vulgarly, held in dread, chiefly as operating through the acts of the public authorities. But reflecting persons perceived that when society is itself the tyrant—society collectively, over the separate individuals who compose it—its means of tyrannizing are not restricted to the acts which it may do by the hands of its political functionaries. Society can

and does execute its own mandates: and if it issues wrong mandates instead of right, or any mandates at all in things with which it ought not to meddle, it practices a social tyranny more formidable than many kinds of political oppression, since, though not usually upheld by such extreme penalties, it leaves fewer means of escape, penetrating much more deeply into the details of life, and enslaving the soul itself. Protection, therefore, against the tyranny of the magistrate is not enough: there needs protection also against the tyranny of the prevailing opinion and feeling; against the tendency of society to impose, by other means than civil penalties, its own ideas and practices as rules of conduct on those who dissent from them; to fetter the development, and, if possible, prevent the formation, of any individuality not in harmony with its ways, and compel all characters to fashion themselves upon the model of its own. There is a limit to the legitimate interference of collective opinion with individual independence: and to find that limit, and maintain it against encroachment, is as indispensable to a good condition of human affairs, as protection against political despotism.

But though this proposition is not likely to be contested in general terms, the practical question, where to place the limit—how to make the fitting adjustment between individual independence and social control—is a subject on which nearly everything remains to be done.

The object of this Essay is to assert one very simple principle, as entitled to govern absolutely the dealings of society with the individual in the way of compulsion and control, whether the means used be physical force in the form of legal penalties, or the moral coercion of public opinion. That principle is that the sole end for which mankind are warranted, individually or collectively in interfering with the liberty of action of any of their number, is self-protection. That the only purpose for which power can be rightfully exercised over any member of a civilized community, against his will, is to prevent harm to others. His own good, either physical or moral, is not a sufficient warrant. He cannot rightfully be compelled to do or forbear because it will be better for him to do so, because it will make him happier, because, in the opinions of others, to do so would be wise, or even right. These are good reasons for remonstrating with him, or reasoning with him, or persuading him, or entreating him, but not for compelling him, or visiting him with any evil, in case he do otherwise. To justify that, the conduct from which it is desired to deter him, must be calculated to produce evil to some one else. The only part of the conduct of any one, for which he is amenable to society, is that which concerns others. In the part which merely concerns himself, his independence is, of right, absolute. Over himself, over his own body and mind, the individual is sovereign.

It is, perhaps, hardly necessary to say that this doctrine is meant to apply only to human beings in the maturity of their faculties. We are not speaking of children, or of young persons below the age which the law may fix as that of manhood or womanhood. Those who are still in a state to require being taken care of by others, must be protected against their own actions as well as against external injury. For the same reason, we may leave out of consideration those backward states of society in which the race itself may be considered as in its nonage. The early difficulties in the way of spontaneous progress are so great, that there is seldom any choice of means for overcoming them; and a ruler full of the spirit of improvement is warranted in the use of any expedients that will attain an end, perhaps otherwise unattainable. Despotism is a legitimate mode of government in dealing with barbarians, provided the end be their improvement, and the means justified by actually effecting that end. Liberty, as a principle, has no application to any state of things anterior to the time when mankind have become capable of being improved by free and equal discussion. Until then, there is nothing for them but implicit obedience to an Akbar or a Charlemagne, if they are so fortunate as to find one. But as soon as mankind have attained the capacity of being guided to their own improvement by conviction or persuasion (a period long since reached in all nations with whom we need here concern ourselves), compulsion, either in the direct form or in that of pains and penalties for non-compliance, is no longer admissible as a means to their own good, and justifiable only for the security of others.

It is proper to state that I forego any advantage which could be derived to my argument from the idea of abstract right, as a thing independent of utility. I regard utility as the ultimate appeal on all ethical questions; but it must be utility in the largest sense, grounded on the permanent interests of man as a progressive being. Those interests, I contend, authorize the subjection of individual spontaneity to external control, only in respect to those actions of each, which concern the interest of other people. If any one does an act hurtful to others, there is a prima facie case for punishing him, by law, or, where legal penalties are not safely applicable, by general disapprobation. There are also many positive acts for the benefit of others, which he may rightfully be compelled to perform; such as, to give evidence in a court of justice; to bear his fair share in the common defense, or in any other joint work necessary to the interest of the society of which he enjoys the protection; and to perform certain acts of individual beneficence, such as saving a fellow-creature's life, or interposing to protect the defenseless against ill-usage, things which whenever it is obviously a man's duty to do, he may rightfully be made responsible to society for not doing. A person may cause evil to others not only by his actions but by his inaction, and in neither case he is justly accountable to them for the injury. The latter case, it is true, requires a much more cautious exercise of compulsion than the former. To make any one answerable for doing evil to others, is the rule; to make him answerable for not preventing evil, is, comparatively speaking, the exception. Yet there are many cases clear enough and grave enough to justify that exception. In all things which regard the external relations of the individual, he is *de jure* amenable to those whose interests are concerned, and if need be, to society as their protector. There are often good reasons for not holding him to the responsibility; but these reasons must arise from the special expediencies of the case: either because it is a kind of case in which he is on the whole likely to act better, when left to his own discretion, than when controlled in any way in which society have it in their power to control him; or because the attempt to exercise control would produce other evils, greater than those which it would prevent. When such reasons as these preclude the enforcement of responsibility, the conscience of the agent himself should step into the vacant judgment-seat, and protect those interests of others which have no external protection; judging himself all the more rigidly, because the case does not admit of his being made accountable to the judgment of his fellow creatures.

10   But there is a sphere of action in which society, as distinguished 10
from the individual, has, if any, only an indirect interest: comprehending all that portion of a person's life and conduct which affects only himself, or if it also affects others, only with their free, voluntary, and undeceived consent and participation. When I say only himself, I mean directly, and in the first instance: for whatever affects himself, may affect others through himself; and the objection which may be grounded on this contingency will receive consideration in the sequel. This, then, is the appropriate region of human liberty. It comprises, first, the inward domain of consciousness; demanding liberty of conscience, in the most comprehensive sense; liberty of thought and feeling; absolute freedom of opinion and sentiment on all subjects, practical or speculative, scientific, moral, or theological. The liberty of

expressing and publishing opinions may seem to fall under a different principle, since it belongs to that part of the conduct of an individual which concerns other people; but, being almost of as much importance as the liberty of thought itself, and resting in great part on the same reasons, is practically inseparable from it. Secondly, the principle requires liberty of tastes and pursuits; of framing the plan of our life to suit our own character; of doing as we like, subject to such consequences as may follow: without impediment from our fellow-creatures, so long as what we do does not harm them, even though they should think our conduct foolish, perverse, or wrong. Thirdly, from this liberty of each individual, follows the liberty, within the same limits, of combination among individuals; freedom to unite, for any purpose not involving harm to others: the persons combining being supposed to be of full age, and not forced or deceived.

No society in which these liberties are not, on the whole, respected, is free, whatever may be its form of government; and none is completely free in which they do not exist absolute and unqualified. The only freedom which deserves the name, is that of pursuing our own good in our own way, so long as we do not attempt to deprive others of theirs, or impede their efforts to obtain it. Each is the proper guardian of his own health, whether bodily, or mental and spiritual. Mankind are greater gainers by suffering each other to live as seems good to themselves, than by compelling each to live as seems good to the rest.

Liberty of Thought and Discussion

The time, it is to be hoped, is gone by when any defense would be necessary of the "liberty of the press" as one of the securities against corrupt or tyrannical government. No argument, we may suppose, can now be needed, against permitting a legislature or an executive, not identified in interest with the people, to prescribe opinions to them, and determine what doctrines or what arguments they shall be allowed to hear. This aspect of the question, besides, has been so often and so triumphantly enforced by preceding writers, that it needs not be specially insisted on in this place. Though the law of England, on the subject of the press, is as servile to this day as it was in the time of the Tudors, there is little danger of its being actually put in force against political discussion, except during some temporary panic, when fear of insurrection drives ministers and judges from their propriety; and, speaking generally, it is not, in constitutional countries, to be apprehended, that the government, whether completely responsible to the people or not, will often attempt to control the expression of opinion, except when in doing so it makes itself the organ of the general intolerance of the public. Let us suppose, therefore, that the government is entirely at one with the people, and never thinks of exerting any power of coercion unless in agreement with what it conceives to be their voice. But I deny the right of the people to exercise such coercion, either by themselves or by their government. The power itself is illegitimate. The best government has no more title to it than the worst. It is as noxious, or more noxious, when exerted in accordance with public opinion, than when in opposition to it. If all mankind minus one, were of one opinion, and only one person were of the contrary opinion, mankind would be no more justified in silencing that one person, than he, if he had the power, would be justified in silencing mankind. Were an opinion a personal possession of no value except to the owner; if to be obstructed in the enjoyment of it were simply a private injury, it would make some difference whether the injury was inflicted only on a few persons or on many. But the peculiar evil of silencing the expression of an opinion is, that it is robbing the human race; posterity as well as the existing generation; those who dissent from the opinion, still more than those who hold it. If the opinion is right, they are deprived of the opportunity of exchanging error for truth: if wrong, they lose, what is almost as great a benefit, the clearer perception and livelier impression of truth, produced by its collision with error.

It is necessary to consider separately these two hypotheses, each of which has a distinct branch of the argument corresponding to it. We can never be sure that the opinion we are endeavouring to stifle is a false opinion; and if we were sure, stifling it would be an evil still.

First: the opinion which it is attempted to suppress by authority may possibly be true. Those who desire to suppress it, of course deny its truth; but they are not infallible. They have no authority to decide the question for all mankind, and exclude every other person from the means of judging. To refuse a hearing to an opinion, because they are sure that it is false, is to assume that *their* certainty is the same thing as *absolute* certainty. All silencing of discussion is an assumption of infallibility. Its condemnation may be allowed to rest on this common argument, not the worse for being common.

15   Unfortunately for the good sense of mankind, the fact of their   15
fallibility is far from carrying the weight in their practical judgment,
which is always allowed to it in theory; for while every one well
knows himself to be fallible, few think it necessary to take any precautions against their own fallibility, or admit the supposition that any
opinion, of which they feel very certain, may be one of the examples
of the error to which they acknowledge themselves to be liable.
Absolute princes, or others who are accustomed to unlimited defer-
ence, usually feel this complete confidence in their own opinions on
nearly all subjects. People more happily situated, who sometimes hear
their opinions disputed, and are not wholly unused to be set right
when they are wrong, place the same unbounded reliance only on
such of their opinions as are shared by all who surround them, or to
whom they habitually defer: for in proportion to a man's want of confidence in his own solitary judgment, does he usually repose, with
implicit trust, on the infallibility of "the world" in general. And the
world, to each individual, means the part of it with which he comes
in contact; his party, his sect, his church, his class of society: the man
may be called, by comparison, almost liberal and largeminded to
whom it means anything so comprehensive as his own country or his
own age. Nor is his faith in this collective authority at all shaken by
his being aware that other ages, countries, sects, churches, classes, and
parties have thought, and even now think, the exact reverse. He
devolves upon his own world the responsibility of being in the right
against the dissentient worlds of other people; and it never troubles
him that mere accident has decided which of these numerous worlds
is the object of his reliance, and that the same causes which make him
a Churchman in London, would have made him a Buddhist or a
Confucian in Peking. Yet it is as evident in itself as any amount of
argument can make it, that ages are no more infallible than individuals; every age having held many opinions which subsequent ages have
deemed not only false but absurd; and it is as certain that many opinions, now general, will be rejected by future ages, as it is that many,
once general, are rejected by the present.

The objection likely to be made to this argument would probably
take some such form as the following. There is no greater assumption
of infallibility in forbidding the propagation of error, than in any
other thing which is done by public authority on its own judgment
and responsibility. Judgment is given to men that they may use it.
Because it may be used erroneously, are men to be told that they

ought not to use it at all? To prohibit what they think pernicious, is not claiming exemption from error, but fulfilling the duty incumbent on them, although fallible, of acting on their conscientious conviction. If we were never to act on our opinions, because those opinions may be wrong, we should leave all our interests uncared for, and all our duties unperformed. An objection which applies to all conduct, can be no valid objection to any conduct in particular. It is the duty of governments, and of individuals, to form the truest opinions they can; to form them carefully, and never impose them upon others unless they are quite sure of being right. But when they are sure (such reasoners may say), it is not conscientiousness but cowardice to shrink from acting on their opinions, and allow doctrines which they honestly think dangerous to the welfare of mankind, either in this life or in another, to be scattered abroad without restraint, because other people, in less enlightened times, have persecuted opinions now believed to be true. Let us take care, it may be said, not to make the same mistake: but governments and nations have made mistakes in other things, which are not denied to be fit subjects for the exercise of authority: they have laid on bad taxes, made unjust wars. Ought we therefore to lay on no taxes, and, under whatever provocation, make no wars? Men, and governments, must act to the best of their ability. There is no such thing as absolute certainty, but there is assurance sufficient for the purposes of human life. We may, and must, assume our opinion to be true for the guidance of our own conduct: and it is assuming no more when we forbid bad men to pervert society by the propagation of opinions which we regard as false and pernicious.

I answer, that it is assuming very much more. There is the greatest difference between presuming an opinion to be true, because, with every opportunity for contesting it, it has not been refuted, and assuming its truth for the purpose of not permitting its refutation. Complete liberty of contradicting and disproving our opinion, is the very condition which justifies us in assuming its truth for purposes of action; and on no other terms can a being with human faculties have any rational assurance of being right.

When we consider either the history of opinion, or the ordinary conduct of human life, to what is it to be ascribed that the one and the other are no worse than they are? Not certainly to the inherent force of the human understanding; for, on any matter not self-evident, there are ninety-nine persons totally incapable of judging of it, for one who is capable; and the capacity of the hundredth person is only comparative; for the majority of the eminent men of every past generation held many opinions now known to be erroneous, and did or approved numerous things which no one will now justify. Why is it, then, that there is on the whole a preponderance among mankind of rational opinions and rational conduct? If there really is this pre-ponderance—which there must be, unless human affairs are, and have always been, in an almost desperate state—it is owing to a qual-ity of the human mind, the source of everything respectable in man either as an intellectual or as a moral being, namely, that his errors are corrigible. He is capable of rectifying his mistakes by discussion and experience. Not by experience alone. There must be discussion, to show how experience is to be interpreted. Wrong opinions and prac-tices gradually yield to fact and argument: but facts and arguments, to produce any effect on the mind, must be brought before it. Very few facts are able to tell their own story, without comments to bring out their meaning. The whole strength and value, then, of human judg-ment, depending on the one property, that it can be set right when it is wrong, reliance can be placed on it only when the means of setting it right are kept constantly at hand. In the case of any person whose judgment is really deserving of confidence, how has it become so? Because he has kept his mind open to criticism of his opinions and conduct. Because it has been his practice to listen to all that could be said against him; to profit by as much of it as was just, and expound to himself, and upon occasion to others, the fallacy of what was falla-cious. Because he has felt, that the only way in which a human being can make some approach to knowing the whole of a subject, is by hearing what can be said about it by persons of every variety of opin-ion, and studying all modes in which it can be looked at by every character of mind. No wise man ever acquired his wisdom in any mode but this; nor is it in the nature of human intellect to become wise in any other manner. The steady habit of correcting and com-pleting his own opinion by collating it with those of others, so far from causing doubt and hesitation in carrying it into practice, is the only stable foundation for a just reliance on it: for, being cognizant of all that can, at least obviously, be said against him, and having taken up his position against all gainsayers—knowing that he has sought for objections and difficulties, instead of avoiding them, and has shut out no light which can be thrown upon the subject from any quarter—he has a right to think his judgment better than that of any person, or any multitude, who have not gone through a similar process.

It is not too much to require that what the wisest of mankind, those who are best entitled to trust their own judgment, find necessary to warrant their relying on it, should be submitted to by that miscellaneous collection of a few wise and many foolish individuals, called the public. The most intolerant of churches, the Roman Catholic Church, even at the canonization of a saint, admits, and listens patiently to, a "devil's advocate." The holiest of men, it appears, cannot be admitted to posthumous honors, until all that the devil could say against him is known and weighed. If even the Newtonian philosophy were not permitted to be questioned, mankind could not feel as complete assurance of its truth as they now do. The beliefs which we have most warrant for, have no safeguard to rest on, but a standing invitation to the whole world to prove them unfounded. If the challenge is not accepted, or is accepted and the attempt fails, we are far enough from certainty still; but we have done the best that the existing state of human reason admits of; we have neglected nothing that could give the truth a chance of reaching us: if the lists are kept open, we may hope that if there be a better truth, it will be found when the human mind is capable of receiving it; and in the meantime we may rely on having attained such approach to truth, as is possible in our own day. This is the amount of certainty attainable by a fallible being, and this the sole way of attaining it.

20   Strange it is, that men should admit the validity of the arguments   20
for free discussion, but object to their being "pushed to an extreme"; not seeing that unless the reasons are good for an extreme case, they are not good for any case. Strange that they should imagine that they are not assuming infallibility, when they acknowledge that there should be free discussion on all subjects which can possibly be *doubtful*, but think that some particular principle or doctrine should be forbidden to be questioned because it is so *certain*, that is, because *they are certain* that it is certain. To call any proposition certain, while there is any one who would deny its certainty if permitted, but who is not permitted, is to assume that we ourselves, and those who agree with us, are the judges of certainty, and judges without hearing the other side.

In the present age—which has been described as "destitute of faith, but terrified at scepticism"—in which people feel sure, not so much that their opinions are true, as that they should not know what to do without them—the claims of an opinion to be protected from public attack are rested not so much on its truth, as on its importance to society. There are, it is alleged, certain beliefs, so useful, not to say indispensable to well-being, that it is as much the duty of governments to uphold those beliefs, as to protect any other of the interests of society. In a case of such necessity, and so directly in the line of their duty, something less than infallibility may, it is maintained, warrant, and even bind, governments, to act on their own opinion, confirmed by the general opinion of mankind. It is also often argued, and still oftener thought, that none but bad men would desire to weaken these salutary beliefs; and there can be nothing wrong, it is thought, in restraining bad men, and prohibiting what only such men would wish to practise. This mode of thinking makes the justification of restraints on discussion not a question of the truth of doctrines, but of their usefulness; and flatters itself by that means to escape the responsibility of claiming to be an infallible judge of opinions. But those who thus satisfy themselves, do not perceive that the assumption of infallibility is merely shifted from one point to another. The usefulness of an opinion is itself matter of opinion: as disputable, as open to discussion, and requiring discussion as much, as the opinion itself. There is the same need of an infallible judge of opinions to decide an opinion to be noxious, as to decide it to be false, unless the opinion condemned has full opportunity of defending itself. And it will not do to say that the heretic may be allowed to maintain the utility or harmlessness of his opinion, though forbidden to maintain its truth. The truth of an opinion is part of its utility. If we would know whether or not it is desirable that a proposition should be believed, is it possible to exclude the consideration of whether or not it is true? In the opinion, not of bad men, but of the best men, no belief which is contrary to truth can be really useful: and can you prevent such men from urging that plea, when they are charged with culpability for denying some doctrine which they are told is useful, but which they believe to be false? Those who are on the side of received opinions, never fail to take all possible advantage of this plea; you do not find *them* handling the question of utility as if it could be completely abstracted from that of truth: on the contrary, it is, above all, because their doctrine is "the truth," that the knowledge or the belief of it is held to be so indispensable. There can be no fair discussion of the question of usefulness, when an argument so vital may be employed on one side, but not on the other. And in point of fact, when law or public feeling do not permit the truth of an opinion to be disputed, they are just as little tolerant of a denial of its usefulness.

The utmost they allow is an extenuation of its absolute necessity or of the positive guilt of rejecting it.

In order more fully to illustrate the mischief of denying a hearing to opinions because we, in our own judgment, have condemned them, it will be desirable to fix down the discussion to a concrete case; and I choose, by preference, the cases which are least favorable to me—in which the argument against freedom of opinion, both on the score of truth and on that of utility, is considered the strongest. Let the opinions impugned be the belief in a God and in a future state, or any of the commonly received doctrines of morality. To fight the battle on such ground, gives a great advantage to an unfair antagonist; since he will be sure to say (and many who have no desire to be unfair will say it internally), are these the doctrines which you do not deem sufficiently certain to be taken under the protection of law? Is the belief in a God one of the opinions, to feel sure of which, you hold to be assuming infallibility? But I must be permitted to observe, that it is not the feeling sure of a doctrine (be it what it may) which I call an assumption of infallibility. It is the undertaking to decide that question *for others*, without allowing them to hear what can be said on the contrary side. And I denounce and reprobate this pretension not the less, if put forth on the side of my most solemn convictions. However positive any one's persuasion may be, not only of the falsity but of the pernicious consequences—not only of the pernicious consequences, but (to adopt expressions which I altogether condemn) the immorality and impiety of an opinion; yet if, in pursuance of that private judgment, though backed by the public judgment of his country or his cotemporaries, he prevents the opinion from being heard in its defense, he assumes infallibility. And so far from the assumption being less objectionable or less dangerous because the opinion is called immoral or impious, this is the case of all others in which it is most fatal. These are exactly the occasions on which the men of one generation commit those dreadful mistakes, which excite the astonishment and horror of posterity. It is among such that we find the instances memorable in history, when the arm of the law has been employed to root out the best men and the noblest doctrines; with deplorable success as to the men, though some of the doctrines have survived to be (as if in mockery) invoked, in defense of similar conduct towards those who dissent from *them*, or from their received interpretation.

Mankind can hardly be too often reminded, that there was once a man named Socrates, between whom and the legal authorities and public opinion of his time, there took place a memorable collision. Born in an age and country abounding in individual greatness, this man has been handed down to us by those who best knew both him and the age, as the most virtuous man in it; while *we* know him as the head and prototype of all subsequent teachers of virtue, the source equally of the lofty inspiration of Plato and the judicious utilitarianism of Aristotle, *i maestri di color che sanno*, the two headsprings of ethical as of all other philosophy. This acknowledged master of all the eminent thinkers who have since lived—whose fame, still growing after more than two thousand years, all but outweighs the whole remainder of the names which make his native city illustrious—was put to death by his countrymen, after a judicial conviction, for impiety and immorality. Impiety, in denying the gods recognized by the State; indeed his accuser asserted (see the *Apologia*) that he believed in no gods at all. Immorality, in being, by his doctrines and instructions, a "corrupter of youth." Of these charges the tribunal, there is every ground for believing, honestly found him guilty, and condemned the man who probably of all then born had deserved best of mankind, to be put to death as a criminal.

To pass from this to the only other instance of judicial iniquity, the mention of which, after the condemnation of Socrates, would not be an anti-climax: the event which took place on Calvary rather more than eighteen hundred years ago. The man who left on the memory of those who witnessed his life and conversation, such an impression of his moral grandeur, that eighteen subsequent centuries have done homage to him as the Almighty in person, was ignominiously put to death, as what? As a blasphemer. Men did not merely mistake their benefactor; they mistook him for the exact contrary of what he was, and treated him as that prodigy of impiety, which they themselves are now held to be, for their treatment of him. The feelings with which mankind now regard these lamentable transactions, especially the latter of the two, render them extremely unjust in their judgment of the unhappy actors. These were, to all appearance, not bad men—not worse than men most commonly are, but rather the contrary: men who possessed in a full, or somewhat more than a full measure, the religious, moral, and patriotic feelings of their time and people: the very kind of men who, in all times, our own included, have every chance of passing through life blameless and respected. The high-priest who rent his garments when the words were pronounced, which, according to all the ideas of his country, constituted the blackest guilt, was in all probability quite as sincere in his horror and indignation, as the generality of respectable and pious men now are in the religious and moral sentiments they profess; and most of those who now shudder at his conduct, if they had lived in his time, and been born Jews, would have acted precisely as he did. Orthodox Christians who are tempted to think that those who stoned to death the first martyrs must have been worse men than they themselves are, ought to remember that one of those persecutors was Saint Paul.

25   Let us add one more example, the most striking of all, if the 25 impressiveness of an error is measured by the wisdom and virtue of him who falls into it. If ever any one, possessed of power, had grounds for thinking himself the best and most enlightened among his cotemporaries, it was the Emperor Marcus Aurelius. Absolute monarch of the whole civilized world, he preserved through life not only the most unblemished justice, but what was less to be expected from his Stoical breeding, the tenderest heart. The few failings which are attributed to him, were all on the side of indulgence: while his writings, the highest ethical product of the ancient mind, differ scarcely perceptibly, if they differ at all, from the most characteristic teachings of Christ. This man, a better Christian in all but the dogmatic sense of the word, than almost any of the ostensibly Christian sovereigns who have since reigned, persecuted Christianity. Placed at the summit of all the previous attainments of humanity, with an open, unfettered intellect, and a character which led him of himself to embody in his moral writings the Christian ideal, he yet failed to see that Christianity was to be a good and not an evil to the world, with his duties to which he was so deeply penetrated. Existing society he knew to be in a deplorable state. But such as it was, he saw or thought he saw, that it was held together and prevented from being worse, by belief and reverence of the received divinities. As a ruler of mankind, he deemed it his duty not to suffer society to fall in pieces; and saw not how, if its existing ties were removed, any others could be formed which could again knit it together. The new religion openly aimed at dissolving these ties: unless, therefore, it was his duty to adopt that religion, it seemed to be his duty to put it down. Inasmuch then as the theology of Christianity did not appear to him true or of divine origin; inasmuch as this strange history of a crucified God was not credible to him, and a system which purported to rest entirely upon a foundation to him so wholly unbelievable, could not be foreseen by him to be that renovating agency which, after all abatements, it has in fact

proved to be; the gentlest and most amiable of philosophers and rulers, under a solemn sense of duty, authorized the persecution of Christianity. To my mind this is one of the most tragical facts in all history. It is a bitter thought, how different a thing the Christianity of the world might have been, if the Christian faith had been adopted as the religion of the empire under the auspices of Marcus Aurelius instead of those of Constantine. But it would be equally unjust to him and false to truth, to deny, that no one plea which can be urged for punishing anti-Christian teaching, was wanting to Marcus Aurelius for punishing, as he did, the propagation of Christianity. No Christian more firmly believes that Atheism is false, and tends to the dissolution of society, than Marcus Aurelius believed the same things of Christianity; he who, of all men then living, might have been thought the most capable of appreciating it. Unless any one who approves of punishment for the promulgation of opinions, flatters himself that he is a wiser and better man than Marcus Aurelius— more deeply versed in the wisdom of his time, more elevated in his intellect above it—more earnest in his search for truth, or more sin-gle-minded in his devotion to it when found;—let him abstain from that assumption of the joint infallibility of himself and the multitude, which the great Antoninus made with so unfortunate a result.

Aware of the impossibility of defending the use of punishment for restraining irreligious opinions, by any argument which will not justify Marcus Antoninus, the enemies of religious freedom, when hard pressed, occasionally accept this consequence, and say, with Dr. Johnson, that the persecutors of Christianity were in the right; that persecution is an ordeal through which truth ought to pass, and always passes successfully, legal penalties being, in the end, powerless against truth, though sometimes beneficially effective against mischie-vous errors. This is a form of the argument for religious intolerance, sufficiently remarkable not to be passed without notice.

A theory which maintains that truth may justifiably be perse-cuted because persecution cannot possibly do it any harm, cannot be charged with being intentionally hostile to the reception of new truths; but we cannot commend the generosity of its dealing with the persons to whom mankind are indebted for them. To discover to the world something which deeply concerns it, and of which it was previ-ously ignorant; to prove to it that it had been mistaken on some vital point of temporal or spiritual interest, is as important a service as a human being can render to his fellow-creatures, and in certain cases, as in those of the early Christians and of the Reformers, those who think with Dr. Johnson believe it to have been the most precious gift which could be bestowed on mankind. That the authors of such splendid benefits should be requited by martyrdom; that their reward should be to be dealt with as the vilest of criminals, is not, upon this theory, a deplorable error and misfortune, for which humanity should mourn in sackcloth and ashes, but the normal and justifiable state of things. The propounder of a new truth, according to this doctrine, should stand, as stood, in the legislation of the Locrians, the proposer of a new law, with a halter round his neck, to be instantly tightened if the public assembly did not, on hearing his reasons, then and there adopt his proposition. People who defend this mode of treating bene-factors, cannot be supposed to set much value on the benefit; and I believe this view of the subject is mostly confined to the sort of per-sons who think that new truths may have been desirable once, but that we have had enough of them now.

But, indeed, the dictum that truth always triumphs over persecu-tion, is one of those pleasant falsehoods which men repeat after one another till they pass into commonplaces, but which all experience refutes. History teems with instances of truth put down by persecu-tion. If not suppressed forever, it may be thrown back for centuries. To speak only of religious opinions: the Reformation broke out at least twenty times before Luther, and was put down. Arnold of Bres-cia was put down. Fra Dolcino was put down. Savonarola was put down. The Albigeois were put down. The Vaudois were put down. The Lollards were put down. The Hussites were put down. Even after the era of Luther, wherever persecution was persisted in, it was suc-cessful. In Spain, Italy, Flanders, the Austrian empire, Protestantism was rooted out; and, most likely, would have been so in England, had Queen Mary lived, or Queen Elizabeth died. Persecution has always succeeded, save where the heretics were too strong a party to be effec-tually persecuted. No reasonable person can doubt that Christianity might have been extirpated in the Roman empire. It spread, and became predominant, because the persecutions were only occasional, lasting but a short time, and separated by long intervals of almost undisturbed propagandism. It is a piece of idle sentimentality that truth, merely as truth, has any inherent power denied to error, of pre-vailing against the dungeon and the stake. Men are not more zealous for truth than they often are for error, and a sufficient application of legal or even of social penalties will generally succeed in stopping the propagation of either. The real advantage which truth has, consists in this, that when an opinion is true, it may be extinguished once, twice, or many times, but in the course of ages there will generally be found persons to rediscover it, until some one of its reappearances falls on a time when from favourable circumstances it escapes persecution until it has made such head as to withstand all subsequent attempts to suppress it.

What is boasted of at the present time as the revival of religion, is always, in narrow and uncultivated minds, at least as much the revival of bigotry; and where there is the strongest permanent leaven of intolerance in the feelings of a people, which at all times abides in the middle classes of this country, it needs but little to provoke them into actively persecuting those whom they have never ceased to think proper objects of persecution. For it is this—it is the opinions men entertain, and the feelings they cherish, respecting those who disown the beliefs they deem important, which makes this country not a place of mental freedom. For a long time past, the chief mischief of the legal penalties is that they strengthen the social stigma. It is that stigma which is really effective, and so effective is it, that the profession of opinions which are under the ban of society is much less common in England, than is, in many other countries, the avowal of those which incur risk of judicial punishment. In respect to all persons but those whose pecuniary circumstances make them independent of the good will of other people, opinion, on this subject, is as efficacious as law; men might as well be imprisoned, as excluded from the means of earning their bread. Those whose bread is already secured, and who desire no favors from men in power, or from bodies of men, or from the public, have nothing to fear from the open avowal of any opinions, but to be ill-thought of and ill-spoken of, and this it ought not to require a very heroic mould to enable them to bear. There is no room for any appeal *ad misericordiam* in behalf of such persons. But though we do not now inflict so much evil on those who think differently from us, as it was formerly our custom to do, it may be that we do ourselves as much evil as ever by our treatment of them. Socrates was put to death, but the Socratic philosophy rose like the sun in heaven, and spread its illumination over the whole intellectual firmament. Christians were cast to the lions, but the Christian Church grew up a stately and spreading tree, overtopping the older and less vigorous growths, and stifling them by its shade. Our merely social intolerance kills no one, roots out no opinions, but induces men to disguise them, or to abstain from any active effort for their diffusion. With us, heretical opinions do not perceptibly gain or even lose, ground in each decade or generation; they never blaze out far and wide, but continue to smolder in the narrow circles of thinking and studious persons among whom they originate, without ever lighting up the general affairs of mankind with either a true or a deceptive light. And thus is kept up a state of things very satisfactory to some minds, because, without the unpleasant process of fining or imprisoning anybody, it maintains all prevailing opinions outwardly undisturbed, while it does not absolutely interdict the exercise of reason by dissentients afflicted with the malady of thought. A convenient plan for having peace in the intellectual world, and keeping all things going on therein very much as they do already. But the price paid for this sort of intellectual pacification, is the sacrifice of the entire moral courage of the human mind. A state of things in which a large portion of the most active and inquiring intellects find it advisable to keep the genuine principles and grounds of their convictions within their own breasts, and attempt, in what they address to the public, to fit as much as they can of their own conclusions to premises which they have internally renounced, cannot send forth the open, fearless characters, and logical, consistent intellects who once adorned the thinking world. The sort of men who can be looked for under it, are either mere conformers to commonplace, or time-servers for truth whose arguments on all great subjects are meant for their hearers, and are not those which have convinced themselves. Those who avoid this alternative, do so by narrowing their thoughts and interests to things which can be spoken of without venturing within the region of principles, that is, to small practical matters, which would come right of themselves, if but the minds of mankind were strengthened and enlarged, and which will never be made effectually right until then: while that which would strengthen and enlarge men's minds, free and daring speculation on the highest subjects, is abandoned.

30   Those in whose eyes this reticence on the part of heretics is no 30 evil, should consider in the first place, that in consequence of it there is never any fair and thorough discussion of heretical opinions; and that such of them as could not stand such a discussion, though they may be prevented from spreading, do not disappear. But it is not the minds of heretics that are deteriorated most, by the ban placed on all inquiry which does not end in the orthodox conclusions. The greatest

harm done is to those who are not heretics, and whose whole mental development is cramped, and their reason cowed, by the fear of heresy. Who can compute what the world loses in the multitude of promising intellects combined with timid characters, who dare not follow out any bold, vigorous, independent train of thought, lest it should land them in something which would admit of being considered irreligious or immoral? Among them we may occasionally see some man of deep conscientiousness, and subtle and refined understanding, who spends a life in sophisticating with an intellect which he cannot silence, and exhausts the resources of ingenuity in attempting to reconcile the promptings of his conscience and reason with orthodoxy, which yet he does not, perhaps, to the end succeed in doing. No one can be a great thinker who does not recognize, that as a thinker it is his first duty to follow his intellect to whatever conclusions it may lead. Truth gains more even by the errors of one who, with due study and preparation, thinks for himself, than by the true opinions of those who only hold them because they do not suffer themselves to think. Not that it is solely, or chiefly, to form great thinkers, that freedom of thinking is required. On the contrary, it is as much and even more indispensable, to enable average human beings to attain the mental stature which they are capable of. There have been, and may again be, great individual thinkers, in a general atmosphere of mental slavery. But there never has been, nor ever will be, in that atmosphere, an intellectually active people. Where any people has made a temporary approach to such a character, it has been because the dread of heterodox speculation was for a time suspended. Where there is a tacit convention that principles are not to be disputed; where the discussion of the greatest questions which can occupy humanity is considered to be closed, we cannot hope to find that generally high scale of mental activity which has made some periods of history so remarkable. Never when controversy avoided the subjects which are large and important enough to kindle enthusiasm, was the mind of a people stirred up from its foundations, and the impulse given which raised even persons of the most ordinary intellect to something of the dignity of thinking beings. Of such we have had an example in the condition of Europe during the times immediately following the Reformation; another, though limited to the Continent and to a more cultivated class, in the speculative movement of the latter half of the eighteenth century; and a third, of still briefer duration, in the intellectual fermentation of Germany during the

Goethian and Fichtean period. These periods differed widely in the particular opinions which they developed; but were alike in this, that during all three the yoke of authority was broken. In each, an old mental despotism had been thrown off, and no new one had yet taken its place. The impulse given at these three periods has made Europe what it now is. Every single improvement which has taken place either in the human mind or in institutions, may be traced distinctly to one or other of them. Appearances have for some time indicated that all three impulses are well-nigh spent; and we can expect no fresh start, until we again assert our mental freedom.

Let us now pass to the second division of the argument, and dismissing the supposition that any of the received opinions may be false, let us assume them to be true, and examine into the worth of the manner in which they are likely to be held, when their truth is not freely and openly canvassed. However unwillingly a person who has a strong opinion may admit the possibility that his opinion may be false, he ought to be moved by the consideration that however true it may be, if it is not fully, frequently, and fearlessly discussed, it will be held as a dead dogma, not a living truth.

There is a class of persons (happily not quite so numerous as formerly) who think it enough if a person assents undoubtingly to what they think true, though he has no knowledge whatever of the grounds of the opinion, and could not make a tenable defense of it against the most superficial objections. Such persons, if they can once get their creed taught from authority, naturally think that no good, and some harm, comes of its being allowed to be questioned. Where their influence prevails, they make it nearly impossible for the received opinion to be rejected wisely and considerately, though it may still be rejected rashly and ignorantly; for to shut out discussion entirely is seldom possible and, when it once gets in, beliefs not grounded on conviction are apt to give way before the slightest semblance of an argument. Waiving, however, this possibility—assuming that the true opinion abides in the mind, but abides as a prejudice, a belief independent of, and proof against, argument—this is not the way in which truth ought to be held by a rational being. This is not knowing the truth. Truth, thus held, is but one superstition the more accidentally clinging to the words which enunciate a truth.

If the intellect and judgment of mankind ought to be cultivated, a thing which Protestants at least do not deny, on what can these faculties be more appropriately exercised by any one, than on the things which concern him so much that it is considered necessary for him to hold opinions on them? If the cultivation of the understanding consists in one thing more than in another, it is surely in learning the grounds of one's own opinions. Whatever people believe, on subjects on which it is of the first importance to believe rightly, they ought to be able to defend against at least the common objections. But, some one may say, "Let them be *taught* the grounds of their opinions. It does not follow that opinions must be merely parroted because they are never heard controverted. Persons who learn geometry do not simply commit the theorems to memory, but understand and learn likewise the demonstrations; and it would be absurd to say that they remain ignorant of the grounds of geometrical truths, because they never hear any one deny, and attempt to disprove them." Undoubtedly, and such teaching suffices on a subject like mathematics, where there is nothing at all to be said on the wrong side of the question. The peculiarity of the evidence of mathematical truths is that all the argument is on one side. There are no objections, and no answers to objections. But on every subject on which difference of opinion is possible, the truth depends on a balance to be struck between two sets of conflicting reasons. Even in natural philosophy, there is always some other explanation possible of the same facts; some geocentric theory instead of heliocentric, some phlogiston instead of oxygen; and it has to be shown why that other theory cannot be the true one: and until this is shown and until we know how it is shown, we do not understand the grounds of our opinion. But when we turn to subjects infinitely more complicated, to morals, religion, politics, social relations, and the business of life, three-fourths of the arguments for every disputed opinion consist in dispelling the appearances which favor some opinion different from it. The greatest orator, save one, of antiquity, has left it on record that he always studied his adversary's case with as great, if not with still greater, intensity than even his own. What Cicero practiced as the means of forensic success, requires to be imitated by all who study any subject in order to arrive at the truth. He who knows only his own side of the case, knows little of that. His reasons may be good, and no one may have been able to refute them. But if he is equally unable to refute the reasons on the opposite side; if he does not so much as know what they are, he has no ground for preferring either opinion. The rational position for him would be suspension of judgment, and unless he contents himself with that, he is either led by authority, or adopts, like the generality of the world, the side to which he feels most inclination. Nor is it enough that he should hear the arguments of adversaries from his own teachers, presented as they state them, and accompanied by what they offer as refutations. This is not the way to do justice to the arguments, or bring them into real contact with his own mind. He must be able to hear them from persons who actually believe them; who defend them in earnest, and do their very utmost for them. He must know them in their most plausible and persuasive form; he must feel the whole force of the difficulty which the true view of the subject has to encounter and dispose of else he will never really possess himself of the portion of truth which meets and removes that difficulty. Ninety-nine in a hundred of what are called educated men are in this condition; even of those who can argue fluently for their opinions. Their conclusion may be true, but it might be false for anything they know: they have never thrown themselves into the mental position of those who think differently from them, and considered what such persons may have to say; and consequently they do not, in any proper sense of the word, know the doctrine which they themselves profess. They do not know those parts of it which explain and justify the remainder; the considerations which show that a fact which seemingly conflicts with another is reconcilable with it, or that, of two apparently strong reasons, one and not the other ought to be preferred. All that part of the truth which turns the scale, and decides the judgment of a completely informed mind, they are strangers to; nor is it ever really known, but to those who have attended equally and impartially to both sides, and endeavored to see the reasons of both in the strongest light. So essential is this discipline to a real understanding of moral and human subjects, that if opponents of all important truths do not exist, it is indispensable to imagine them and supply them with the strongest arguments which the most skillful devil's advocate can conjure up.

To abate the force of these considerations, an enemy of free discussion may be supposed to say, that there is no necessity for mankind in general to know and understand all that can be said against or for their opinions by philosophers and theologians. That it is not needful for common men to be able to expose all the misstatements or fallacies of an ingenious opponent. That it is enough if there is always somebody capable of answering them, so that nothing likely to mislead uninstructed persons remains unrefuted. That simple minds, having been taught the obvious grounds of the truths inculcated on them, may trust to authority for the rest, and being aware that they have neither knowledge nor talent to resolve every difficulty which can be raised, may repose in the assurance that all those which have been raised have been or can be answered, by those who are specially trained to the task.

35   Conceding to this view of the subject the utmost that can be   35 claimed for it by those most easily satisfied with the amount of understanding of truth which ought to accompany the belief of it; even so, the argument for free discussion is no way weakened. For even this doctrine acknowledges that mankind ought to have a rational assurance that all objections have been satisfactorily answered; and how are they to be answered if that which requires to be answered is not spoken? or how can the answer be known to be satisfactory, if the objectors have no opportunity of showing that it is unsatisfactory? If not the public, at least the philosophers and theologians who are to resolve the difficulties, must make themselves familiar with those difficulties in their most puzzling form; and this cannot be accomplished unless they are freely stated, and placed in the most advantageous light which they admit of. The Catholic Church has its own way of dealing with this embarrassing problem. It makes a broad separation between those who can be permitted to receive its doctrines on conviction, and those who must accept them on trust. Neither, indeed, are allowed any choice as to what they will accept; but the clergy, such at least as can be fully confided in, may admissibly and meritoriously make themselves acquainted with the arguments of opponents, in order to answer them, and may, therefore, read heretical books; the laity, not unless by special permission, hard to be obtained. This discipline recognizes a knowledge of the enemy's case as beneficial to the teachers, but finds means, consistent with this, of denying it to the rest of the world: thus giving to the *élite* more mental culture, though not more mental freedom, than it allows to the mass. By this device it succeeds in obtaining the kind of mental superiority which its purposes require; for though culture without freedom never made a large and liberal mind, it can make a clever *nisi prius* advocate of a cause. But in countries professing Protestantism, this resource is denied; since Protestants hold, at least in theory, that the responsibility for the choice of a religion must be borne by each for himself, and cannot be thrown off upon teachers. Besides, in the present state of the world, it is practically impossible that writings which are read by the instructed can be kept from the uninstructed. If the teachers of mankind are to

be cognizant of all that they ought to know, everything must be free to be written and published without restraint.

If, however, the mischievous operation of the absence of free discussion, when the received opinions are true, were confined to leaving men ignorant of the grounds of those opinions, it might be thought that this, if an intellectual, is no moral evil, and does not affect the worth of the opinions, regarded in their influence on the character. The fact, however, is that not only the grounds of the opinion are forgotten in the absence of discussion, but too often the meaning of the opinion itself. The words which convey it cease to suggest ideas, or suggest only a small portion of those they were originally employed to communicate. Instead of a vivid conception and a living belief, there remain only a few phrases retained by rote; or, if any part, the shell and husk only of the meaning is retained, the finer essence being lost. The great chapter in human history which this fact occupies and fills, cannot be too earnestly studied and meditated on.

It is illustrated in the experience of almost all ethical doctrines and religious creeds. They are all full of meaning and vitality to those who originate them, and to the direct disciples of the originators. Their meaning continues to be felt in undiminished strength, and is perhaps brought out into even fuller consciousness, so long as the struggle lasts to give the doctrine or creed an ascendency over other creeds. At last it either prevails, and becomes the general opinion, or its progress stops; it keeps possession of the ground it has gained, but ceases to spread further. When either of these results has become apparent, controversy on the subject flags, and gradually dies away. The doctrine has taken its place, if not as a received opinion, as one of the admitted sects or divisions of opinion: those who hold it have generally inherited, not adopted it; and conversion from one of these doctrines to another, being now an exceptional fact, occupies little place in the thoughts of their professors. Instead of being, as at first, constantly on the alert either to defend themselves against the world, or to bring the world over to them, they have subsided into acquiescence, and neither listen, when they can help it, to arguments against their creed, nor trouble dissentients (if there be such) with arguments in its favor. From this time may usually be dated the decline in the living power of the doctrine. We often hear the teachers of all creeds lamenting the difficulty of keeping up in the minds of believers a lively apprehension of the truth which they nominally recognize, so that it may penetrate the feelings, and acquire a real mastery over the conduct. No such difficulty is complained of while the creed is still fighting for its existence: even the weaker combatants then know and feel what they are fighting for, and the difference between it and other doctrines; and in that period of every creed's existence, not a few persons may be found, who have realized its fundamental principles in all the forms of thought, have weighed and considered them in all their important bearings, and have experienced the full effect on the character, which belief in that creed ought to produce in a mind thoroughly imbued with it. But when it has come to be an hereditary creed, and to be received passively, not actively—when the mind is no longer compelled, in the same degree as at first, to exercise its vital powers on the questions which its belief presents to it, there is a progressive tendency to forget all of the belief except the formularies, or to give it a dull and torpid assent, as if accepting it on trust dispensed with the necessity of realizing it in consciousness, or testing it by personal experience; until it almost ceases to connect itself at all with the inner life of the human being. Then are seen the cases, so frequent in this age of the world as almost to form the majority, in which the creed remains as it were outside the mind, encrusting and petrifying it against all other influences addressed to the higher parts of our nature; manifesting its power by not suffering any fresh and living conviction to get in, but itself doing nothing for the mind or heart, except standing sentinel over them to keep them vacant.

To what an extent doctrines intrinsically fitted to make the deepest impression upon the mind may remain in it as dead beliefs, without being ever realized in the imagination, the feelings, or the understanding, is exemplified by the manner in which the majority of believers hold the doctrines of Christianity. By Christianity I here mean what is accounted such by all churches and sects—the maxims and precepts contained in the New Testament. These are considered sacred, and accepted as laws, by all professing Christians. Yet it is scarcely too much to say that not one Christian in a thousand guides or tests his individual conduct by reference to those laws. The standard to which he does refer it, is the custom of his nation, his class, or his religious profession. He has thus, on the one hand, a collection of ethical maxims, which he believes to have been vouchsafed to him by infallible wisdom as rules for his government; and on the other, a set of every-day judgments and practices, which go a certain length with some of those maxims, not so great a length with others, stand in direct opposition to some, and are, on the whole, a compromise between the Christian creed and the interests and suggestions of worldly life. To the first of these standards he gives his homage; to the other his real allegiance. All Christians believe that the blessed are the poor and humble, and those who are ill-used by the world; that it is easier for a camel to pass through the eye of a needle than for a rich man to enter the kingdom of heaven; that they should judge not, lest they be judged; that they should swear not at all; that they should love their neighbor as themselves; that if one take their cloak, they should give him their coat also; that they should take no thought for the morrow; that if they would be perfect, they should sell all that they have and give it to the poor. They are not insincere when they say that they believe these things. They do believe them, as people believe what they have always heard lauded and never discussed. But in the sense of that living belief which regulates conduct, they believe these doctrines just up to the point to which it is usual to act upon them. The doctrines in their integrity are serviceable to pelt adversaries with; and it is understood that they are to be put forward (when possible) as the reasons for whatever people do that they think laudable. But any one who reminded them that the maxims require an infinity of things which they never even think of doing, would gain nothing but to be classed among those very unpopular characters who affect to be better than other people. The doctrines have no hold on ordinary believers—are not a power in their minds. They have an habitual respect for the sound of them, but no feeling which spreads from the words to the things signified, and forces the mind to take *them* in, and make them conform to the formula. Whenever conduct is concerned, they look round for Mr. A and B to direct them how far to go in obeying Christ.

Now we may be well assured that the case was not thus, but far otherwise, with the early Christians. Had it been thus, Christianity never would have expanded from an obscure sect of the despised Hebrews into the religion of the Roman empire. When their enemies said, "See how these Christians love one another" (a remark not likely to be made by anybody now), they assuredly had a much livelier feeling of the meaning of their creed than they have ever had since. And to this cause, probably, it is chiefly owing that Christianity now makes so little progress in extending its domain, and after eighteen centuries, is still nearly confined to Europeans and the descendants of Europeans. Even with the strictly religious, who are much in earnest about their doctrines, and attach a greater amount of meaning to many of them than people in general, it commonly happens that the part which is thus comparatively active in their minds is that which was made by Calvin, or Knox, or some such person much nearer in character to themselves. The sayings of Christ coexist passively in their minds, producing hardly any effect beyond what is caused by mere listening to words so amiable and bland. There are many reasons, doubtless, why doctrines which are the badge of a sect retain more of their vitality than those common to all recognized sects, and why more pains are taken by teachers to keep their meaning alive; but one reason certainly is, that the peculiar doctrines are more questioned, and have to be oftener defended against open gainsayers. Both teachers and learners go to sleep at their post, as soon as there is no enemy in the field.

40   The same thing holds true, generally speaking, of all traditional   40
doctrines—those of prudence and knowledge of life, as well as of morals or religion. All languages and literatures are full of general observations on life, both as to what it is, and how to conduct oneself in it; observations which everybody knows, which everybody repeats, or hears with acquiescence, which are received as truisms, yet of which most people first truly learn the meaning, when experience, generally of a painful kind, has made it a reality to them. How often, when smarting under some unforeseen misfortune or disappointment, does a person call to mind some proverb or common saying, familiar to him all his life, the meaning of which, if he had ever before felt it as he does now, would have saved him from the calamity. There are indeed reasons for this, other than the absence of discussion: there are many truths of which the full meaning *cannot* be realized, until personal experience has brought it home. But much more of the meaning even of these would have been understood, and what was understood would have been far more deeply impressed on the mind, if the man had been accustomed to hear it argued *pro* and *con* by people who did understand it. The fatal tendency of mankind to leave off thinking about a thing when it is no longer doubtful, is the cause of half their errors. A contemporary author has well spoken of "the deep slumber of a decided opinion."

But what! (it may be asked) Is the absence of unanimity an indispensable condition of true knowledge? Is it necessary that some part of mankind should persist in error, to enable any to realize the truth? Does a belief cease to be real and vital as soon as it is generally received—and is a proposition never thoroughly understood and felt unless some doubt of it remains? As soon as mankind have unanimously accepted a truth, does the truth perish within them? The highest aim and best result of improved intelligence, it has hitherto been thought, is to unite mankind more and more in the acknowledgment of all important truths: and does the intelligence only last as long as it has not achieved its object? Do the fruits of conquest perish by the very completeness of the victory?

I affirm no such thing. As mankind improve, the number of doctrines which are no longer disputed or doubted will be constantly on the increase: and the well-being of mankind may almost be measured by the number and gravity of the truths which have reached the point of being uncontested. The cessation, on one question after another, of serious controversy, is one of the necessary incidents of the consolidation of opinion; a consolidation as salutary in the case of true opinions, as it is dangerous and noxious when the opinions are erroneous. But though this gradual narrowing of the bounds of diversity of opinion is necessary in both senses of the term, being at once inevitable and indispensable, we are not therefore obliged to conclude that all its consequences must be beneficial. The loss of so important an aid to the intelligent and living apprehension of a truth, as is afforded by the necessity of explaining it to, or defending it against, opponents, though not sufficient to outweigh, is no trifling drawback from, the benefit of its universal recognition. Where this advantage can no longer be had, I confess I should like to see the teachers of mankind endeavoring to provide a substitute for it; some contrivance for making the difficulties of the question as present to the learner's consciousness, as if they were pressed upon him by a dissentient champion, eager for his conversion.

But instead of seeking contrivances for this purpose, they have lost those they formerly had. The Socratic dialectics, so magnificently exemplified in the dialogues of Plato, were a contrivance of this description. They were essentially a negative discussion of the great questions of philosophy and life, directed with consummate skill to the purpose of convincing any one who had merely adopted the commonplaces of received opinion, that he did not understand the subject—that he as yet attached no definite meaning to the doctrines he professed; in order that, becoming aware of his ignorance, he might be put in the way to attain a stable belief, resting on a clear apprehension both of the meaning of doctrines and of their evidence. The school disputations of the Middle Ages had a somewhat similar object. They were intended to make sure that the pupil understood his own opinion, and (by necessary correlation) the opinion opposed to it, and could enforce the grounds of the one and confute those of the other. These last-mentioned contests had indeed the incurable defect, that the premises appealed to were taken from authority, not from reason; and, as a discipline to the mind, they were in every respect inferior to the powerful dialectics which formed the intellects of the "Socratici viri": but the modern mind owes far more to both than it is generally willing to admit, and the present modes of education contain nothing which in the smallest degree supplies the place either of the one or of the other. A person who derives all his instruction from teachers or books, even if he escape the besetting temptation of contenting himself with cram, is under no compulsion to hear both sides; accordingly it is far from a frequent accomplishment, even among thinkers, to know both sides; and the weakest part of what everybody says in defense of his opinion, is what he intends as a reply to antagonists. It is the fashion of the present time to disparage negative logic—that which points out weaknesses in theory or errors in practice, without establishing positive truths. Such negative criticism would indeed be poor enough as an ultimate result; but as a means to attaining any positive knowledge or conviction worthy the name, it cannot be valued too highly; and until people are again systematically trained to it, there will be few great thinkers, and a low general average of intellect, in any but the mathematical and physical departments of speculation. On any other subject no one's opinions deserve the name of knowledge, except so far as he has either had forced upon him by others, or gone through of himself, the same mental process which would have been required of him in carrying on an active controversy with opponents. That, therefore, which when absent, it is so indispensable, but so difficult, to create, how worse than absurd is it to forego, when spontaneously offering itself! If there are any persons who contest a received opinion, or who will do so if law or opinion will let them, let us thank them for it, open our minds to listen to them, and rejoice that there is some one to do for us what we otherwise ought, if we have any regard for either the certainty or the vitality of our convictions, to do with much greater labor for ourselves.

It still remains to speak of one of the principal causes which make diversity of opinion advantageous, and will continue to do so until mankind shall have entered a stage of intellectual advancement which at present seems at an incalculable distance. We have hitherto considered only two possibilities: that the received opinion may be false, and some other opinion, consequently, true; or that, the received opinion being true, a conflict with the opposite error is essential to a clear apprehension and deep feeling of its truth. But there is a commoner case than either of these; when the conflicting doctrines, instead of being one true and the other false, share the truth between them; and the nonconforming opinion is needed to supply the remainder of the truth, of which the received doctrine embodies only a part. Popular opinions, on subjects not palpable to sense, are often true, but seldom or never the whole truth. They are a part of the truth; sometimes a greater, sometimes a smaller part, but exaggerated, distorted, and disjoined from the truths by which they ought to be accompanied and limited. Heretical opinions, on the other hand, are generally some of these suppressed and neglected truths, bursting the bonds which kept them down, and either seeking reconciliation with the truth contained in the common opinion, or fronting it as enemies, and setting themselves up, with similar exclusiveness, as the whole truth. The latter case is hitherto the most frequent, as, in the human mind, one-sidedness has always been the rule, and many-sidedness the exception. Hence, even in revolutions of opinion, one part of the truth usually sets while another rises. Even progress, which ought to superadd, for the most part only substitutes one partial and incomplete truth for another; improvement consisting chiefly in this, that the new fragment of truth is more wanted, more adapted to the needs of the time, than that which it displaces. Such being the partial character of prevailing opinions, even when resting on a true foundation, every opinion which embodies somewhat of the portion of truth which the common opinion omits, ought to be considered precious, with whatever amount of error and confusion that truth may be blended. No sober judge of human affairs will feel bound to be indignant because those who force on our notice truths which we should otherwise have overlooked, overlook some of those which we see. Rather, he will think that so long as popular truth is one-sided, it is more desirable than otherwise that unpopular truth should have one-sided asserters too; such being usually the most energetic, and the most likely to compel reluctant attention to the fragment of wisdom which they proclaim as if it were the whole.

45   Thus, in the eighteenth century, when nearly all the instructed,   45 and all those of the uninstructed who were led by them, were lost in admiration of what is called civilization, and of the marvels of modern science, literature, and philosophy, and while greatly overrating the amount of unlikeness between the men of modern and those of ancient times, indulged the belief that the whole of the difference was in their own favor; with what a salutary shock did the paradoxes of Rousseau explode like bombshells in the midst, dislocating the compact mass of one-sided opinion, and forcing its elements to recombine in a better form and with additional ingredients. Not that the current opinions were on the whole farther from the truth than Rousseau's were; on the contrary, they were nearer to it; they contained more of positive truth, and very much less of error. Nevertheless there lay in Rousseau's doctrine, and has floated down the stream of opinion along with it, a considerable amount of exactly those truths which the popular opinion wanted; and these are the deposit which was left behind when the flood subsided. The superior worth of simplicity of life, the enervating and demoralizing effect of the trammels and hypocrisies of artificial society, are ideas which have never been entirely absent from cultivated minds since Rousseau wrote; and they will in time produce their due effect, though at present needing to be asserted as much as ever, and to be asserted by deeds, for words, on this subject, have nearly exhausted their power.

In politics, again, it is almost a commonplace, that a party of order or stability, and a party of progress or reform, are both necessary elements of a healthy state of political life; until the one or the other shall have so enlarged its mental grasp as to be a party equally of order and of progress, knowing and distinguishing what is fit to be preserved from what ought to be swept away. Each of these modes of thinking derives its utility from the deficiencies of the other; but it is in a great measure the opposition of the other that keeps each within the limits of reason and sanity. Unless opinions favorable to democracy and to aristocracy, to property and to equality, to co-operation and to competition, to luxury and to abstinence, to sociality and individuality, to liberty and discipline, and all the other standing antagonisms of practical life, are expressed with equal freedom, and enforced and defended with equal talent and energy, there is no chance of both elements obtaining their due; one scale is sure to go up, and the other down. Truth, in the great practical concerns of life, is so much a question of the reconciling and combining of opposites, that very few have minds sufficiently capacious and impartial to make the adjustment with an approach to correctness, and it has to be made by the rough process of a struggle between combatants fighting under hostile banners. On any of the great open questions just enumerated, if either of the two opinions has a better claim than the other, not merely to be tolerated, but to be encouraged and countenanced, it is the one which happens at the particular time and place to be in a minority. That is the opinion which, for the time being, represents the neglected interests, the side of human well-being which is in danger of obtaining less than its share. I am aware that there is not, in this country, any intolerance of differences of opinion on most of these topics. They are adduced to show, by admitted and multiplied examples, the universality of the fact, that only through diversity of opinion is there, in the existing state of human intellect, a chance of fair play to all sides of the truth. When there are persons to be found, who form an exception to the apparent unanimity of the world on any subject, even if the world is in the right, it is always probable that dissentients have something worth hearing to say for themselves, and that truth would lose something by their silence.

It may be objected, "But *some* received principles, especially on the highest and most vital subjects, are more than half-truths. The Christian morality, for instance, is the whole truth on that subject, and if any one teaches a morality which varies from it, he is wholly in error." As this is of all cases the most important in practice, none can be fitter to test the general maxim. But before pronouncing what Christian morality is or is not, it would be desirable to decide what is meant by Christian morality. If it means the morality of the New Testament, I wonder that any one who derives his knowledge of this from the book itself, can suppose that it was announced, or intended, as a complete doctrine of morals. The Gospel always refers to a preexisting morality, and confines its precepts to the particulars in which that morality was to be corrected, or superseded by a wider and higher; expressing itself, moreover, in terms most general, often impossible to be interpreted literally, and possessing rather the impressiveness of poetry or eloquence than the precision of legislation.

To extract from it a body of ethical doctrine, has never been possible without eking it out from the Old Testament, that is, from a system elaborate indeed, but in many respects barbarous, and intended only for a barbarous people. St. Paul, a declared enemy to this Judaical mode of interpreting the doctrine and filling up the scheme of his Master, equally assumes a preexisting morality, namely, that of the Greeks and Romans; and his advice to Christians is in a great measure a system of accommodation to that even to the extent of giving an apparent sanction to slavery. What is called Christian, but should rather be termed theological, morality, was not the work of Christ or the Apostles, but is of much later origin, having been gradually built up by the Catholic Church of the first five centuries, and though not implicitly adopted by moderns and Protestants, has been much less modified by them than might have been expected. For the most part, indeed, they have contented themselves with cutting off the additions which had been made to it in the Middle Ages, each sect supplying the place by fresh additions, adapted to its own character and tendencies. That mankind owe a great debt to this morality, and to its early teachers, I should be the last person to deny; but I do not scruple to say of it, that it is, in many important points, incomplete and one-sided, and that unless ideas and feelings, not sanctioned by it, had contributed to the formation of European life and character, human affairs would have been in a worse condition than they now are. Christian morality (so called) has all the characters of a reaction; it is, in great part, a protest against Paganism. Its ideal is negative rather than positive; passive rather than active; Innocence rather than Nobleness; Abstinence from Evil, rather than energetic Pursuit of Good: in its precepts (as has been well said) "thou shalt not" predominates unduly over "thou shalt." In its horror of sensuality, it made an idol of asceticism, which has been gradually compromised away into one of legality. It holds out the hope of heaven and the threat of hell, as the appointed and appropriate motives to a virtuous life: in this falling far below the best of the ancients, and doing what lies in it to give to human morality an essentially selfish character, by disconnecting each man's feelings of duty from the interests of his fellow-creatures, except so far as a self-interested inducement is offered to him for consulting them. It is essentially a doctrine of passive obedience; it inculcates submission to all authorities found established; who indeed are not to be actively obeyed when they command what religion forbids, but who are not to be resisted, far less rebelled against, for any amount of wrong to ourselves. And while, in the morality of the best Pagan nations, duty to the State holds even a disproportionate place, infringing on the just liberty of the individual; in purely Christian ethics that grand department of duty is scarcely noticed or acknowledged. It is in the Koran, not the New Testament, that we read the maxim—"A ruler who appoints any man to an office, when there is in his dominions another man better qualified for it, sins against God and against the State." What little recognition the idea of obligation to the public obtains in modern morality, is derived from Greek and Roman sources, not from Christian; as, even in the morality of private life, whatever exists of magnanimity, high-mindedness, personal dignity, even the sense of honor, is derived from the purely human, not the religious part of our education, and never could have grown out of a standard of ethics in which the only worth, professedly recognized, is that of obedience.

I am as far as any one from pretending that these defects are necessarily inherent in the Christian ethics, in every manner in which it can be conceived, or that the many requisites of a complete moral doctrine which it does not contain, do not admit of being reconciled with it. Far less would I insinuate this of the doctrines and precepts of Christ himself. I believe that the sayings of Christ are all, that I can see any evidence of their having been intended to be; that they are irreconcilable with nothing which a comprehensive morality requires; that everything which is excellent in ethics may be brought within them, with no greater violence to their language than has been done to it by all who have attempted to deduce from them any practical system of conduct whatever. But it is quite consistent with this, to believe that they contain and were meant to contain, only a part of the truth; that many essential elements of the highest morality are among the things which are not provided for, nor intended to be provided for, in the recorded deliverances of the Founder of Christianity, and which have been entirely thrown aside in the system of ethics erected on the basis of those deliverances by the Christian Church. And this being so, I think it a great error to persist in attempting to find in the Christian doctrine that complete rule for our guidance, which its author intended it to sanction and enforce, but only partially to provide. I believe, too, that this narrow theory is becoming a grave practical evil, detracting greatly from the value of the moral training and instruction, which so many well-meaning persons are now at length exerting themselves to promote. I much fear that by attempting to form the mind and feelings on an exclusively religious type, and discarding those secular standards (as for want of a better name they may be called) which heretofore coexisted with and supplemented the Christian ethics, receiving some of its spirit, and infusing into it some of theirs, there will result, and is even now resulting, a low, abject, servile type of character, which, submit itself as it may to what it deems the Supreme Will, is incapable of rising to or sympathizing in the conception of Supreme Goodness. I believe that other ethics than any one which can be evolved from exclusively Christian sources, must exist side by side with Christian ethics to produce the moral regeneration of mankind; and that the Christian system is no exception to the rule that in an imperfect state of the human mind, the interests of truth require a diversity of opinions. It is not necessary that in ceasing to ignore the moral truths not contained in Christianity, men should ignore any of those which it does contain. Such prejudice, or oversight, when it occurs, is altogether an evil; but it is one from which we cannot hope to be always exempt, and must be regarded as the price paid for an inestimable good. The exclusive pretension made by a part of the truth to be the whole, must and ought to be protested against, and if a reactionary impulse should make the protestors unjust in their turn, this one-sidedness, like the other, may be lamented, but must be tolerated. If Christians would teach infidels to be just to Christianity, they should themselves be just to infidelity. It can do truth no service to blink the fact, known to all who have the most ordinary acquaintance with literary history, that a large portion of the noblest and most valuable moral teaching has been the work, not only of men who did not know, but of men who knew and rejected, the Christian faith.

I do not pretend that the most unlimited use of the freedom of enunciating all possible opinions would put an end to the evils of religious or philosophical sectarianism. Every truth which men of narrow capacity are in earnest about, is sure to be asserted, inculcated, and in many ways even acted on, as if no other truth existed in the world, or at all events none that could limit or qualify the first. I acknowledge that the tendency of all opinions to become sectarian is not cured by the freest discussion, but is often heightened and exacerbated thereby; the truth which ought to have been, but was not, seen, being rejected all the more violently because proclaimed by persons regarded as opponents. But it is not on the impassioned partisan, it is on the calmer and more disinterested bystander, that this collision of opinions works its salutary effect. Not the violent conflict between parts of the truth, but the quiet suppression of half of it, is the formidable evil; there is always hope when people are forced to listen to both sides; it is when they attend only to one that errors harden into prejudices, and truth itself ceases to have the effect of truth, by being exaggerated into falsehood. And since there are few mental attributes more rare than that judicial faculty which can sit in intelligent judgment between two sides of a question, of which only one is represented by an advocate before it, truth has no chance but in proportion as every side of it, every opinion which embodies any fraction of the truth, not only finds advocates, but is so advocated as to be listened to.

50   We have now recognized the necessity to the mental well-being of 50 mankind (on which all their other well-being depends) of freedom of opinion, and freedom of the expression of opinion, on four distinct grounds, which we will now briefly recapitulate.

First, if any opinion is compelled to silence, that opinion may, for aught we can certainly know, be true. To deny this is to assume our own infallibility.

Secondly, though the silenced opinion be an error, it may, and very commonly does, contain a portion of truth; and since the general or prevailing opinion on any object is rarely or never the whole truth, it is only by the collision of adverse opinions that the remainder of the truth has any chance of being supplied.

Thirdly, even if the received opinion be not only true, but the whole truth, unless it is suffered to be, and actually is, vigorously and earnestly contested, it will, by most of those who receive it, be held in the manner of a prejudice, with little comprehension or feeling of its rational grounds. And not only this, but, fourthly, the meaning of the doctrine itself will be in danger of being lost, or enfeebled, and deprived of its vital effect on the character and conduct: the dogma becoming a mere formal profession, inefficacious for good, but cumbering the ground, and preventing the growth of any real and heartfelt conviction, from reason or personal experience.

Questions

1. Is liberty valuable mostly for achieving goals such as peace, individual fulfillment, and wealth, or is liberty a legitimate end in itself?
2. To what extent does open and free expression of ideas guarantee that the truth will emerge in any particular situation?
3. Would Mill agree with highway speed limits?

Letter from Birmingham Jail

Martin Luther King, Jr.

Martin Luther King, Jr. (1929–1968) was born in Atlanta, Georgia. The son and grandson of Baptist ministers, he attended Moorhouse College, Crozer Theological Seminary, and Boston University where he received a Ph.D. (1955) and met his future wife, Coretta Scott. King's active involvement in the civil rights movement began in 1955, when he led a boycott of segregated buses in Montgomery, Alabama. From the mid 1950s until he was shot and killed in Memphis, Tennessee, while supporting striking city workers, King organized boycotts, sit-ins, mass demonstrations, and other protest activities. As a black civil rights leader, King was arrested, jailed, stoned, stabbed, and beaten; his house was bombed; he was placed under secret surveillance by Federal Bureau of Investigation (FBI) director J. Edgar Hoover; and in 1966 he was awarded the Nobel Peace Prize. Through his leadership—always underscored by his nonviolent beliefs—King's name has become synonymous with the watersheds of the civil rights movement in the United States: Rosa Parks; the Southern Christian Leadership Conference (which King founded); Selma, Alabama; the Civil Rights Act; the Voting Rights Act; and the 1963 civil rights march on Washington, D. C. His published works include Strength to Love *(1963) and* Conscience for Change *(1967). This essay—published in a revised form in* Why We Can't Wait *(1964)—is King's stern response to eight clergymen from Alabama who were asking civil rights activists to give up public demonstrations in Birmingham, Alabama, and*

412

turn to the courts. Read the clergymen's public statement first, then King's detailed rebuttal (printed here as it appeared originally). Keep in mind that King wrote these words four months before he delivered his famous "I Have a Dream" speech during the August 1963 civil rights march on Washington; after long years of activism, he was clearly impatient with the slow progress of the civil rights movement.

Public Statement by Eight Alabama Clergymen

(April 12, 1963)

1   We the undersigned clergymen are among those who, in January, issued "An Appeal for Law and Order and Common Sense," in dealing with racial problems in Alabama. We expressed understanding that honest convictions in racial matters could properly be pursued in the courts, but urged that decisions of those courts should in the meantime be peacefully obeyed.

Since that time there had been some evidence of increased forbearance and a willingness to face facts. Responsible citizens have undertaken to work on various problems which cause racial friction and unrest. In Birmingham, recent public events have given indication that we all have opportunity for a new constructive and realistic approach to racial problems.

However, we are now confronted by a series of demonstrations by some of our Negro citizens, directed and led in part by outsiders. We recognize the natural impatience of people who feel that their hopes are slow in being realized. But we are convinced that these demonstrations are unwise and untimely.

We agree rather with certain local Negro leadership which has called for honest and open negotiation of racial issues in our area. And we believe this kind of facing of issues can best be accomplished by citizens of our own metropolitan area, white and Negro, meeting with their knowledge and experience of the local situation. All of us need to face that responsibility and find proper channels for its accomplishment.

5   Just as we formerly pointed out that "hatred and violence have no   5
sanction in our religious and political traditions," we also point out
that such actions as incite to hatred and violence, however technically
peaceful those actions may be, have not contributed to the resolution
of our local problems. We do not believe that these days of new hope
are days when extreme measures are justified in Birmingham.

We commend the community as a whole, and the local news
media and law enforcement officials in particular, on the calm manner in which these demonstrations have been handled. We urge the
public to continue to show restraint should the demonstrations continue, and the law enforcement officials to remain calm and continue
to protect our city from violence.

We further strongly urge our own Negro community to withdraw
support from these demonstrations, and to unite locally in working
peacefully for a better Birmingham. When rights are consistently denied, a cause should be pressed in the courts and in negotiations
among local leaders, and not in the streets. We appeal to both our
white and Negro citizenry to observe the principles of law and order
and common sense.

Signed by:

C.C. J. CARPENTER, D.D., LL.D., *Bishop of Alabama*
JOSEPH A. DURICK, D.D., *Auxiliary Bishop, Diocese of
    Mobile, Birmingham*
RABBI MILTON L. GRAFMAN, *Temple Emanu-El,
    Birmingham, Alabama*
BISHOP PAUL HARDIN, *Bishop of the Alabama-West Florida
    Conference of the Methodist Church*
BISHOP NOLAN B. HARMON, *Bishop of the North Alabama
    Conference of the Methodist Church*
GEORGE M. MURRAY, D.D., LL.D., *Bishop Coadjutor,
    Episcopal Diocese of Alabama*
EDWARD V. RAMAGE, *Moderator, Synod of the Alabama
    Presbyterian Church in the United States*
EARL STALLINGS, *Pastor, First Baptist Church, Birmingham,
    Alabama*

Letter from Birmingham Jail

MARTIN LUTHER KING, JR.
Birmingham City Jail
April 16, 1963

Bishop C. C. J. Carpenter
Bishop Joseph A. Durick
Rabbi Milton L. Grafman
Bishop Paul Hardin
Bishop Nolan B. Harmon
The Rev. George M. Murray
The Rev. Edward V. Ramage
The Rev. Earl Stallings

My dear Fellow Clergymen,

While confined here in the Birmingham City Jail, I came across your recent statement calling our present activities "unwise and untimely." Seldom, if ever, do I pause to answer criticism of my work and ideas. If I sought to answer all of the criticisms that cross my desk, my secretaries would be engaged in little else in the course of the day and I would have no time for constructive work. But since I feel that you are men of genuine good will and your criticisms are sincerely set forth, I would like to answer your statement in what I hope will be patient and reasonable terms.

I think I should give the reason for my being in Birmingham, since you have been influenced by the argument of "outsiders coming in." I have the honor of serving as president of the Southern Christian Leadership Conference, an organization operating in every Southern state with headquarters in Atlanta, Georgia. We have some eighty-five affiliate organizations all across the South—one being the Alabama Christian Movement for Human Rights. Whenever necessary and possible we share staff, educational, and financial resources with our affiliates. Several months ago our local affiliate here in Birmingham invited us to be on call to engage in a nonviolent direct action program if such were deemed necessary. We readily consented, and when the hour came we lived up to our promises. So I, along with several members of my staff, am here, because I was invited here. I am here because I have basic organizational ties here.

10   But more basically, I am in Birmingham because injustice is here.   10 Just as the eighth century prophets left their little villages and carried their "thus saith the Lord" far beyond the boundaries of their home town, and just as the Apostle Paul left his little village of Tarsus and carried the gospel of Jesus Christ to practically every hamlet and city of the Greco-Roman world, I too am compelled to carry the gospel of freedom beyond my particular home town. Like Paul, I must constantly respond to the Macedonian call for aid.

Moreover, I am cognizant of the interrelatedness of all communities and states. I cannot sit idly by in Atlanta and not be concerned about what happens in Birmingham. Injustice anywhere is a threat to justice everywhere. We are caught in an inescapable network of mutuality, tied in a single garment of destiny. Whatever affects one directly affects all indirectly. Never again can we afford to live with the narrow, provincial "outside agitator" idea. Anyone who lives inside the United States can never be considered an outsider anywhere in this country.

You deplore the demonstrations that are presently taking place in Birmingham. But I am sorry that your statement did not express a similar concern for the conditions that brought the demonstrations into being. I am sure that each of you would want to go beyond the superficial social analyst who looks merely at effects, and does not grapple with underlying causes. I would not hesitate to say that it is unfortunate that so-called demonstrations are taking place in Birmingham at this time, but I would say in more emphatic terms that it is even more unfortunate that the white power structure of this city left the Negro community with no other alternative.

In any nonviolent campaign there are four basic steps: (1) collection of the facts to determine whether injustices are alive; (2) negotiation; (3) self-purification; and (4) direct action. We have gone through all of these steps in Birmingham. There can be no gainsaying of the fact that racial injustice engulfs this community. Birmingham is probably the most thoroughly segregated city in the United States. Its ugly record of police brutality is known in every section of this country. Its unjust treatment of Negroes in the courts is a notorious reality. There have been more unsolved bombings of Negro homes and churches in Birmingham than any city in this nation. These are the hard, brutal, and unbelievable facts. On the basis of these conditions, Negro leaders sought to negotiate with the city fathers. But the political leaders consistently refused to engage in good faith negotiation.

Then came the opportunity last September to talk with some of the leaders of the economic community. In these negotiating sessions certain promises were made by the merchants—such as the promise to remove the humiliating racial signs from the stores. On the basis of these promises Rev. Shuttlesworth and the leaders of the Alabama Christian Movement for Human Rights agreed to call a moratorium on any type of demonstrations. As the weeks and months unfolded we realized that we were the victims of a broken promise. The signs remained. As in so many experiences of the past we were confronted with blasted hopes, and the dark shadow of a deep disappointment settled upon us. So we had no alternative except that of preparing for direct action, whereby we would present our very bodies as a means of laying our case before the conscience of the local and national community. We were not unmindful of the difficulties involved. So we decided to go through a process of self-purification. We started having workshops on nonviolence and repeatedly asked ourselves the questions, "Are you able to accept blows without retaliating?" "Are you able to endure the ordeals of jail?"

15 We decided to set our direct action program around the Easter season, realizing that with the exception of Christmas, this was the largest shopping period of the year. Knowing that a strong economic withdrawal program would be the by-product of direct action, we felt that this was the best time to bring pressure on the merchants for the needed changes. Then it occurred to us that the March election was ahead, and so we speedily decided to postpone action until after election day. When we discovered that Mr. Connor was in the run-off, we decided again to postpone so that the demonstrations could not be used to cloud the issues. At this time we agreed to begin our nonviolent witness the day after the run-off.

This reveals that we did not move irresponsibly into direct action. We too wanted to see Mr. Connor defeated; so we went through postponement after postponement to aid in this community need. After this we felt that direct action could be delayed no longer.

You may well ask, "Why direct action? Why sit-ins, marches, etc.? Isn't negotiation a better path?" You are exactly right in your call for negotiation. Indeed, this is the purpose of direct action. Nonviolent direct action seeks to create such a crisis and establish such creative tension that a community that has constantly refused to negotiate is forced to confront the issue. It seeks so to dramatize the issue that it can no longer be ignored. I just referred to the creation of tension as a part of the work of the nonviolent resister. This may sound rather shocking. But I must confess that I am not afraid of the word tension. I have earnestly worked and preached against violent tension, but there is a type of constructive nonviolent tension that is necessary for growth. Just as Socrates felt that it was necessary to create a tension in the mind so that individuals could rise from the bondage of myths and half-truths to the unfettered realm of creative analysis and objective appraisal, we must see the need of having nonviolent gadflies to create the kind of tension in society that will help men rise from the dark depths of prejudice and racism to the majestic heights of understanding and brotherhood. So the purpose of the direct action is to create a situation so crisis-packed that it will inevitably open the door to negotiation. We, therefore, concur with you in your call for negotiation. Too long has our beloved Southland been bogged down in the tragic attempt to live in monologue rather than dialogue.

One of the basic points in your statement is that our acts are untimely. Some have asked, "Why didn't you give the new administration time to act?" The only answer that I can give to this inquiry is that the new administration must be prodded about as much as the outgoing one before it acts. We will be sadly mistaken if we feel that the election of Mr. Boutwell will bring the millennium to Birmingham. While Mr. Boutwell is much more articulate and gentle than Mr. Connor, they are both segregationists dedicated to the task of maintaining the status quo. The hope I see in Mr. Boutwell is that he will be reasonable enough to see the futility of massive resistance to desegregation. But he will not see this without pressure from the devotees of civil rights. My friends, I must say to you that we have not made a single gain in civil rights without determined legal and nonviolent pressure. History is the long and tragic story of the fact that privileged groups seldom give up their privileges voluntarily. Individuals may see the moral light and voluntarily give up their unjust posture; but as Reinhold Niebuhr has reminded us, groups are more immoral than individuals.

We know through painful experience that freedom is never voluntarily given by the oppressor; it must be demanded by the oppressed. Frankly I have never yet engaged in a direct action movement that was

He speaks from experiences

Ability to bring the reader to feel **empathy**

The fact that he's writing in jail

"well timed," according to the timetable of those who have not suffered unduly from the disease of segregation. For years now I have heard the word "Wait!" It rings in the ear of every Negro with a piercing familiarity. This "wait" has almost always meant "never." It has been a tranquilizing thalidomide, relieving the emotional stress for a moment, only to give birth to an ill-formed infant of frustration. We must come to see with the distinguished jurist of yesterday that "justice too long delayed is justice denied." We have waited for more than three hundred and forty years for our constitutional and God-given rights. The nations of Asia and Africa are moving with jet-like speed toward the goal of political independence, and we still creep at horse and buggy pace toward the gaining of a cup of coffee at a lunch counter.

20   I guess it is easy for those who have never felt the stinging darts   20
of segregation to say wait. But when you have seen vicious mobs lynch your mothers and fathers at will and drown your sisters and brothers at whim; when you have seen hate filled policemen curse, kick, brutalize, and even kill your black brothers and sisters with impunity; when you see the vast majority of your twenty million Negro brothers smothering in an air-tight cage of poverty in the midst of an affluent society; when you suddenly find your tongue twisted and your speech stammering as you seek to explain to your six-year-old daughter why she can't go to the public amusement park that has just been advertised on television, and see tears welling up in her little eyes when she is told that Funtown is closed to colored children, and see the depressing clouds of inferiority begin to form in her little mental sky, and see her begin to distort her little personality by unconsciously developing a bitterness toward white people; when you have to concoct an answer for a five-year-old son asking in agonizing pathos: "Daddy, why do white people treat colored people so mean?"; when you take a cross country drive and find it necessary to sleep night after night in the uncomfortable corners of your automobile because no motel will accept you; when you are humiliated day in and day out by nagging signs reading "white" and "colored"; when your first name becomes "nigger" and your middle name becomes "boy" (however old you are) and your last name becomes "John," and when your wife and mother are never given the respected title "Mrs."; when you are harried by day and haunted by night by the fact that you are a Negro, living constantly at tip-toe stance never quite knowing what to expect next, and plagued with inner fears and outer resentments; when you are forever

fighting a degenerating sense of "nobodiness";——then you will understand why we find it difficult to wait. There comes a time when the cup of endurance runs over, and men are no longer willing to be plunged into an abyss of injustice where they experience the bleakness of corroding despair. I hope, sirs, you can understand our legitimate and unavoidable impatience.

You express a great deal of anxiety over our willingness to break laws. This is certainly a legitimate concern. Since we so diligently urge people to obey the Supreme Court's decision of 1954 outlawing segregation in the public schools, it is rather strange and paradoxical to find us consciously breaking laws. One may well ask, "How can you advocate breaking some laws and obeying others?" The answer is found in the fact that there are two types of laws. There are *just* laws and there are *unjust* laws. I would be the first to advocate obeying just laws. One has not only a legal but moral responsibility to obey just laws. Conversely, one has a moral responsibility to disobey unjust laws. I would agree with Saint Augustine that "An unjust law is no law at all."

Now what is the difference between the two? How does one determine when a law is just or unjust? A just law is a man-made code that squares with the moral law or the law of God. An unjust law is a code that is out of harmony with the moral law. To put it in the terms of Saint Thomas Aquinas, an unjust law is a human law that is not rooted in eternal and natural law. Any law that uplifts human personality is just. Any law that degrades human personality is unjust. All segregation statutes are unjust because segregation distorts the soul and damages the personality. It gives the segregator a false sense of superiority and the segregated a false sense of inferiority. To use the words of Martin Buber, the great Jewish philosopher, segregation substitutes an "I-it" relationship for the "I-thou" relationship, and ends up relegating persons to the status of things. So segregation is not only politically, economically, and sociologically unsound, but it is morally wrong and sinful. Paul Tillich has said that sin is separation. Isn't segregation an existential expression of man's tragic separation, an expression of his awful estrangement, his terrible sinfulness? So I can urge men to obey the 1954 decision of the Supreme Court because it is morally right, and I can urge them to disobey segregation ordinances because they are morally wrong.

Let us turn to a more concrete example of just and unjust laws. An unjust law is a code that a majority inflicts on a minority that is not binding on itself. This is *difference* made legal. On the other hand a just law is a code that a majority compels a minority to follow that it is willing to follow itself. This is *sameness* made legal.

Let me give another explanation. An unjust law is a code inflicted upon a minority which that minority had no part in enacting or creating because they did not have the unhampered right to vote. Who can say the legislature of Alabama which set up the segregation laws was democratically elected? Throughout the state of Alabama all types of conniving methods are used to prevent Negroes from becoming registered voters and there are some counties without a single Negro registered to vote despite the fact that the Negro constitutes a majority of the population. Can any law set up in such a state be considered democratically structured?

25   These are just a few examples of unjust and just laws. There are   25
some instances when a law is just on its face but unjust in its application. For instance, I was arrested Friday on a charge of parading without a permit. Now there is nothing wrong with an ordinance which requires a permit for a parade, but when the ordinance is used to preserve segregation and to deny citizens the First Amendment privilege of peaceful assembly and peaceful protest, then it becomes unjust.

I hope you can see the distinction I am trying to point out. In no sense do I advocate evading or defying the law as the rabid segregationist would do. This would lead to anarchy. One who breaks an unjust law must do it *openly, lovingly* (not hatefully as the white mothers did in New Orleans when they were seen on television screaming "nigger, nigger, nigger") and with a willingness to accept the penalty. I submit that an individual who breaks a law that conscience tells him is unjust, and willingly accepts the penalty by staying in jail to arouse the conscience of the community over its injustice, is in reality expressing the very highest respect for law.

Of course there is nothing new about this kind of civil disobedience. It was seen sublimely in the refusal of Shadrach, Meshach, and Abednego to obey the laws of Nebuchadnezzar because a higher moral law was involved. It was practiced superbly by the early Christians who were willing to face hungry lions and the excruciating pain of chopping blocks, before submitting to certain unjust laws of the Roman Empire. To a degree academic freedom is a reality today because Socrates practiced civil disobedience.

We can never forget that everything Hitler did in Germany was "legal" and everything the Hungarian freedom fighters did in Hungary was "illegal." It was "illegal" to aid and comfort a Jew in Hitler's Germany. But I am sure that, if I had lived in Germany during that time, I would have aided and comforted my Jewish brothers even though it was illegal. If I lived in a communist country today where certain principles dear to the Christian faith are suppressed, I believe I would openly advocate disobeying those antireligious laws.

I must make two honest confessions to you, my Christian and Jewish brothers. First I must confess that over the last few years I have been gravely disappointed with the white moderate. I have almost reached the regrettable conclusion that the Negroes' great stumbling block in the stride toward freedom is not the White Citizens' "Counciler" or the Ku Klux Klanner, but the white moderate who is more devoted to "order" than to justice; who prefers a negative peace which is the absence of tension to a positive peace which is the presence of justice; who constantly says "I agree with you in the goal you seek, but I can't agree with your methods of direct action;" who paternalistically feels that he can set the timetable for another man's freedom; who lives by the myth of time and who constantly advises the Negro to wait until a "more convenient season." Shallow understanding from people of good will is more frustrating than absolute misunderstanding from people of ill will. Lukewarm acceptance is much more bewildering than outright rejection.

30   I had hoped that the white moderate would understand that law 30 and order exist for the purpose of establishing justice, and that when they fail to do this they become the dangerously structured dams that block the flow of social progress. I had hoped that the white moderate would understand that the present tension in the South is merely a necessary phase of the transition from an obnoxious negative peace, where the Negro passively accepted his unjust plight, to a substance-filled positive peace, where all men will respect the dignity and worth of human personality. Actually, we who engage in nonviolent direct action are not the creators of tension. We merely bring to the surface the hidden tension that is already alive. We bring it out in the open where it can be seen and dealt with. Like a boil that can never be cured as long as it is covered up but must be opened with all its pus-flowing ugliness to the natural medicines of air and light, injustice must likewise be exposed, with all of the tension its exposing creates, to the light

of human conscience and the air of national opinion before it can be cured.

In your statement you asserted that our actions, even though peaceful, must be condemned because they precipitate violence. But can this assertion be logically made? Isn't this like condemning the robbed man because his possession of money precipitated the evil act of robbery? Isn't this like condemning Socrates because his unswerving commitment to truth and his philosophical delvings precipitated the misguided popular mind to make him drink the hemlock? Isn't this like condemning Jesus because His unique God consciousness and never-ceasing devotion to His will precipitated the evil act of crucifixion? We must come to see, as federal courts have consistently affirmed, that it is immoral to urge an individual to withdraw his efforts to gain his basic constitutional rights because the quest precipitates violence. Society must protect the robbed and punish the robber.

I had also hoped that the white moderate would reject the myth of time. I received a letter this morning from a white brother in Texas which said: "All Christians know that the colored people will receive equal rights eventually, but is it possible that you are in too great of a religious hurry? It has taken Christianity almost 2,000 years to accomplish what it has. The teachings of Christ take time to come to earth." All that is said here grows out of a tragic misconception of time. It is the strangely irrational notion that there is something in the very flow of time that will inevitably cure all ills. Actually time is neutral. It can be used either destructively or constructively. I am coming to feel that the people of ill will have used time much more effectively than the people of good will. We will have to repent in this generation not merely for the vitriolic words and actions of the bad people, but for the appalling silence of the good people. We must come to see that human progress never rolls in on wheels of inevitability. It comes through the tireless efforts and persistent work of men willing to be co-workers with God, and without this hard work time itself becomes an ally of the forces of social stagnation.

We must use time creatively, and forever realize that the time is always ripe to do right. Now is the time to make real the promise of democracy, and transform our pending national elegy into a creative psalm of brotherhood. Now is the time to lift our national policy from the quicksand of racial injustice to the solid rock of human dignity.

You spoke of our activity in Birmingham as extreme. At first I was rather disappointed that fellow clergymen would see my nonviolent efforts as those of the extremist. I started thinking about the fact that I stand in the middle of two opposing forces in the Negro community. One is a force of complacency made up of Negroes who, as a result of long years of oppression, have been so completely drained of self-respect and a sense of "somebodiness" that they have adjusted to segregation, and of a few Negroes in the middle class who, because of a degree of academic and economic security, and because at points they profit by segregation, have unconsciously become insensitive to the problems of the masses. The other force is one of bitterness and hatred and comes perilously close to advocating violence. It is expressed in the various black nationalist groups that are springing up over the nation, the largest and best known being Elijah Muhammad's Muslim movement. This movement is nourished by the contemporary frustration over the continued existence of racial discrimination. It is made up of people who have lost faith in America, who have absolutely repudiated Christianity, and who have concluded that the white man is an incurable "devil." I have tried to stand between these two forces saying that we need not follow the "do-nothingism" of the complacent or the hatred and despair of the black nationalist. There is the more excellent way of love and nonviolent protest. I'm grateful to God that, through the Negro church, the dimension of nonviolence entered our struggle. If this philosophy had not emerged I am convinced that by now many streets of the South would be flowing with floods of blood. And I am further convinced that if our white brothers dismiss us as "rabble rousers" and "outside agitators"—those of us who are working through the channels of nonviolent direct action—and refuse to support our nonviolent efforts, millions of Negroes, out of frustration and despair, will seek solace and security in black nationalist ideologies, a development that will lead inevitably to a frightening racial nightmare.

35   Oppressed people cannot remain oppressed forever. The urge for   35
freedom will eventually come. This is what has happened to the American Negro. Something within has reminded him of his birthright of freedom; something without has reminded him that he can gain it. Consciously and unconsciously, he has been swept in by what the Germans call the *Zeitgeist*, and with his black brothers of Africa, and his brown and yellow brothers of Asia, South America, and the

Caribbean, he is moving with a sense of cosmic urgency toward the promised land of racial justice. Recognizing this vital urge that has engulfed the Negro community, one should readily understand public demonstrations. The Negro has many pent-up resentments and latent frustrations. He has to get them out. So let him march sometime; let him have his prayer pilgrimages to the city hall; understand why he must have sit-ins and freedom rides. If his repressed emotions do not come out in these nonviolent ways, they will come out in ominous expressions of violence. This is not a threat; it is a fact of history. So I have not said to my people, "Get rid of your discontent." But I have tried to say that this normal and healthy discontent can be channeled through the creative outlet of nonviolent direct action. Now this approach is being dismissed as extremist. I must admit that I was initially disappointed in being so categorized.

But as I continued to think about the matter I gradually gained a bit of satisfaction from being considered an extremist. Was not Jesus an extremist in love? "Love your enemies, bless them that curse you, pray for them that despitefully use you." Was not Amos an extremist for justice— "Let justice roll down like waters and righteousness like a mighty stream." Was not Paul an extremist for the gospel of Jesus Christ— "I bear in my body the marks of the Lord Jesus." Was not Martin Luther an extremist— "Here I stand; I can do none other so help me God." Was not John Bunyan an extremist— "I will stay in jail to the end of my days before I make a butchery of my conscience." Was not Abraham Lincoln an extremist— "This nation cannot survive half slave and half free." Was not Thomas Jefferson an extremist— "We hold these truths to be self evident that all men are created equal." So the question is not whether we will be extremist but what kind of extremist will we be. Will we be extremists for hate or will we be extremists for love? Will we be extremists for the preservation of injustice or will we be extremists for the cause of justice? In that dramatic scene on Calvary's hill three men were crucified. We must never forget that all three were crucified for the same crime—the crime of extremism. Two were extremists for immorality, and thus fell below their environment. The other, Jesus Christ, was an extremist for love, truth, and goodness, and thereby rose above His environment. So, after all, maybe the South, the nation, and the world are in dire need of creative extremists.

I had hoped that the white moderate would see this. Maybe I was too optimistic. Maybe I expected too much. I guess I should have realized that few members of a race that has oppressed another race can understand or appreciate the deep groans and passionate yearnings of those that have been oppressed, and still fewer have the vision to see that injustice must be rooted out by strong, persistent, and determined action. I am thankful, however, that some of our white brothers have grasped the meaning of this social revolution and committed themselves to it. They are still all too small in quantity, but they are big in quality. Some like Ralph McGill, Lillian Smith, Harry Golden, and James Dabbs have written about our struggle in eloquent, prophetic, and understanding terms. Others have marched with us down nameless streets of the South. They have languished in filthy, roach-infested jails, suffering the abuse and brutality of angry policemen who see them as "dirty nigger lovers." They, unlike so many of their moderate brothers and sisters, have recognized the urgency of the moment and sensed the need for powerful "action" antidotes to combat the disease of segregation.

Let me rush on to mention my other disappointment. I have been so greatly disappointed with the white Church and its leadership. Of course there are some notable exceptions. I am not unmindful of the fact that each of you has taken some significant stands on this issue. I commend you, Rev. Stallings, for your Christian stand on this past Sunday, in welcoming Negroes to your worship service on a nonsegregated basis. I commend the Catholic leaders of this state for integrating Springhill College several years ago.

But despite these notable exceptions I must honestly reiterate that I have been disappointed with the Church. I do not say that as one of those negative critics who can always find something wrong with the Church. I say it as a minister of the gospel, who loves the Church; who was nurtured in its bosom; who has been sustained by its spiritual blessings and who will remain true to it as long as the cord of life shall lengthen.

40 I had the strange feeling when I was suddenly catapulted into the 40
leadership of the bus protest in Montgomery several years ago that we would have the support of the white Church. I felt that the white ministers, priests, and rabbis of the South would be some of our strongest allies. Instead, some have been outright opponents, refusing to understand the

freedom movement and misrepresenting its leaders; all too many others have been more cautious than courageous and have remained silent behind the anesthetizing security of stained glass windows.

In spite of my shattered dreams of the past, I came to Birmingham with the hope that the white religious leadership of the community would see the justice of our cause and, with deep moral concern, serve as the channel through which our just grievances could get to the power structure. I had hoped that each of you would understand. But again I have been disappointed.

I have heard numerous religious leaders of the South call upon their worshippers to comply with a desegregation decision because it is the law, but I have longed to hear white ministers say follow this decree because integration is morally right and the Negro is your brother. In the midst of blatant injustices inflicted upon the Negro, I have watched white churches stand on the sideline and merely mouth pious irrelevancies and sanctimonious trivialities. In the midst of a mighty struggle to rid our nation of racial and economic injustice, I have heard so many ministers say, "Those are social issues with which the Gospel has no real concern," and I have watched so many churches commit themselves to a completely otherworldly religion which made a strange distinction between body and soul, the sacred and the secular.

So here we are moving toward the exit of the twentieth century with a religious community largely adjusted to the status quo, standing as a tail light behind other community agencies rather than a headlight leading men to higher levels of justice.

I have travelled the length and breadth of Alabama, Mississippi, and all the other Southern states. On sweltering summer days and crisp autumn mornings I have looked at her beautiful churches with their spires pointing heavenward. I have beheld the impressive outlay of her massive religious education buildings. Over and over again I have found myself asking: "Who worships here? Who is their God? Where were their voices when the lips of Governor Barnett dripped with words of interposition and nullification? Where were they when Governor Wallace gave the clarion call for defiance and hatred? Where were their voices of support when tired, bruised, and weary Negro men and women decided to rise from the dark dungeons of complacency to the bright hills of creative protest?"

45 Yes, these questions are still in my mind. In deep disappointment, 45 I have wept over the laxity of the Church. But be assured that my tears

have been tears of love. There can be no deep disappointment where there is not deep love. Yes, I love the Church; I love her sacred walls. How could I do otherwise? I am in the rather unique position of being the son, the grandson, and the great grandson of preachers. Yes, I see the Church as the body of Christ. But, oh! How we have blemished and scarred that body through social neglect and fear of being non-conformists.

There was a time when the Church was very powerful. It was during that period when the early Christians rejoiced when they were deemed worthy to suffer for what they believed. In those days the Church was not merely a thermometer that recorded the ideas and principles of popular opinion; it was a thermostat that transformed the mores of society. Wherever the early Christians entered a town the power structure got disturbed and immediately sought to convict them for being "disturbers of the peace" and "outside agitators." But they went on with the conviction that they were a "colony of heaven" and had to obey God rather than man. They were small in number but big in commitment. They were too God-intoxicated to be "astronomically intimidated." They brought an end to such ancient evils as infanticide and gladiatorial contest.

Things are different now. The contemporary Church is so often a weak, ineffectual voice with an uncertain sound. It is so often the arch-supporter of the status quo. Far from being disturbed by the presence of the Church, the power structure of the average community is consoled by the Church's silent and often vocal sanction of things as they are.

But the judgment of God is upon the Church as never before. If the Church of today does not recapture the sacrificial spirit of the early Church, it will lose its authentic ring, forfeit the loyalty of millions, and be dismissed as an irrelevant social club with no meaning for the twentieth century. I am meeting young people every day whose disappointment with the Church has risen to outright disgust.

Maybe again I have been too optimistic. Is organized religion too inextricably bound to the status quo to save our nation and the world? Maybe I must turn my faith to the inner spiritual Church, the church within the Church, as the true *ecclesia* and the hope of the world. But again I am thankful to God that some noble souls from the ranks of organized religion have broken loose from the paralyzing chains of conformity and joined us as active partners in the struggle for freedom. They have left their secure congregations and walked the streets of Albany, Georgia, with us. They have gone through the highways of the South on torturous rides for freedom. Yes, they have gone to jail with us. Some have been kicked out of their churches and lost the support of their bishops and fellow ministers. But they have gone with the faith that right defeated is stronger than evil triumphant. These men have been the leaven in the lump of the race. Their witness has been the spiritual salt that has preserved the true meaning of the Gospel in these troubled times. They have carved a tunnel of hope through the dark mountain of disappointment.

50   I hope the Church as a whole will meet the challenge of this decisive hour. But even if the Church does not come to the aid of justice, I have no despair about the future. I have no fear about the outcome of our struggle in Birmingham, even if our motives are presently misunderstood. We will reach the goal of freedom in Birmingham and all over the nation, because the goal of America is freedom. Abused and scorned though we may be, our destiny is tied up with the destiny of America. Before the pilgrims landed at Plymouth, we were here. Before the pen of Jefferson etched across the pages of history the majestic words of the Declaration of Independence, we were here. For more than two centuries our foreparents labored in this country without wages; they made cotton "king"; and they built the homes of their masters in the midst of brutal injustice and shameful humiliation—and yet out of a bottomless vitality they continued to thrive and develop. If the inexpressible cruelties of slavery could not stop us, the opposition we now face will surely fail. We will win our freedom because the sacred heritage of our nation and the eternal will of God are embodied in our echoing demands.

I must close now. But before closing I am impelled to mention one other point in your statement that troubled me profoundly. You warmly commended the Birmingham police force for keeping "order" and "preventing violence." I don't believe you would have so warmly commended the police force if you had seen its angry violent dogs literally biting six unarmed, nonviolent Negroes. I don't believe you would so quickly commend the policemen if you would observe their ugly and inhuman treatment of Negroes here in the city jail; if you would watch them push and curse old Negro women and young Negro girls; if you would see them slap and kick old Negro men and young Negro boys; if you will observe them, as they did on two occasions, refuse to give us food because we wanted to sing our grace together. I'm sorry that I can't join you in your praise for the police department.

It is true that they have been rather disciplined in their public handling of the demonstrators. In this sense they have been rather publicly "nonviolent." But for what purpose? To preserve the evil system of segregation. Over the last few years I have consistently preached that nonviolence demands that the means we use must be as pure as the ends we seek. So I have tried to make it clear that it is wrong to use immoral means to attain moral ends. But now I must affirm that it is just as wrong, or even more so, to use moral means to preserve immoral ends. Maybe Mr. Connor and his policemen have been rather publicly nonviolent, as Chief Pritchett was in Albany, Georgia, but they have used the moral means of nonviolence to maintain the immoral end of flagrant racial injustice. T. S. Eliot has said that there is no greater treason than to do the right deed for the wrong reason.

I wish you had commended the Negro sit-inners and demonstrators of Birmingham for their sublime courage, their willingness to suffer, and their amazing discipline in the midst of the most inhuman provocation. One day the South will recognize its real heroes. They will be the James Merediths, courageously and with a majestic sense of purpose, facing jeering and hostile mobs and the agonizing loneliness that characterizes the life of the pioneer. They will be old, oppressed, battered Negro women, symbolized in a seventy-two year old woman of Montgomery, Alabama, who rose up with a sense of dignity and with her people decided not to ride the segregated buses, and responded to one who inquired about her tiredness with ungrammatical profundity: "My feets is tired, but my soul is rested." They will be young high school and college students, young ministers of the gospel and a host of the elders, courageously and nonviolently sitting in at lunch counters and willingly going to jail for conscience sake. One day the South will know that when these disinherited children of God sat down at lunch counters they were in reality standing up for the best in the American dream and the most sacred values in our Judeo-Christian heritage, and thus carrying our whole nation back to great wells of democracy which were dug deep by the founding fathers in the formulation of the Constitution and the Declaration of Independence.

Never before have I written a letter this long (or should I say a book?). I'm afraid that it is much too long to take your precious time.

I can assure you that it would have been much shorter if I had been writing from a comfortable desk, but what else is there to do when you are alone for days in the dull monotony of a narrow jail cell other than write long letters, think strange thoughts, and pray long prayers!

55   If I have said anything in this letter that is an overstatement of the truth and is indicative of an unreasonable impatience, I beg you to forgive me. If I have said anything in this letter that is an understatement of the truth and is indicative of my having a patience that makes me patient with anything less than brotherhood, I beg God to forgive me.

I hope this letter finds you strong in the faith. I also hope that circumstances will soon make it possible for me to meet each of you, not as an integrationist or a civil rights leader, but as a fellow clergyman and a Christian brother. Let us all hope that the dark clouds of racial prejudice will soon pass away and the deep fog of misunderstanding will be lifted from our fear-drenched communities and in some not too distant tomorrow the radiant stars of love and brotherhood will shine over our great nation with all of their scintillating beauty.

Yours for the cause of
Peace and Brotherhood
MARTIN LUTHER KING, JR.

Questions on Meaning

1. At the time that this essay was written, King had been active in the civil rights movement for nearly 10 years. How had he usually handled criticisms of his work and ideas? Why?
2. The public statement by the eight clergymen exhibits a distrust for *outsiders*. How does King address that common fear and skepticism? If you had been one of the *local* clergymen, how do you think you would have reacted to King's explanation? Would you have respected his convictions? Embraced his beliefs?
3. Often in this essay, King addresses the issue of the timeliness of nonviolent demonstrations and other political activities. This urgency of action is a common theme of King's. "For years I have heard the word 'Wait!' " he writes. "It rings in the ear of every Negro with a piercing familiarity." What does the word *wait* mean to King?

Questions on Rhetorical Strategy and Style

1. King's dominant rhetorical strategy is clear: persuasion. He is not telling a story; he is not using flowery language or a preacher's oratory. This essay is logos and ethos: a sound argument supported by credibility, integrity, and experience. Analyze how he builds the argument one step at a time through the essay.
2. Repetition helps to drive home an argument. Show two places in this essay where King effectively uses repetition. Rewrite one of the passages without the repeated phrase and compare its effectiveness with the original.
3. Find King's discussion of just and unjust laws and locate the two paragraphs in which he gives examples of these laws ("Let us turn to a more concrete example . . . " and "Let me give another explanation . . . "). What is your reaction to his use of examples here?

Writing Assignments

1. A student of Gandhi, King based his political activities on nonviolent confrontation. In this essay, King outlines four steps of nonviolent activism: collect facts, negotiate, self-purify, and take direct action. Identify an injustice in your lifetime that people are trying or have tried to change through nonviolent activism.

Examples may include a physical barrier to people with physical handicaps, an employment restriction that discriminates against elderly people, or a city ordinance that unfairly restricts the activities of teenagers. Describe the political activity that has occurred, then relate it to King's four steps. Were these steps applied? If not, discuss how the outcome might have been different if these steps had been applied.

2. In this essay, King responds to the charge of being an extremist by admitting that he initially was put off by the label, but then realized that he wore it proudly. What is your reaction to the term? Does "extremist" hold negative or positive connotations for you? Is it used to credit or discredit? Identify some current political figures who are called extremists. Write an essay defining the term and describing how it is commonly applied, using current extremist political figures as examples.

3. King writes that one "has a moral responsibility to disobey unjust laws." Do you agree? Reread his defense of that statement. Does King's stance help overturn unjust laws or create anarchy? Choose a "law" that affects your life that you feel is unjust—perhaps a dormitory rule or campus restriction or a local law. Would you, or do you, intentionally break it? Write an essay describing the "law" and your action, arguing your viewpoint on obeying or disobeying it.

Second Inaugural Address (March 4, 1865)

Abraham Lincoln

Fellow Countrymen:

1   At this second appearing to take the oath of the presidential office, there is less occasion for an extended address than there was at the first. Then a statement, somewhat in detail, of a course to be pursued, seemed fitting and proper. Now, at the expiration of four years, during which public declarations have been constantly called forth on every point and phase of the great contest which still absorbs the attention, and engrosses the energies [sic] of the nation, little that is new could be presented. The progress of our arms, upon which all else chiefly depends, is as well known to the public as to myself; and it is, I trust, reasonably satisfactory and encouraging to all. With high hope for the future, no prediction in regard to it so ventured.

On the occasion corresponding to this four years ago, all thoughts were anxiously directed to an impending civil-war. All dreaded it—all sought to avert it. While the inaugural address was being delivered from this place, devoted altogether to saving the Union without war, insurgent agents were in the city seeking to destroy it without war— seeking to dissolve the Union, and divide effects, by negotiation. Both parties deprecated war; but one of them would make war rather than let the nation survive; and others would accept war rather than let it perish. And the war came.

One eighth of the whole population were colored slaves, not distributed generally over the Union, but localized in the Southern part of it. These slaves constituted a peculiar and powerful interest. All knew that this interest was somehow, the cause of the war. To strengthen, perpetuate, and extend this interest was the object for which the insurgents would rend the Union, even by war; while the government claimed no right to do more than to restrict the territorial enlargement of it. Neither party expected for the war, the magnitude, or the duration, which it has already attained. Neither anticipated that the cause of the conflict might cease with, or even before, the conflict itself should cease. Each looked for an easier triumph, and a result less fundamental and astounding. Both read the same Bible, and pray to the same God; and each invokes His aid against the other. It may seem strange that any men should dare ask a just Gods assistance in wringing their bread from the sweat of other men's faces; but let us judge not that we will be not judged.[1] The prayers of both could not be answered; that of neither has been answered fully. The Almighty has His own purposes. Woe unto the world because of offenses! for it must needs be that offenses come; but woe to that man by whom the offense cometh![2] If we shall suppose that American Slavery is one of those offenses which, in the providence of God, must needs come, but which, having continued through His appointed time, He now wills to remove, and that He gives to both North and South, this terrible war, as the woe due to those by whom the offense came, shall we discern therein any departure from those divine attributes which the believers in a Living God always ascribe to Him? Fondly do we hope—fervently do we pray—that this mighty scourge of war may speedily pass away. Yet, if God wills that it continue, until all the wealth piled by the bond-man's two hundred and fifty years of unrequited toil shall be sunk, and until every drop of blood drawn with the lash, shall be paid by another drawn with the sword, as was said three thousand years ago, so still it must be said the judgments of the Lord, are true and righteous altogether.[3]

With malice toward none; with charity for all; with firmness in the right, as God gives us to see the right, let us strive on to finish the work we are in, to bind up the nation's wounds; to care for him who shall have borne the battle, and for his widow, and his orphan—to do all which may achieve and cherish a just, and a lasting peace, among ourselves, and with all nations.

End Notes

1. See Matthew 7:1.
2. Matthew 18:7.
3. Psalms 19:9

The Declaration of Independence
Thomas Jefferson

Thomas Jefferson (1743–1826) was born in Virginia in a well-to-do land-owning family. He graduated from the College of William and Mary and then studied law. When he was elected at age 26 to the Virginia legislature, he had already begun forming his revolutionary views. As a delegate to the Second Continental Congress in 1775, he was the principal writer of the Declaration of Independence, which was adopted on July 4, 1776. After the Revolution he was Governor of Virginia from 1775 to 1777. From then until 1801, when he was elected the third President of the United States, Jefferson served in various federal positions, including secretary of state and ambassador to France. Jefferson was influential as an advocate of democracy in the early years of the United States, although his ideas were more typical of the eighteenth century "enlightened man" than original. The Declaration of Independence shows his ideas and style as well as those of the times and remains not merely an important historical document but also an eloquent statement of the founding principles of this country.

1 When in the course of human events, it becomes necessary for one people to dissolve the political bands which have connected them with another, and to assume among the powers of the earth, the separate and equal station to which the Laws of Nature and of Nature's God entitle them, a decent respect to the opinions of mankind requires that they should declare the causes which impel them to the separation.

We hold these truths to be self-evident, that all men are created equal, that they are endowed by their Creator with certain inalienable rights, that among these are life, liberty, and the pursuit of happiness. That to secure these rights, governments are instituted among men, deriving their just powers from the consent of the governed. That whenever any form of government becomes destructive of these ends, it is the right of the people to alter or to abolish it, and to institute new government, laying its foundation on such principles and organizing its powers in such form, as to them shall seem most likely to effect their safety and happiness. Prudence, indeed, will dictate that governments long established should not be changed for light and transient causes; and accordingly all experience hath shown, that mankind are more disposed to suffer, while evils are sufferable, than to right themselves by abolishing the forms to which they are accustomed. But when a long train of abuses and usurpations, pursuing invariably the same object, evinces a design to reduce them under absolute despotism, it is their right, it is their duty, to throw off such government, and to provide new guards for their future security. Such has been the patient sufferance of these Colonies; and such is now the necessity which constrains them to alter their former systems of government. The history of the present King of Great Britain is a history of repeated injuries and usurpations, all having in direct object the establishment of an absolute tyranny over these States. To prove this, let facts be submitted to a candid world.

He has refused his assent to laws, the most wholesome and necessary for the public good.

He has forbidden his Governors to pass laws of immediate and pressing importance, unless suspended in their operation till his assent should be obtained; and when so suspended, he has utterly neglected to attend to them.

5 He has refused to pass other laws for the accommodation of large 5 districts of people, unless those people would relinquish the right of representation in the legislature, a right inestimable to them and formidable to tyrants only.

He has called together legislative bodies at places unusual, uncomfortable, and distant from the depository of their public records, for the sole purpose of fatiguing them into compliance with his measures.

He has dissolved representative houses repeatedly, for opposing with manly firmness his invasions on the rights of the people.

He has refused for a long time, after such dissolutions, to cause others to be elected; whereby the legislative powers, incapable of annihilation, have returned to the people at large for their exercise; the State remaining in the meantime exposed to all the dangers of invasion from without and convulsions within.

He has endeavoured to prevent the population of these states; for that purpose obstructing the laws for naturalization of foreigners; refusing to pass others to encourage their migration hither, and raising the conditions of new appropriations of lands.

10   He has obstructed the administration of justice, by refusing his assent to laws for establishing judiciary powers.

He has made judges dependent on his will alone, for the tenure of their offices, and the amount and payment of their salaries.

He has erected a multitude of new offices, and sent hither swarms of officers to harass our people, and eat out their substance.

He has kept among us, in times of peace, standing armies without the consent of our legislatures.

He has affected to render the military independent of and superior to the civil power.

15   He has combined with others to subject us to a jurisdiction foreign of our constitution, and unacknowledged by our laws; giving his assent to their acts of pretended legislation:

For quartering large bodies of armed troops among us:

For protecting them, by a mock trial, from punishment for any murders which they should commit on the inhabitants of these States:

For cutting off our trade with all parts of the world:

For imposing taxes on us without our consent:

20   For depriving us in many cases of the benefits of trial by jury:

For transporting us beyond seas to be tried for pretended offences:

For abolishing the free system of English laws in a neighbouring Province, establishing therein an arbitrary government, and enlarging its boundaries so as to render it at once an example and fit instrument for introducing the same absolute rule into these Colonies:

For taking away our Charters, abolishing our most valuable laws, and altering fundamentally the forms of our governments:

For suspending our own legislatures, and declaring themselves invested with power to legislate for us in all cases whatsoever.

25   He has abdicated government here, by declaring us out of his protection and waging war against us.

He has plundered our seas, ravaged our coasts, burnt our towns, and destroyed the lives of our people.

He is at this time transporting large armies of foreign mercenaries to complete the works of death, desolation, and tyranny, already begun with circumstances of cruelty and perfidy scarcely paralleled in the most barbarous ages, and totally unworthy the head of a civilized nation.

He has constrained our fellow citizens taken captive on the high seas to bear arms against their country, to become the executioners of their friends and brethren, or to fall themselves by their hands.

He has excited domestic insurrections amongst us, and has endeavoured to bring on the inhabitants of our frontiers, the merciless Indian savages, whose known rule of warfare, is an undistinguished destruction of all ages, sexes, and conditions.

30   In every stage of these oppressions we have petitioned for redress   30 in the most humble terms: our repeated petitions have been answered only by repeated injury. A prince whose character is thus marked by every act which may define a tyrant is unfit to be the ruler of a free people.

Nor have we been wanting in attention to our British brethren. We have warned them from time to time of attempts by their legislature to extend an unwarrantable jurisdiction over us. We have reminded them of the circumstances of our emigration and settlement here. We have appealed to their native justice and magnanimity, and we have conjured them by the ties of our common kindred to disavow these usurpations, which would inevitably interrupt our connections and correspondence. They too have been deaf to the voice of justice and of consanguinity. We must, therefore, acquiesce in the necessity, which denounces our separation, and hold them, as we hold the rest of mankind, enemies in war, in peace friends.

We, therefore, the Representatives of the United States of America, in General Congress assembled, appealing to the Supreme Judge of the world for the rectitude of our intentions, do, in the name, and by authority of the good people of these Colonies, solemnly publish and declare, That these United Colonies are, and of right ought to be, Free and Independent States; that they are absolved from all allegiance to the British Crown, and that all political connection between them and the state of Great Britain, is and ought to be totally dissolved; and that as Free and Independent States, they have full power to levy war, conclude peace, contract alliances, establish commerce, and to do all other acts and things which Independent States may of right do. And for the support of this declaration, with a firm reliance on the protection of Divine Providence, we mutually pledge to each other our lives, our fortunes, and our sacred honor.

Questions on Meaning

1. Most readers will recall the historical purpose of the Declaration of Independence, but unless you've had cause to read it in recent years you've probably forgotten much of its substance. As you just read it, what feelings did it evoke? What aspects had you forgotten? What is your impression of it now as a work of literature rather than as a historical document?
2. To whom is the Declaration of Independence addressed? What leads you to that conclusion?
3. Explain in your own words Jefferson's justification for democratic government.

Questions on Rhetorical Strategy and Style

1. The Declaration frequently uses dramatic language such as "sent hither swarms of officers to harass our people" and "plundered our seas, ravaged our coasts, burnt our towns, and destroyed the lives of our people." Find several other examples of similar powerful language. What is the purpose of such language in this document?
2. Note that the part of the Declaration that enumerates the long list of "facts . . . submitted to a candid world" comprises the greatest part of its length. Why is that?
3. Jefferson uses the rhetorical strategy of persuasion, to craft the Declaration. Identify at least two aspects of persuasion in this writing and explain their effect.

Writing Assignments

1. "Pursuit of happiness" is a phrase much used in the two centuries since it was written. Think about what that phrase implies about a government's power over people. Write an essay in which you define the right to pursue happiness in the modern world. Make sure you clarify with examples both what that right should guarantee and what it should not guarantee.
2. If the Colonies were justified in declaring their independence from what they saw as an oppressive England, were the Southern states also justified in declaring their independence when they seceded from the Union (thus beginning the Civil War)? Do some basic research if necessary to understand both situations, and then write an essay building your argument by comparing and contrasting these two situations.

Talking Back

bell hooks

*bell hooks (1952–), the pseudonym of Gloria Watkins, was
born in Kentucky. She received a B.A. from Stanford University and a Ph.D. from the University of California,
Santa Cruz. An advocate for African-American women in
the feminist movement as well as a critic of the white male-
dominated U.S. power structure, hooks has taught at Ober-
lin College and Yale University. Her books include* Ain't I a
Woman: Black Women and Feminism *(1981),* Feminist
Theory: From Margin to Center *(1984),* Talking Back:
Thinking Feminist, Thinking Black *(1989),* Yearning:
Race, Gender, and Cultural Politics *(1990),* Breaking
Bread: Insurgent Black Intellectual Life *(1992),* Black
Looks: Race and Representation *(1992),* Outlaw Cul-
ture *(1994),* Teaching to Transgress: Education as the
Practice of Freedom *(1994),* Reel to Real: Race, Sex,
and Class at the Movies *(1996), and* Remembering
Rapture *(1999). hooks describes her confrontations
throughout life with rules of speech—and the role of
silence—in this excerpt from* Talking Back.

1   In the world of the southern black community I grew up in, "back
talk" and "talking back" meant speaking as an equal to an authority figure. It meant daring to disagree and sometimes it just meant
having an opinion. In the "old school," children were meant to be
seen and not heard. My great-grandparents, grandparents, and parents were all from the old school. To make yourself heard if you were
a child was to invite punishment, the back-hand lick, the slap across
the face that would catch you unaware, or the feel of switches stinging
your arms and legs.

To speak then when one was not spoken to was a courageous act—an act of risk and daring. And yet it was hard not to speak in warm rooms where heated discussions began at the crack of dawn, women's voices filling the air, giving orders, making threats, fussing. Black men may have excelled in the art of poetic preaching in the male-dominated church, but in the church of the home, where the everyday rules of how to live and how to act were established, it was black women who preached. There, black women spoke in a language so rich, so poetic, that it felt to me like being shut off from life, smothered to death if one were not allowed to participate.

It was in that world of woman talk (the men were often silent, often absent) that was born in me the craving to speak, to have a voice, and not just any voice but one that could be identified as belonging to me. To make my voice, I had to speak, to hear myself talk—and talk I did—darting in and out of grown folks' conversations and dialogues, answering questions that were not directed at me, endlessly asking questions, making speeches. Needless to say, the punishments for these acts of speech seemed endless. They were intended to silence me—the child—and more particularly the girl child. Had I been a boy, they might have encouraged me to speak believing that I might someday be called to preach. There was no "calling" for talking girls, no legitimized rewarded speech. The punishments I received for "talking back" were intended to suppress all possibility that I would create my own speech. That speech was to be suppressed so that the "right speech of womanhood" would emerge.

Within feminist circles, silence is often seen as the sexist "right speech of womanhood"—the sign of woman's submission to patriarchal authority. This emphasis on woman's silence may be an accurate remembering of what has taken place in the households of women from WASP backgrounds in the United States, but in black communities (and diverse ethnic communities), women have not been silent. Their voices can be heard. Certainly for black women, our struggle has not been to emerge from silence into speech but to change the nature and direction of our speech, to make a speech that compels listeners, one that is heard.

5 Our speech, "the right speech of womanhood," was often the soliloquy, the talking into thin air, the talking to ears that do not hear you—the talk that is simply not listened to. Unlike the black male preacher whose speech was to be heard, who was to be listened to,

whose words were to be remembered, the voices of black women—giving orders, making threats, fussing—could be tuned out, could become a kind of background music, audible but not acknowledged as significant speech. Dialogue—the sharing of speech and recognition—took place not between mother and child or mother and male authority figure but among black women. I can remember watching fascinated as our mother talked with her mother, sisters, and women friends. The intimacy and intensity of their speech—the satisfaction they received from talking to one another, the pleasure, the joy. It was in this world of woman speech, loud talk, angry words, women with tongues quick and sharp, tender sweet tongues, touching our world with their words, that I made speech my birthright—and the right to voice, to authorship, a privilege I would not be denied. It was in that world and because of it that I came to dream of writing, to write.

Writing was a way to capture speech, to hold onto it, keep it close. And so I wrote down bits and pieces of conversations, confessing in cheap diaries that soon fell apart from too much handling, expressing the intensity of my sorrow, the anguish of speech—for I was always saying the wrong thing, asking the wrong questions. I could not confine my speech to the necessary corners and concerns of life. I hid these writings under my bed, in pillow stuffings, among faded underwear. When my sisters found and read them, they ridiculed and mocked me—poking fun. I felt violated, ashamed, as if the secret parts of my self had been exposed, brought into the open, and hung like newly clean laundry, out in the air for everyone to see. The fear of exposure, the fear that one's deepest emotions and innermost thoughts will be dismissed as mere nonsense, felt by so many young girls keeping diaries, holding and hiding speech, seems to me now one of the barriers that women have always needed and still need to destroy so that we are no longer pushed into secrecy or silence.

Despite my feelings of violation, of exposure, I continued to speak and write, choosing my hiding places well, learning to destroy work when no safe place could be found. I was never taught absolute silence, I was taught that it was important to speak but to talk a talk that was in itself a silence. Taught to speak and yet beware of the betrayal of too much heard speech, I experienced intense confusion and deep anxiety in my efforts to speak and write. Reciting poems at Sunday afternoon church service might be rewarded. Writing a poem (when one's time could be "better" spent sweeping, ironing, learning to cook) was luxurious activity, indulged in at the expense of others. Questioning authority, raising issues that were not deemed appropriate subjects, brought pain, punishments—like telling mama I wanted to die before her because I could not live without her—that was crazy talk, crazy speech, the kind that would lead you to end up in a mental institution. "Little girl," I would be told, "if you don't stop all this crazy talk and crazy acting you are going to end up right out there at Western State."

Madness, not just physical abuse, was the punishment for too much talk if you were female. Yet even as this fear of madness haunted me, hanging over my writing like a monstrous shadow, I could not stop the words, making thought, writing speech. For this terrible madness which I feared, which I was sure was the destiny of daring women born to intense speech (after all, the authorities emphasized this point daily), was not as threatening as imposed silence, as suppressed speech.

Safety and sanity were to be sacrificed if I was to experience defiant speech. Though I risked them both, deep-seated fears and anxieties characterized my childhood days. I would speak but I would not ride a bike, play hardball, or hold the gray kitten. Writing about the ways we are traumatized in our growing-up years, psychoanalyst Alice Miller makes the point in *For Your Own Good* that it is not clear why childhood wounds become for some folk an opportunity to grow, to move forward rather than backward in the process of self-realization. Certainly, when I reflect on the trials of my growing-up years, the many punishments, I can see now that in resistance I learned to be vigilant in the nourishment of my spirit, to be tough, to courageously protect that spirit from forces that would break it.

10   While punishing me, my parents often spoke about the necessity   10
of breaking my spirit. Now when I ponder the silences, the voices that are not heard, the voices of those wounded and/or oppressed individuals who do not speak or write, I contemplate the acts of persecution, torture—the terrorism that breaks spirits, that makes creativity impossible. I write these words to bear witness to the primacy of resistance struggle in any situation of domination (even within family life); to the strength and power that emerges from sustained resistance and the profound conviction that these forces can be healing, can protect us from dehumanization and despair.

These early trials, wherein I learned to stand my ground, to keep my spirit intact, came vividly to mind after I published *Ain't I A Woman* and the book was sharply and harshly criticized. While I had expected a climate of critical dialogue, I was not expecting a critical avalanche that had the power in its intensity to crush the spirit, to push one into silence. Since that time, I have heard stories about black women, about women of color, who write and publish (even when the work is quite successful) having nervous breakdowns, being made mad because they cannot bear the harsh responses of family, friends, and unknown critics, or becoming silent, unproductive. Surely, the absence of a humane critical response has tremendous impact on the writer from any oppressed, colonized group who endeavors to speak. For us, true speaking is not solely an expression of creative power; it is an act of resistance, a political gesture that challenges politics of domination that would render us nameless and voiceless. As such, it is a courageous act—as such, it represents a threat. To those who wield oppressive power, that which is threatening must necessarily be wiped out, annihilated, silenced.

Recently, efforts by black women writers to call attention to our work serve to highlight both our presence and absence. Whenever I peruse women's bookstores, I am struck not by the rapidly growing body of feminist writing by black women, but by the paucity of available published material. Those of us who write and are published remain few in number. The context of silence is varied and multidimensional. Most obvious are the ways racism, sexism, and class exploitation act to suppress and silence. Less obvious are the inner struggles, the efforts made to gain the necessary confidence to write, to re-write, to fully develop craft and skill—and the extent to which such efforts fail.

Although I have wanted writing to be my life-work since childhood, it has been difficult for me to claim "writer" as part of that which identifies and shapes my everyday reality. Even after publishing books, I would often speak of wanting to be a writer as though these works did not exist. And though I would be told, "you are a writer," I was not yet ready to fully affirm this truth. Part of myself was still held captive by domineering forces of history, of familial life that had charted a map of silence, of right speech. I had not completely let go of the fear of saying the wrong thing, of being punished. Somewhere in the deep recesses of my mind, I believed I could avoid both responsibility and punishment if I did not declare myself a writer.

One of the many reasons I chose to write using the pseudonym bell hooks, a family name (mother to Sarah Oldham, grandmother to Rosa Bell Oldham, great-grandmother to me), was to construct a writer-identity that would challenge and subdue all impulses leading me away from speech into silence. I was a young girl buying bubble gum at the corner store when I first really heard the full name bell hooks. I had just "talked back" to a grown person. Even now I can recall the surprised look, the mocking tones that informed me I must be kin to bell hooks—a sharp-tongued woman, a woman who spoke her mind, a woman who was not afraid to talk back. I claimed this legacy of defiance, of will, of courage, affirming my link to female ancestors who were bold and daring in their speech. Unlike my bold and daring mother and grandmother, who were not supportive of talking back, even though they were assertive and powerful in their speech, bell hooks as I discovered, claimed, and invented her was my ally, my support.

15   That initial act of talking back outside the home was empowering. It was the first of many acts of defiant speech that would make it possible for me to emerge as an independent thinker and writer. In retrospect, "talking back" became for me a rite of initiation, testing my courage, strengthening my commitment, preparing me for the days ahead—the days when writing, rejection notices, periods of silence, publication, ongoing development seem impossible but necessary.

Moving from silence into speech is for the oppressed, the colonized, the exploited, and those who stand and struggle side by side a gesture of defiance that heals, that makes new life and new growth possible. It is that act of speech, of "talking back," that is no mere gesture of empty words, that is the expression of our movement from object to subject—the liberated voice.

Questions on Meaning

1. How does hooks define "back talk" and "talking back"? How does she describe her reaction to her first act of "talking back" outside her house?
2. What does hooks mean by "true speak"? Who is the "us" she is referring to when she discusses "true speak"?
3. Even though hooks learned as a young girl that writing was her life, why has she had such a difficult time accepting that she *is* a writer? How has her "map of silence" affected her ability to grow into her role as a writer?

Questions on Rhetorical Strategy and Style

1. How does hooks compare and contrast "silence" with "speech"? What are the various "contexts" of silence that she reveals—from quieting the "girl child" to suppressing the expression of women to talking a talk that is silence to the "right speech of womanhood"? What examples does she provide to illustrate the differences between silence and speech?
2. How does she compare and contrast the woman talk of black women with the talk of black men? The talk of black women and other women of color with the talk of white women? Explain how your experience confirms or contradicts these observations.

Writing Assignments

1. What has been your experience when you have spoken out or expressed yourself (perhaps in writing) in terms that might offend some people. What kind of criticism have you received? How has it affected you? Has it affected your subsequent "talking out": did it silence you or increase your resolve to continue to express yourself?
2. Write an essay comparing and contrasting "talking back" (as hooks defines it) with rudeness and disrespect. When is a comment by a child to an adult applauded as a forthright child speaking up for what is right, and when is it criticized as being contentious, argumentative, or nasty? Is it possible to create *rules* of speech? How do language, mannerisms, and context affect whether a spoken word is "acceptable" or "unacceptable"?

The New Community

Amitai Etzioni

[handwritten annotations: ✱ New communities - independent wall st + dep small town economic progress — self reliance — new social relationships — intellectual technological — community neighborhood value shared resources relationships — 2nd story — This American Life — Crybabies — they talk to var street guys — Jim wallis @ wheaton October 28th]

Amitai Etzioni (1929–) was born in Cologne, Germany. Educated at Hebrew University in Jerusalem (B.A., 1954) and the University of California at Berkeley (M.A., 1956, and Ph.D., 1958), Etzioni has directed the Center for Policy Research at Columbia University and taught at George Washington University. Published widely, Etzioni has written for both scholarly and lay audiences. He also has edited a journal, Responsive Community. *His books include* The Spirit of Community: Rights, Responsibilities, and the Communitarian Agenda *(1993). In this essay, Etzioni compares and contrasts two sociological concepts, one having to do with close-knit communities based on relationship and the other having to do with diverse communities based on social contracts.*

1   It's hard to believe now, but for a long time the loss of community was considered to be liberating. Societies were believed to progress from closely knit, "primitive," or rural villages to unrestrictive, "modern," or urban societies. The former were depicted as based on kinship and loyalty in an age in which both were suspect; the latter, however, were seen as based on reason (or "rationality") in an era in which reason's power to illuminate was admired with little attention paid to the deep shadows it casts. The two types of social relations have often been labeled with the terms supplied by a German sociologist, Ferdinand Tönnies. One is gemeinschaft, the German term for community, and the other is gesellschaft, the German word for society, which he used to refer to people who have rather few bonds, like people in a crowd or a mass society (*Community and Society*).

Reprinted from *The Spirit of Community: Rights, Responsibilities, and the Communitarian Agenda* (1993), by permission of Crown Publishers, a division of Random House, Inc.

Far from decrying the loss of community, this sanguine approach to the rise of modernity depicted small towns and villages as backward places that confined behavior. American writers such as Sinclair Lewis and John O'Hara satirized small towns as insular, claustrophobic places, inhabited by petty, mean-spirited people. They were depicted as the opposite of "big cities," whose atmosphere was said to set people free. Anonymity would allow each person to pursue what he or she wished rather than what the community dictated. It was further argued that relations in the *gesellschaft* would be based not on preexisting, "ascribed" social bonds, such as between cousins, but on contractual relations, freely negotiated among autonomous individuals.

Other major forms of progress were believed to accompany the movement from a world of villages to one of cities. Magic, superstition, alchemy, and religion—"backward beliefs"—would be replaced by bright, shining science and technology. There would be no more villagers willing to sell their wares only to their own kind and not to outsiders—a phenomenon anthropologists have often noted. Old-fashioned values and a sense of obligation were expected to yield to logic and calculation. Social bonds dominating all relations (you did not charge interest on a loan to members of your community because such a charge was considered indecent usury) were pushed aside to make room for a free market, with prices and interest rates set according to market logic. By the same token, the network of reciprocal obligations and care that is at the heart of communities would give way to individual rights protected by the state. The impersonal right to social services and welfare payments, for instance, would replace any reliance on members of one's family, tribe, or ethnic benevolent association.

The sun, moon, and stars of the new universe would be individuals, not the community. In a typical case, the U.S. Supreme Court ruled that the Sierra Club had no legal standing to argue for the preservation of parkland as a community resource (Glendon 112). Rather, if the Sierra Club wished to show standing, it would have to demonstrate that particular individuals were harmed.

5 Throughout twentieth-century America, as the transition to *gesellschaft* evolved, even its champions realized that it was not the unmitigated blessing they had expected. Although it was true that those who moved from villages and small towns into urban centers often shed tight social relations and strong community bonds, the

result for many was isolation, lack of caring for one another, and exposure to rowdiness and crime.

Criminologists report that young farmhands in rural America in the early nineteenth-century did not always work on their parents' land. However, when they were sent to work outside their home they usually lived with other farmers and were integrated into their family life. In this way they were placed in a community context that sustained the moral voice, reinforced the values of their upbringing, and promoted socially constructive behavior. It was only when these farmhands went to work in factories in cities—and were housed on their own in barracks without established social networks, elders, and values—that rowdy and criminal behavior, alcoholism, and prostitution became common. Even in those early days attempts to correct these proclivities were made not by returning these young people to their families and villages, but by trying to generate Communitarian elements in the cities. Among the best analysts of these developments is James Q. Wilson, a leading political scientist. He notes that associations such as the Young Men's Christian Association (YMCA), temperance societies, and the Children's Aid society sought to provide a socially appropriate, morality-sustaining context for young people ("Rediscovery" 13).

Other experiences paralleled those of the factory hands. The migration to the American West, for example, is usually thought of as a time when individuals were free to venture forth and carve out a life of their own in the Great Plains. Actually, many people traveled in caravans and settled as communities, although each family claimed its own plot of land. Mutual assistance in such rough terrain was an absolute requirement. Mining towns and trading posts, however, in which rampant individualism often did prevail, were places of much chicanery. People who had mined gold often lost their stakes to unscrupulous traders; those who owned land were driven off it with little compensation by railroad companies, among others. Fly-by-night banks frequently welshed on notes that they themselves had issued. An unfettered market, one without a community context, turned out to lack the essential moral underpinnings that trade requires, and not just by sound social relations.

In many ways these frontier settlements—with their washed-out social bonds, loose morals, and unbridled greed—were the forerunners of Wall Street in the 1980s. The Street became a "den of thieves," thick with knaves who held that anything went as long as you made millions more than the next guy. Moreover, the mood of self-centered "making it" of the me generation spilled over into large segments of society. It was celebrated by the White House and many in Congress, who saw in an unfettered pursuit of self-interest the social force that revitalizes economies and societies. By the end of the eighties even some of the proponents of me-ism felt that the pursuit of greed had run amok.

By the early nineties the waning of community, which had long concerned sociologists, became more pronounced and drew more attention. As writer Jonathan Rowe put it: "It was common to think about the community as we used to think about air and water. It is there. It takes care of itself, and it can and will absorb whatever we unleash into it" ("Left and Right"). Now it became evident that the social environment needed fostering just as nature did. Responding to the new cues, George Bush evoked the image of a "kinder, gentler" society as a central theme for his first presidential campaign in 1988. The time was right to return to community and the moral order it harbored. Bill Clinton made the spirit of community a theme of his 1992 campaign.

10 The prolonged recession of 1991–1992 and the generally low 10 and slowing growth of the American economy worked against this new concern with we-ness. Interracial and interethnic tensions rose considerably, not only between blacks and whites, but also between blacks and Hispanics and among various segments of the community and Asian-Americans. This is one more reason why the United States will have to work its way to a stronger, growing, more competitive economy: interracial and ethnic peace are much easier to maintain in a rising than in a stagnant economy. However, it does not mean that community rebuilding has to be deferred until the economy is shored up. It does indicate that enhancing we-ness will require greater commitment and effort from both the government and the people, if community rebuilding is to take place in a sluggish economy.

Does this mean that we all have to move back to live in small towns and villages in order to ensure the social foundations of morality, to rebuild and shore up we-ness? Can one not bring up decent young people in the city? Isn't it possible to have a modern society, which requires a high concentration of labor and a great deal of geographic mobility—and still sustain a web of social bonds, a Communitarian nexus? There is more than one sociological answer to these queries.

First, many cities have sustained (or reclaimed) some elements of community. Herbert Gans, a Columbia University sociologist, observed that within cities there were what he called "urban villages." He found communities where, generally speaking, "neighbors were friendly and quick to say hello to each other," where the various ethnic groups, transients, and bohemians "could live together side by side without much difficulty." Gans further noted that "for most West Enders (in Boston) . . . life in the area resembled that found in the village or small town, and even in the suburb" (*The Urban Villagers*, 14–15). Even in large metropolises, such as New York City, there are neighborhoods in which many people know their neighbors, their shopkeepers, and their local leaders. They are likely to meet one another in neighborhood bars, bowling alleys, and places of worship. They watch out for each other's safety and children. They act in concert to protect their parks and bus stops. They form political clubs and are a force in local politics. (Jim Sleeper's *Closest of Strangers* provides a fine description of these New York City communities.)

In some instances members of one ethnic group live comfortably next to one another, as in New York City's Chinatown and Miami's Little Havana. In other cities ethnic groups are more geographically dispersed but sustain ethnic-community bonds around such institutions as churches and synagogues, social clubs, and private schools. In recent decades a measure of return to community has benefited from the revival of loyalty to ethnic groups. While the sons and daughters of immigrants, the so-called second generation, often sought to assimilate, to become Americanized to the point that their distinct backgrounds were lost in a new identity, *their* children, the third generation and onward, often seek to reestablish their ethnic identity and bonds.

How does one reconcile the two sociological pictures—the James Q. Wilson concept of the city as *gesellschaft*, with little community or moral base, and the Herbert Gans image of *gemeinschaft*, of urban villages? The answer, first of all, is that both exist side by side. Between the urban villages, in row houses and high rises, you find large pockets of people who do not know their next-door neighbors, with whom they may have shared a floor, corridors, and elevators for a generation. Elderly people especially, who have no social bonds at work and are largely abandoned by their families, often lead rather isolated lives. In 1950 14.4 percent of those sixty-five years of age and older lived alone (Monk 534); by 1990 the percentage stood at nearly 31 percent (U.S. Bureau of the Census, table L, 12).

15   Also, to some extent a welcome return to small-town life of sorts 15 has been occurring in modern America. Although not all suburbs, which attracted millions of city dwellers, make for viable communities, as a rule the movement to the suburbs has enhanced the Communitarian nexus.

In addition, postmodern technology helps. More people are again able to work at home or nearby, and a high concentration of labor is less and less necessary, in contrast with the industrial age. People can use their computers and modems at home to do a good part of their office work, from processing insurance claims to trading worldwide commodities, stocks, and bonds. Architects can design buildings and engineers monitor faraway power networks from their places of residence.

It used to be widely observed that Americans, unlike Europeans, move around so much that they are hard-pressed to put down real community roots. On average, it is said, the whole country moves about once every five years. These figures, however, may be a bit obsolete. For various reasons, in recent years Americans seem to move somewhat less often (Barringer A16). One explanation is a growing desire to maintain the bonds of friendship and local social roots of their children, spouses, and themselves. In effect there is little reason to believe that the economy will suffer if this trend continues, and it may actually benefit from less shuttling around of people. Surely the Communitarian nexus will benefit.

Finally, there are new, nongeographic, communities made up of people who do not live near one another. Their foundations may not be as stable and deep-rooted as residential communities, but they fulfill many of the social and moral functions of traditional communities. Work-based and professional communities are among the most common of these. That is, people who work together in a steel mill or a high-tech firm such as Lotus or Microsoft often develop work-related friendships and community webs; groups of co-workers hang around together, help one another, play and party together, and go on joint outings. As they learn to know and care for one another, they also form and reinforce moral expectations.

Other communities are found in some law firms, on many campuses (although one community may not encompass everyone on campus), among physicians at the same hospital or with the same specialty in a town, and among some labor union members.

20 Some critics have attacked these communities as being artificially 20 constructed, because they lack geographical definition or because they are merely social networks, without a residential concentration. Ray Oldenburg, author of *The Great Good Place*, decries the new definitions of community that encompass co-workers and even radio call-in show audiences. "Can we really create a satisfactory community apart from geography?" he asks (Baldwin 17). "My answer is 'no.'" But people who work every day in the same place spend more hours together and in closer proximity than people who live on the same village street. Most important, these nongeographic communities often provide at least some elements of the Communitarian nexus, and hence they tend to have the moral infrastructure we consider essential for a civil and humane society.

In short, our society is neither without community nor sufficiently Communitarian; it is neither *gemeinschaft* nor *gesellschaft*, but a mixture of the two sociological conditions. America does not need a simple return to gemeinschaft, to the traditional community. Modern economic prerequisites preclude such a shift, but even if it were possible, such backpedaling would be undesirable because traditional communities have been too constraining and authoritarian. Such traditional communities were usually homogeneous. What we need now are communities that balance both diversity and unity. As John W. Gardner has noted: "To prevent the wholeness from smothering diversity, there must be a philosophy of pluralism, an open climate for dissent, and an opportunity for subcommunities to retain their identity and share in the setting of larger group goals" (*Building Community* 11). Thus, we need to strengthen the communitarian elements in the urban and suburban centers, to provide the social bonds that sustain the moral voice, but at the same time avoid tight networks that suppress pluralism and dissent. James Pinkerton, who served in the Bush White House, speaks eloquently about a new paradigm focused around what he calls a "new *gemeinschaft*." It would be, he says, neither oppressive nor hierarchical. In short, we need new communities in which people have choices and readily accommodate divergent *sub*communities but still maintain common bonds.

" American Outlaws "

Notes

Deborah Baldwin, "Creating Community," *Common Cause Magazine*, July/August 1990, 17.

Felicity Barringer, "18 Percent of Households in U.S. Moved in '89," *New York Times*, December 20, 1991, A16.

Herbert Gans, *The Urban Villagers: Group and Class in the Life of Italian-Americans* (New York: The Free Press, 1962, 1982), 14–15.

John W. Gardner, *Building Community* (Washington, D.C.: Independent Sector, 1991), 11.

Mary Ann Glendon, *Rights Talk* (New York: The Free Press, 1991), 112.

Abraham Monk, "Aging, Loneliness, and Communications," *American Behavioral Scientist* 31 (5): 534.

Jonathan Rowe, "Left and Right: The Emergence of a New Politics in the 1990s?" sponsored by the Heritage Foundation and the Progressive Foundation, October 30, 1991, Washington, D.C.

Jim Sleeper, *Closest of Strangers: Liberalism and the Politics of Race in New York* (New York: W. W. Norton & Company, 1990).

Ferdinand Tönnies, *Community and Society*, translated and edited by Charles P. Loomis (East Lansing: Michigan State University Press, 1957).

communitygroup

society - indv

Questions on Meaning

1. The essay begins by setting up a sociological concept that comes from sociologist Ferdinand Tönnies: humans live either in close communities or they live in large distant societies. He then says that in the past Americans have tended to move toward these distant societies, with big cities and strong rule of law rather than social agreements. How does he support this perspective?

2. What was American society like in the days of family farms? How did people relate then? What was the frontier like? Why did people have to depend closely on one another?

3. How have American cities kept some of the close relationships from the past? What have technology and professional networking done to enhance relationship-based communities?

Questions on Rhetorical Strategy and Style

1. This essay has an academic structure. What is the professional and scholarly base for the essay (that is, how is Tönnies used to set up the structure of the essay)?

2. Next the essay gives a history of the America that lives by close relationships. How does this section represent a more personal and feeling-based perspective?

3. Finally, the essay comes together with a synthesis that shows a combination of previously separate concepts. How does the synthesis complete the essay?

Writing Assignments

1. Describe the community in which you live or where you grew up. Write about whether it was based on personal relationships or on following the rule of law. Where did the two overlap? Would you have had it any differently?

2. Describe the Internet communities in which you participate. On what are these communities based? Who are your friends and co-workers online? Is this a kind of relationship-based community for you? How?

3. How often has your family moved in your life? Write about the stability of your experience. Did you move every five years (as has been the national norm), or did you live in one place all your life, or a mix of the two? Describe your experience and evaluate that experience.

Tour of the City: Encounters between East and West

Pico Iyer

*Pico Iyer (1957–) was born in Oxford, England and ex-
perienced the education reserved for Britain's elite: at Eton,
an exclusive prep school; at Oxford, the most distinguished
university in England; and later at Harvard, the most
revered university in America. Iyer writes for* Time, The
Village Voice, *and other magazines. His travel book,*
Video Night in Kathmandu, and Other Reports from
the Not-so-far-East *(1988), was widely praised. He has
written two more travel books,* The Lady and the Monk
(1991) and Falling Off the Map *(1993). He currently
lives in Santa Barbara, California. As you read his essay
from* Video Night, *note the carefully detailed record of
perception, the mark of someone who has traveled widely
and observed keenly.*

1   To mention, however faintly, the West's cultural assault on the
East is, inevitably, to draw dangerously close to the fashionable belief that the First World is corrupting the Third. And
to accept that AIDS and Rambo are the two great "Western" exports
of 1985 is to encourage some all too easy conclusions: that the West's
main contributions to the rest of the world are sex and violence, a
cureless disease and a killer cure; that America is exporting nothing
but a literal kind of infection and a bloody sort of indoctrination. In
place of physical imperialism, we often assert a kind of sentimental
colonialism that would replace Rambo myths with Sambo myths and
conclude that because the First World feels guilty, the Third World

must be innocent—what Pascal Bruckner refers to as "compassion as contempt."

This, however, I find simplistic—both because corruption often says most about those who detect it and because the developing world may often have good reason to assent in its own transformation.

This is not to deny that the First World has indeed inflicted much damage on the Third, especially through the inhuman calculations of geopolitics. If power corrupts, superpowers are super-corrupting, and the past decade alone has seen each of the major powers destroy a self-contained Asian culture by dragging it into the cross fire of the Real World: Tibet was invaded for strategic reasons by the Chinese, and now the dreamed-of Shangri-La is almost lost forever; Afghanistan was overrun by Soviet tanks, and now the Michauds' photographic record of its fugitive beauties must be subtitled, with appropriate melancholy, "Paradise Lost"; Cambodia, once so gentle a land that cyclo drivers were said to tip their passengers, fell into the sights of Washington and is now just a land of corpses.

On an individual level too, Western tourists invariably visit destruction on the places they visit, descending in droves on some "authentic Eastern village" until only two things are certain: it is neither Eastern nor authentic. Each passing season (and each passing tourist) brings new developments to the forgotten places of the world—and in a never-never land, every development is a change for the worse. In search of a lovely simplicity, Westerners saddle the East with complexities; in search of peace, they bring agitation. As soon as Arcadia is seen as a potential commodity, amenities spring up on every side to meet outsiders' needs, and paradise is not so much lost as remaindered. In Asia alone, Bali, Tahiti, Sri Lanka and Nepal have already been so taken over by Paradise stores, Paradise hotels and Paradise cafés that they sometimes seem less like utopias than packaged imitations of utopia; Ladakh, Tibet and Ko Samui may one day follow. No man, they say, is an island; in the age of international travel, not even an island can remain an island for long.

Like every tourist, moreover, I found myself spreading corruption even as I decried it. In northern Thailand, I joined a friend in giving hill tribesmen tutorials in the songs of Sam Cooke until a young Thai girl was breaking the silence of the jungle with a piercing refrain of "She was sixteen, too young to love, and I was too young to know." In China, I gave a local boy eager for some English-language reading matter a copy of the only novel I had on hand—Gore Vidal's strenu-ously perverse *Duluth*. And in a faraway hill station in Burma, a group of cheery black marketeers treated me to tea and I, in return, taught them the words "lesbian" and "skin flicks," with which they seemed much pleased.

Yet that in itself betrays some of the paradoxes that haunt our talk of corruption. For often, the denizens of the place we call paradise long for nothing so much as news of that "real paradise" across the seas—the concrete metropolis of skyscrapers and burger joints. And often what we call corruption, they might be inclined to call progress or profit. As tourists, we have reason to hope that the quaint anachro-nism we have discovered will always remain "unspoiled," as fixed as a museum piece for our inspection. It is perilous, however, to assume that its inhabitants will long for the same. Indeed, a kind of imperial arrogance underlies the very assumption that the people of the devel-oping world should be happier without the TVs and motorbikes that we find so indispensable ourselves. If money does not buy happiness, neither does poverty.

In other ways too, our laments for lost paradises may really have much more to do with our own state of mind than with the state of the place whose decline we mourn. Whenever we recall the places we have seen, we tend to observe them in the late afternoon glow of nos-talgia, after memory, the mind's great cosmetician, has softened out rough edges, smoothed out imperfections and removed the whole to a lovely abstract distance. Just as a good man, once dead, is remem-bered as a saint, so a pleasant place, once quit, is recalled as a utopia. Nothing is ever what it used to be.

If the First World is not invariably corrupting the Third, we are sometimes apt to leap to the opposite conclusion: that the Third World, in fact, is hustling the First. As tourists, moreover, we are so bombarded with importunities from a variety of locals—girls who live off their bodies and touts who live off their wits, merchants who use friendship to lure us into their stores and "students" who attach themselves to us in order to improve their English—that we begin to regard ourselves as beleaguered innocents and those we meet as shame-less predators.

To do so, however, is to ignore the great asymmetry that governs every meeting between tourist and local: that we are there by choice and they largely by circumstance; that we are traveling in the spirit of pleasure, adventure and romance, while they are mired in the more urgent business of trying to survive; and that we, often courted by the government, enjoy a kind of unofficial diplomatic immunity, which gives us all the perks of authority and none of the perils of responsibility, while they must stake their hopes on every potential transaction.

Descending upon native lands quite literally from the heavens, *dei ex machinae* from an alien world of affluence, we understandably strike many locals in much the same way that movie stars strike us. And just as some of us are wont to accost a celebrity glimpsed by chance at a restaurant, so many people in developing countries may be tempted to do anything and everything possible to come into contact with the free-moving visitors from abroad and their world of distant glamour. They have nothing to lose in approaching a foreigner—at worst, they will merely be insulted or pushed away. And they have everything to gain: a memory, a conversation, an old copy of *Paris Match,* perhaps even a friendship or a job opportunity. Every foreigner is a messenger from a world of dreams.

"Do you know Beverly Hills?" I was once asked by a young Burmese boy who had just spent nine months in jail for trying to escape his closed motherland. "Do you know Hollywood? Las Vegas? The Potomac, I think, is very famous. Am I right? Detroit, Michigan, is where they make cars. Ford. General Motors. Chevrolet. Do you know Howard Hughes? There are many Jewish people in New York. Am I right? And also at *Time* magazine? Am I right?" Tell us about life behind the scenes, we ask the star, and which is the best place in the whole wide world, and what is Liz Taylor really like.

The touts that accost us are nearly always, to be sure, worldly pragmatists. But they are also, in many cases, wistful dreamers, whose hopes are not so different from the ones our culture encourages: to slough off straitened circumstances and set up a new life and a new self abroad, underwritten by hard work and dedication. American dreams are strongest in the hearts of those who have seen America only in their dreams.

I first met Maung-Maung as I stumbled off a sixteen-hour third-class overnight train from Rangoon to Mandalay. He was standing outside the station, waiting to pick up tourists; a scrawny fellow in his late twenties, with a sailor's cap, a beard, a torn white shirt above his *longyi* and an open, rough-hewn face—a typical tout, in short. Beside him stood his bicycle trishaw. On one side was painted the legend "My Life"; on the other, "B.Sc. (Maths)."

We haggled for a few minutes. Then Maung-Maung smilingly persuaded me to part with a somewhat inflated fare—twenty cents— for the trip across town, and together we began cruising through the wide, sunny boulevards of the city of kings. As we set off, we began to exchange the usual questions—age, place of birth, marital status and education—and before long we found that our answers often jibed. Soon, indeed, the conversation was proceeding swimmingly. A little while into our talk, my driver, while carefully steering his trishaw with one hand, sank the other into his pocket and handed back to me a piece of jade. I admired it dutifully, then extended it back in his direction. "No," he said. "This is present."

15   Where, I instantly wondered, was the catch—was he framing me, or bribing me, or cunningly putting me in his debt? What was the small print? What did he want?

"I want you," said Maung-Maung, "to have something so you can always remember me. Also, so you can always have happy memories of Mandalay." I did not know how to respond. "You see," he went on, "if I love other people, they will love me. It is like Newton's law, or Archimedes."

This was not what I had expected. "I think," he added, "it is always good to apply physics to life."

That I did not doubt. But still I was somewhat taken aback. "Did you study physics at school?"

"No, I study physics in college. You see, I am graduate from University of Mandalay—B.Sc. Mathematics." He waved with pride at the inscription on the side of his trishaw.

20   "And you completed all your studies?"

"Yes. B.Sc. Mathematics."

"Then why are you working in this kind of job?"

"Other jobs are difficult. You see, here in Burma, a teacher earns only two hundred fifty kyats [$30] in a month. Managing director has only one thousand kyats [$125]. Even President makes only four thousand kyats [$500]. For me, I do not make much money. But in this job, I can meet tourist and improve my English. Experience, I believe, is the best teacher."

"But surely you could earn much more just by driving a horse cart?"

25 "I am Buddhist," Maung-Maung reminded me gently, as he went 25
pedaling calmly through the streets. "I do not want to inflict harm on
any living creature. If I hit horse in this life, in next life I come back
as horse."

"So"—I was still skeptical—"you live off tourists instead?"

"Yes," he said, turning around to give me a smile. My irony, it
seems, was wasted. "Until two years ago, in my village in Shan States,
I had never seen a tourist."

"Never?"

"Only in movies." Again he smiled back at me.

30 I was still trying to puzzle out why a university graduate would be 30
content with such a humble job when Maung-Maung, as he pedaled,
reached into the basket perched in front of his handlebars and pulled
out a thick leather book. Looking ahead as he steered, he handed it
back to me to read. Reluctantly, I opened it, bracing myself for porno
postcards or other illicit souvenirs. Inside, however, was nothing but
a series of black-and-white snapshots. Every one of them had been
painstakingly annotated in English: "My Headmaster," "My Monk,"
"My Brothers and Sisters," "My Friend's Girlfriend." And his own
girlfriend? "I had picture before. But after she broke my heart, and fall
in love with other people, I tear it out."

At the very back of his book, in textbook English, Maung-Maung
had carefully inscribed the principles by which he lived.

1. Abstain from violence.
2. Abstain from illicit sexual intercourse.
3. Abstain from intoxicants of all kinds.
4. Always be helpful.
5. Always be kind.

"It must be hard," I said dryly, "to stick to all these rules."

"Yes. It is not always easy," he confessed. "But I must try. If people
ask me for food, my monk tell me, I must always give them money.
But if they want money for playing cards, I must give them no help.
My monk also explain I must always give forgiveness—even to people
who hurt me. If you put air into volleyball and throw it against wall,
it bounces back. But if you do not put in air, what happens? It col-
lapses against wall."

Faith, in short, was its own vindication.

35   I was now beginning to suspect that I would find no more en-   35
gaging guide to Mandalay than Maung-Maung, so I asked him if he
would agree to show me around. "Yes, thank you very much. But first,
please, I would like you to see my home."

Ah, I thought, here comes the setup. Once I'm in his house, far
from the center of a city I don't know, he will drop a drug in my tea
or pull out a knife or even bring in a few accomplices. I will find out
too late that his friendliness is only a means to an end.

Maung-Maung did nothing to dispel these suspicions as he pedaled the trishaw off the main street and we began to pass through dirty
alleyways, down narrow lanes of run-down shacks. At last we pulled
up before a hut, fronted with weeds. Smiling proudly, he got off and
asked me to enter.

There was not much to see inside his tiny room. There was a cot,
on which sat a young man, his head buried in his hands. There was
another cot, on which Maung-Maung invited me to sit as he introduced me to his roommate. The only other piece of furniture was a
blackboard in a corner on which my host had written out the statement reproduced in the epigraph to this book, expressing his lifelong
pledge to be of service to tourists.

I sat down, not sure what was meant to happen next. For a few
minutes, we made desultory conversation. His home, Maung-Maung
explained, cost 30 kyats ($4) a month. This other man was also a uni-
versity graduate, but he had no job: every night, he got drunk. Then,
after a few moments of reflection, my host reached down to the floor
next to his bed and picked up what I took to be his two most valuable belonging18   s.

40   Solemnly, he handed the first of them to me. It was a sociology   40
textbook from Australia. Its title was *Life in Modern America.* Then,
as gently as if it were his Bible, Maung-Maung passed across the other
volume, a dusty old English-Burmese dictionary, its yellowed pages
falling from their covers. "Every night," he explained, "after I am finished on trishaw, I come here and read this. Also, every word I do not
know I look up." Inside the front cover, he had copied out a few spec-
imen sentences. *If you do this, you may end up in jail. My heart is lac-
erated by what you said. What a lark.*

I was touched by his show of trust. But I also felt as uncertain as
an actor walking through a play he hasn't read. Perhaps, I said a little

uneasily, we should go now, so we can be sure of seeing all the sights of Mandalay before sundown. "Do not worry," Maung-Maung assured me with a quiet smile, "we will see everything. I know how long the trip will take. But first, please, I would like you to see this."

Reaching under his bed, he pulled out what was clearly his most precious treasure of all. With a mixture of shyness and pride, he handed over a thick black notebook. I looked at the cover for markings and, finding none, opened it up. Inside, placed in alphabetical order, was every single letter he had ever received from a foreign visitor. Every one was meticulously dated and annotated; many were accompanied by handwritten testimonials or reminiscences from the tourists Maung-Maung had met. On some pages, he had affixed wrinkled passport photos of his foreign visitors by which he could remember them.

Toward the end of the book, Maung-Maung had composed a two-page essay, laboriously inscribed in neat and grammatical English, called "Guide to Jewelry." It was followed by two further monographs, "For You" and "For the Tourists." In them, Maung-Maung warned visitors against "twisty characters," explained something of the history and beauty of Mandalay and told his readers not to trust him until he had proved worthy of their trust.

Made quiet by this labor of love, I looked up. "This must have taken you a long time to write."

45 "Yes," he replied with a bashful smile. "I have to look many times 45 at dictionary. But it is my pleasure to help tourists."

I went back to flipping through the book. At the very end of the volume, carefully copied out, was a final four-page essay, entitled "My Life."

He had grown up, Maung-Maung wrote, in a small village, the eldest of ten children. His mother had never learned to read, and feeling that her disability made her "blind," she was determined that her children go to school. It was not easy, because his father was a farmer and earned only 300 kyats a month. Still, Maung-Maung, as the eldest, was able to complete his education at the local school.

When he finished, he told his parents that he wanted to go to university. Sorrowfully, they told him that they could not afford it—they had given him all they had for his schooling. He knew that was true, but still he was set on continuing his studies. "I have hand. I have head. I have legs," he told them. "I wish to stand on my own legs."

With that, he left his village and went to Mandalay. Deeply wounded by his desertion, his parents did not speak to him for a year.

In Mandalay, Maung-Maung's narrative continued, he had begun to finance his studies by digging holes—he got 4 kyats for every hole. Then he got a job cleaning clothes. Then he went to a monastery and washed dishes and clothes in exchange for board and lodging. Finally, he took a night job as a trishaw driver.

When they heard of that, his parents were shocked. "They think I go with prostitutes. Everyone looks down on trishaw driver. Also other trishaw drivers hate me because I am a student. I do not want to quarrel with them. But I do not like it when they say dirty things or go with prostitutes." Nevertheless, after graduation Maung-Maung decided to pay 7 kyats a day to rent a trishaw full-time. Sometimes, he wrote, he made less than 1 kyat a day, and many nights he slept in his vehicle in the hope of catching the first tourists of the day. He was a poor man, he went on, but he made more money than his father. Most important, he made many friends. And through riding his trishaw he had begun to learn English.

His dream, Maung-Maung's essay concluded, was to buy his own trishaw. But that cost four hundred dollars. And his greatest dream was, one day, to get a "Further Certificate" in mathematics. He had already planned the details of that far-off moment when he could invite his parents to his graduation. "I must hire taxi. I must buy English suit. I must pay for my parents to come to Mandalay. I know that it is expensive, but I want to express my gratitude to my parents. They are my lovers."

When I finished the essay, Maung-Maung smiled back his gratitude, and gave me a tour of the city as he had promised.

The American empire in the East: that was my grand theme as I set forth. But as soon as I left the realm of abstract labels and generalized forces, and came down to individuals—to myself, Maung-Maung and many others like him—the easy contrasts began to grow confused. If cultures are only individuals writ large, as Salman Rushdie and Gabriel García Márquez have suggested, individuals are small cultures in themselves. Everyone is familiar with the slogan of Kipling's "Oh, East is East, and West is West, and never the twain shall meet." But few recall that the lines that conclude the refrain, just a few syllables later, exclaim, "But there is neither East nor West, border, nor breed, nor birth, / When two strong men stand face to face, though they come from the ends of the earth!"

On a grand collective level, the encounters between East and West might well be interpreted as a battle; but on the human level, the meeting more closely resembled a mating dance (even Rambo, while waging war against the Vietnamese, had fallen in love with a Vietnamese girl). Whenever a Westerner meets an Easterner, each is to some extent confronted with the unknown. And the unknown is at once an enticement and a challenge; it awakens in us both the lover and the would-be conqueror. When Westerner meets Easterner, therefore, each finds himself often drawn to the other, yet mystified; each projects his romantic hopes on the stranger, as well as his designs; and each pursues both his illusions and his vested interests with a curious mix of innocence and calculation that shifts with every step.

55 Everywhere I went in Asia, I came upon variations on this same 55 uncertain pattern: in the streets of China, where locals half woo, half recoil from Westerners whose ways remain alien but whose goods are now irresistible; in the country-and-western bars of Manila, where former conqueror and former conquest slow-dance cheek to cheek with an affection, and a guilt, born of longtime familiarity; in the high places of the Himalayas, where affluent Westerners eager to slough off their riches in order to find religion meet local wise men so poor that they have made of riches a religion; and, most vividly of all, in the darkened bars of Bangkok, where a Western man and a Thai girl exchange shy questions and tentative glances, neither knowing whether either is after love or something else. Sometimes, the romance seemed like a blind date, sometimes like a passionate attachment; sometimes like a back-street coupling, sometimes like the rhyme of kindred spirits. Always, though, it made any talk of winners and losers irrelevant.

Usually, too, the cross-cultural affairs developed with all the contradictory twists and turns of any romance in which opposites attract and then retract and then don't know exactly where they stand. The Westerner is drawn to the tradition of the Easterner, and almost covets his knowledge of suffering, but what attracts the Easterner to the West is exactly the opposite—his future, and his freedom from all hardship. After a while, each starts to become more like the other, and somewhat less like the person the other seeks. The New Yorker disappoints the locals by turning into a barefoot ascetic dressed in bangles and beads, while the Nepali peasant frustrates his foreign supplicants by turning out to be a traveling salesman in Levi's and Madonna

T-shirt. Soon, neither is quite the person he was, or the one the other wanted. The upshot is confusion. "You cannot have pineapple for breakfast," a Thai waitress once admonished me. "Why?" I asked. "What do *you* have for breakfast?" "Hot dog."

It is never hard, in such skewed exchanges, to find silliness and self-delusion. "Everybody thought that everybody else was ridiculously exotic," writes Gita Mehta of East-West relations in *Karma Cola,* "and everybody got it wrong." Yet Mehta's cold-eyed perspective does justice to only one aspect of this encounter. For the rest, I prefer to listen to her wise and very different compatriot, R. K. Narayan, whose typical tale "God and the Cobbler" describes a chance meeting in a crowded Indian street between a Western hippie and a village cobbler. Each, absurdly, takes the other to be a god. Yet the beauty of their folly is that each, lifted by the other's faith, surprises himself, and us, by somehow rising to the challenge and proving worthy of the trust he has mistakenly inspired: each, taken out of himself, becomes, not a god perhaps, but something better than a dupe or fraud. Faith becomes its own vindication. And at the story's end, each leaves the other with a kind of benediction, the more valuable because untypical.

Every trip we take deposits us at the same forking of the paths: it can be a shortcut to alienation—removed from our home and distanced from our immediate surroundings, we can afford to be contemptuous of both; or it can be a voyage into renewal, as, leaving our selves and pasts at home and traveling light, we recover our innocence abroad. Abroad, we are all Titanias, so bedazzled by strangeness that we comically mistake asses for beauties; but away from home, we can also be Mirandas, so new to the world that our blind faith can become a kind of higher sight. "After living in Asia," John Krich quotes an old hand as saying, "you trust nobody, but you believe everything." At the same time, as Edmond Taylor wrote, Asia is "the school of doubt in which one learns faith in man." If every journey makes us wiser about the world, it also returns us to a sort of childhood. In alien parts, we speak more simply, in our own or some other language, move more freely, unencumbered by the histories that we carry around at home, and look more excitedly, with eyes of wonder. And if every trip worth taking is both a tragedy and a comedy, rich with melodrama and farce, it is also, at its heart, a love story. The romance with the foreign must certainly be leavened with a spirit of keen and unillusioned realism; but it must also be observed with a measure of faith.

Questions on Meaning

1. Iyer is a tough-minded writer, one who refuses to accept easy answers but always searches for the complexity beneath the surface of things. One example of this trait is in the essay's first sentence. "To mention, however faintly, the West's cultural assault on the East is, inevitably, to draw dangerously close to the fashionable belief that the First World is corrupting the Third." He does not want to succumb to merely "fashionable" beliefs, but to investigate and test his theories about other cultures. Find several more of his tough-minded statements and explain them.
2. Describe the character of Maung-Maung as Iyer perceives it.
3. List some of the common misconceptions people of Eastern and Western cultures carry about each other. Add the qualifications and complexities that Iyer mentions.

Questions on Rhetorical Strategy and Style

1. Iyer writes for "high-brow" publications like the *Times Literary Supplement* as well as more "middle-brow" publications like *Time* magazine and *The Village Voice*. As a writer for relatively educated readers, is he a trustworthy correspondent concerning Third World cultures? What are his strengths and weaknesses?
2. Iyer's skeptical and analytical style sometimes masks tender feelings. Note a passage in which he is clearly affected by what is happening, and explain how the language or content gives him away.
3. Reread Iyer's concluding paragraph. What is its relation to the rest of the essay?

Writing Assignments

1. Write an essay that recounts your contact with a foreign culture—in travel or in moving to a new place or in some change in your social circumstances. What features of your own and your new culture's life seem most important to you? Language, manners, money, safety, lifestyle? Detail your expectations and stereotypical attitudes, your intentions, the inevitable conflicts and confusions that arise from difference.
2. Go to a library, newstand or bookstore that carries travel magazines. Read a few essays in those magazines and compose a travel

essay concerning one of your own recent trips. Try to imitate the style of presentation you find in the magazine.

How Social Movements Matter

David S. Meyer

Were the activists who protested the Iraq War successful? Social movement activists are often discouraged when their immediate goals are not attained. However, this article reports research that shows that social movements of all types can have deep and long lasting consequences for politics, the larger society, and the activists themselves.

In January 2003, tens if not hundreds of thousands of people assembled in Washington, D.C. to try to stop the impending invasion of Iraq. It did not look good for the demonstrators. Months earlier, Congress authorized President Bush to use force to disarm Iraq, and Bush repeatedly said that he would not let the lack of international support influence his decision about when—or whether—to use military force. Opposition to military action grew in the intervening months; the Washington demonstration coincided with sister events in San Francisco, Portland, Tampa, Tokyo, Paris, Cairo and Moscow. Protests, albeit smaller and less frequent, continued after the war began. Did any of them change anything? Could they have? How? And how would we know if they did?

Such questions are not specific to this latest peace mobilization, but are endemic to protest movements more generally. Social movements are organized challenges to authorities that use a broad range of tactics, both inside and outside of conventional politics, in an effort to promote social and political change. Opponents of the Iraq War wrote letters to elected officials and editors of newspapers, called talk radio shows and contributed money to antiwar groups. Many also invited arrest by civil disobedience; some protesters, for example, blocked entrances to government offices and military bases. A group of 50 "Unreasonable Women of West Marin" lay naked on a

Reprinted from *Contexts* 2, no. 4 (2003), by permission of the University of California Press.

northern California beach, spelling out "Peace" with their bodies for a photographer flying overhead. Besides using diverse methods of protest, opponents of the war also held diverse political views. Some opposed all war, some opposed all U.S. military intervention, while others were skeptical only about this particular military intervention. This is a familiar social movement story: broad coalitions stage social movements, and differences within a movement coalition are often nearly as broad as those between the movement and the authorities it challenges.

Political activists and their targets act as if social movements matter, and sociologists have been trying, for the better part of at least four decades, to figure out why, when and how. It is too easy—and not very helpful—to paint activists as heroes or, alternatively, as cranks. It is similarly too easy to credit them for social change or, alternatively, to dismiss their efforts by saying that changes, such as advances in civil rights or environmental protections, would have happened anyway. What we have learned is that social movements are less a departure from conventional institutional politics than an extension of them—a "politics by other means." In the end, we find that movements crest and wane, often failing to attain their immediate goals, but they can lastingly change political debates, governmental institutions and the wider culture.

It is often difficult to tell whether activism makes a difference because the forces that propel people to mobilize are often the same forces responsible for social change. For example, it is difficult to decide whether the feminist movement opened new opportunities to women or whether economic changes fostered both the jobs and feminism. Also, authorities challenged by movements deny that activism influenced their decisions. What politicians want to admit that their judgments can be affected by "mobs"? Why risk encouraging protesters in the future? Finally, movements virtually never achieve all that their partisans demand, and so activists are quick to question their own influence. As a result, proving that movements influence politics and policy involves difficult detective work.

5 But research shows that social movements can affect government policy, as well as how it is made. And movement influence extends further. Activism often profoundly changes the activists, and through them, the organizations in which they participate, as well as the broader culture. The ways that movements make a difference are

complex, veiled, and take far longer to manifest themselves than the news cycle that covers a single demonstration, or even a whole protest campaign.

When Movements Emerge

Activists protest when they think it might help them achieve their goals—goals they might not accomplish otherwise. Organizers successfully mobilize movements when they convince people that the issue at hand is urgent, that positive outcomes are possible and that their efforts could make a difference. In the case of the war on Iraq, for example, President Bush set the agenda for a broad range of activists by explicitly committing the country to military intervention. More conventional politics—elections, campaign contributions and letter-writing—had already played out and it became clear that none of these activities were sufficient, in and of themselves, to stop the war. In addition, the President's failure to build broad international or domestic support led activists to believe that direct pressure might prevent war. The rapid worldwide growth of the movement itself encouraged activism, assuring participants that they were part of something larger than themselves, something that might matter. In effect, President Bush's actions encouraged anti-war activism to spread beyond a small group of perpetual peace activists to a broader public.

With peace movements, it is clear that threat of war helps organizers mobilize people. Threats generally help political opposition grow beyond conventional politics. Movements against nuclear armaments, for example, emerge strongly when governments announce they are building more weapons. Similarly, environmental movements expand when government policies toward forests, pesticides, or toxic wastes become visibly negligent. In the case of abortion politics, each side has kept the other mobilized for more than 30 years by periodically threatening to take control of the issue. In each of these cases, those who lose in traditional political contests such as elections or lobbying campaigns often take to the streets.

Other sorts of movements grow when the promise of success arises. American civil rights activists, for example, were able to mobilize most broadly when they saw signals that substantial change was possible. Rosa Parks knew about Jackie Robinson and *Brown v Board of Education*—as well as Gandhian civil disobedience—before deciding not to move to the back of the bus in Montgomery, Alabama. Government responsiveness to earlier activism—such as President Truman's desegregation of the armed forces and calling for an anti-lynching law—though limited, fitful, and often strategic, for a time encouraged others in their efforts. And the success of African-American activists encouraged other ethnic groups, as well as women, to pursue social change through movement politics.

As social movements grow, they incorporate more groups with a broader range of goals and more diverse tactics. Absent a focus like an imminent war, activists inside and political figures outside compete with one another to define movement goals and objectives. Political authorities often respond with policy concessions designed to diminish the breadth and depth of a movement. While such tactics can divide a movement, they are also one way of measuring a movement's success.

How Movements Matter: Public Policy

By uniting, however loosely, a broad range of groups and individuals, and taking action, social movements can influence public policy, at least by bringing attention to their issues. Newspaper stories about a demonstration pique political, journalistic and public interest in the demonstrators' concerns. By bringing scrutiny to a contested policy, activists can promote alternative thinking. By displaying a large and engaged constituency, social movements provide political support for leaders sympathetic to their concerns. Large demonstrations show that there are passionate citizens who might also donate money, work in campaigns, and vote for candidates who will speak for them. Citizen mobilization against abortion, taxes, and immigration, for example, has encouraged ambitious politicians to cater to those constituencies. In these ways, social movement activism spurs and supports more conventional political action.

Activism outside of government can also strengthen advocates of minority positions within government. Social movements—just like presidential administrations and congressional majorities—are coalitions. Anti-war activists in the streets may have strengthened the bargaining position of the more internationalist factions in the Bush administration, most notably Colin Powell, and led, at least temporarily, to diplomatic action in the United Nations. Mobilized opposition also, for a time, seemed to embolden Congressional critics, and encouraged lesser-known candidates for the Democratic presidential nomination to vocally oppose the war.

Social movements, by the popularity of their arguments, or more frequently, the strength of their support, can convince authorities to re-examine and possibly change their policy preferences. Movements can demand a litmus test for their support. Thus, George H. W. Bush, seeking the Republican nomination for president in 1980, revised his prior support for abortion rights. A few years later, Jesse Jackson likewise reconsidered his opposition to abortion. Movements raised the profile of the issue, forcing politicians not only to address their concerns, but to accede to their demands.

Although movement activists promote specific policies—a nuclear freeze, an equal rights amendment, an end to legal abortion, or, more recently, a cap on malpractice awards—their demands are usually so absolute that they do not translate well into policy. (Placards and bumper stickers offer little space for nuanced debate.) Indeed, the clearest message that activists can generally send is absolute rejection: no to nuclear weapons, abortion, pesticides or taxes. These admonitions rarely become policy, but by promoting their programs in stark moral terms, activists place the onus on others to offer alternative policies that are, depending on one's perspective, more moderate or complex. At the same time, politicians often use such alternatives to capture, or at least defuse, social movements. The anti-nuclear weapons movement of the late 1950s and early 1960s did not end the arms race or all nuclear testing. It did, however, lead to the Limited Test Ban Treaty, which ended atmospheric testing. First Eisenhower, then Kennedy, offered arms control proposals and talks with the Soviet Union, at least in part as a response to the movement. This peace movement established the framework for arms control in superpower relations, which subsequently spread to the entire international community.

In these ways, activists shape events—even if they do not necessarily get credit for their efforts or achieve everything they want. The movement against the Vietnam War, for instance, generated a great deal of attention which, in turn, changed the conduct of that war and much else in domestic politics. President Johnson chose bombing targets with attention to minimizing political opposition; President Nixon, elected at least partly as a result of the backlash against the antiwar movement nonetheless tailored his military strategy to respond to some of its concerns. In later years, he suggested that the anti-war movement made it unthinkable for him to threaten nuclear escalation in Vietnam—even as a bluff. In addition, the movement helped end the draft, institutionalizing all-volunteer armed forces. And, according to Colin Powell, the Vietnam dissenters provoked a new military approach for the United States, one that emphasized the use of overwhelming force to minimize American casualties. Thus, the military execution of the 1991 Persian Gulf war was influenced by an anti-war movement that peaked more than three decades earlier. This is significant, if not the effect most anti-war activists envisioned.

Political Institutions

15 Social movements can alter not only the substance of policy, but also   15
how policy is made. It is not uncommon for governments to create new institutions, such as departments and agencies, in response to activists' demands. For example, President Kennedy responded to the nuclear freeze movement by establishing the Arms Control and Disarmament Agency, which became a permanent voice and venue in the federal bureaucracy for arms control. A glance at any organizational chart of federal offices turns up numerous departments, boards, and commissions that trace their origins to popular mobilization. These include the Department of Labor, the Department of Housing and Urban Development, the National Labor Relations Board, the Environmental Protection Agency, the National Council on Disability, the Consumer Product Safety Commission and the Equal Employment Opportunity Commission. Although these offices do not always support activist goals, their very existence represents a permanent institutional concern and a venue for making demands. If, as environmentalists argue, the current Environmental Protection Agency is often more interested in facilitating exploitation of the environment than in preventing it, this does not negate the fact that the environmental movement established a set of procedures through which environmental concerns can be addressed.

Government responses to movement demands also include ensuring that diverse voices are heard in decision-making. In local zoning decisions, for example, environmental impact statements are a now a routine part of getting a permit for construction. Congress passed legislation establishing this requirement in 1970 in response to the growing environmental movement. Indeed, movement groups, including Greenpeace and the Sierra Club, negotiated directly with congressional sponsors. Similarly, juries and judges now routinely hear victim impact statements before pronouncing sentences in criminal cases, the product of the victims' rights movement. Both public and private organizations have created new departments to manage and, perhaps more importantly, document personnel practices, such as hiring and firing, to avoid being sued for discrimination on the basis of gender, ethnicity or disability. Workshops on diversity, tolerance, and sexual harassment are commonplace in American universities and corporations, a change over just two decades that would have been impossible to imagine without the activism of the 1960s and 1970s. In such now well-established bureaucratic routines, we can see how social movements change practices, and through them, beliefs.

Social movements also spawn dedicated organizations that generally survive long after a movement's moment has passed. The environmental movement, for example, firmly established a "big ten" group of national organizations, such as the Wildlife Defense Fund, which survives primarily by raising money from self-defined environmentalists. It cultivates donors by monitoring and publicizing government actions and environmental conditions, lobbying elected officials and administrators, and occasionally mobilizing supporters to do something more than mail in their annual membership renewals. Here, too, the seemingly permanent establishment of "movement organizations" in Washington, D.C. and in state capitals across the United States has—even if these groups often lose—fundamentally changed policymaking. Salaried officers of the organizations routinely screen high-level appointees to the judiciary and government bureaucracy and testify before legislatures. Mindful of this process, policymakers seek to preempt their arguments by modifying policy—or at least their rhetoric.

Political Activists

Social movements also change the people who participate in them, educating as well as mobilizing activists, and thereby promoting ongoing awareness and action that extends beyond the boundaries of one movement or campaign. Those who turn out at anti-war demonstrations today have often cut their activist teeth mobilizing against globalization, on behalf of labor, for animal rights or against welfare reform. By politicizing communities, connecting people, and promoting personal loyalties, social movements build the infrastructure not only of subsequent movements, but of a democratic society more generally.

Importantly, these consequences are often indirect and difficult to document. When hundreds of thousands of activists march to the Supreme Court to demonstrate their support for legal abortion, their efforts might persuade a justice. More likely, the march signals commitment and passion to other activists and inspires them to return home and advocate for abortion rights in their communities across the country, thereby affecting the shape of politics and culture more broadly.

20   The 2003 anti-Iraq War movement mobilized faster, with better   20 organizational ties in the United States and transnationally, than, for example, the movement against the 1991 Persian Gulf War. But how are we to assess its influence? Many activists no doubt see their efforts as having been wasted, or at least as unsuccessful. Moreover, supporters of the war point to the rapid seizure of Baghdad and ouster of Saddam Hussein's regime as evidence of the peace movement's naïveté. But a movement's legacy extends through a range of outcomes beyond a government's decision of the moment. It includes consequences for process, institutional practices, organizations and individuals. This anti-war movement changed the rhetoric and international politics of the United States' preparation for war, leading to a detour through the United Nations that delayed the start of war. The activists who marched in Washington, San Francisco and Los Angeles may retreat for awhile, but they are likely to be engaged in politics more intensively in the future. This may not be much consolation to people who marched to stop a war, but it is true. To paraphrase a famous scholar: activists make history, but they do not make it just as they please. In fighting one political battle, they shape the conditions of the next one.

Questions

1. Describe the elements that assist the growth of social movements.
2. Provide examples from the reading, and beyond the reading, that show how social movements matter to politics. How can politicians defuse social movements? Provide an example.
3. The author reports that social movements often "spawn dedicated organizations that generally survive long after a movement's moment has passed." For example, they mention the Wildlife Defense Fund as an outgrowth of the environmental movement. Visit the Amy Biehl Foundation Web site at: *http://www.amybiehl.org/*. Study the organization's -history and current focus. What social movement was Amy Biehl committed to? Where has the organization continued in the aftermath of her death and now that the movement's moment has passed.
4. How do social movements change the people who participate in them?

Recommended Resources

Arkin, William M. "The Dividends of Delay." *Los Angeles Times,* February 23, 2003. Arkin details the influence of the peace movement on U.S. military strategy in the Iraq War.

Giugni, Marco, Doug McAdam, and Charles Tilly. *How Social Movements Matter.* Minneapolis, MN: University of Minnesota Press, 1999. This collection employs diverse approaches in examining the outcomes of social movements across a range of cases.

Klatch, Rebecca. *A Generation Divided: The New Left, The New Right, and the 1960s.* Berkeley, CA: University of California Press, 1999. Klatch traces individual life stories of activists on both ends of the political spectrum during a turbulent period and beyond.

Meyer, David S. "Protest Cycles and Political Process: American Peace Movements in the Nuclear Age." *Political Research Quarterly* 46 (1993): 451–79. This article details how government responses to peace movements affect policy and subsequent political mobilization.

Meyer, David S., Nancy Whittier, and Belinda Robnett, eds. *Social Movements: Identity, Culture, and the State.* New York: Oxford University Press, 2002. A collection that addresses the link between protesters and context across different settings and times.

McAdam, Doug and Yang Su. "The War at Home: Antiwar Protests and Congressional Voting, 1965 to 1973." *American Sociological Review* 67 (2002): 696–721. Antiwar protests set an agenda for Congress, forcing resolutions about the war, but could not influence the outcomes of those votes.

Rochon, Thomas. *Culture Moves: Ideas, Activism, and Changing Values.* Princeton, NJ: Princeton University Press, 1998. Rochon looks at social movements as a primary way to promote new ideas and alter culture.

Tarrow, Sidney. *Power in Movement.* New York: Cambridge University Press, [1994] 1998. A broad and comprehensive review of scholarship on movements, synthesized in a useful framework.

"Called Home" from *Animal, Vegetable, Miracle*

Barbara Kingsolver spellbound

Michael Moore Sicko
the Cave

*When Barbara Kingsolver (1955–) was seven years old,
her father, a physician, took the family from their rural
Kentucky home to the Congo for two years. Her recollec-
tion of those two years lent credibility to the details of
everyday African life found in her award-winning novel*
The Poisonwood Bible *(1998). Although Kingsolver wrote
stories and kept journals throughout her childhood and
adolescence, she never considered becoming a professional
writer until her thirties. After earning a biology degree
from DePauw University and a master's degree in ecology
from the University of Arizona, she traveled and worked
at jobs ranging from archaeologist to x-ray technician to
translator of medical documents. In her thirties she spent
two years as a freelance journalist, and began writing fiction by night. Her first novel,* The Bean Trees, *was published to wide critical and popular acclaim in 1988; since
that time she has written poetry and essays as well as articles,
stories, and book reviews. Kingsolver has been the recipient
of numerous awards, including the Pen/USA West Fiction
Award, the Physicians for Social Responsibility National
Award, and the National Humanities Medal. Several years
ago Kingsolver and her family embarked on an experiment in living simply, making as little impact on the environment as possible. With her husband and daughter she
recorded this venture, which was published in 2007 as*
Animal, Vegetable, Miracle. *The following selection is the
introductory chapter of that book.*

Reprinted from *Animal, Vegetable, Miracle: A Year of Food Life* (2007), by permission
of HarperCollins, Inc.

1   This story about good food begins in a quick-stop convenience   1
market. It was our family's last day in Arizona, where I'd lived
half my life and raised two kids for the whole of theirs. Now
we were moving away forever, taking our nostalgic inventory of the
things we would never see again: the bush where the roadrunner built
a nest and fed lizards to her weird-looking babies; the tree Camille
crashed into learning to ride a bike; the exact spot where Lily touched
a dead snake. Our driveway was just the first tributary on a memory
river sweeping us out.

One person's picture postcard is someone else's normal. This was
the landscape whose every face we knew: giant saguaro cacti, coyotes,
mountains, the wicked sun reflecting off bare gravel. We were leaving
it now in one of its uglier moments, which made good-bye easier, but
also seemed like a cheap shot—like ending a romance right when
your partner has really bad bed hair. The desert that day looked like a
nasty case of prickly heat caught in a long, naked wince.

This was the end of May. Our rainfall since Thanksgiving had
measured less than *one inch*. The cacti, denizens of deprivation,
looked ready to pull up roots and hitch a ride out if they could. The
prickly pears waved good-bye with puckered, grayish pads. The tall,
dehydrated saguaros stood around all teetery and sucked-in like very
prickly supermodels. Even in the best of times desert creatures live on
the edge of survival, getting by mostly on vapor and their own life
savings. Now, as the southern tier of U.S. states came into a third
consecutive year of drought, people elsewhere debated how seriously
they should take global warming. We were staring it in the face.

Away went our little family, like rats leaping off the burning ship.
It hurt to think about everything at once: our friends, our desert, old
home, new home. We felt giddy and tragic as we pulled up at a little
gas-and-go market on the outside edge of Tucson. Before we set off to
seek our fortunes we had to gas up, of course, and buy snacks for the
road. We did have a cooler in the back seat packed with respectable
lunch fare. But we had more than two thousand miles to go. Before
we crossed a few state lines we'd need to give our car a salt treatment
and indulge in some things that go crunch.

5   This was the trip of our lives. We were ending our existence out-   5
side the city limits of Tucson, Arizona, to begin a rural one in southern Appalachia. We'd sold our house and stuffed the car with the
most crucial things: birth certificates, books-on-tape, and a dog on

drugs. (Just for the trip, I swear.) All other stuff would come in the moving van. For better or worse, we would soon be living on a farm.

For twenty years Steven had owned a piece of land in the southern Appalachians with a farmhouse, barn, orchards and fields, and a tax zoning known as "farm use." He was living there when I met him, teaching college and fixing up his old house one salvaged window at a time. I'd come as a visiting writer, recently divorced, with something of a fixer-upper life. We proceeded to wreck our agendas in the predictable fashion by falling in love. My young daughter and I were attached to our community in Tucson; Steven was just as attached to his own green pastures and the birdsong chorus of deciduous eastern woodlands. My father-in-law to be, upon hearing the exciting news about us, asked Steven, "Couldn't you find one closer?"

Apparently not. We held on to the farm by renting the farmhouse to another family, and maintained marital happiness by migrating like birds: for the school year we lived in Tucson, but every summer headed back to our rich foraging grounds, the farm. For three months a year we lived in a tiny, extremely crooked log cabin in the woods behind the farmhouse, listening to wood thrushes, growing our own food. The girls (for another child came along shortly) loved playing in the creek, catching turtles, experiencing real mud. I liked working the land, and increasingly came to think of this place as my home too. When all of us were ready, we decided, we'd go there for keeps.

We had many conventional reasons for relocation, including extended family. My Kingsolver ancestors came from that county in Virginia; I'd grown up only a few hours away, over the Kentucky line. Returning now would allow my kids more than just a hit-and-run, holiday acquaintance with grandparents and cousins. In my adult life I'd hardly shared a phone book with anyone else using my last name. Now I could spend Memorial Day decorating my ancestors' graves with peonies from my backyard. Tucson had opened my eyes to the world and given me a writing career, legions of friends, and a taste for the sensory extravagance of red hot chiles and five-alarm sunsets. But after twenty-five years in the desert, I'd been called home.

There is another reason the move felt right to us, and it's the purview of this book. We wanted to live in a place that could feed us: where rain falls, crops grow, and drinking water bubbles right up out of the ground. This might seem an abstract reason for leaving beloved friends and one of the most idyllic destination cities in the United

States. But it was real to us. As it closes in on the million-souls mark, Tucson's charms have made it one of this country's fastest-growing cities. It keeps its people serviced across the wide, wide spectrum of daily human wants, with its banks, shops, symphonies, colleges, art galleries, city parks, and more golf courses than you can shake a stick at. By all accounts it's a bountiful source of everything on the human-need checklist, save for just the one thing—the stuff we put in our mouths every few hours to keep us alive. Like many other modern U.S. cities, it might as well be a space station where human sustenance is concerned. Virtually every unit of food consumed there moves into town in a refrigerated module from somewhere far away. Every ounce of the city's drinking, washing, and goldfish-bowl-filling water is pumped from a nonrenewable source—a fossil aquifer that is dropping so fast, sometimes the ground crumbles. In a more recent development, some city water now arrives via a three-hundred-mile-long open canal across the desert from the Colorado River, which—owing to our thirsts—is a river that no longer reaches the ocean, but peters out in a sand flat near the Mexican border.

10   If it crosses your mind that water running through hundreds of   10
miles of open ditch in a desert will evaporate and end up full of concentrated salts and muck, then let me just tell you, that kind of negative thinking will never get you elected to public office in the state of Arizona. When this giant new tap turned on, developers drew up plans to roll pink stucco subdivisions across the desert in all directions. The rest of us were supposed to rejoice as the new flow rushed into our pipes, even as the city warned us this water was kind of special. They said it was okay to drink, but don't put it in an aquarium because it would *kill the fish*.

Drink it we did, then, filled our coffee makers too, and mixed our children's juice concentrate with fluid that would gag a guppy. Oh, America the Beautiful, where are our standards? How did Europeans, ancestral cultures to most of us, whose average crowded country would fit inside one of our national parks, somehow hoard the market share of Beautiful? They'll run over a McDonald's with a bulldozer because it threatens the way of life of their fine cheeses. They have international trade hissy fits when we try to slip modified genes into their bread. They get their favorite ham from Parma, Italy, along with a favorite cheese, knowing these foods are linked in an ancient connection the farmers have crafted between the milk and the hogs. Oh.

We were thinking *Parmesan* meant, not "coming from Parma," but "coming from a green shaker can." Did they kick us out for bad taste?

No, it was mostly for vagrancy, poverty, or being too religious. We came here for the freedom to make a *Leaves of Grass* kind of culture and hear America singing to a good beat, pierce our navels as needed, and eat whatever we want without some drudge scolding: "You don't know where that's been!" And boy howdy, we do not.

The average food item on a U.S. grocery shelf has traveled farther than most families go on their annual vacations. True fact. Fossil fuels were consumed for the food's transport, refrigeration, and processing, with the obvious environmental consequences. The option of getting our household's food from closer to home, in Tucson, seemed no better to us. The Sonoran desert historically offered to humans baked dirt as a construction material, and for eats, a corn-and-beans diet organized around late summer monsoons, garnished in spring with cactus fruits and wild tubers. The Hohokam and Pima were the last people to live on that land without creating an environmental overdraft. When the Spaniards arrived, they didn't rush to take up the Hohokam diet craze. Instead they set about working up a monumental debt: planting orange trees and alfalfa, digging wells for irrigation, withdrawing millions more gallons from the water table each year than a dozen inches of annual rainfall could ever restore. Arizona is still an agricultural state. Even after the population boom of the mid-nineties, 85 percent of the state's water still went to thirsty crops like cotton, alfalfa, citrus, and pecan trees. Mild winters offer the opportunity to create an artificial endless summer, as long as we can conjure up water and sustain a chemically induced illusion of topsoil.

Living in Arizona on borrowed water made me nervous. We belonged to a far-flung little community of erstwhile Tucson homesteaders, raising chickens in our yards and patches of vegetables for our own use, frequenting farmers markets to buy from Arizona farmers, trying to reduce the miles-per-gallon quotient of our diets in a gasoholic world. But these gardens of ours had a drinking problem. So did Arizona farms. That's a devil of a choice: Rob Mexico's water or guzzle Saudi Arabia's gas?

15   Traditionally, employment and family dictate choices about where   15
to live. It's also legitimate to consider weather, schools, and other quality-of-life indices. We added one more wish to our list: more than one out of three of the basic elements necessary for human life.

Oily Food

Americans put almost as much fossil fuel into our refrigerators as our cars. We're consuming about 400 gallons of oil a year per citizen—about 17 percent of our nation's energy use—for agriculture, a close second to our vehicular use. Tractors, combines, harvesters, irrigation, sprayers, tillers, balers, and other equipment all use petroleum. Even bigger gas guzzlers on the farm are not the machines, but so-called inputs. Synthetic fertilizers, pesticides, and herbicides use oil and natural gas as their starting materials, and in their manufacturing. More than a quarter of all farming energy goes into synthetic fertilizers.

But getting the crop from seed to harvest takes only one-fifth of the total oil used for our food. The lion's share is consumed during the trip from the farm to your plate. Each food item in a typical U.S. meal has traveled an average of 1,500 miles. In addition to direct transport, other fuel-thirsty steps include processing (drying, milling, cutting, sorting, baking), packaging, warehousing, and refrigeration. Energy calories consumed by production, packaging, and shipping far outweigh the energy calories we receive from the food.

A quick way to improve food-related fuel economy would be to buy a quart of motor oil and drink it. More palatable options are available. If every U.S. citizen ate just one meal a week (any meal) composed of locally and organically raised meats and produce, we would reduce our country's oil consumption by over 1.1 million barrels of oil *every week*. That's not gallons, but barrels. Small changes in buying habits can make big differences. Becoming a less energy-dependent nation may just need to start with a good breakfast.

—Steven L. Hopp

(*Oxygen* Arizona has got.) If we'd had family ties, maybe we'd have felt more entitled to claim a seat at Tucson's lean dining table. But I moved there as a young adult, then added through birth and marriage three more mouths to feed. As a guest, I'd probably overstayed my welcome. So, as the U.S. population made an unprecedented dash for the Sun Belt, one carload of us dog-paddled against the tide, heading for the Promised Land where water falls from the sky and green stuff grows all around. We were about to begin the adventure of realigning our lives with our food chain.

Naturally, our first stop was to buy junk food and fossil fuel.

In the cinder-block convenience mart we foraged the aisles for blue corn chips and Craisins. Our family's natural-foods teenager scooped up a pile of energy bars big enough to pass as a retirement plan for a hamster. Our family's congenitally frugal Mom shelled out two bucks for a fancy green bottle of about a nickel's worth of iced tea. As long as we were all going crazy here, we threw in some 99-cent bottles of what comes free out of drinking fountains in places like Perrier, France. In our present location, 99 cents for good water seemed like a bargain. The goldfish should be so lucky.

As we gathered our loot onto the counter the sky darkened suddenly. After two hundred consecutive cloudless days, you forget what it looks like when a cloud crosses the sun. We all blinked. The cashier frowned toward the plate-glass window.

"*Dang,*" she said, "it's going to rain."

20   "I hope so," Steven said.   20

She turned her scowl from the window to Steven. This bleached-blond guardian of gas pumps and snack food was not amused. "It better not, is all I can say."

"But we need it," I pointed out. I am not one to argue with cashiers, but the desert was dying, and this was my very last minute as a Tucsonan. I hated to jinx it with bad precipitation-karma.

"I know that's what they're saying, but I don't care. Tomorrow's my first day off in two weeks, and I want to wash my car."

For three hundred miles we drove that day through desperately parched Sonoran badlands, chewing our salty cashews with a peculiar guilt. We had all shared this wish, in some way or another: that it wouldn't rain on our day off. Thunderheads dissolved ahead of us, as if honoring our compatriot's desire to wash her car as the final benediction pronounced on a dying land. In our desert, we would not see rain again.

25   It took us five days to reach the farm. On our first full day there we   25 spent ten hours mowing, clearing brush, and working on the farmhouse. Too tired to cook, we headed into town for supper, opting for a diner of the southern type that puts grits on your plate until noon and biscuits after, whether you ask for them or not. Our waitress was young and chatty, a student at the junior college nearby studying to be a nurse or else, if she doesn't pass the chemistry, a television broadcaster. She said she was looking forward to the weekend, but smiled broadly nevertheless at the clouds gathering over the hills outside. The wooded mountainsides and velvet pastures of southwestern Virginia looked

remarkably green to our desert-scorched eyes, but the forests and fields were suffering here too. Drought had plagued most of the southern United States that spring.

A good crack of thunder boomed, and the rain let loose just as the waitress came back to clear our plates. "Listen at that," she clucked. "Don't we need it!"

We do, we agreed. The hayfields aren't half what they should be.

"Let's hope it's a good long one," she said, pausing with our plates balanced on her arm, continuing to watch out the window for a good long minute. "And that it's not so hard that it washes everything out."

It is not my intention here to lionize country wisdom over city ambition. I only submit that the children of farmers are likely to know where food comes from, and that the rest of us might do well to pay attention. For our family, something turned over that evening in the diner: a gas-pump cashier's curse of drought was lifted by a waitress's simple, agricultural craving for rain. I thought to myself: There is hope for us.

30   Who is *us*, exactly? I live now in a county whose economic base is   30
farming. A disastrous summer will mean some of our neighbors will lose their farms. Others will have to keep farming *and* go looking for a job at the end of a long commute. We'll feel the effects in school enrollments, local businesses, shifts in land use and tax structure. The health of our streams, soils, and forests is also at stake, as lost farms get sold to developers whose business is to rearrange (drastically) the topsoil and everything on it. When I recognize good agricultural sense, though, I'm not just thinking of my town but also my species. It's not a trivial difference: praying for or against rainfall during a drought. You can argue that wishes don't count, but humans are good at making our dreams manifest and we do, historically speaking, get what we wish for. What are the just deserts for a species too selfish or preoccupied to hope for rain when the land outside is dying? Should we be buried under the topsoil in our own clean cars, to make room for wiser creatures?

We'd surely do better, if only we *knew* any better. In two generations we've transformed ourselves from a rural to an urban nation. North American children begin their school year around Labor Day and finish at the beginning of June with no idea that this arrangement was devised to free up children's labor when it was needed on the farm.

Most people of my grandparents' generation had an intuitive sense of agricultural basics: when various fruits and vegetables come into season, which ones keep through the winter, how to preserve the others. On what day autumn's first frost will likely fall on their county, and when to expect the last one in spring. Which crops can be planted before the last frost, and which must wait. Which grains are autumn-planted. What an asparagus patch looks like in August. Most importantly: what animals and vegetables thrive in one's immediate region and how to live well on those, with little else thrown into the mix beyond a bag of flour, a pinch of salt, and a handful of coffee. Few people of my generation, and approximately none of our children, could answer any of those questions, let alone all. This knowledge has vanished from our culture.

We also have largely convinced ourselves it wasn't too important. Consider how Americans might respond to a proposal that agriculture was to become a mandatory subject in all schools, alongside reading and mathematics. A fair number of parents would get hot under the collar to see their kids' attention being pulled away from the essentials of grammar, the all-important trigonometry, to make room for down-on-the-farm stuff. The baby boom psyche embraces a powerful presumption that education is a key to moving *away* from manual labor, and dirt—two undeniable ingredients of farming. It's good enough for us that somebody, somewhere, knows food production well enough to serve the rest of us with all we need to eat, each day of our lives.

If that is true, why isn't it good enough for someone else to know multiplication and the contents of the Bill of Rights? Is the story of bread, from tilled ground to our table, less relevant to our lives than the history of the thirteen colonies? Couldn't one make a case for the relevance of a subject that informs choices we make *daily*—as in, What's for dinner? Isn't ignorance of our food sources causing problems as diverse as overdependence on petroleum, and an epidemic of diet-related diseases?

If this book is not exactly an argument for reinstating food-production classes in schools (and it might be), it does contain a lot of what you might learn there. From our family's gas-station beginnings we have traveled far enough to discover ways of taking charge of one's food, and even knowing where it has been. This is the story of a year in which we made every attempt to feed ourselves animals and vegetables whose provenance we really knew. We tried to wring most of the petroleum out of our food chain, even if that meant giving up some things. Our highest shopping goal was to get our food from so close to home, we'd know the person who grew it. Often that turned out to be *us*, as we learned to produce more of what we needed, starting with dirt, seeds, and enough knowledge to muddle through. Or starting with baby animals and enough sense to refrain from naming them.

35   This is not a how-to book aimed at getting you cranking out your own food. We ourselves live in a region where every other house has a garden out back, but to many urban people the idea of growing your food must seem as plausible as writing and conducting your own symphonies for your personal listening pleasure. If that is your case, think of the agricultural parts of the story as a music appreciation course for food—acquainting yourself with the composers and con-ductors can improve the quality of your experience. Knowing the secret natural history of potatoes, melons, or asparagus gives you a leg up on detecting whether those in your market are wholesome kids from a nearby farm, or vagrants who idled away their precious youth in a boxcar. Knowing how foods grow is to know how and when to look for them; such expertise is useful for certain kinds of people, namely, the ones who eat, no matter where they live or grocery shop.

Absence of that knowledge has rendered us a nation of wary label-readers, oddly uneasy in our obligate relationship with the things we eat. We call our food animals by different names after they're dead, pre-sumably sparing ourselves any vision of the beefs and the porks running around on actual hooves. Our words for unhealthy contamination—"soiled" or "dirty"—suggest that if we really knew the number-one ingredient of a garden, we'd all head straight into therapy. I used to take my children's friends out to the garden to warm them up to the idea of eating vegetables, but this strategy sometimes backfired: they'd back away slowly saying, "Oh *man*, those things touched *dirt*!" Adults do the same by pretending it all comes from the clean, well-lighted grocery store. We're like petulant teenagers rejecting our mother. We *know* we came out of her, but *ee-ew*.

We don't know beans about beans. Asparagus, potatoes, turkey drumsticks—you name it, we don't have a clue how the world makes it. I usually think I'm exaggerating the scope of the problem, and then I'll encounter an editor (at a well-known nature magazine) who's nix-ing the part of my story that refers to pineapples growing from the ground. She insisted they grew on trees. Or, I'll have a conversation like this one:

"What's new on the farm?" asks my friend, a lifelong city dweller who likes for me to keep her posted by phone. She's a gourmet cook, she cares about the world, and has been around a lot longer than I have. This particular conversation was in early spring, so I told her what was up in the garden: peas, potatoes, spinach.

"Wait a minute," she said. "When you say, 'The potatoes are up,' what do you mean?" She paused, formulating her question: "What part of a potato comes *up*?"

"Um, the plant part," I said. "The stems and leaves."

"Wow," she said. "I never knew a potato *had* a plant part."

Many bright people are really in the dark about vegetable life. Biology teachers face kids in classrooms who may not even believe in the metamorphosis of bud to flower to fruit and seed, but rather, some continuum of pansies becoming petunias becoming chrysanthemums; that's the only reality they witness as landscapers come to campuses and city parks and surreptitiously yank out one flower before it fades from its prime, replacing it with another. (My biology-professor brother pointed this out to me.) The same disconnection from natural processes may be at the heart of our country's shift away from believing in evolution. In the past, principles of natural selection and change over time made sense to kids who'd watched it all unfold. Whether or not they knew the terms, farm families understood the processes well enough to imitate them: culling, selecting, and improving their herds and crops. For modern kids who intuitively believe in the spontaneous generation of fruits and vegetables in the produce section, trying to get their minds around the slow speciation of the plant kingdom may be a stretch.

Steven, also a biology professor, grew up in the corn belt of Iowa but has encountered his share of agricultural agnostics in the world. As a graduate student he lived in an urban neighborhood where his little backyard vegetable garden was a howling curiosity for the boys who ran wild in the alley. He befriended these kids, especially Malcolm, known throughout the neighborhood as "Malcolm-get-your-backside-in-here-now-or-you-won't-be-*having*-no-dinner!" Malcolm liked hanging around when Steven was working in the garden, but predictably enough, had a love-hate thing with the idea of the vegetables touching the dirt. The first time he watched Steven pull long, orange carrots out of the ground, he demanded: "How'd you get them *in* there?"

Steven held forth with condensed Intro Botany. Starts with a seed, grows into a plant. Water, sunlight, leaves, roots. "A carrot," Steven concluded, "is actually a root."

45 "Uh-huh . . ." said Malcolm doubtfully.

A crowd had gathered now. Steven engaged his audience by asking, "Can you guys think of other foods that might be root vegetables?"

Malcolm checked with his pals, using a lifeline before confidently submitting his final answer: "Spaghetti?"

We can't know what we haven't been taught. Steven couldn't recognize tobacco in vivo before moving in his twenties to southwestern Virginia, where the tobacco leaf might as well be the state flag. One Saturday morning soon after he'd moved, he was standing on a farmer's porch at a country yard sale when a field of giant, pale leaves and tall pink flower spikes caught his eye. He asked the farmer the name of this gorgeous plant. The man grinned hugely and asked, "You're not *from* here, are you, son?"

That farmer is probably still telling this story; Steven is his Malcolm. Every one of us is somebody's Malcolm. Country folks can be as food-chain-challenged as the city mice, in our own ways. Rural southern cooking is famous for processed-ingredient recipes like Coca-Cola cake, and plenty of rural kids harbor a potent dread of compost and earthworms. What we all don't know about farming could keep the farmers laughing until the cows come home. Except that they are barely making a living, while the rest of us play make-believe about the important part being the grocery store.

50 When we walked as a nation away from the land, our knowledge of food production fell away from us like dirt in a laundry-soap commercial. Now, it's fair to say, the majority of us don't want to be farmers, see farmers, pay farmers, or hear their complaints. Except as straw-chewing figures in children's books, we don't quite believe in them anymore. When we give it a thought, we mostly consider the food industry to be a *thing* rather than a person. We obligingly give 85 cents of our every food dollar to that thing, too—the processors, marketers, and transporters. And we complain about the high price of organic meats and vegetables that might send back more than three nickels per buck to the farmers: those actual humans putting seeds in the ground, harvesting, attending livestock births, standing in the

fields at dawn casting their shadows upon our sustenance. There seems to be some reason we don't want to compensate or think about these hardworking people. In the grocery store checkout corral, we're more likely to learn which TV stars are secretly fornicating than to inquire as to the whereabouts of the people who grew the cucumbers and melons in our carts.

This drift away from our agricultural roots is a natural consequence of migration from the land to the factory, which is as old as the Industrial Revolution. But we got ourselves uprooted entirely by a drastic reconfiguration of U.S. farming, beginning just after World War II. Our munitions plants, challenged to beat their swords into plowshares, retooled to make ammonium nitrate surpluses into chemical fertilizers instead of explosives. The next explosions were yields on midwestern corn and soybean fields. It seemed like a good thing, but some officials saw these new surpluses as reason to dismantle New Deal policies that had helped farmers weather the economic uncertainties notorious to their vocation. Over the next decades, nudged by industry, the government rewrote the rules on commodity subsidies so these funds did not safeguard farmers, but instead guaranteed a supply of cheap corn and soybeans.

These two crops, formerly food for people and animals, became something entirely new: a standardized raw material for a new extractive industry, not so different from logging or mining. Mills and factories were designed for a multibranched production line as complex as the one that turns iron and aluminum ores into the likes of automobiles, paper clips, and antiperspirants. But instead, this new industry made piles of corn and soybeans into high-fructose corn syrup, hydrogenated oils, and thousands of other starch- or oil-based chemicals. Cattle and chickens were brought in off the pasture into intensely crowded and mechanized CAFOs (concentrated animal feeding operations) where corn—which is no part of a cow's natural diet, by the way—could be turned cheaply and quickly into animal flesh. All these different products, in turn, rolled on down the new industrial food pipeline to be processed into the soft drinks, burgers, and other cheap foods on which our nation now largely runs—or sits on its bottom, as the case may be.

This is how 70 percent of all our midwestern agricultural land shifted gradually into single-crop corn or soybean farms, each one of them now, on average, the size of Manhattan. Owing to synthetic fertilizers and pesticides, genetic modification, and a conversion of farming from a naturally based to a highly mechanized production system, U.S. farmers now produce 3,900 calories per U.S. citizen, per day. That is twice what we need, and 700 calories a day more than they grew in 1980. Commodity farmers can only survive by producing their maximum yields, so they do. And here is the shocking plot twist: as the farmers produced those extra calories, the food industry figured out how to get them into the bodies of people who didn't really *want* to eat 700 more calories a day. That is the well-oiled machine we call Late Capitalism.

Most of those calories enter our mouths in forms hardly recognizable as corn and soybeans, or even vegetable in origin: high-fructose corn syrup (HFCS) owns up to its parentage, but lecithin, citric acid, maltodextrin, sorbitol, and xanthan gum, for example, are also manufactured from corn. So are beef, eggs, and poultry, in a different but no less artificial process. Soybeans also become animal flesh, or else a category of ingredient known as "added fats." If every product containing corn or soybeans were removed from your grocery store, it would look more like a hardware store. Alarmingly, the lightbulbs might be naked, since many packaging materials also now contain cornstarch.

With so many extra calories to deliver, the packages have gotten bigger. The shapely eight-ounce Coke bottle of yesteryear became twenty ounces of carbonated high-fructose corn syrup and water; the accompanying meal morphed similarly. So did the American waistline. U.S. consumption of "added fats" has increased by one-third since 1975, and our HFCS is up by 1000 percent. About a third of all our calories now come from what is known, by community consent, as junk food.

No cashier held a gun to our heads and made us supersize it, true enough. But humans have a built-in weakness for fats and sugar. We evolved in lean environments where it was a big plus for survival to gorge on calorie-dense foods whenever we found them. Whether or not they understand the biology, food marketers know the weakness and have exploited it without mercy. Obesity is generally viewed as a failure of personal resolve, with no acknowledgment of the genuine conspiracy in this historical scheme. People actually did sit in strategy meetings discussing ways to get all those surplus calories into people who neither needed nor wished to consume them. Children have been targeted especially; food companies spend over $10 billion a year selling food brands to kids, and it isn't broccoli they're pushing. Overweight children are a demographic in many ways similar to minors addicted to cigarettes, with one notable exception: their parents are usually their suppliers. We all subsidize the cheap calories with our tax dollars, the strategists make fortunes, and the overweight consumers get blamed for the violation. The perfect crime.

All industrialized countries have experienced some commodification of agriculture and increased consumption of processed foods. But nowhere else on earth has it become normal to layer on the love handles as we do. (Nude beaches are still popular in Europe.) Other well-fed populations have had better luck controlling caloric excess through culture and custom: Italians eat Italian food, the Japanese eat Japanese, and so on, honoring ancient synergies between what their land can give and what their bodies need. Strong food cultures are both aesthetic and functional, keeping the quality and quantity of foods consumed relatively consistent from one generation to the next. And so, while the economies of many Western countries expanded massively in the late twentieth century, their citizens did not.

Here in the U.S. we seem puzzled by these people who refrain from gluttony in the presence of a glut. We've even named a thing we call the French Paradox: How can people have such a grand time eating cheese and fattened goose livers and still stay slim? Having logged some years in France, I have some hunches: they don't suck down giant sodas; they consume many courses in a meal but the portions of the fatty ones tend to be tiny; they smoke like chimneys (though that's changing); and they draw out meals sociably, so it's not just about shoveling it in. The all-you-can-eat buffet is an alien concern to the French, to put it mildly. Owing to certain rules about taste and civility in their heads, their bodies seem to know when enough is enough. When asked, my French friends have confided with varying degrees of tact that the real paradox is how people manage to consume, so very much, the scary food of America.

Why do we? Where are *our* ingrained rules of taste and civility, our ancient treaties between our human cravings and the particular fat of our land? Did they perhaps fly out the window while we were eating in a speeding car?

60 Food culture in the United States has long been cast as the property 60
of a privileged class. It is nothing of the kind. Culture is the property of a species. Humans don't do everything we crave to do—that is

arguably what makes us human. We're genetically predisposed toward certain behaviors that we've collectively decided are unhelpful; adultery and racism are possible examples. With reasonable success, we mitigate those impulses through civil codes, religious rituals, maternal warnings—the whole bag of tricks we call culture. Food cultures concentrate a population's collective wisdom about the plants and animals that grow in a place, and the complex ways of rendering them tasty. These are mores of survival, good health, and control of excess. Living without such a culture would seem dangerous.

And here we are, sure enough in trouble. North America's native cuisine met the same unfortunate fate as its native people, save for a few relics like the Thanksgiving turkey. Certainly, we still have regional specialties, but the Carolina barbecue will almost certainly have California tomatoes in its sauce (maybe also Nebraska-fattened feedlot hogs), and the Louisiana gumbo is just as likely to contain Indonesian farmed shrimp. If either of these shows up on a fast-food menu with lots of added fats or HFCS, we seem unable either to discern or resist the corruption. We have yet to come up with a strong set of generalized norms, passed down through families, for savoring and sensibly consuming what our land and climate give us. We have, instead, a string of fad diets convulsing our bookstores and bellies, one after another, at the scale of the national best seller. Nine out of ten nutritionists (unofficial survey) view this as evidence that we have entirely lost our marbles. A more optimistic view might be this: these sets of mandates captivate us because we're looking hard for a food culture of our own. A profit-driven food industry has exploded and nutritionally bankrupted our caloric supply, and we long for a Food Leviticus to save us from the sinful roil of cheap fats and carbs.

What the fad diets don't offer, though, is any sense of national and biological integrity. A food culture is not something that gets *sold* to people. It arises out of a place, a soil, a climate, a history, a temperament, a collective sense of belonging. Every set of fad-diet rules is essentially framed in the negative, dictating what you must give up. Together they've helped us form powerfully negative associations with the very act of eating. Our most celebrated models of beauty are starved people. But we're still an animal that must eat to live. To paraphrase a famous campaign slogan: it's the biology, stupid. A food culture of anti-eating is worse than useless.

People hold to their food customs because of the *positives*: comfort, nourishment, heavenly aromas. A sturdy food tradition even calls to outsiders; plenty of red-blooded Americans will happily eat Italian, French, Thai, Chinese, you name it. But try the reverse: hand the Atkins menu to a French person, and run for your life.

Will North Americans ever have a food culture to call our own? Can we find or make up a set of rituals, recipes, ethics, and buying habits that will let us love our food and eat it too? Some signs point to "yes." Better food—more local, more healthy, more sensible—is a powerful new topic of the American conversation. It reaches from the epicurean quarters of Slow Food convivia to the matter-of-fact Surgeon General's Office; from Farm Aid concerts to school lunch programs. From the rural routes to the inner cities, we are staring at our plates and wondering where that's *been*. For the first time since our nation's food was ubiquitously local, the point of origin now matters again to some consumers. We're increasingly wary of an industry that puts stuff in our dinner we can't identify as animal, vegetable, mineral, or what. The halcyon postwar promise of "better living through chemistry" has fallen from grace. "No additives" is now often considered a plus rather than the minus that, technically, it is.

We're a nation with an eating disorder, and we know it. The multiple maladies caused by bad eating are taking a dire toll on our health—most tragically for our kids, who are predicted to be this country's first generation to have a *shorter* life expectancy than their parents. That alone is a stunning enough fact to give us pause. So is a government policy that advises us to eat more fruits and vegetables, while doling out subsidies *not* to fruit and vegetable farmers, but to commodity crops destined to become soda pop and cheap burgers. The Farm Bill, as of this writing, could aptly be called the Farm Kill, both for its effects on small farmers and for what it does to us, the consumers who are financing it. The Green Revolution of the 1970s promised that industrial agriculture would make food cheaper and available to more people. Instead, it has helped more of us become less healthy.

A majority of North Americans do understand, at some level, that our food choices are politically charged, affecting arenas from rural culture to international oil cartels and global climate change. Plenty of consumers are trying to get off the petroleum-driven industrial food wagon: banning fast food from their homes and schools, avoiding

---

Hungry World

All these heirloom eggplants and artisan cheeses from the farmers' market are great for weekend dinner parties, but don't we still need industrial farming to feed the hungry?

In fact, all the world's farms currently produce enough food to make every person on the globe fat. Even though 800 million people are chronically underfed (6 will die of hunger-related causes while you read this article), it's because they lack money and opportunity, not because food is unavailable in their countries. The UN Food and Agriculture Organization (FAO) reports that current food production can sustain world food needs even for the 8 billion people who are projected to inhabit the planet in 2030. This will hold even with anticipated increases in meat consumption, and without adding genetically modified crops.

Is all this the reliable bounty of industrial production? Yes and no—with the "no" being more of a problem in the near future. Industrial farming methods, wherever they are practiced, promote soil erosion, salinization, desertification, and loss of soil fertility. The FAO estimates that over 25 percent of arable land in the world is already compromised by one or more of these problems. The worst-affected areas are those with more arid climates or sloped terrain. Numerous field trials in both the United States and the United Kingdom have shown that organic practices can produce commodity crop yields (corn, soybeans, wheat) comparable to those of industrial farms. By using cover crops or animal manures for fertilizer, these practices improve soil fertility and moisture-holding capacity over seasons, with cumulative benefits. These techniques are particularly advantageous in regions that lack the money and technology for industrial approaches.

(*continued on the next page*)

---

the unpronounceable ingredient lists. However, *banning* is negative and therefore fails as a food culture per se.

Something positive is also happening under the surface of our nation's food preference paradigm. It could be called a movement. It includes gardeners who grow some of their own produce—one-quarter of all U.S. households, according to the U.S. Census Bureau. Just as importantly, it's the city dwellers who roll their kids out of bed on Saturday mornings and head down to the farmers' markets to pinch the tomatoes and inhale the spicy-sweet melons—New York, alone, has about a quarter million such shoppers. It involves the farmers' markets themselves, along with a new breed of restaurant owner (and customer) dedicated to buying locally produced food. It has

Conventional methods are definitely producing huge quantities of corn, wheat, and soybeans, but not to feed the poor. Most of it becomes animal feed for meat production, or the ingredients of processed foods for wealthier consumers who are already getting plenty of calories. Food sellers prefer to market more food to people who have money, rather than those who have little. World food trade policies most often favor developed countries at the expense of developing countries; distributors, processors, and shippers reap most of the benefits. Even direct food aid for disasters (a small percentage of all the world's hunger) is most profitable for grain companies and shippers. By law, 75 percent of such aid sent from the United States to other nations must be grown, packaged, and shipped by U.S. companies. This practice, called "tied aid," delays shipments of food by as much as six months, increases the costs of the food by over 50 percent, and directs over two-thirds of the aid money to the distributors.

If efficiency is the issue, resources go furthest when people produce their own food, near to where it is consumed. Many hunger-relief organizations provide assistance not in the form of bags of food, but in programs that teach and provide support technology for locally appropriate, sustainable farming. These programs do more than alleviate hunger for a day and send a paycheck to a multinational. They provide a livelihood to the person in need, addressing the real root of hunger, which is not about food production, but about poverty.

For more information, visit www.wn.org, www.journeytoforever.org, or www.heifer.org.

—Steve L. Hopp

been embraced by farmers who manage to keep family farms by thinking outside the box, learning to grow organic peppers or gourmet mushrooms. It engages schoolchildren and teachers who are bringing food-growing curricula into classrooms and lunchrooms from Berkeley, California, to my own county in southern Appalachia. It includes the kids who get dirty in those outdoor classrooms planting tomatoes and peppers at the end of third grade, then harvesting and cooking their own pizza when they start back into fourth. And it owes a debt to parents who can watch those kids getting dirty, and not make a fuss.

At its heart, a genuine food culture is an affinity between people and the land that feeds them. Step one, probably, is to *live* on the land that feeds them, or at least on the same continent, ideally the same region. Step two is to be able to countenance the ideas of "food" and "dirt" in the same sentence, and three is to start poking into one's supply chain to learn where things are coming from. In the spirit of this adventure, our family set out to find ourselves a real American culture of food, or at least the piece of it that worked for us, and to describe it for anyone who might be looking for something similar. This book tells the story of what we learned, or didn't; what we ate, or couldn't; and how our family was changed by one year of deliberately eating food produced in the same place where we worked, loved our neighbors, drank the water, and breathed the air. It's not at all necessary to live on a food-producing farm to participate in this culture. But it is necessary to know such farms exist, understand something about what they do, and consider oneself basically in their court. This book is about those things.

The story is pegged, as we were, to a one-year cycle of how and when foods become available in a temperate climate. Because food cultures affect everyone living under the same roof, we undertook this project—both the eating and the writing—as a family. Steven's sidebars are, in his words, "fifty-cent buckets of a dollar's worth of goods" on various topics I've mentioned in the narrative. Camille's essays offer a nineteen-year-old's perspective on the local-food project, plus nutritional information, recipes, and meal plans for every season. Lily's contributions were many, including more than fifty dozen eggs and a willingness to swear off Pop-Tarts for the duration, but she was too young to sign a book contract.

70   Will our single-family decision to step off the nonsustainable food   70
grid give a big black eye to that petroleum-hungry behemoth? Keep reading, but don't hold your breath. We only knew, when we started, that similar choices made by many families at once were already making a difference: organic growers, farmers' markets, and small exurban food producers now comprise the fastest-growing sector of the U.S. food economy. A lot of people at once are waking up to a troublesome truth about cheap fossil fuels: we are going to run out of them. Our jet-age dependence on petroleum to feed our faces is a limited-time-only proposition. Every food calorie we presently eat has used dozens or even hundreds of fossil-fuel calories in its making: grain milling, for example, which turns corn into the ingredients of packaged foods, costs ten calories for every one food calorie produced. That's *before* it gets shipped anywhere. By the time my children are my age, that version of dinnertime will surely be an unthinkable extravagance.

I enjoy denial as much as the next person, but this isn't rocket science: our kids will eventually have to make food differently. They could be assisted by some familiarity with how vegetables grow from seeds, how animals grow on pasture, and how whole ingredients can be made into meals, gee whiz, right in the kitchen. My husband and I decided our children would not grow up without knowing a potato has a plant part. We would take a food sabbatical, getting our hands dirty in some of the actual dying arts of food production. We hoped to prove—at least to ourselves—that a family living on or near green land need not depend for its life on industrial food. We were writing our Dear John letter to a roomie that smells like exhaust fumes and the feedlot.

But sticking it to the Man (whoever he is) may not be the most inspired principle around which to organize one's life. We were also after tangible, healthy pleasures, in the same way that boycotting tobacco, for example, brings other benefits besides the satisfaction of withholding your money from Philip Morris. We hoped a year away from industrial foods would taste so good, we might actually enjoy it. The positives, rather than the negatives, ultimately nudged us to step away from the agribusiness supply line and explore the local food landscape. Doing the right thing, in this case, is not about abstinence-only, throwing out bread, tightening your belt, wearing a fake leather belt, or dragging around feeling righteous and gloomy. Food is the rare moral arena in which the ethical choice is generally the one more likely to make you groan with pleasure. Why resist that?

In Nikos Kazantzakis's novel *Zorba the Greek*, the pallid narrator frets a lot about his weaknesses of the flesh. He lies awake at night worrying about the infinite varieties of lust that call to him from this world; for example, cherries. He's way too fond of cherries. Zorba tells him, Well then, I'm afraid what you must do is stand under the tree, collect a big bowl full, and stuff yourself. Eat cherries like they're going out of season.

This was approximately the basis of our plan: the Zorba diet.

Questions on Meaning

1. What is Kingsolver's primary purpose in writing her book? How does this selection establish that purpose?
2. Why, after recounting the incidents with the city cashier and the rural waitress, does Kingsolver conclude, "There is hope for us"?
3. Explain what Kingsolver means by a "food culture." On what basis doe she conclude that other countries enjoy food cultures, while the United States does not?

Questions on Rhetorical Strategy and Style

1. Effective argument employs *logos* (logical reasoning), *pathos* (emotional appeal), and *ethos* (the writer's credible, ethical character). Using examples from the selection, explain how Kingsolver uses all three to persuade the reader.
2. Kingsolver employs figurative language, including *simile* (stated comparison), *metaphor* (implied comparison), and *personification* (attributing human characteristics to non-human entities). Identify at least two examples of each and explain their impact on you as a reader.

Writing Assignments

1. Kingsolver is particularly critical of regimented diets. Gather information on several popular diet plans (e.g., Atkins, South Beach, Jenny Craig), focusing on such features as prohibited foods, limited foods, approved foods, and nutritional information. Write a report on these diets, evaluating their effectiveness with regard to what Kingsolver would call a healthy food culture.
2. Create a guide for consumers in your area, providing information on growing their own vegetables, finding organic and locally grown foods in shops and farmers' markets, and identifying restaurants that emphasize locally grown and raised produce and animals.
3. Visit the web sites listed at the end of the "Hungry World" box. Using information from these sites, write a proposal that addresses the inequities in food distribution. Cite specific evidence from the sites to support your proposal.

Online Communities: Networks that Nurture Long-distance Relationships and Local Ties

John B. Horrigan

This fascinating report on online communities challenges assertions made by sociologists, journalists, and other social observers who predicted that Internet use would cause people to withdraw from social engagement and become increasingly isolated, alienated, and disengaged. Through his analysis of telephone interviews with 3,002 people over the age of eighteen who use the Internet, John B. Horrigan found evidence that challenges these assertions. He learned that the Internet allows users to enjoy satisfying contact with diverse communities—communities with whom the users might not interact offline.

1   When ARPANET, the Internet's precursor, came online in 1969, it did not have a foundational moment like the telephone's, where Alexander Graham Bell ordered his associate Thomas Watson: "Mr. Watson, come here, I want you." That sentence signaled an era of person-to-person communication over distance. In contrast, ARPANET connected a community. In its earliest days, it was a community of computer researchers at major U.S. universities working on similar problems.[1] Since then, the Internet's capability of allowing many-to-many communications has fostered communities of various sizes and sorts.

In this report, we assess the scope of online communities in the United States and the impact they are having on people's lives. We examine two kinds of communities—those that are primarily cyber-based with no inherently geographic aspect (i.e., online communities)

Reprinted from *Pew Internet and American Life Project*, Pew Internet & American Life Project.

and those in which people use the Internet to connect with groups based in the community in which they live (i.e., communities online). We call members of the former group "Cyber Groupies." We define people who belong to any group having to do with their community as "Local Groupies" and analyze how they use the Internet to stay in touch with local affairs.

Our survey suggests that going online to connect with a group is a central part of Americans' Internet experience. More people have used the Internet to contact an online group than have done extremely popular activities, such as getting news online, health information, or financial information. More people participate in online groups than have bought things online. Fully 84% of all Internet users have contacted an online group at one time or another. We call them Cyber Groupies and there are about 90 million of them. Some 79% of Cyber Groupies identify a particular group with which they remain in contact. Additionally, Cyber Groupies often surf to more than one online group; the average Cyber Groupie has gone to about four different online groups at one time or another. Finally, a quarter

The Cyber Groupie Population

The Percent of Internet users in each group who are . . .	Cyber Groupies	Non-Cyber Groupies
Sex . . .		
Male	51%	40%
Female	49	60
Age . . .		
18–24	17	15
25–34	24	19
35–44	28	22
45–54	20	16
55+	11	28
Internet experience . . .		
Online in last 6 months	8	19
Online for about 1 year	17	23
Online for 2–3 years	33	32
Online for > 3 years	41	25
Number of Observations	N=1,426	N=271

Source: Pew Internet & American Life Project, Jan.–Feb. 2001 Survey, Internet users, n=1,697. Margin of error is ±3%.

of Internet users (26%) say they have used email and the Web to contact or get information about groups and organizations in their communities. These Local Groupies number more than 28 million.

The demographics of the Cyber Groupie population are fairly close to the overall Internet population. Where differences do emerge, the pattern suggests that early adopters of the Internet are more likely to have contacted online groups. This means that Cyber Groupies are more likely to be men and to have college educations or better. Cyber Groupies also tend to be younger than non-groupies. This no doubt is linked to the fact that online groups play a minor role in the lives of people over the age of 55.

5   The broad appeal of online groups and the youthful tilt of the   5
Cyber Groupie population—especially among those active in online groups and those who have recently joined them—suggests that the Internet is providing an important place for associational activity for some of the most enthusiastic online Americans. This is occurring in the context of widespread worry that Americans are less and less willing to get involved in community affairs and group activities. It is too soon to say that use of the Internet is reversing that trend. But the findings from this survey indicate that group activity is flourishing online and it is a place that attracts Internet users to new group activity.

The Internet, Communities, and the Virtual "Third Place"

Social scientists cite any number of indicators to illustrate that Americans' level of civic engagement is on the decline. Membership in organizations whose health may be seen as an indicator of strong community involvement—such as the Parent-Teachers Association (PTA)—has declined steadily over the past several decades.[2] The share of Americans voting in presidential elections has fallen since the 1960s, with voting rates in some local elections no higher than 10%.[3] There has been some evidence of growth in certain kinds of organization called "tertiary associations," but that has not been encouraging to those who worry about the decline of community in America. Tertiary organizations have members spread throughout the country, rarely have local chapters, and usually ask members only for a membership check in exchange for an occasional newsletter. These organizations expect little of their members besides their financial contributions.

While concurring that community involvement is on the wane, many activists believe that the Internet might be able to reverse the trend. Since the early days of the Web, activists have argued that "community networks" could bind increasingly fragmented communities together and provide a voice for segments of society that have been traditionally ignored. Such electronic communities can lower the barriers to democratic participation. Advocates hope lower barriers, coupled with deliberate activities that bring all segments of a town or city into the planning process for building community networks, can help revive the community spirit in America.[4] These advocates do not argue that it is inevitable that the Internet will create community involvement, but rather that the Internet presents an opportunity to build community at a time when the need is great.[5]

Though often focused on the opportunities the Internet presents for a renaissance of local places, technology activists also recognize that virtual communities (i.e., online groups that connect people with common interests without any concern about distance) can play an important role in users' lives.[6] One of the earliest proponents of virtual communities, Howard Rheingold, argues that "people anywhere . . . inevitably build virtual communities" as "informal public spaces disappear from our real lives."[7] Rheingold holds out hope that virtual communities can revive democratic participation, in part by increasing the diversity of sources of information and by sparking public debate that is not mediated by large corporations or special interests.

The hopes for the Internet and community are tempered by the acknowledgement that it is a technology that has the potential to undermine community. As author Andrew Shapiro points out, the Internet's potential to give people more control also allows them to restrict the flow of information they receive. By giving people a choice to block out information that somehow does not "fit" with a community's beliefs or norms, the Internet could exacerbate existing trends toward community fragmentation.[8] Nothing about this is inevitable, but Shapiro notes that the evidence on online communities suggests that some degree of face-to-face interaction is necessary for an online community to be sustainable.[9] As Katie Hafner points out in her new account of the pioneering online community. "The Well," this cyber group really gained vitality once members, most of whom lived in the San Francisco Bay Area, had met face-to-face.[10]

The findings of the Pew Internet & American Life Project survey indicate that something positive is afoot with respect to the Internet and community life in the United States. People's use of the Internet to participate in organizations is not necessarily evidence of a revival of civic engagement, but it has clearly stimulated new associational activity. And, because they have been both physical and virtual, these group interactions are richer than those found in "tertiary associations." This type of activity might be likened to what sociologist Ray Oldenburg calls the "third place"—the corner bar, café, or bookstore where people hang out to talk about things that are going on in their lives and neighborhood.[11]

Although Oldenburg very clearly has physical interaction in mind in talking about third places, the Internet has spurred in cyberspace the types of conversations that Oldenburg describes in third places. Our survey suggests that significant numbers of Cyber Groupies are enjoying new relationships because of their use of the Internet. One-quarter (27%) of Cyber Groupies say the Net has helped them connect with people of different economic and ethnic backgrounds and 37% say it has helped them connect with people of different generations. Whether through cyber groups or online groups grounded in local communities, the Internet's "virtual third places" appear to be building bridges among their participants.

Patterns of chatter

If online communites are to have "third place" characteristics, chatter and connection have to be part of what is occurring when people access these groups. Our survey findings suggest that online communities, far from having passive members who lurk on email lists, are environments where a healthy number of members email others and interact on a frequent basis. This is especially true for non-local cyber communities, where a quarter of members routinely email other members.

Approximately 23 million Internet users engage in email exchanges with other online group members several times a week. This is about one-quarter of Cyber Groupies. While much of this emailing (76%) is simply seeking out membership news and group information, a lot of it (68%) involves discussing issues with other group members. And fully half (49%) of those who email an online group say that one of their main reasons to do so is to create or maintain personal relationships with members.

How people engage with their online groups

The percent of each group who responded "yes" to the following questions	Cyber Groupies	Local Groupies
Did you belong to this group before you started communicating with them online?	42%	80%
Do you ever send or receive email with this group or its members?	60	38
Do you email your online group at least several times a week?	43	33
Has communicating with this group through the Internet allowed you to get to know people you otherwise would not have met?	50	35
Does your group or association have a Web site?	73	40
Do you find your group's Web site VERY useful?	50	40
Number of observations	N=1,350	N=438

Source: Pew Internet & American Life Project, Jan.–Feb. 2001 Survey, Internet users, n=1,697. Margin of error is ±3% for Cyber Groupies, ±5% for Local Groupies

For Local Groupies—the 68% of Internet users who belong to a group with some connection to the community where they live—there are lower levels of online chatter, perhaps because physical proximity enables face-to-face communication. Three out of eight (38%) Local Groupies use email to communicate with others in the group. This is conspicuously less than the 60% who email non-local cyber groups. Of these local emailers, however, one-third (33%) send messages to other group members at least several times a week. This means that one in eight (13%) of members of online groups that are close to home routinely exchange e-communications with group members. That comes to 10 million Americans.

It is not surprising that Local Groupies report lower levels of engagement with their online groups than Cyber Groupies. Local groups can rely on physical proximity for interaction and members may be accustomed to face-to-face or telephone contact. Most Local Groupies belonged to their principal local organization *before* they started using the Internet to deal with the group, while most Cyber Groupies did not belong to their main group before they started communicating with it online. Still, one-third (35%) of Local Groupies who go to their group's Web site or email the group say that participation online with a favorite local group has enabled them to meet new people. This is not as striking as the 50% of Cyber Groupies who report they have gotten to know someone new through their online group, but it illustrates that even in local areas many people use the Internet to make new contacts.

The behavior of people on listservs of their online groups is another indication that chatter is a popular activity in online communities. For people who go to their online groups' Web sites, about two-thirds (64%) report that the group has a listserv. Among Internet users whose main online group has a listserv, 60% read and post messages to it. Roughly a third (33%) of those active on listservs (i.e., those who have ever posted messages) write messages at least several times a week. This emailing and listserv activity is reflected in how connected people feel to other people group members. Half (50%) of online group members say that participation with group through the Internet has enabled them to meet new people, and nearly half (47%) say the group has made them feel connected to other group members. About one in five (22%) say that they have arranged to meet in person someone in the group that they first met online.

About half of those who use the Internet to connect to local groups (49%) say these groups have listservs. Overall, about one-third (35%) of people who email a local online group have met someone new in their community with the help of the Internet, and 38% of these emailers say communicating with the local group through the Internet has increased their involvement in their local community.

Reasons for chatter

Internet users were also asked about the reasons they communicate with their principal online group. They were most likely to report that liked discussing issues with others and creating and maintaining personal relationships with other group members. About two-thirds

Why people communicate with online groups

The reasons cited by Cyber Groupies for emailing an online group ...	% who say it is important
Getting general membership news and information	76%
Getting involved with or learning more about group activities	71
Discussing issues with others	68
Creating or maintaining relationships with others in group	49

Source: Pew Internet & American Life Project, Jan.–Feb. 2001 Survey, Internet users, n=1,697. Margin of error is ±3%

say an important reason they email others in the group is to discuss issues affecting the group, while half say emailing the group helps build relationships with others in the group.

New Community Participants

Net Joiners: The people who find groups on the Internet, then become members

In addition to fostering chatter, the Net is drawing people to groups they had not previously encountered. In part of our survey we asked respondents about the online group they most frequently contacted via the Internet. We enquired whether they belonged to this group before they started using the Internet. More than half of Cyber Groupies (56%) joined the group after having begun communicating with it over the Internet. For Local Groupies, 20% joined the group after they begun communicating with it on the Internet. We call the people who have joined a group after being in contact via the Internet

Cyber Groupies: The online groups Net Joiners and Long-timers go to . . .

Which of these groups are you MOST in contact with through the Internet?	All Cyber Groupies (%)	Net Joiners* (%)	Long-timers** (%)
Trade association or professional group	21%	17%	30%
A group for people who share a hobby or interest	17	23	18
A religious organization	6	3	8
A group of people who share your lifestyle	6	5	6
A fan group of a particular team	6	7	6
A sports team or league in which you participate	5	5	6
A group of people who share your beliefs	4	3	5
A local community group or association	4	2	5
A political group	3	2	4
A fan group of a TV show or entertainer	3	10	3
A support group for a medical condition or personal problem	2	6	2
Ethnic or cultural group	1	2	2
Labor Union	1	1	1
NOT in contact with any particular group	16	16	9

*Those who join online groups after they encountered the group online.
**Those who already belong to a group before they use the Internet to communicate with it.
Source: Pew Internet & American Life Project, Jan.–Feb. 2001 Survey, Internet users, n=1,697. Margin of error is ±3%

"Net Joiners." The people who already belong to a group and who then begin to use the Internet to stay in touch with group activities are "Long-timers."

20   Net Joiners generally have less Internet experience than Long-   20
timers. Net Joiners are also more demographically diverse than Long-time group members. Notably, the joiners as a group are younger than the overall Internet population. Although Net Joiners tend to report lower levels of frequent participation in online groups than Long-timers do, there does not appear to be pervasive lurking among either Net Joiners or Long-timers. Many people, when thinking about the group with which they are most involved, report they are active participants in online discussions.

Joiners of online groups, whether they are cyber groups or local groups, have different membership patterns. Net Joiners are drawn principally to hobbyist groups, whereas Long-timers are most involved with trade or professional associations. For Local Groupies, the differences are more striking. While most Long-time members of local groups are most engaged with religious groups, Net Joiners are evenly split among religious groups and local youth groups. Moreover, they are interested in charitable groups, neighborhood associations, and local sports leagues.

On average, Cyber Groupies are most likely to say that a trade or professional group is the online group with which they most closely stay in touch (21% say this), followed closely by hobby groups (17%). In contrast, Net Joiners of online groups are most involved with a group having to do with a hobby.

Net Joiners are less involved with their online group than Long-time members, if involvement is measured by email traffic with the group, new acquaintances made, and perceptions about overall engagement with the group. About half of all Net Joiners (49%) say they use email to communicate with an online group, well below the three-quarters (78%) of Long-timers who use the Internet to keep in touch with it. However, when measured by frequency of email contact, Net Joiners are about as likely as the Long-time members to send or receive an email from the group at least several times a week (41% for Net Joiners to 45% for Long-timers). . . .

Demographically, Net Joiners of cyber groups are more likely than Long-timers to be female, young, non-white, come from households with modest incomes, and relatively new to the Internet. Net Joiners are far less likely to have a college education than Long-timers

A Profile of Net Joiners of Cyber Groups and Long-timers in those groups

	Net Joiners* (%)	Long-timers** (%)
Where they live . . .		
Rural Areas	20%	17%
Suburban Areas	46	54
Urban Areas	33	29
Sex . . .		
Male	48	53
Female	52	47
Age . . .		
18–24	21	13
25–34	25	24
35–44	27	29
44–55	16	23
55+	10	11
Race/Ethnicity . . .		
White, not Hispanic	74	81
Black, not Hispanic	10	6
Hispanic	11	5
Other	4	6
Education . . .		
High school grad or less	39	25
Some college	30	27
College grad	30	48
Income . . .		
Less than 30K	22	11
$30K–$50K	24	21
$50K–$75K	16	21
Over $75K	17	25
Don't know/refused	20	21
Internet experience . . .		
Online in last 6 months	11	5
Online for about 1 year	18	15
Online for 2–3 years	33	34
Online for >3 years	38	47
Number of observations	N=798	N=613

*Those who join online groups **after** they encountered the group online.

Those who already belong to a group **before they use the Internet to communicate with it.

Source: Pew Internet & American Life Project, Jan.–Feb. 2001 Survey.

and twice as likely to be in a household making less than $30,000 per year. Net Joiners are also about twice as likely as Long-Timers to be Hispanic or African-American. Another notable difference comes in Internet experience. These figures suggest that not only are cyber groups a magnet for Internet users, they are especially attractive to novice Internet users. . . .

Building new ties; strengthening existing ones

25 For millions, use of the Internet cuts two ways in their social lives: It helps them find others who share their passions or lifestyles or professional interests. It also helps them feel more connected to groups or people they already know.

The table below summarizes Internet users' persepctives on how the Internet allows them to connect to different groups or people. The Internet's strongest bridges are relatively short ones. Online Americans most often say that the Internet has helped them connect to groups with which they are already involved or people or groups with common interests. Still, between one-quarter and one-third of Cyber Groupies say that the Net has helped them connect with people of different ages, ethnic backgrounds, or economic backgrounds. One bridge that the Internet does not build, at least to a large extent, is to local community groups. Of the 26% of Cyber Groupies who said it has helped connect them to nearby groups, only 6% says it has helped them "a lot" in getting them in touch with locally-based groups.

Cyber Groupies who are active in their online group are more likely to use the Net to connect with new people or groups. These users—defined as those who are members of a local and cyber group *and* who exchange emails with the group—are substantially more likely than other Internet users to report that the Internet has deepened their ties to groups to which they already belong or to local community groups. They enjoy a kind of "participatory premium."

The effect is also significant when survey respondents are asked how effective the Internet is in helping them find people who share their interests or beliefs. Those active in online communities are more likely than other Internet users to say their online activities help them connect with people of different backgrounds. Given that the pool of active online community members is among the Internet elite (the technology's early adopters who tend to be white, wealthy, and educated) this last finding is understandable. These users are accustomed

Who are the Net Joiners and Long-timers in Local Groups?

	Net Joiners (%)	Long-timers (%)
Where they live . . .		
Rural Areas	11%	16%
Suburban Areas	49	53
Urban Areas	41	31
Sex . . .		
Male	52	50
Female	48	50
Age . . .		
18–24	21	15
25–24	22	22
35–44	33	25
44–55	17	23
55+	7	15
Race/Ethnicity . . .		
White, not Hispanic	68	85
Black, not Hispanic	10	5
Hispanic	11	4
Other	10	5
Education . . .		
High school grad or less	27	20
Some college	37	30
College grad	36	50
Income . . .		
Less than 30K	17	12
$30K–$50K	29	18
$50K–$75K	18	22
Over $75K	21	27
Don't know/refused	15	21
Internet/experience . . .		
Online in last 6 months	5	4
Online for about 1 year	14	13
Online for 2–3 years	28	34
Online for >3 years	51	48
Number of observations	n=106	n=450

Source: Pew Internet & American Life Project, Jan.–Feb. 2001 Survey.

to talking to those people and groups with whom they have conversed since they came to the Internet. On average, these people are not too different from each other.

As Internet adoption continues, it might be the case that new users are more likely to connect with people of different backgrounds than their predecessors in large part because the Internet population continues to diversify. Although difficult to predict, there is some evidence that this broadening of users' social universes might increase as the Internet population grows.

30   The behavior of Local Groupies who joined an online community 30
after making initial Internet contact illustrates this hopeful scenario. They are fairly diverse set of Internet veterans, with 11% Hispanics, 10% African-Americans, and 68% whites. This subset of Local Groupies is much more likely than active online community members in general to connect with people of different backgrounds. When asked whether the Internet has helped them connect with people from different generations, 53% said it had "a lot" or "some"; 41% said it had helped them connect with people from different racial or ethnic backgrounds; and 46% said the Internet had helped them connect with people from different economic backgrounds. And more than half (54%) said the Internet helped them connect to groups in their local community. In each case, these numbers represent about a 10-point increase over the average for active online community members.

How the Internet makes them feel connected

The percent of who say their use of the Internet has helped them "a lot" or "some" ...	Cyber Groupies	Very active online community members
Find people or groups who share your interests	49%	61%
Become more involved with organizations or groups to which you already belong	40	58
Connect with people of different ages or generations	37	44
Find people or groups who share your beliefs	32	46
Connect with people from different economic backgrounds	29	37
Connect with people from different racial or ethnic backgrounds	27	33
Connect with groups based in your local community	26	43

Source: Pew Internet & American Life Project, Jan.–Feb. 2001 Survey, Internet users, n=1,697. Margin of error is ±3%.

The Internet is also a bridge for younger members of online communities. Many in the 18-to-24 age bracket say the Internet helps them reach out to people of different ages, economic backgrounds, and ethnicity. Nearly half (47%) of online community members between the ages of 18 and 24 say the Internet helps "a lot" or "some" to connect them to people in different generations, 42% say it has helped make connections with people in different ethnic groups, and 36% say it has helped them reach out to people from different economic backgrounds. And 29% say it has helped them connect to groups in their local community. For the young who are quite active in online communities (i.e., those who email their groups), the results are more striking. Fully 60% say the Internet has helped connect them to people of different generations, 54% say that about ethnic groups, and 44% say it has helped them connect to local community groups.

In sum, online communities are enabling Internet users to build bridges to other groups and people, while at the same time deepening ties to groups and ideas with which people are already involved. As the Internet draws people to online groups, it is notable that these people (i.e., Net Joiners among Local Groupies) are ethnically more diverse than other Internet users. As the Internet disseminates more broadly throughout the population, there are signs that online groups may facilitate new connections across ethnic, economic, and generational categories. It is also worth underscoring that young people seem especially interested in taking advantage of the Internet's bridge building potential in online groups. As noted at the outset, there is pervasive worry that young people shy away from group activity and civic engagement. With the online groups drawing young people into groups involved with their local community, this survey suggests that the Internet may develop into an important new avenue for civic engagement among young people. . . .

End Notes

1. Michael Hiltzik, *Dealers of Lightning: Xerox PARC and the Dawn of the Computer Age*. New York: HarperCollins, 1999, p. 43.
2. Robert D. Putnam, *op. cit.* p. 57. About 47% of families with children belonged to the PTA in 1960, while 18% belonged in 1997.
3. *Ibid*, p. 31–33. Putnam points out that 63% of eligible voters cast ballots in 1960, and 49% did so in 1996.

4. Douglas Schuler, *New Community Networks: Wired for Change*. New York: Addison-Wesley Publishing, 1996, p. 142.
5. Steven E. Miller, *Civilizing Cyberspace: Policy, Power, and the Information Superhighway*. New York: Addison-Wesley Publishing, 1996, p. 329.
6. *Ibid*. p. 333.
7. Howard Rheingold, *The Virtual Community*, 1993, chapter 1.
8. Andrew Shapiro, *The Control Revolution: How the Internet is Putting Individuals in Charge and Changing the World We Know*. New York: Century Foundation, 1999, p. 116–117.
9. *Ibid*. p. 211–212.
10. Katie Hafner, *The Well: A Story of Love, Death & Real Life in the Seminal Online Community*, New York: Carroll and Graf, 2001.
11. Ray Oldenburg, *The Great Good Place: Cafés, Coffee Shops, Bookstores, Bars, Hair Salons, and Other Hangouts at the Heart of a Community*. New York: Marlowe & Company, 3rd Edition, 1999. For Oldenburg, people's "first place" is home and "second place" work.

Questions

1. Distinguish between Cyber Groupies and Local Groupies. Which, if either, best describes you? If you do not belong to either group, why not?
2. What factors might allow the Internet to increase community solidarity? What factors might cause it to undermine community solidarity?
3. Define "Net Joiners" and "Long-timers." Which, if either, best describes you?
4. What does Horrigan mean by patterns of chatter? How do patterns of chatter create community between Net Joiners and Long-timers?